AMERICAN
WARS

ISSUES &
CONTROVERSIES
━━ IN ━━
AMERICAN HISTORY

AMERICAN WARS

BALLARD C. CAMPBELL, PH.D.
BALLARD C. CAMPBELL, PH.D., SERIES EDITOR

Facts On File
An Infobase Learning Company

Issues and Controversies in American History: American Wars

Facts On File, Inc.
An imprint of Infobase Learning
132 West 31st Street
New York NY 10001

Library of Congress Cataloging-in-Publication Data

Campbell, Ballard C., 1940–
    American wars / Ballard C. Campbell.
      p. cm.—(Issues and controversies in American history)
    Includes bibliographical references and index.
    ISBN 978-0-8160-7727-4
    1. United States—History, Military, I. Title.
    E181.C25 2011
    355.00973—dc23 2011017577

Facts On File books are available at special discounts when purchased in bulk quantities for businesses, associations, institutions, or sales promotions. Please call our Special Sales Department in New York at (212) 967-8800 or (800) 322-8755.

You can find Facts On File on the World Wide Web at http://www.infobaselearning.com

Text design by Kerry Casey
Composition by Hermitage Publishing Services
Cover printed by Yurchak Printing, Landisville, Pa.
Book printed and bound by Yurchak Printing, Landisville, Pa.
Date printed: September 2012
Printed in the United States of America

This book is printed on acid-free paper.

CONTENTS

ᚚᚚᚚLIST OF DOCUMENTSᚚᚚᚚ

Chapter 12   The Iraq War: Will the American Invasion of Iraq Reduce Terrorism?

⸘ABOUT THE AUTHOR⸘

Ballard C. Campbell is professor of history and public policy at Northeastern University in Boston. He holds a B.S. in political science from Northwestern University, an M.A. in history from Northeastern University, and a Ph.D. in history from the University of Wisconsin, Madison. In addition to *American Wars*, Professor Campbell has written or edited five books, including *Disasters, Accidents, and Crises in American History: A Reference Guide to the Nation's Most Catastrophic Events* (2008); *The Growth of American Government: Governance from the Cleveland Era to the Present* (1995); and *Representative Democracy: Public Policy and Midwestern Legislatures in the Late Nineteenth Century* (1980). He has written numerous articles and book chapters for academic and nonacademic publications, as well as three dozen book reviews. He serves as general editor of the Facts On File series Issues and Controversies in American History, in which *American Wars* is included. Professor Campbell is past president of both the Society for Historians of the Gilded Age and Progressive Era and the New England Historical Association. The Organization of American Historians appointed him a Distinguished Lecturer in 2006 and reappointed him through 2015. He teaches courses in American and comparative governmental history, and economic and business history. Born in East Orange, New Jersey, and a former resident of Newton, Massachusetts, Professor Campbell now lives in Portland, Maine, with his wife, Eugenie B. Campbell.

PREFACE

From a distance we tend to see history as a continuous narrative that flows from one period to another. When the largest building blocks of history are considered, such as the American Revolution, slavery, the Civil War, industrialization, the role of women, and the degradation of the environment, history indeed can be viewed as a nearly seamless web of events, with only an occasional sharp shift in direction. On closer inspection, however, we see that historical development entailed numerous conflicts, controversies, and choices. And at virtually every crossroad in American history the future hung in the balance until the key issues were confronted and resolved. It was at these times that individuals debated the central issues at stake. History didn't just happen. Individuals made it happen.

The *Issues and Controversies in American History* series focuses on these critical disputes. The authors believe that historical understanding is furthered by studying the choices that contemporaries debated, how they envisioned these options, and how their decisions influenced the way history unfolded. This approach to history helps us to see the contingency in historical causation – that the directions that individuals, groups, and society took depended in large measure on the outcome of debates at critical junctures in the nation's history. When studied closely, history reveals a landscape of controversies. Some of these issues remained subjects of dispute decades after their initial resolution. Yet every major debate shaped the future course of the nation's history.

The *Issues and Controversies* series is constructed to illuminate the great debates in American history and to illustrate the contingency by which it unfolded. Each volume focuses on an important topic in American history and is composed of chapters, usually arranged chronologically, that address major controversies about the subject. Every chapter opens with a summary of the issue and the debate about it, and then lays out the historical background of the chapter's subject. Two short essays in each chapter provide fuller glimpses of selected subjects. The heart of each chapter contains a summary of the debate on the controversy. Theses discourses are illustrated by primary sources, which present the opposing arguments of the two sides. These documents also offer a sampling of the tone, flavor, and logic of the participants. The conclusion to each chapter examines the impact of the debate and offers thoughts on how different decisions could have produced different outcomes. These "What If?" sections are intended to illustrate contingency and dependency in history—that history isn't inevitable but is shaped by the decisions people make. A list of discussion questions in each chapter is designed to provoke reflection about the issues that contemporaries faced. The bibliography and list of websites for each chapter will help students locate additional resources about each controversy.

Ballard Campbell's volume on American Wars is especially appropriate for this series. The United States fought a dozen major armed conflicts between 1775 and 2012. Each of these military actions raised fundamental questions about whether to go to war, how to conduct military operations, or in 1775–76, at the onset of the American Revolution, whether to separate from Great Britain. Debate wracked Congress and the nation over whether the United States should declare war in 1812, 1846, 1898, and 1917. President Abraham Lincoln's decision to emancipate slaves and when to do so generated impassioned discussion in 1862 and 1863 and had an important bearing on the prosecution of the Civil War. The United States remained neutral during the opening years of World War II, yet President Franklin Roosevelt's aid to Great Britain sparked a national controversy over the extent to which the Axis powers threatened the nation. Decisions that led to a cold war with Russia in 1947 and 1948 prompted critics to question the wisdom of President Harry Truman's policy toward the Soviet Union. The disagreement between General Douglas MacArthur and President Truman over expanding the Korean War into China became a national controversy in 1951. A prolonged debate ensued over the insertion of American ground troops into the Vietnam War during the 1960s. The deployment of American forces in the Persian Gulf in 1991 and for an invasion of Iraq in 2003 raised questions over the appropriateness of these interventions and whether the president needed congressional approval to authorize these actions. Congress narrowly supported the president on both occasions, but critics challenged the claim that the invasion of Iraq would lessen terrorism. The history of these 12 military conflicts demonstrates that making war was never taken for granted in the United States. Each intervention became a contested issue in which participants drew on partisanship, ideology, and circumstances in arguing differing views. Professor Campbell's analysis in *American Wars* reviews these debates and explains how they shaped the course of the nation's history.

Ballard C. Campbell
Series Editor

﹅﹅﹅INTRODUCTION ﹅﹅﹅

The history of American wars presents several paradoxes. Americans like to think of themselves as a peaceful people, but they have engaged in numerous military conflicts. Since 1775, they have fought 12 major wars, which works out to be, roughly, one each generation. Numerous smaller conflicts took place between these larger ones. From the American Revolution to World War II, the political tradition of the United States warned of the dangers of maintaining a large standing army. And in fact, the nation's peacetime military establishment was minuscule, at least by world standards. Yet Americans have been able to field sufficient means when circumstances called for military force.

The nation's constitutional system dictated that civilian authority would be superior to military authority, but the greatest presidents of the United States—Abraham Lincoln and Franklin D. Roosevelt, to cite two—served during major wars. Many of America's greatest war heroes—George Washington, Andrew Jackson, Ulysses S. Grant, Dwight D. Eisenhower—became presidents. On another theme, the culture of the United States has venerated capitalism and private initiative. Nonetheless, government has had an enormous impact on the nation's economy, in good measure because of the demands of war. Government contracts to businesses and research institutes during military emergencies have stimulated commercial development and technological innovation. In many respects, to study war in America requires unraveling its paradoxes.

This book examines the 12 most important wars in the history of the United States, beginning with the American Revolution and concluding with the Iraq War. Each of these conflicts had four phases, beginning with the circumstances that involved the nation in the war. A second phase entailed the home front during wartime and governmental support of military operations. A third phase concerned the mobilization of military forces and their activity in the field. And fourth, each war ended with a peace treaty or settlement, which together with the war itself, conveyed enormous consequences.

American Wars gives some attention to each of these phases of war. The circumstances in which each war unfolded provoked sharply debated issues. This book concentrates on these debates, selecting one major controversy in each war for close examination. The book traces how these controversies arose, identifies the several sides of the debate, reviews these arguments, and summarizes the outcome of the disagreement. An assessment of each war's legacy and a speculation concerning how events might have turned out differently conclude each chapter.

The 12 wars can be grouped into three chronological periods, each of which possesses distinctive historical characteristics. The era between 1775 and 1877, when the American Revolution, the War of 1812, the Mexican War, and the Civil War occurred, touched concerns linked to the formation of the republic. Each of these conflicts forced Americans to confront critical questions concerning the form and purpose of the United States. During the Revolution, colonists debated whether they should separate from Great Britain and declare independence. Thirty-six years later, Americans debated whether the United States should declare war on Great Britain. Some historians call the war that followed—the War of 1812—the second American Revolution. During 1846–47, Americans disagreed about going to war against Mexico, a venture that some saw as a ruse to expand slavery. During the Civil War, Lincoln wrestled with the question of whether to free slaves who resided in the areas of rebellion against the Union. The answers to these issues had profound consequences in shaping the history of the nation.

The second era of American wars, which spans from the late 19th century to the end of World War II, embodied the projection of American power beyond the borders of the nation. Conflict with Spain over Cuba in 1898 sparked a debate in Congress and the country over whether the United States should free the island from colonial rule. When World War I began in Europe in 1914, the United States remained neutral. The critical issue in 1917, when America became entangled with Germany over maritime trading rights, was whether the United States should abandon neutrality and enter the European war against Germany. World War II erupted in September 1939, once again leading to a period of American neutrality. Before Japan attacked Pearl Harbor on December 7, 1941, a debate raged in the United States over whether the security and national interest of the United States was linked to the ability of Great Britain to hold off its German adversary.

The third era of American Wars dates from end of World War II in 1945 and continues to the present, a period sometimes termed the *Pax Americana*. During these years, the United States possessed unparalleled power, which was used to achieve world political stability. The chapter on the origins of the cold war centers on whether the Soviet Union started this decades-long conflict. During the Korean War of the early 1950s, political and military leaders debated whether to invade China, which had entered the conflict in support of North Korea. Whether the United States should put combat troops in Vietnam was the key question debated during the nation's protracted struggle in Indochina. Iraq's invasion of Kuwait in 1990 spawned a national debate over whether the United States should use its military to expel the Iraqi invaders. Joined by a broad international coalition, the United States did so in the Persian Gulf War. Following the 9/11 attacks on the United States in 2001, a debate arose over whether a U.S. invasion of Iraq would reduce the threat of terrorism. President George W. Bush approved an incursion in 2003. The Persian Gulf and Iraq Wars constitute a realignment of the challenges to world security following World War II. The cold war occurred in the early decades of the post–World War II era (1946–89), when the Soviet Union and China were seen as America's top adversaries. After the fall of communism in Eastern Europe, the central focus of U.S. foreign policy shifted to fighting terrorism and achieving political stability in the Middle East.

Dividing American wars into these three broad eras helps to identify how each cluster of military conflicts influenced the course of American history. The century between 1776 and 1876 constitutes the building of the American republic into a major nation-state. The American Revolution broke the bonds of British colonialism and confirmed U.S. control of territory between the Atlantic Ocean and the Mississippi River. The War of 1812 removed the British barrier around the Great Lakes, a presence that had discouraged American penetration into the center of the continent. Victory over Mexico in 1848 transferred a huge expanse of territory, including California, to the United States. The Civil War threatened to split the Union into two rival nations. President Lincoln's leadership during war against the southern Confederacy preserved the Union and barred slavery from any part of it. Adding the Spanish-American War to this process of nation-building completes the history of territorial acquisitions. Victory over Spain in 1898 resulted in the transfer of Puerto Rico and several Pacific islands (including the Philippines temporarily) to the United States and confirmed the nation's dominant presence in the Caribbean region. The wars of this nation-building era and also World War I (1917–18) had a marked impact on stimulating nationalistic pride in the United States as a nation. These surges of patriotism were critical in fusing diffuse places and peoples into a more unified national culture, although local identities and ethnic differences remained hallmarks of the United States.

World War I constitutes a transitional event in the history of the United States. This conflict certified that the United States had built a powerful continental republic and could project this might throughout most of the world. World War II extended this capability further, with the nation emerging from this struggle in 1945 as the dominant military organization in the world. The United States used its immense influence and power to thwart the aspirations of the Communist nations during the cold war. The Korean and Vietnam wars represented active military campaigns in this quest to contain communism. Since the collapse of the Soviet Union in 1991, non-state violence (terrorism), religious hostilities (mainly between radical Islamic and the Judeo-Christian traditions), and access to oil in the Middle East arose as dominant challenges to U.S. foreign policy. The two wars with Iraq are central events in this new chapter of American military and diplomatic history.

Besides influencing relations with the rest of the world, wars had important effects on American society. America's three greatest presidents—Washington, Lincoln, and Franklin Roosevelt—all served as either commander in chief or as president during major wars. All three were two-term presidents (and Roosevelt a four-term president). Washington was a general and war hero, as were Presidents William Henry Harrison, Zachary Taylor, Ulysses Grant, and Dwight D. Eisenhower. Other generals ran for president but lost: Winfield Scott (1852), George McClellan (1864), and Winfield Scott Hancock (1880). John C. Frémont (1856), Barry Goldwater (1964), and John Kerry (2004) had had military experience and lost presidential races. President Theodore Roosevelt was a hero of the Spanish-American War, and President Harry Truman served in France during World War I. Presidents Rutherford B. Hayes, James Garfield, Benjamin Harrison, William McKinley, John F.

Kennedy, Richard Nixon, Gerald Ford, Jimmy Carter, and George H. W. Bush were military veterans. In the post–World War II era, Generals Douglas MacArthur, Colin Powell, and Wesley Clark were aspirants for the presidency, but none was nominated. Clearly, service in the armed forces incubated presidential prospects. Chances of nomination and election were even better if one were a military hero.

American wars affected the outcome of elections, especially for national offices. Federalist opposition to the War of 1812 hastened the party's demise. Zachary Taylor's presidential nomination in 1848 was designed, in part, to keep the Whig Party from fracturing over the issue of slavery. Lincoln's reelection in 1864 was tied to developments on the battlefield during the Civil War. Woodrow Wilson's missteps over the Versailles Treaty that concluded World War I had disastrous consequences for the Democratic Party in 1918 and 1920. President Truman's tough stand against the Soviet Union at the onset of the cold war helped his election in 1948, keeping the presidency in the hands of the Democratic Party. But the unpopularity of the Korean War, which began during the Truman administration, was instrumental in the 1952 election of Dwight D. Eisenhower, the Republican candidate for president. The Vietnam War was a critical factor in ending President Lyndon Johnson's hope for reelection in 1968. The Vietnam conflict also contributed to Nixon's resignation as president in 1974 during the throes of the Watergate scandal. President George W. Bush's unwavering support for the war in Iraq was a key factor in Democrat Barack Obama's victory over Republican candidate John McCain (a Vietnam veteran and prisoner of war) in the 2008 presidential election. Once again, a war helped to shift power between the two major political parties.

These highlights of American elections suggest the impact that wars have had on American government. One conduit of this influence lay in veterans' organizations. The Grand Army of the Republic (GAR), formed by Union veterans in 1866, was a reliable source of votes for Republicans for decades after the Civil War. Confederate veterans had their own organization. The Veterans of Foreign Wars formed after the Spanish-American War, and the American Legion followed World War I. John Kerry, Democratic nominee for president in 2004, was a prominent member of Vietnam Veterans Against the War, formed in 1967. Candidates for elective office, especially Republicans, have made it a point to address gatherings of veterans' groups during their political campaigns.

Wars also have had profound effects on the economy. This relationship is reciprocal, in that, on the one hand, the ability to wage war depends to a large degree on the capacity of the economy to sustain the military. This requirement not only entails the provision of weapons and supplies but also depends on raising the funds to pay for these goods, as well as military pay and veterans' benefits. On the other hand, government purchases during war have stimulated the private sector of the economy. The British embargo of American trade during the War of 1812 was instrumental in encouraging domestic manufacturing, especially of cotton textiles. The federal government consumed massive amounts of goods during the Civil War, leading some historians to credit the conflict with providing a major boost to industrialization. The impact of government war orders on the domestic economy is perhaps best illustrated by World War II. Federal spending to win this war helped to raise the United States out of the Great Depression and left the country richer after the war than before the economic downturn began. The Defense Department poured billions of dollars into electronics, aircraft, and other industries during the cold war, helping to fuel a quarter-century of economic growth after 1948. The Iraq War turned out to be highly profitable for private firms that contracted with the government to provide goods and services overseas.

Government has promoted new technologies in its quest to improve its military capacity. In the 19th century, military leaders sought improved weapons, beginning with the replacement of flintlock rifles for smoothbore muskets. A little known aspect of the U.S. Army's role in the early phase of American industrialization was its loan of engineers to private canal and railroad firms. The army also built roads in the federal territories, thus facilitating the immigration of settlers in the trans-Mississippi West. World War I stimulated the development of radio, aircraft, and research on electrical-magnetic detection systems that led to sonar and radar. Researchers during World War II produced penicillin, nylon, and computers as well as harnessed nuclear energy, to name some key innovations of these years. The defense establishment during the cold war created the first version of the Internet and launched satellites that enabled advanced communications and global positioning systems (GPS). These illustrations demonstrate the range of inventions initially intended for military functions that became fixtures of the civilian economy.

The cost of developing new technologies added to the financial demands of sustaining the nation's military establishment. Peace tends to generate pressures for cutting defense spending. Wars, by contrast, rally support for increased financing for the military. Every major war has caused a dramatic upward spike in spending during the conflict. Government borrowed heavily to finance its 19th-century wars. In the 20th century, tax increases covered a substantial portion of war-related costs. World War II introduced major changes in the nation's capacity to raise revenue, including the withholding of income taxes "at the source" (meaning employers). Reluctance to raise taxes during some wars, such as the Vietnam War and the two wars in the Middle East, has added billions of dollars to the national debt. From the Revolution through the Civil War, military conflicts have played central roles in the creation and development of American banking. The initial deposits of the first Bank of the United States (1791–1811) rested heavily on debt instruments resulting from Revolutionary war loans.

The transformative effect of war on finance and business has an analogy in war-induced changes to the American presidency. The Constitution of the United States invests the president with powers to act as the nation's chief diplomat and as commander in chief of the military. This dual allocation of authority gives the chief executive far more power over foreign affairs than over domestic matters. Congress plays a considerably smaller role in shaping foreign policy compared to domestic affairs. Presidents in the 19th century paid heed to the dictum that Congress proposes and the president disposes public policy. Deference to this tradition waned in the 20th century as presidents came to wield more and more independent power over military action. World War II was the last American conflict in which Congress voted a formal declaration of war, a power that the Constitution grants to the legislature. Since 1950, presidents have contended that they could deploy U.S. soldiers in foreign wars without the formal approval of Congress. This assertion of executive prerogative is a major reason that presidential power has grown in the 20th and 21st centuries.

While the scope of presidential action in military matters has changed over time, the constitutional dictum that civilian officials have control over the military has not. George Washington was instrumental in shaping this tradition, which became firmly rooted in American political practice. Presidents have the power to fire generals, and they have, including some very popular military figures. Moreover, controversial issues concerning strategy and diplomacy have arisen in all major American wars. Army, navy, and air force leaders have provided advice on these issues, but the final decision for broad strategy and wartime objectives always has rested with civilian policy makers. At the center of this circle of leaders is the president of the United States. In certain respects, a study of the controversial decisions that have surrounded each American war focuses first and foremost on the president.

How presidents, political leaders, and military figures confronted the thorny issues surrounding American wars is the central focus of this book. Each war posed a controversial issue that literally held life-and-death consequences. The question of whether the American colonies should declare their independence from Great Britain had enormous implications, not only for the members of the Continental Congress who wrestled with the issue, but for the American colonists generally. Once they formally separated from Britain, the delegates to the Continental Congress became traitors subject to hanging if they failed. An influential inducement to decide in favor of independence was the news that a British naval armada containing 30,000 troops had sailed into New York Harbor. This development made it crystal clear that the king of England would not bargain with his North American subjects; he would force their obedience.

The connection between the British fleet's arrival and the Continental Congress's decision to separate from Britain illustrates the *contingency* of historical decisions. This idea holds that the actions of individuals are, in large measure, due to the circumstances they confront. Humans can see the future only dimly, yet they must make decisions within a sequence of unfolding events, many of which are unanticipated and usually imperfectly understood at the time they occur. Historians usually cannot pinpoint the precise set of causes that led decision makers to select a particular course of action, but it is a good bet that the circumstances that surrounded the decision played a part, perhaps the critical part, in shaping it. Because the concept of historical contingency can help decipher how decisions are reached, we have included counterfactual "what if" reflections in each chapter. The chapter on the American Revolution asks: *What if* the king and British officials had shown a willingness to negotiate a reconciliation of differ-ences with the American colonists? Would the Continental Congress have then chosen a different course of action? Because counterfactual questions cannot be answered with certainty, we can only speculate about what *did not* happen. But reflections on these questions shed some light on how decisions were influenced by the contexts in which they were made.

The influence of contextual circumstances on political and military decisions means that the historian of war must reconstruct the events that preceded each conflict. This book does so, beginning with the American Revolution and concluding with the Iraq War. Each chapter summarizes the background of the war, focuses in greater detail on the debate over a critical issue about the war, and reviews the outcome and legacy of the conflict. Two short essays (sidebars) illuminate subjects that played instrumental roles in each war. Each chapter concludes with a "what if" counterfactual essay. This last section reminds us that the unpredictable unfolding of events formed patterns we call history.

1

THE AMERICAN REVOLUTION:
Should the Colonies Separate from Great Britain?

—ɯ—

THE CONTROVERSY

The Issue

Victory over the French in the Seven Years' War changed the harmonious relationship between Britain's North American colonies and the mother country. New taxes and regulations imposed on the Americans produced a series of protests and crises between 1763 and 1775. These confrontations spurred Britain to suppress disobedience to Parliamentary policy with military force. Beginning with the Battle of Lexington and Concord in April 1775, the colonists mounted armed resistance to British "coercion." After a year of military conflict, American patriots issued a Declaration of Independence that withdrew the United States from the British Empire. Did the Americans make the right decision?

- ♦ *Arguments for separation from Great Britain:* Thomas Paine, the author of *Common Sense*, thought so, as did most members of the Continental Congress, which assigned the task of drafting a Declaration of Independence to Thomas Jefferson. Yet even on the eve of the announcement of independence, some members of Congress hoped for reconciliation. For them and other residents of the colonies, breaking the bonds with their mother country was emotionally painful and politically dangerous.

- ♦ *Arguments against separation from Great Britain:* A large number of colonists, many of them learned and respected figures in North America, rejected separation. They argued that the benefits of remaining within the British Empire outweighed the disadvantages, even with Parliament's newly imposed taxes. Many of these "loyalists" expressed resentment of the Massachusetts "radicals" who turned a family dispute into a movement for independence. Thousands of loyalists voluntarily departed their homeland or were driven out. The American Revolution was also a civil war.

—ɯ—

Thomas Jefferson drafted the Declaration of Independence for the Continental Congress in early June 1776. (© North Wind Picture Archives/Alamy)

INTRODUCTION

Early in the morning of April 19, 1775, six companies of Redcoats from Boston marched from Lexington to Concord, Massachusetts. They were the advance units of a British force instructed to commandeer store-houses of weapons and ammunition and to arrest leaders of the provincial resistance to military government in the colony. Concord had a welcoming party for the king's men. Waiting in town were 400 min-utemen and other militiamen—local citizens who performed military service—from Concord and surrounding towns. The minutemen were specially selected to be ready for action at a minute's notice. Word that "the regulars are coming out" had reached Concord in time to assembly a sizeable force. The provincials knew that the Redcoats had already vis-ited Lexington, looking for leaders of the resistance to British military rule. They did not know that American blood had been spilled there.

When British soldiers entered Concord, the provincials withdrew to the heights overlooking the North Bridge over the Concord River. There they waited impatiently until smoke from the center of town spurred them to action. As militiamen approached the North Bridge, British soldiers unleashed a fusillade of shots, killing two Americans. The minutemen returned fire, killing three Redcoats and wounding others. These were the shots "heard round the world," as the poet Ralph Waldo Emerson later commemorated the start of the American Rev-olution. And the Americans fired many more times during April 19. Thousands of provincial militiamen gathered from far and wide in Mid-dlesex County to harass the British column as it returned to Charles-town, just outside of Boston. Brutal hand-to-hand combat took place in Menotomy (now Arlington). Fighting in unorthodox, guerrilla style, the Americans killed 73 British soldiers and wounded 174.

Few Americans who took part in the fight on April 19 were rev-olutionaries. They had not taken the field to win independence for a new nation or to replace the parliamentary monarchy with a repub-lic. Rather, the New Englanders saw their action as a defense of their homes and their rights as Englishmen from a regime that had turned oppressive. However, the patriot stand at the old North Bridge set the wheels of change in motion. Less than two months after Lexington and Concord, an assembly of delegates from the colonies appointed George Washington commander in chief of "all the continental forces," and

New Englanders had fought a pitched battle against British regulars at Bunker Hill in Charlestown, Massachusetts. A little over a year later, the colonists declared their independence from Great Britain.

Today, most Americans probably assume that Americans who fought British Redcoats at Concord struck a blow for independence. The assumption is inaccurate, at least in a literal sense. Most residents of British North America, and particularly those of English background, considered themselves British subjects of King George III. These Britishers by sentiment and tradition severed their political ties with the "mother country" only with great reluctance. They argued that they did so by necessity, as the Crown and his ministers left them no alternative. The king had cavalierly turned aside colonial petitions for reconciliation of grievances and launched a plan to crush resistance and instill obedience to Parliament with brute force. King George, many said, was stripping citizens of their liberties and reducing them to "slavery."

Many colonists urged reconciliation with Britain until the vote for independence was cast. Yet even then, a substantial number of people in the American colonies remained loyal to the king of England. These Tories, as loyalists were called, argued that membership in the British Empire brought important benefits. British subjects possessed unsurpassed political rights. The English army and navy offered military security and protection for trade. Resistance to this military force promised destruction of their homes and commerce, and perhaps a trip to the gallows. They were right. Until Washington's victory over the British army at Yorktown in 1781, the British considered Americans traitors, for whom the penalty was death.

BACKGROUND

The British Colonies in North America

The events at Lexington and Concord occurred more than a century and a half after the initial settlement of Virginia (1607) and Massachusetts (1620), the oldest of the 13 colonies that became the United States of America. Emigration and expanding settlements had brought the white population of these colonies to 2.5 million by 1775. Colonists were spread out along the Atlantic seaboard from southern Maine (then part of Massachusetts Bay Colony) to Georgia. These inhabitants, mainly

British in background, with some Europeans and half a million Africans (most of whom were slaves), lived within the authority of the British Empire. Parliament imposed a variety of commercial regulations on the Americans, which most deemed acceptable, and occasionally disallowed laws passed in colonial assemblies. While formidable in theory, British rule of the North American colonies through 1763 was benign. The Americans elected their own legislatures, which enacted laws in each colony. Most day-to-day governance proceeded in the towns of New England and New York and at the county level.

The Seven Years' War changed this cooperative relationship. Between 1689 and 1763, Britain fought four wars against France and its various European allies in a struggle for world power and empire. The last of these conflicts, known in the colonies as the French and Indian War, began in North America in 1754. Between 1756 and 1763, the war spread to the Indian subcontinent, the Caribbean, and Africa. British victories over the French in Canada in 1760 hastened the signing of a peace treaty in 1763, which ceded Canada and the Mississippi Valley to Great Britain. The fruits of victory over France and Spain, however, planted seeds of discontent in the colonies.

Americans had taken part in the campaigns against the French and their Native American allies, but the British shouldered the bulk of the cost of war, which doubled the country's national debt. A sharp depression at the end of the war made it politically difficult to raise taxes, which many people in England protested. Besides its war debt, Britain now administered a huge new region in the Americas, which added to its financial obligations. To help manage its new territories and to pacify Native Americans, the British ministry announced a proclamation in 1763 that barred further American settlement into the region west of the Appalachian Mountains.

Aware that Americans paid far less taxes than British residents, the king's ministers resolved to have Americans help pay the costs of defense in North America. Agreeable to this goal, Parliament enacted a Revenue Act of 1764, which increased import duties on sugar into the colonies and legislated new trade regulations. The Crown administration tightened the enforcement of customs collections by stationing the British navy in the colonies and establishing British-run "Vice Admiralty" courts that functioned without juries. Americans cried foul, protesting the new regulations. James Otis, a Boston lawyer, wrote that no part of "his majesty's dominions" could be taxed "without their consent." His pamphlet began 12 years of protest over new British taxation of Americans. The colonial legislature in Massachusetts urged a boycott of certain items imported from Britain. The Seven Years' War had set in motion events that undermined the more or less harmonious political accord between colony and mother country.

Three Crises, 1765–1774

Protests over the Revenue Act and Proclamation of 1763 were under way when Britain issued an additional shock by enactment of the Stamp Act in 1765. This measure placed taxes on items such as legal documents, newspapers, and playing cards that circulated in the colonies. Compounding this insult was a new Quartering Act, which obligated colonials to house British troops, now stationed in North America. At the urging of Patrick Henry, the Virginia House of Burgesses issued a resolve that condemned the Stamp Act. Other colonial legislatures followed suit. Delegates from 11 colonies met at a Stamp Act Congress in New York, which issued "resolutions" that rejected the premises of the new tax. The statement asserted that colonists were entitled to the "rights and liberties" afforded to "subjects within the kingdom of Great Britain." These freedoms included the principle that "no taxation be imposed on them but with their own consent." As the colonists were not actually represented in Parliament, they were unable to participate directly in the legislative process. The resolution added a protest against the Vice Admiralty courts, arguing that trial by jury was an inherent right of "every British subject."

Some colonists protested the Stamp Act through a group called the Sons of Liberty. Rioting occurred in colonial cities, and the homes of Stamp Act collectors were looted. Faced with physical danger, tax collectors resigned their commissions. Parliament conceded its inability to collect stamp taxes by repealing the act in 1766, yet the British ministry was not impressed with the colonial legal complaint. Parliament made this point emphatic in the Declaratory Act (1766), which stated that Parliament had authority to make laws for the colonies "in all cases whatsoever."

The Stamp Act imbroglio was the first of three crises that raised tensions between Parliament and colonist to a dangerous level between 1765 and 1774. Each set of confrontations prompted the formation of local organizations to counter new British policy. These protest groups stimulated intercolonial cooperation among colonists, who previously had acted largely in isolation from each other. The resolutions of the Stamp Act Congress set forth arguments that would be repeated and enhanced in the coming years, thus laying an ideological foundation for resistance to British administration.

The second crisis occurred over the Townshend Duties, levied in 1767. Making use of a presumed distinction between internal and external taxes, this measure imposed duties only on imported goods, such as glass, paper, and tea. Colonists balked again. John Dickinson, a Pennsylvania lawyer, wrote that the imports taxed were tantamount to internal taxation because Britain prohibited the manufacture of certain items in the colonies, thus making them available only through imports. Because of the physical inability for colonists to send representatives to Parliament, taxing them without their consent threatened to reduce them to "abject slaves." Merchants in Boston and New York spearheaded nonimportation agreements that applied economic pressure on Britain, which repealed the Townshend duties, except on tea. In the meantime, General Thomas Gage, commander of British forces in North America, had moved his headquarters and warships to Boston, a center of resistance to the new British policy. The presence of "lobsterbacks" on the city streets sparked confrontations with locals, culminating in the Boston Massacre in 1770, when British soldiers fatally shot five colonials in an unruly and threatening crowd. Paul Revere's etching of the incident, widely distributed in the colonies, dramatized the armed assault on American civilians. Tension was elevated another notch with the publication of the *Boston Pamphlet* (1772–73), in which the Boston Town Meeting charged that a plot was afoot to deprive Americans of their rights and "enslave" them. The immediate provocation had been the British decision to pay the salaries of royal officials from revenue duties rather than from monies voted by colonial legislatures, a step that would undermine the authority of Massachusetts lawmakers.

The Tea Act of 1773 ignited a third crisis. This measure granted a special tax dispensation to the British East India Company, a step that gave its tea business an advantage over rival colonial importers of this popular drink. Bay Colony residents signified their distaste for the act by holding the Boston Tea Party, in which revelers disguised as Indians boarded three merchant vessels and threw several hundred chests of tea into the harbor. Protesters used committees of correspondence to communicate with citizens in Massachusetts and other colonies, urging a boycott of British tea.

In the eyes of the king's ministers and Parliament, Bostonians had crossed a critical line. British officials saw these acts of defiance as the breakdown of civil order in the colonies and deliberate challenges to the sovereignty of Parliament. The British response took the form of four punitive laws, collectively known as the Coercive Acts—Americans called them the Intolerable Acts—of 1774. These measures shut down the port of Boston to outside commerce (until the destroyed tea was paid for), revoked the right to elect representatives to the Massachusetts legislature, limited town meetings to one a year, and protected soldiers and judges from trials by the Sons of Liberty. In addition to these actions, which revised Massachusetts' royal charter, Parliament enacted a broader quartering policy for the housing of soldiers. General Gage assumed the dual role as head of the British military and governor of Massachusetts. Clearly, the Crown had responded to events in its most unruly American colony with a heavy hand. Adding insult to injury, a separate law (the Quebec Act) recognized the Catholic Church as a legal entity in Canada. The law was an affront to Protestants in the colonies.

The residents of Massachusetts did not sheepishly acquiesce to these punitive measures. An extra-legal session of the Boston Town Meeting called for an intercolonial meeting to address the latest British oppression. Other colonies heeded the call. In September 1774, delegates from 12 colonies met in Philadelphia to review the situation. The next month, this (first) Continental Congress adopted a Declaration of Rights and Resolves that reviewed the complaints of the colonists, such as levying taxes without the consent of citizens and transporting colonists to England for trial. These transgressions, the delegates stated, violated the laws of nature and the rights of British subjects, which the declaration enumerated. (See "First Continental Congress, Declaration and Resolves, October 14, 1774," on page 27 in the Primary Sources section.) The tradition of self-governance in the colonies was manifestly apparent in the declaration of rights. The fourth right set forth reminded the king that "the foundation of English liberty . . . is a right in the people to participate in their legislative council." The congress approved a Continental Association to boycott British products, passed resolutions urging colonies to prepare their militaries, and planned to meet again the following spring.

1775: From Protest to Confrontation

The conflict between the colonies and Great Britain evolved from protest to military confrontation as 1775 unfolded. Boston was placed under martial law, and General Thomas Gage acted as the military governor of Massachusetts. Towns throughout New England and elsewhere stockpiled guns and ammunition, some of which were smuggled into America, and drilled their militias. Committees of safety monitored British troop movements in the Boston region and watched for Tory (colonists loyal to the King) spies in their communities.

Neither the king nor his ministers nor Parliament showed any willingness to compromise. King George III brushed aside colonial petitions for negotiated reconciliation. The British view was that Parliamentary jurisdiction included all dominions of the Crown and that the American colonies now veered toward rebellion. The British demanded full obedience to the laws of Parliament. In April 1775, General Gage received instructions from the ministry: Arrest the rebel leaders, and act quickly to crush the insurrection with force. Gage doubted that he had sufficient manpower to do the job, but he followed orders.

On the evening of April 18, 1775, Gage dispatched a detachment of Redcoat regular troops in Boston to make a nighttime march to Lexington and Concord. The next morning, Redcoats opened fire on militia "minutemen" (citizen soldiers) who had gathered on Lexington Common, killing several. Patriot leaders John Hancock and Samuel Adams escaped the clutches of the British search party, having been warned by Paul Revere. (See the sidebar "The Midnight Ride of Paul Revere" on page 10.) that "the regulars are coming." British troops then marched on to Concord, where Redcoats and minutemen exchanged fire with fatal results at the old North Bridge. Protests had given way to armed confrontation.

Thousands of militiamen from Massachusetts and surrounding colonies gathered around Boston, where Gage had withdrawn his force. Penned up in a city under siege, General Gage, under pressure from the ministry, decided to occupy the heights on the Charlestown peninsula, which overlooked Boston and the harbor. Word of Gage's plan slipped out, allowing the patriots to fortify several hills, including Bunker Hill and Breed's Hill, near the village of Charlestown. On June 17, 1775, Redcoats crossed the narrow strip of water from Boston to Charlestown and stormed up Breed's Hill into the withering

THE MIDNIGHT RIDE OF PAUL REVERE

LISTEN, my children, and you shall hear
Of the midnight ride of Paul Revere,
On the eighteenth of April, in Seventy-Five;
Hardly a man is now alive
Who remembers that famous day and year.

He said to his friend, "If the British march
By land or sea from the town to-night,
Hang a lantern aloft in the belfry arch
Of the North Church tower, as a signal light,—
One, if by land, and two, if by sea;
And I on the opposite shore will be,
Ready to ride and spread the alarm
Through every Middlesex village and farm,
For the country-folk to be up and to arm."

These are the opening stanzas of Henry Wadsworth Longfellow's 1861 poem about "The Midnight Ride of Paul Revere," perhaps the most famous verse ever penned about the United States of America. Longfellow embellished history a little in his rendition of Paul Revere's part in the Revolution. Revere did rouse John Hancock and Samuel Adams from their beds in Lexington, where militiamen formed to confront British soldiers. The first shots of the Revolutionary war were fired early in the morning of April 19 on the town green in Lexington, Massachusetts. However, Revere was captured by a British patrol en route to Concord, the ultimate objective of the Redcoat foray into Boston's hinterland. Dr. Samuel Prescott, another patriot rider, delivered the warning to minutemen in Concord. Yet

fire of colonial militiamen. Although the British eventually routed the colonials from their hilltop bunkers, the Redcoats suffered tremendous casualties in the fight, known as the Battle of Bunker Hill. Patriots demonstrated that they could stand up to the strongest military in the world.

Longfellow certainly captured in a figurative way that "The fate of a nation was riding that night."

Paul Revere was a silversmith in Boston, born in the city in 1734. He followed his father's trade and on his death took over the Boston shop at age 19. A versatile craftsman, Revere also engraved etchings, including the famous picture of the Boston Massacre. For a time, he engaged in dentistry, a skill that bore some relationship to working with gold and silver wire. Although it is not known if he masqueraded as an Indian in the Boston Tea Party, Revere did participate in the planning of the event. When the British closed the port of Boston, Revere served as a courier for leaders in the resistance to the British occupation. His night ride of April 18–19, 1775, was undertaken as part of this communication network. Patriots kept a close eye on General Thomas Gage, who was instructed to capture the ringleaders of the colonial resistance and its store of weapons and ammunition kept in Concord. Revere was part of the team that sped out from Boston and other towns to spread the news that Gage had given orders to march out of the city. The rest of the story, as Longfellow suggested in his poem, is history.

Revere served in the Massachusetts militia during the Revolutionary War, taking part in the futile effort to dislodge the British in Castine, Maine, in 1779. He achieved greater success in his business ventures after the revolution. Turning the goldsmith business over to his eldest son, Revere opened an iron foundry in Boston in 1788. He specialized in casting bells, one of which was mounted on the USS *Constitution*. Later, Revere opened a copper-rolling mill in Canton, Massachusetts. Copper from his works was used on the dome of the new Massachusetts statehouse and in boilers for Robert Fulton's early steamboats. By the time he died in 1818, Revere had enjoyed many decades as a successful businessman. Some 43 years later, he would be immortalized in verse for his role in the opening shots of the American Revolution.

A Second Continental Congress had assembled in Philadelphia in May. Two days prior to the Battle of Bunker Hill, the delegates appointed George Washington, a resident of Virginia and a colonial in its militia, commander in chief of the continental defense forces. Washington did not reach Massachusetts in time for the Battle of Bunker Hill, but once

Battle of Bunker Hill and the Siege of Boston, June 1775–March 1776

Mystic R.

January 1776

Hog Island

Bunker Hill

Breed's Hill

June 17, 1775

Noddles Island

Cambridge

January 1776

Charlestown

Boston Harbor

March 17, 1776

Boston

Long Wharf

Charles R.

Brookline

Boston Neck

May 1775

Dorchester Flats (dry at low tide)

Nook's Hill

January 1776

Dorchester Heights

Roxbury

Roxbury Hill

Dorchester

— American troops

— British troops

ЛЛЛ American fortification

ЛЛЛ British fortification

British navy

Elevation

N

0   1 mile
0   1 km

© Infobase Learning

in Cambridge, he got right to work trying to mold a ragtag collection of New Englanders into an army. (See the sidebar "George Washington Takes Command" on page 14.) In the meantime, the congress acted decisively to meet the crisis. First, the delegates drafted a petition seeking reconciliation of their differences with the Crown and Parliament. The document stated explicitly that colonists remained proudly loyal British subjects. Second, the congress set forth why colonists had taken up arms in the Declaration of Causes and Necessity (July 6, 1775). Denouncing Gage's "warlike" foray into Lexington and Concord, where his troops "murdered eight of the inhabitants," the congress stated boldly that "We are reduced to the alternative of choosing an unconditional submission to the tyranny of irritated ministers or resistance by force. The latter is our choice." The congress advised the colonies to form temporary governments, free of royal control, to manage affairs in their regions. Then, delegates got to work assembling items required for the military confrontation with the British in Boston, where General William Howe, who had replaced Gage, wintered his garrison. The king responded by declaring that colonists who supported armed resistance were "rebels." Despite these setbacks, however, resistance leaders in America clung to the hope of reconciliation with Great Britain through 1775. Resistance to Britain's iron-fisted policy had not yet become revolution.

1776: From Confrontation to Separation

The Second Continental Congress worked feverishly in the early months of 1776. It functioned as a de facto national government, giving first priority to supporting an army that could resist the British incursion. "Independency," however, as the question of separation was called, had not been the primary reason that colonial leaders called a second meeting. But events rapidly altered its purpose—and perhaps loyalty to the king and Britain. In the eyes of most delegates assembled in Philadelphia, Parliament had displayed its intention of crushing the colonial "rebellion." Furthermore, delegates understood the seriousness of their military situation, even its desperateness, notwithstanding Washington's success in forcing the redcoats out of Boston in March 1776. In a daring maneuver during the dead of winter, Washington's men had transported cannon from Fort Ticonderoga on Lake Champlain to Dorchester Heights overlooking Boston. Seeing the vulnerability of his position, General Howe and the British invasion force departed for Halifax, Nova Scotia. The retreat was Washington's first major triumph, but he knew that the British would be back, most likely headed to New York.

During the siege of Boston (fall 1775–winter 1776), the Royal Navy had leveled the town of Falmouth, Maine's, leading seaport (now

GEORGE WASHINGTON TAKES COMMAND

George Washington was 43 years old when the Continental Congress appointed him commander of "all the continental forces, raised or to be raised, for the defense of American liberty." Some observers questioned the choice. Although Washington was an officer in the Virginia militia, he had never commanded a unit larger than a regiment. He had no experience with artillery or cavalry, nor had he led troops in a large-scale battle. The task ahead of him promised confrontation with battle-tested troops trained by the most powerful military organization in the world. Washington's mediocre performance in the French and Indian War, especially his surrender at Fort Necessity near present-day Pittsburgh, offered little assurance that he could overcome these liabilities. At the time of his appointment on June 15, 1775, there was no regular Patriot army. Washington himself acknowledged his shortcomings to the Continental Congress when he accepted the post.

But Washington was clearly capable of handling the job. He was born in Westmoreland County, Virginia, on February 22, 1734, a fourth-generation Virginian in a line of descendents from England. He had inherited a 2,500-acre plantation named Mount Vernon from his half-brother. His marriage to Martha Dandridge Custis in 1759, perhaps the wealthiest widow in Virginia, expanded his holdings. Eventually he put more than 3,200 acres into cultivation, planting mainly grains. Scores of slaves did most of the farm labor. Washington was a careful manager of this extensive plantation, inspecting his five working farms regularly as well as attending to his other economic ventures, such as a grain mill and fishing. As was common for a Virginia gentleman of his statute, Washington served in the Virginia legislature.

Washington was also a Patriot. He opposed the British effort to coerce the colonies into obedience following the Intolerable Acts, serving as one of Virginia's representatives to the First and Second Continental Congresses. He

named Portland). Lord John Dunmore, the royal governor of Virginia, burned Norfolk. More menacing to southern planters, Dunmore had offered freedom to slaves who fought Virginia rebels. Early in 1776, the congress learned that the king was sending reinforcements, including "foreign mercenaries," to the colonies. These acts of royal "brutality" strained hopes for reconciliation.

arrived at the second intercolonial meeting in Philadelphia in 1775 dressed in his military uniform. Although he did not expressly acknowledge his interest in leading an army of Patriots, Washington was clearly ready to lead the fight. The congress recognized Washington's assets. Physically impressive, he stood at least six feet two inches tall, with a muscular frame. He seldom spoke yet possessed a demeanor that radiated confidence. The Pennsylvania physician Benjamin Rush said "He has so much martial dignity in his deportment." These qualities became legendary during the seven years that "His Excellency" commanded the Patriot army. Washington's Virginia connection was also significant in the fight against the British. The fighting initially began in New England. Patriot leaders understood that all the colonies needed to cooperate if Americans were to have a chance of repelling a British invasion. Washington's selection was critical in fusing cooperation between the northern and southern colonies.

Washington greatest quality was recognition of how the Revolution could be won. He brought two critical elements to this task. First, Washington preserved the American army by avoiding pitched battles against the more experienced British. If the Patriot army remained in the field, the American cause remained alive. Second, Washington retained faith in eventual triumph despite repeated adversity and setbacks. Washington was not a great strategist, but he had an extraordinary mental toughness and learned by experience. His natural ability to radiate these attributes led his troops, officers in particular, to idolize him. So did a grateful nation when the American army and its French allies forced the British to surrender at Yorktown in 1781. Washington was heralded as America's greatest Revolutionary hero. This halo of adulation contributed to Washington's selection as president of the convention that wrote the Constitution of the United States in 1787 and his election as the first president of the United States in 1789.

That an amicable resolution of differences was even a desirable goal was directly challenged by Thomas Paine in January 1776. A recent emigrant from Britain, Paine authored a pamphlet entitled *Common Sense*, which argued that rule by a monarchy was burdened by contradictions. Americans would be much better off, in Paine's opinion, by declaring independence and establishing a republic. Written in a popular style

John Adams was a forceful advocate of separation from Great Britain when the question was debated in the Continental Congress in June 1776. (© Archive Images/ Alamy)

and weaving together arguments already in circulation, *Common Sense* was an immediate hit and best-seller. Most historians have credited Paine's treatise with immense influence in persuading the colonists that separation from England was logical and desirable—and possible.

Paine's ideas helped to frame the debate in the congress and among colonists over how to respond to British military coercion. Some delegates to the congress, such as John Adams of Massachusetts, urged independence. Moderates, such as John Dickinson, held on to hopes for reconciliation, even as fighting raged. By spring 1776, few in Congress thought reconciliation possible, but delegates from New York, Pennsylvania, and Maryland hung back from lending their support to independence. Other states, such as New Hampshire and South Carolina, forged ahead of the congress by writing their own constitutions, which were, in effect, declarations of independence. In May, the congress recommended that all colonies form new governments. On June 7, Richard Henry Lee moved a resolution for independence in the congress, which appointed a committee to draft a declaration of independence. By then, it was known that the British fleet had departed Halifax and soon would land an army, including German mercenaries, to fight Americans. The advance flotilla of this fleet arrived in New York on June 29. Three days later, delegates at the Continental Congress approved a Declaration of Independence, despite some lingering negative votes. The congress made the declaration public on July 4, 1776.

THE DEBATE

The Argument for Separation from Britain

Thomas Paine's *Common Sense* put the proposition of separation from the mother country before American colonists in plain and compelling language. He attacked the idea that monarchs were best suited to maintain liberty. (See "Thomas Paine, *Common Sense,* January 1776," on page 29 in the Primary Sources section.) In the first place, monarchs received their authority through heredity, which opened up the possibilities that weak candidates could come to the throne. Second, a monarch's broad power nurtured ambition, which was difficult to restrain. Staying with the empire would surely thrust Americans frequently into wars among Europe's many kingdoms. Liberty was more secure in a government based on the people themselves, thus, in a "republic." Other factors, including geography, pointed to the folly of staying within the empire. "There is something very absurd," Paine wrote, "in supposing a continent to be perpetually governed by an island." The historian Pauline Maier has observed (in *American Scripture*) that Paine did more than devise a powerful constitutional argument. He spoke to the pride most Americans had in being British, challenging their assumption that Britain had the most perfect form of government. Recent events, Paine argued, demonstrated the folly of that notion.

The delegates to the Second Continental Congress and Americans in the colonies had five months to reflect on Paine's treatise prior to the debate on Richard Henry Lee's resolution for independence on June 8, 1776. John Adams, Lee, and other delegates pointed out that no delegate now believed it was possible to restore traditional relations with Britain; the commencement of hostilities had dissolved the accords and sentiments that once prevailed. (See "Debate in Congress over Independence Resolution, June 8, 1776," on page 30 in the Primary Sources section.) Further delay, they argued, would jeopardize foreign assistance, especially from France. Moreover, separation would permit Americans to reopen trade with nations that currently observed Britain's ban of commerce with its rebellious colonies.

The debate in the congress on separation was as much about timing as it was about the merits of establishing an independent sovereignty. Moreover, separation meant the creation of a new government. The Declaration of Independence spoke to all of these issues and did so in elegant language, drafted by Thomas Jefferson, with editorial help from members of the congress. A decision for separation, Jefferson argued, should not occur for "light and transient causes" but only "when a long train of abuses and usurpations, pursuing invariably the same object" makes the alternative unpalatable. (See "Declaration of Independence, July 4, 1776," on page 31 in the Primary Sources section.) That "design," the declaration charged, was to place the colonies under "absolute despotism." Several sentences later, the congress substituted the word *tyranny* for *despotism,* repeating language the congress had used in the Declaration of Causes for Taking Up Arms and in earlier remonstrances to Britain. The Declaration and Resolves adopted by the First Continental Congress had used the term *enslave* to convey the same complaints about "the present King of Great Britain." These were powerful metaphors, reflecting both the anger of colonial leaders and their hope to convince fellow Americans that their rights were in jeopardy.

How did Jefferson document the king's conspiracy to strip Americans of their liberties? His evidence consisted of a list of 27 indictments against the Crown. Some of these charges, such as suspending colonial legislatures, imposing taxes without the consent of the inhabitants, and holding trials without the benefit of juries, directly undermined liberties that colonists assumed were inviolate. Offensive, too, was the maintenance of standing armies in the colonies, waging war against Americans, and ravaging towns along their coastline. Particularly damning was the observation that George III "is, at this time, transporting large armies of foreign mercenaries to complete the works of death, desolation, and tyranny . . . with . . . perfidy . . . unworthy the head of a civilized nation." Summing up these "oppressions," Jefferson said, made the king a tyrant and "unfit to be the ruler of a free people."

The declaration was more than a catalog of sins by the Crown against the liberties of American colonists. It also was a superbly styled version

John Trumbull's painting of the presentation of the Declaration of Independence to the Continental Congress shows John Adams, Roger Sherman, Robert R. Livingston, Thomas Jefferson, and James Madison in front of the desk. (© INTERFOTO/Alamy)

of John Locke's political philosophy that articulated reasons for placing restraints on the power of rulers. Men have unalienable rights, including "life, liberty and the pursuit of happiness," Jefferson wrote. Governments are instituted to secure these rights; public officials get their powers from the "consent of the governed." The Declaration of Independence was revolutionary not only because it cut the colonial bond with British rule and established an independent nation, but also because it articulated a philosophy that justified the formation of a republic (a political system based on popular consent). These were innovative and courageous steps, which required compelling arguments to overcome anxieties about venturing into uncharted territory. Jefferson is rightly remembered for hitting the right cadence and pitch in scripting this famous statement. Members of the congress amended the document, which probably helped to persuade 55 delegates to sign it.

The Argument Against Separation from Britain

The proposal to break from Britain did not find universal agreement. Far from it. When the Second Continental Congress entertained debate on Lee's independence resolution on June 8, 1776, only five states had authorized their delegates to vote for separation. The argument to delay approval of the motion was led by James Wilson (PA), Robert R. Livingston (NY), Edward Rutledge (SC), and John Dickinson (PA). According to Jefferson's notes on the proceedings, naysayers claimed that the "voice of the people" had not yet demanded that the congress agree to separation. Better to wait for a clear public signal, especially in the middle colonies, where opinions "were not yet ripe for bidding adieu to the British connection." (See "Debate in Congress over Independence Resolution, June 8, 1776," on page 33 in the Primary Sources section.) Doubts were expressed that delegates from several colonies lacked authorization from their colonies to approve independence. Hence, a premature declaration of separation could lead some colonies to break the unified front currently opposing British oppression, a development that could prove disastrous for recruiting foreign assistance. Disunity, the moderates warned, invited partitioning by European powers.

The opponents of independence in Congress on June 8 were probably more much concerned about the timing of a decision than with its underlying logic and, perhaps, even its inevitability. Wilson, Rutledge and Livingston went on to sign the declaration; the latter was a member of the committee that drafted the document, along with Jefferson and Benjamin Franklin. Dickinson did not sign but remained a Patriot during the Revolution. A substantial number of American colonists turned in the other direction, however. Most of these "loyalists" took their oaths of allegiance to the king as solemn and irrevocable commitments and took pride in the British Empire. They were well represented among royal officials in the colonies, Anglican clergymen, and successful merchants, especially in the coastal cities. The colonies of New York, New Jersey, Maryland, and Pennsylvania were strongholds of Loyalist sentiment, as were some communities of Germans and Irish, who questioned how far American liberty would go on their behalf. Some individuals, such as Joseph Galloway, who had been speaker of the Pennsylvania Assembly, and William Franklin, Benjamin's son and governor of New Jersey, were articulate and influential men. But the Loyalists never developed the network of communication that the colonial committees of correspondence created or matched the organizational zeal of a Samuel Adams of Boston.

Loyalists and others who opposed separation saw the colonists headed toward disaster. William Eddis, the secretary to the governor of Maryland, argued as much. Writing in the *Maryland Gazette* in February 1775, Eddis thought that American defiance of Great Britain was unnecessary and unwise. (See "William Eddis in *Maryland Gazette*, February 14, 1775," on page 34 in the Primary Sources section.) He expressed the opinion, as did others, that Britain did not intend to reduce the provinces "to a state of abject servility, by force of arms. . . ." But American defiance of Parliamentary authority would lead to a British blockade, which would produce impoverishment and promote divisions within the colonies. In large measure, he was right, although we know that the Patriots prevailed over wartime hardships and hounded many Loyalists out of the new country.

Charles Inglis, an Anglican clergymen attached to Trinity Church in New York when the Revolution erupted, also saw separation as a mistake. (See "Charles Inglis, *The True Interest of America Impartially Stated*, 1776," on page 35 in the Primary Sources section.) In 1776, he published a pamphlet that rebutted Paine's *Common Sense* point by point. He argued that a break with Britain would deprive colonial commerce of the protection of "the greatest naval power in the world." Waging war, he argued, would cost the colonists more than if they helped to pay for British naval security. He warned that the king and Parliament might parcel out parts of the American continent to

European powers as a way of forestalling further rebellions once the rebellion was crushed. He further opined that a "limited monarchy is the form of government that was most favorable to liberty." Other Loyalists thought that Britain offered wide protection for rights, more than any other nation-state. They were no doubt correct in this observation. Inglis went further, alleging that America was too large to contain a successful republic. Reservations about the ability of a republic to survive over an extensive area resurfaced during the debate over approval of the Constitution of the United States in 1788. Inglis had articulated a broadly held view in the Western world during the late 18th century about the fragility of a citizen-based polity.

Inglis remained in America until 1783, when he was banished from the new nation. Many Loyalists suffered a similar fate. Some had argued during the debate over the conflict with Britain that separation was led by hotheads from New England, who brandished their own version of moral certitude. Independence, this argument warned, might diminish American religious and cultural tolerance. Other doubters worried that separation from Britain opened up the possibilities of a revolution from below—wherein the poor and propertyless would seize the opportunity to even the score with their wealthy betters. The fear of anarchy and mob disorder haunted both Patriots and Loyalists. In the end, Patriots clamped down on overt opposition to their cause and stripped many Loyalists of their property.

OUTCOME AND IMPACT

The Loyalists remained royalists, meaning that they continued to pledge allegiance to the king of England during his conflict with the colonists. American patriots, by contrast, formed republican governments that dispensed with a monarch. Of the 13 colonies, 11 wrote state constitutions as legal foundations for their governments between 1776 and 1780. Connecticut and Rhode Island continued to use their colonial charters, although with references to the Crown deleted. In 1777, the Continental Congress adopted Articles of Confederation that sought to bind the states into a loose national federation; requiring approval from all the states, the agreement did not go into effect until 1781. The Continental Congress functioned as a national government for most of the war.

Colonial triumph on the battlefield entailed both immense effort and luck. One bit of good fortune was the selection of Washington to lead the Patriots. What Washington lacked in military knowledge he made up for in leadership ability and tenacity in the face of adversity. He never gave up. Washington's great achievement as commander in chief of the continental forces was to keep an army in the field until the most powerful military nation in the world saw the futility of further action against the Americans. Geography was an ally of the Patriot cause. Besides separation from its North American colonies by 3,000 miles of ocean in an era of sailing craft, the British had to conquer and hold locations along 1,300 miles of coastline that stretched from southern Maine to northern Georgia. Adding to British difficulties was the intervention of foreign rivals, a goal that the congress sought when it pondered the Declaration of Independence. France allied with the United States in 1778 and provided critical assistance to the Patriots. Spain declared war on Britain in 1779, and Holland followed suit in 1780. The French landed 7,000 troops to join Washington's siege of the British on the peninsula at Yorktown in October 1781. The French navy prevented the British from being reinforced or escaping by sea. The British surrender at Yorktown persuaded the British ministry that further effort to subdue the rebellious colonies was futile. Articles of peace were signed a year later, and the formal Treaty of Paris, which recognized American independence, was completed in September 1783. During this period, Washington once again proved adept at keeping an army intact until nationhood was officially secured.

These events constitute one of the most impressive achievements in modern history. The Americans not only held off the army of a superpower but also began a "republican" form of government that was based on the consent of the governed rather than on a hereditary monarchy. These dual outcomes sent shock waves through subsequent history. The next 150 years witnessed a host of revolutions against royal government and colonial status throughout the world. Not all of these developments were violent, and not all were successful. Anticolonialism swept through South America in the early 19th century, although Latin nations did not duplicate the democratic arrangement adopted in the United States. All of the English-speaking "settler" colonies of Great Britain (the United States, Canada, South Africa, Australia, and New Zealand) eventually became self-governing nations based on republican principles and parliamentary-style democracies. France underwent a revolution beginning in 1789 that toppled its monarchy and unleashed a new form of popular nationalism, although the new regime ended in a dictatorship under Napoleon. The revolutions of 1848 in Europe against conservative rule rekindled aspirations for constitutional rule.

Citizens of the United States had won stunning victories against colonialism and monarchy, yet not all Americans rejoiced at these achievements. Perhaps half a million residents of the thirteen colonies remained loyal to the king. Some 20,000 fought with his armies in America. States enacted laws during the war that forced residents to declare publicly their support of the Patriot cause or face banishment and loss of property. Up to 100,000 Loyalists emigrated from the United States during and after the war, with 30,000 relocating in Canada. Despite the provisions of the Treaty of Paris, few exiles recovered their property.

WHAT IF?

Of course, American history might have turned out differently. Had Parliament and the Crown not taken such a rigidly hard line toward accommodation with the colonists and recognized the strength of American attachments to Great Britain and the Crown, an alternate scenario is plausible. If British officials had shown more interest in reconciliation, the Continental Congress may have delayed or tabled its decision to separate from Britain. Then the history of the United States would have been written differently. Canada serves as a case in point.

Canada remained a set of separate colonies within the British Empire until the Act of Confederation in 1867. And even at this stage of Canadian history, opposition in the maritime provinces to inclusion in a greater Canada was strong, yet Canada developed a parliamentary style of democracy that afforded broadly based individual rights to its citizens. In many essential respects, its history was similar to that of its southern neighbor. Like the United States, Canada developed a sense of national identity, which helped to explain its resistance to incorporation with its larger southern neighbor. In many respects, the liberties identified by Loyalist writers during the Revolution found a home north of the border, especially in the Canadian maritime provinces. Unlike the United States, Canada eradicated slavery early in its history, sparing its provinces a sectional dispute over bondage.

This counterfactual speculation faces some challenges, of course. The War of 1812 between Britain and the United States poses one of them. Even if the colonies had remained within the British Empire, stresses in the relationship may have provoked armed conflict. The Americans were a sea-faring people, and the renewed war in Europe after 1803 placed American ships and merchants in jeopardy. British efforts to keep peace between pioneers who had migrated west and indigenous Americans in the Mississippi Valley region and the garrisoning of Redcoats on frontier forts remained contentious issues after 1783 and could have flared into serious confrontation between the two nations. In 1812, Britain would face a group of prideful Americans who were more numerous and economically stronger than they had been in 1775. The upshot of these conjectures is that one way or another, the Americans probably would have eventually created a self-governing nation. It is hard to escape the logic of Thomas Paine's conclusion that it was absurd to think that an island could rule a continent *forever.*

CHRONOLOGY

1763	French and Indian War (Seven Years' War) concludes.
1765–66	Stamp Act crisis
1767	Townshend Duties
1770	Boston "massacre"
1773	Boston "tea party"
1774	The Coercive Acts (also known as the Intolerable Acts) Britain dissolves the Massachusetts General Court. *September:* First Continental Congress meets in Philadelphia. *October 14:* Congress issues Declaration and Resolves.
1775	*April 19:* Minutemen engage British at Lexington and Concord. *May:* Second Continental Congress opens deliberations. *June 15:* Continental Congress appoints George Washington military commander. *June 17:* Battle of Bunker Hill *July 6:* Declaration of Causes and Necessity of Taking Up Arms *August 23:* King George III proclaims the colonies in rebellion. *November:* Congress advises colonies to form temporary governments. *December 22:* Parliament passes Prohibitory Act, banning all commerce with colonial ports.
1776	*January:* Thomas Paine publishes *Common Sense.* New Hampshire writes a state constitution. *March:* South Carolina adopts a constitution "independent of Royal authority."

May 10: Congress recommends that colonies form new governments.

May 15: Edmund Pendleton offers resolutions to instruct delegates to Congress to propose independence.

June 7: Richard Henry Lee moves independence resolution in the congress.

June 9: News that British fleet had left Halifax, probably for New York, arrives in the colonies.

June 12: Virginia Bill of Rights

June 29: British war fleet arrives in New York.

July 2: Vote on the Lee Resolution to declare independence

July 4: Declaration of Independence is announced.

1777   *November 17:* Congress adopts Articles of Confederation.

1781   *March:* Maryland becomes the 13th and final state to ratify Articles of Confederation.

October 19: British surrender to Washington at Yorktown.

1783   Treaty of Paris

DISCUSSION QUESTIONS

1. Discuss the role of printing and publication in shaping the dispute between American colonists and British officials.
2. How compelling was the Loyalist argument that independence would cost Americans more than they would gain from separation?
3. What factors were most influential in persuading members of the Continental Congress to decide on independence?
4. How would it have been possible for the British ministry to assert its authority over the American colonies while preventing the colonial decision to separate from the mother country?
5. At what point can it be said that the American colonies established a "republic"?

WEB SITES

Mt. Vernon Association. This site contains numerous stories about George Washington and his Mount Vernon home. Available at http://www.mountvernon.org/.

Paul Revere House, a biography of Revere and an illustrated essay on his famous ride. Available at http://www.paulreverehouse.org/.

BIBLIOGRAPHY

Borden, Morton, and Penn Borden. *The American Tory*. New York: Prentice Hall, 1972.

Fowler, William M., Jr. *Samuel Adams: Radical Puritan*. New York: Longman, 1997.

Gross, Robert A. *The Minutemen and Their World*. New York: Hill and Wang, 1976.

Maier, Pauline. *From Resistance to Revolution*. New York: Random House, 1972.

———. *American Scripture: Making the Declaration of Independence*. New York: Knopf, 1997.

Martin, James K., and Mark Edward Lender. *A Respectable Army: The Military Origins of the Republic, 1763–1789*. 2nd ed. Wheeling, Ill.: Harlan Davidson, 2006.

McCullough, David. *1776*. New York: Simon and Schuster, 2005.

Middlekauff, Robert. *The Glorious Cause: The American Revolution, 1763–1789*. New York: Oxford University Press, 1982.

Nelson, William H. *The American Tory*. New York: Oxford University Press, 1961.

Rakove, Jack N. *The Beginnings of National Politics: An Interpretive History of the Continental Congress*. Baltimore: Johns Hopkins University Press, 1979.

Wood, Gordon. *The Creation of the American Republic*. New York: Norton, 1969.

PRIMARY SOURCES

1. First Continental Congress, Declaration and Resolves, October 14, 1774

Written in response to Britain's imposition of the Intolerable Acts on the Massachusetts Bay colony, the Declaration and Resolves of the First Continental Congress summarized the complaint against British policy toward the colonies and asserted that the colonists' "religion, laws, and liberties, may not be subverted." The document goes on to list the rights of "the inhabitants of the English colonies in North America."

The good people of the several colonies of New-Hampshire, Massa-chusetts-Bay, Rhode Island and Providence Plantations, Connecticut, New-York, New-Jersey, Pennsylvania, Newcastle, Kent, and Sussex on Delaware, Maryland, Virginia, North-Carolina and South-Carolina, justly alarmed at these arbitrary proceedings of parliament and admin-istration, have severally elected, constituted, and appointed deputies to meet, and sit in general Congress, in the city of Philadelphia, in order to obtain such establishment, as that their religion, laws, and liberties, may not be subverted: Whereupon the deputies so appointed being now assembled, in a full and free representation of these colonies, taking into their most serious consideration, the best means of attaining the ends aforesaid, do, in the first place, as Englishmen, their ancestors in like cases have usually done, for asserting and vindicating their rights and liberties, DECLARE,

That the inhabitants of the English colonies in North-America, by the immutable laws of nature, the principles of the English constitution, and the several charters or compacts, have the following RIGHTS:

Resolved, 1. That they are entitled to life, liberty and property: and they have never ceded to any foreign power whatever, a right to dispose of either without their consent.

Resolved, 4. That the foundation of English liberty, and of all free government, is a right in the people to participate in their legislative council: and as the English colonists are not represented, and from their local and other circumstances, cannot properly be represented in the British Parliament, they are entitled to a free and exclusive power of legislation in their several provincial legislatures, where their right of representation can alone be preserved, in all cases of taxation and inter-nal polity, subject only to the negative of their sovereign, in such manner as has been heretofore used and accustomed:

Resolved, 9. That the keeping a standing army in these colonies, in times of peace, without the consent of the legislature of that colony, in which such army is kept, is against law.

Resolved, That the following Acts of Parliament are infringements and violations of the rights of the colonists; and that the repeal of them is essentially necessary, in order to restore harmony between Great Brit-ain and the American colonies, viz.

Also the three acts passed in the last session of Parliament, for stop-ping the port and blocking up the harbour of Boston, for altering the charter and government of Massachusetts-Bay, and that which is entitled, "An act for the better administration of justice, etc."

Also the act passed in the same session for establishing the Roman Catholic religion, in the province of Quebec, abolishing the equitable system of English laws, and erecting a tyranny there, to the great danger (from so total a dissimilarity of religion, law and government) of the neighboring British colonies, by the assistance of whose blood and treasure the said country was conquered from France.

Source: S. E. Morrison, ed., *Sources and Documents Illustrating the American Revolution, 1764–1788.* Oxford: Clarendon Press, 1929, 2d ed., 118–122.

—⁂—

2. Thomas Paine, *Common Sense,* January 1776

Thomas Paine's Common Sense *was written in the heat of the opening armed conflict with England in late 1775 and early 1776. Few publications have had as much impact on subsequent events as this pamphlet. Paine offered numerous argument to support his contention that monarchies were dangerous and the colonies would be better off as a republic, separated from the British Empire.*

I have heard it asserted by some, that as America hath flourished under her former connection with Great Britain, the same connection is necessary towards her future happiness, and will always have the same effect. Nothing can be more fallacious than this kind of argument. We may as well assert that because a child has thriven upon milk, that it is never to have meat, or that the first twenty years of our lives is to become a precedent for the next twenty.

I challenge the warmest advocate for reconciliation to show a single advantage that this continent can reap, by being connected with Great Britain. I repeat the challenge, not a single advantage is derived. Our corn will fetch its price in any market in Europe, and our imported goods must be paid for, buy them where we will.

Europe is too thickly planted with kingdoms to be long at peace, and whenever a war breaks out between England and any foreign power, the trade of America goes to ruin, *because of her connection with Britain.* The next war may not turn out like the last, and should it not, the advocates for reconciliation now will be wishing for separation then, because neutrality in that case would be a safer convoy than a man of war. Everything that is right or natural pleads for separation. The blood of the slain, the weeping voice of nature cries, 'TIS TIME TO PART. Even the distance at which the Almighty hath placed England and America is a strong and natural proof that the authority of the one over the other, was never the design of heaven.

Wherefore, since nothing but blows will do, for God's sake let us come to a final separation, and not leave the next generation to be cutting throats under the violated unmeaning names of parent and child. To say they will never attempt it again is idle and visionary; we thought so at the repeal of the stamp act, yet a year or two undeceived us; as well may we suppose that nations which have been once defeated will never renew the quarrel.

As to government matters, it is not in the power of Britain to do this continent justice: the business of it will soon be too weighty and intricate to be managed with any tolerable degree of convenience, by a power so distant from us, and so very ignorant of us; for if they cannot conquer us, they cannot govern us. To be always running three or four thousand miles with a tale or a petition, waiting four or five months for an answer, which, when obtained, requires five or six more to explain it in, will in a few years be looked upon as folly and childishness.

Small islands not capable of protecting themselves are the proper objects for kingdoms to take under their care; but there is something very absurd in supposing a continent to be perpetually governed by an island.

Source: Thomas Paine. *Common Sense.* 1776, 22–30.

—⁓—

3. Debate in Congress over Independence Resolution, June 8, 1776

Thomas Jefferson took notes on the deliberations in the Second Continental Congress on Richard Henry Lee's resolution to separate from Britain. Jefferson did not document the remarks of particular individuals, but rather provided a general synopsis of the arguments for and against the proposal to declare independence. In this section, Jefferson paraphrased the reasoning of John Adams, Richard Henry Lee, George Wythe, and "others."

On the other side it was by J Adams, Lee, [George] Wythe, and others that no gentleman had argued against the policy or right of separation from Britain, nor had supposed it possible we should ever renew our connection; that they had only opposed is being now declared:

That the question was not whether, by a declaration of independence, we should make ourselves what we are not; but whether we should declare a fact which already exists:

That, as to the people or Parliament of England, we had always been independent of them, their restraints on our trade deriving efficacy from our acquiescence only, and not from any rights they possessed of imposing them; and that, so far, our connection had been federal only, and was now dissolved by the commencement of hostilities.

That, as to the King, we had been bound to him by allegiance but that this bond was now dissolved by his assent to the late act of Parliament, by which he declares us out of his protection, and by his levying war on us—a fact which had long ago provide us out of this protection, it being a certain position in law that allegiance and protection are reciprocal, the one ceasing when the other is withdrawn:

That a *declaration of independence* alone could render it consistent with European delicacy for European powers to treat with us, or even to receive an ambassador from us:

That, till this, they would not receive our vessels into their ports, nor acknowledge the adjudications of our courts of admiralty to be legitimate, in cases of capture by British vessels.

That the present campaign may be unsuccessful, and therefore we had better propose an alliance while our affairs wear a hopeful aspect:

That is would be idle to lose time in settling the terms of alliance till we had first determined we would enter into alliance;

That it is necessary to lose no time in opening a trade for our people, who will want clothes, and will want money, too, for the payment of taxes.

Source: Marion M. Miller, ed. *Great Debates in American History.* New York: Current Literature Publishing Co., 1913, vol. 1, 189–191.

—∞—

4. Declaration of Independence, July 4, 1776

Drafted by Thomas Jefferson and amended by members of the Second Continental Congress, the Declaration of Independence enumerated 27 indictments of the king of England and offered a philosophy in defense of

separation from Britain and the establishment of an independent gov-
ernment. The declaration, excerpts of which are reprinted below, remains
one of the most important documents in the history of the United States.

When in the course of human events, it becomes necessary for one people to dissolve the political bands which have connected them with another, and to assume among the powers of the earth, the separate and equal station to which the laws of nature and of nature's God entitle them, a decent respect to the opinions of mankind requires that they should declare the causes which impel them to the separation.

We hold these truths to be self-evident, that all men are created equal, that they are endowed by their Creator with certain unalienable rights, that among these are life, liberty, and the pursuit of happiness; that, to secure these rights, governments are instituted among men, deriving their just powers from the consent of the governed, that whenever any form of government becomes destructive of these ends, it is the right of the people to alter or to abolish it, and to institute new government, laying its foundation on such principles, and organizing its powers in such form, as to them shall seem most likely to effect their safety and happiness. Prudence, indeed, will dictate that governments long established should not be changed for light and transient causes; and accordingly all experience hath shewn that mankind are more disposed to suffer, while evils are sufferable than to right themselves by abolishing the forms to which they are accustomed. But when a long train of abuses and usurpations, pursuing invariably the same object, evinces a design to reduce them under absolute despotism, it is their right, it is their duty, to throw off such government, and to provide new guards for their future security. Such has been the patient sufferance of these colonies; and such is now the necessity which constrains them to alter their former systems of government. The history of the present King of Great Britain is a history of repeated injuries and usurpations, all having in direct object the establishment of an absolute tyranny over these states. To prove this, let facts be submitted to a candid world.

He has refused his assent to laws, the most wholesome and necessary for the public good. . . .

He has called together legislative bodies at places unusual, uncomfortable, and distant from the depository of their public records, for the sole purpose of fatiguing them into compliance with his measures.

He has dissolved representative houses repeatedly, for opposing with manly firmness his invasions on the rights of the people. . . .

He has made judges dependent on his will alone, for the tenure of their offices, and the amount and payment of their salaries.

He has erected a multitude of new offices, and sent hither swarms of officers to harass our people, and eat out their substance.

He has kept among us, in times of peace, standing armies, without the consent of our legislatures.

He has combined with others to subject us to a jurisdiction foreign to our constitution, and unacknowledged by our laws; giving his assent to their acts of pretended legislation:

For quartering large bodies of armed troops among us;

For protecting them, by a mock trial, from punishment for any murders which they should commit on the inhabitants of these states; . . .

For imposing taxes on us without our consent;

For depriving us, in many cases, of the benefits of trial by jury. . . .

He has abdicated government here, by declaring us out of his protection and waging war against us.

He has plundered our seas, ravaged our coasts, burnt our towns, and destroyed the lives of our people.

He is, at this time, transporting large armies of foreign mercenaries to complete the works of death, desolation, and tyranny, already begun with circumstances of cruelty and perfidy, scarcely paralleled in the most barbarous ages, and totally unworthy the head of a civilized nation.

Source: http://avalon.law.yale.edu/18th_century/declare.asp.

—⟋ɯ⟍—

5. Debate in Congress over Independence Resolution, June 8, 1776

Thomas Jefferson's notes abstracted the arguments against separation made by James Wilson, Robert R. Livingston, Edward Rutledge, and others in the June 8, 1776, debate in the Continental Congress. This group of delegates contended that independence was premature because of the uncertainty over separation from Britain that lingered in some colonies.

They [Congress] proceeded to take it [Lee's resolution] into consideration, and referred it to a committee of the whole. . . . And passed that day and Monday, the 10th, in debating the subject.

It was argued by [James] Wilson, Robert R. Livingston, E. Rutledge, Dickinson, and others—

That, though they were friends to the measures themselves, and saw the impossibility that we should ever again be united with Great Britain, yet they were against adopting them at this time:

That the conduct we had formerly observed was wise and proper now, of deferring to take any capital step till the voice of the people drove us into it:

That they were our power, and without them our declaration could not be carried into effect:

That the people of the middle colonies (Maryland, Delaware, Pennsylvania, the Jerseys, and New York) were not yet ripe for bidding adieu to British connection, but that they were fast ripening, and, in a short time, would join in the general voice of America:

That, if the delegates of any particular colony had no power to declare such colony independent, certain they were the others could not declare it for them; the colonies being as yet perfectly independent of each other:

That the Assembly of Pennsylvania was now sitting above stairs; their convention would sit within a few days; the convention of New York was now sitting; and those of the Jerseys and Delaware counties would meet on the Monday following; and it was probable these bodies would take up the question of independence, and would declare to their delegates the voice of their state;

That, if such a declaration should now be agreed to, these delegates must retire, and possibly their colonies mighty secede from the Union;

That such a secession would weaken us more than could be compensated by any foreign alliance.

That, in the event of such a division, foreign powers would either refuse to join themselves to our fortunes, or, having us so much in their power as that desperate declaration would place us, they would insist on terms proportionably more hard and prejudicial.

Source: Marion M. Miller, ed. *Great Debates in American History.* New York: Current Literature Publishing Co., 1913, vol. 1, 187–189.

---

6. William Eddis in *Maryland Gazette,* February 14, 1775

William Eddis was the secretary to the governor of Maryland. His letter of February 14, 1775, to the Maryland Gazette, *a newspaper, stated that Americans misinterpreted the intentions of Great Britain and that defiance of British control would produce impoverishment and political divisions.*

On deliberate reflection, it can hardly be imagined, that the mother country has formed the least intention of reducing these provinces to a state of abject servility, by the force of arms; the natural connection—the close ties—and nice dependencies, which exist between the different parts of the empire, forbid indulging any conclusions of so melancholy a nature. She will be more just—more tender to her offspring—the voice of reason will prevail—our grievances will be redressed—and she will be found, to the end of time, a kind—a fostering parent! But admitting that Great Britain were determined to enforce a submission to all her mandates; even in that case, we have little cause to apprehend that she will unsheath the sword, and establish her decrees in the blood of thousands. A more safe and certain method is obvious; a small proportion of her naval power would entirely shut up our harbors—suspend trade—impoverish the inhabitants-promote intestine divisions-and involve us in all the horrors of anarchy and confusion. To avoid evils, even great as these, we are not meanly to bend the neck, and submit to every innovation. But when there is no prospect of such calamities, why are we to form ideas of battles and of slaughter?

And friends and Kindred forget the peaceful bonds of amity and love?

Source: Maryland Gazette, February 14, 1775.

—∿—

7. Charles Inglis, *The True Interest of America Impartially Stated,* 1776

Charles Inglis was an Anglican clergyman in New York City. He wrote his 1776 pamphlet in response to Thomas Paine's Common Sense, *published earlier in the year. Inglis enumerated the benefits of remaining within the British empire and the calamities that would probably follow from resistance to British rule.*

I think it no difficult matter to point out many advantages which will certainly attend our reconciliation and connection with Great-Britain, on a firm, constitutional plan. I shall select a few of these; and that their importance may be more clearly discerned, I shall afterwards point out some of the evils which inevitably must attend our separating from Britain, and declaring for independency. On each article I shall study brevity.

1. By a reconciliation with Britain, a period would be put to the present calamitous war, by which so many lives have been lost, and so many more must be lost, if it continues. . . .

3. Agriculture, commerce, and industry would resume their wonted vigor. At present, they languish and droop [sic], both here and in Britain; and must continue to do so, while this unhappy contest remains unsettled.

4. By a connection with Great-Britain, our trade would still have the protection of the greatest naval power in the world. England has the advantage, in this respect, of every other state, whether of ancient or modern times. Her insular situation, her nurseries for seamen, the superiority of those seamen above others—these circumstances to mention no other, combine to make her the first maritime power in the universe-such exactly is the power whose protection we want for our commerce.

5. The protection of our trade, while connected with Britain, will not cost us a *fiftieth* part of what it must cost, were we ourselves to raise a naval force sufficient for this purpose.

6. Whilst connected with Great-Britain, we have a bounty on almost every article of exportation; and we may be better supplied with goods by her, than we could elsewhere. . . . The manufactures of Great-Britain confessedly surpass any in the world—particularly those in every kind of metal, which we want most; and no country can afford linens and woollens, of equal quality cheaper.

7. When a Reconciliation is effected, and things return into the old channel, a few years of peace will restore everything to its pristine state. Emigrants will flow in as usual from the different parts of Europe.

The Americans are properly Britons. They have the manners, habits, and ideas of Britons; and have been accustomed to a similar form of government. But Britons never could bear the extremes, either of monarchy or republicanism. Some of their Kings have aimed at despotism; but always failed. Repeated efforts have been made towards democracy, and they equally failed. . . . After much blood was shed, those confusions would terminate in the despotism of some one successful adventurer; and should the Americans be so fortunate as to emancipate themselves from that thraldom, perhaps the whole would end in a limited monarchy, after shedding as much more blood. Limited monarchy is the form of government which is most favourable to liberty—which is best adapted to the genius and temper of Britons.

Source: Charles Inglis. *The True Interest of America Impartially Stated.* Privately published, 1776.

2

THE WAR OF 1812:

Should the United States Declare War on Great Britain?

—⁊⁊⁊—

THE CONTROVERSY

The Issue

On June 18, 1812, Congress declared war on Great Britain. This action culminated a decade of conflict with Britain over the right of the United States as a neutral nation to trade with Europe. The context of the dispute was Britain's war against Napoléon, whose empire spread over much of the Continent. The Napoleonic Wars included economic warfare in which both England and France interfered with the ships of neutrals headed for ports in Britain and on the Continent. Moreover, Britain imposed a partial blockade of American ports, further ensnaring American merchant vessels in the international struggle. Did Congress make the right call in going to war with Britain?

- ◆ **Arguments for war with Britain:** The proponents of war argued that negotiations with Britain had failed to uphold American rights as a neutral to trade freely with other nations. Further, many Americans denounced the British practice of removing sailors on U.S. ships on the pretext that they were deserters from the British navy. Some war supporters accused the British of spurring on Indians to attack American settlements in the Midwest.

- ◆ **Arguments against war with Britain:** Opponents of war countered that these accusations were overblown and that Americans must wait out the end of the European conflict. Some argued that fighting England only helped Napoléon, who was a power-hungry dictator. As for the Indians, the opponents claimed that U.S. encroachment on traditional Native American homelands explained their hostility.

—⁊⁊⁊—

INTRODUCTION

On June 22, 1807, the USS *Chesapeake,* one of the U.S. Navy's seven frigates and mounting 36 guns, was fired upon and disabled by the HMS *Leopard,* a British naval vessel carrying 56 guns. It was an ignominious defeat for the Americans, made even more galling by occurring within sight of the nation's shores. The *Chesapeake* was only 10 miles out to sea from Norfolk, Virginia, when it was hailed by the *Leopard.* Assuming that some routine matter was at hand, the American captain allowed a British officer to board his vessel, only to be surprised by a message to allow a search of the ship. The Americans refused the request, whereupon the British opened fire, killing three Americans. Unprepared for combat, the captain of the *Chesapeake* surrendered without firing a hostile shot. Then he watched the British remove four of his crew, who were charged with being deserters from the Royal Navy.

The British attack on the *Chesapeake* sparked outrage in the United States. The removal of American sailors from a ship of the U.S. Navy added insult to injury. Calls for war were heard throughout the country. President Thomas Jefferson resisted these demands, but he sympathized with the sentiment. The naval embarrassment off the shores of the United States vividly demonstrated complaints about British harassment of American ships and the "kidnapping" of American seamen. Just as galling, the sovereignty of the nation had been called into question by England's brazen attack on the *Chesapeake.* This challenge to American sovereignty was a key issue in a conflict that had begun four years earlier and festered for five more years until the United States declared war against Great Britain.

On June 1, 1812, President James Madison delivered to Congress a message that highlighted British restrictions of American commerce. The president asked Congress to decide whether the United States should protect its rights as a neutral by confronting Great Britain with armed force. On June 18, Congress voted for war. A substantial proportion of Congress thought the declaration was intemperate and perhaps foolhardy.

America was hardly ready to do battle with one of the military powerhouses of Europe. The United States had only a minuscule army, which lacked trained officers and equipment, and virtually no navy.

Deciding on war meant that the Americans confronted the most formidable naval force yet assembled. Even so, the Americans held Britain at bay for two and a half years, until ratification of the Treaty of Ghent formally ended hostilities in 1815. This good fortune is partially explained by Britain's assignment of the war to a secondary priority. Most of Britain's attention was focused on Napoléon Bonaparte, the French general and emperor, whose ambition to control all of Europe threatened the English and their allies. The American ability to avoid defeat is surprising, too, in light of stiff opposition to the war at home, which hampered the ability of the U.S. military to mount effective campaigns. Numerous American wars have caused dissent at home, but the War of 1812 may have been the most divisive of these foreign conflicts.

Then why did the two nations go to war? Should the United States have declared war against Great Britain? President Madison and his Republican Party colleagues in Congress said yes, war was made inevitable and unavoidable by wanton British disregard for American rights as a neutral nation. Britain had denied Americans commercial access to Europe and the West Indies, seized ships at sea, and "impressed" seamen off vessels that flew the American flag. The British, supporters of the war argued, had virtually confined American commerce to the nation's shorelines and harbors. Proponents of war also claimed that the British encouraged Indians to attack Americans in the Great Lakes region. Waving their list of provocations, prowar advocates saw the honor of the United States held hostage to a self-serving European power.

Opponents questioned these charges and their implications. They argued that it was the pressure of settlers into the American heartland, not the British, that drove Indians to war. They downgraded the significance of the spat with Great Britain, observing that American shippers were making money despite suffering seizures at sea and in European ports. War against Britain was hardly the way to treat a nation that was battling Napoléon, who sought to control all of Europe. Once the European wars came to an end, tensions over America's diplomatic grievances would subside.

The logic of the arguments for and against a war with Great Britain did not reveal the depth of the emotions that existed on both sides of the debate, nor do these claims and counterclaims add up to a clear explanation of the causes of the war. Generations of historians have wrestled with this perplexing question, offering a variety of alternative interpretations for why America fought a "second war of independence" from

Great Britain. The War of 1812 is one of the nation's most challenging historical enigmas.

BACKGROUND

America's foreign policy dilemma in the early 19th century derived first and foremost from one person: Napoléon Bonaparte. His rise to power in 1799 out of the turmoil of the French Revolution and his quest to rearrange the map of Europe put the United States in a difficult position. Napoléon's ambitions produced a renewal of the long-standing rivalry between France and Great Britain, which fought at numerous places around the globe between 1793 and 1802. Following a brief armistice, war between these ancient foes resumed in 1803. The United States remained a neutral nation for the next nine years as the European war unfolded, but with an economy heavily dependent on overseas commerce, America became sucked into the vortex of this dispute. Given the diplomatic and economic circumstances, it was difficult and probably impossible for the United States to have remained fully disentangled from Europe's problems. Less certain is whether these international challenges warranted an American declaration of war against Britain.

Each European power did its best to block the commerce of the other. Toward this goal, both nations seized the ships of neutral countries, including the United States. Besides prohibiting neutrals from trading with French colonies in the Caribbean, a British "order in council" (a regulation adopted by the prime minister and his senior advisers) in 1806 imposed a blockade of Napoleonic Europe. Napoléon responded with his Berlin Decree, which proclaimed a blockade of the British Isles. London fought back with further orders, which, in effect, levied a tax on neutral ships that wished to dock in ports on the European continent. Napoléon followed this action with his Milan Decree, which stated that any ship that paid a monetary tribute to Britain, or stopped at a British port would be considered a British ship, and thus subject to seizure.

Napoléon's order for a blockade of England was an aspiration more than a reality, because the British navy had swept the French from the ocean following its defeat in the Battle of Trafalgar in 1805. French commercial decrees, known as the Continental System, affected primarily European ports under Napoleonic control. Britain's naval advantage allowed its ships to roam the high seas virtually unchallenged. But providing crews for the 600 ships in the Royal Navy required recruiting 10,000 new seamen a year. Life aboard a British warship was close to a prison sentence, with low pay, poor rations, and severe penalties for misconduct. As a consequence, many British seamen deserted and signed on with American vessels, where conditions were better and wages higher. The British retaliated by hailing and searching American ships for British-born deserters from its navy. Britain did not recognize the transference of citizenship to another nations via naturalization, and sometimes British commanders "impressed"—or forcibly removed—U.S. citizens. Americans viewed impressments, especially of U.S. citizens, as an unforgivable violation of liberty. James Monroe, the U.S. secretary of state, estimated that roughly 6,500 Americans had been wrongly impressed in the decade before war with Britain.

So why did the United States not simply stay out of harm's way and avoid trade with nations at war? This was easier said than done, given the way Americans made their living in the first decade of the 19th century. The early decades of the 19th century were the "golden age" of American shipping. The sea had special meaning for most Americans, especially for New Englanders, whose heritage had long derived from a life on or from the ocean. New England shipbuilders became world famous at their craft. Other New Englanders, situated in Boston, Providence, and other seaport towns, were merchant traders and sea captains who bought and sold goods around the world, as well as plying the nation's coastal trade. Many more New Englanders earned their keep as seamen or as dock hands. New England forest products, such as tall pines used for ship masts and cut lumber, were exported to the Caribbean. New York, Maryland, and the Carolinas, too, provided commodities and sea captains for foreign commerce. The United States was the most important neutral carrier of international cargo during the Napoleonic wars. Moreover, the vast majority of both imports into the United States and its exports traveled in American "bottoms."

The ability of Americans to purchase imports depended heavily on their exports of agricultural products. The income from farming was critical to many local economies. Southerners sold cotton to England, as American textile mills were still in their infancy, and tobacco to Europe, whose populations had acquired a taste for the leaf. Grains grown in the middle states, such as Pennsylvania and New York, were shipped to Europe and the Caribbean islands, and Americans imported a wide variety of foreign-produced items that were not made or not made well enough for some tastes in the United States. The only significant manufactured product that Americans exported was ships.

President Thomas Jefferson (1801–09) thought that America's economic importance to Great Britain and the rest of Europe could be used to diplomatic advantage. He proposed an "embargo" that would prohibit the export of American products to all other countries, in hopes this denial of goods would force cessation of offensive trade practices. Congress enacted the measure on December 22, 1807. The embargo failed to force concessions from either Britain or France and was widely condemned. New Englanders, in particular, heaped withering criticism on the policy, which brought a recession to the seacoast region. Paul Revere, the famed Revolutionary rider and Massachusetts resident, who later manufactured copper sheeting, denounced "that cursed Embargo." President Jefferson's decision to bottle up American ships may seem puzzling unless one considers the limitation of the nation's military capabilities. Jefferson and his allies in the Republican Party made a minuscule army and navy as well as low taxes pillars of their political philosophy. (The Republican Party of that era is not related to the present-day Republican Party.) Because the United States lacked a navy that could confront a superpower (see the sidebar "America's Navy" on page 44), use of American sea power against the British was not a viable military option. Jefferson thought his embargo would prove effective within months. He miscalculated. Neither Britain nor France capitulated. On March 1, 1809, three days before Jefferson turned the presidency over to James Madison, a fellow Virginian, Congress repealed the hated embargo. (See the sidebar "'Mr. Jefferson's Embargo'" on page 46.)

With Jefferson retired to Monticello and the embargo no longer in force, Madison inherited the conflict with Europe. The new president proposed alternative restrictions of maritime commerce as a way of leveraging European compliance with American neutral "rights." Congress replaced the embargo with the Non-intercourse Act, which prohibited imports from Britain, though it was largely ineffective. When this measure expired in spring 1810, Congress tried another twist, enacting Macon's Bill No. 2. This law reopened American trade with all nations but allowed the president to suspend trade with either England or France if the other nation ceased its commercial restrictions against the United States. Napoléon's Cadore Letter of August 1810 appeared to signal French assent to American conditions. At least Madison adopted

AMERICA'S NAVY

The United States went to war in 1812 with a navy that consisted of just 16 vessels. Seven of these craft were frigates, which were squared-sailed ships that contained a single deck of guns, usually numbering between 36 and 44, but sometimes more. The remainder of the ocean-going fleet consisted of sloops and brigs (two-masted vessels), which were no match for frigates, or a "ship of the line." The equivalent of the modern battleship, a ship of the line supported two or three decks of 74 or more guns. The United States had no ship of this size, but its navy did include 62 operable gunboats, which were small craft that carried one or two guns and were fit only for operation in harbors or close to the coast. This was the extent of the nation's force at sea when the country confronted an opponent that maintained the strongest navy in the world. Great Britain possessed more than 1,000 ships, dozens of which were ships of the line. If ever there were a military mismatch, this was it.

Why did the United States not bulkup its navy when the nation was harassed at sea after 1803? Part of the reason is the overwhelming dominance of the British navy. American leaders knew that the United States would not be able to compete with Britain. In fact, enlarging the U.S. Navy made it more vulnerable, as Britain might become wary of America's growing potential and take preemptive action, as it had done against the Danish fleet at Copenhagen. Many congressmen regarded fiscal authorization to build warships tantamount to throwing money down the drain. Moreover, the philosophy of the Jeffersonian Republicans who controlled Congress in the early 19th century worshiped cost-consciousness. Voting funds for ships meant raising taxes, which they opposed. Moreover, building a bigger navy meant the creation of a professional cadre of officers, who would seek to put their martial skills into action. Jeffersonians sought to avoid war. They took consolation that North America was separated by the Atlantic Ocean from the powerhouses of Europe, a geographic fact that supported diplomatic isolation and a third-rate military establishment.

this interpretation, as he used the Napoleonic gesture as a pretext to trigger an embargo of trade with Britain. Even France's subsequent seizure of American ships in European ports did not cause the president to revise his reading of Napoléon's Cadore Letter.

Yet the naval situation was not all discouraging. Despite the vast power of the British fleet, America inflicted a few wounds on the naval giant. The United States sent its frigates, its most potent weapon, out to hunt down stray British vessels. Occasionally, the United States got lucky, as when the *Constitution* disabled the HMS *Guerriere* on August 19, 1812, in a gun battle 750 miles east of Boston. The *Constitution* had been launched in 1797, during the undeclared war with France. It was fast, well armed, and sturdily built, as the gunners of the *Guerriere* discovered. Most of its shots failed to penetrate the *Constitution*'s hull, leading to its nickname, *Old Ironsides*. The vessel still floats; it is moored in Boston and open to visitors. But these triumphs were the exception, not the rule. As the War of 1812 progressed, Britain tightened its blockade of the United States, penning up America's warships in the nation's harbors.

Yet, in one of the most astounding feats in American military history, the United States gained the upper hand on inland waters. Both Britain and the United States saw control of the Great Lakes and Lake Champlain as keys to military strategy in the north, where freshwater separated much of the United States from Canada. President Madison ordered the construction of separate naval contingents from scratch—on Lakes Ontario, Champlain, and Erie. All three fleets subsequently out-dueled British opponents, significantly boosting American pride and effectively blocking a British land invasion force. The best-remembered freshwater victory was scored by 27-year-old Oliver Hazard Perry near Put-In Bay on Lake Erie on September 10, 1813. Commodore Perry leaped from his disabled flagship, commandeered a sister vessel in his small fleet, and then raked six British ships with cannon fire, causing the British to surrender. Congress was elated, voting Perry and his crew a lavish financial "prize."

Here was the essence of America' military philosophy—build a fleet or an army when you needed it. Then, let American ingenuity and courage dictate the outcome.

Observing events from his ambassadorial post in Russia, John Quincy Adams saw Madison walking into "a trap to catch us in a war with England." The British also doubted Napoléon's sincerity and refused to

(continues on page 48)

"MR. JEFFERSON'S EMBARGO"

On December 22, 1807, President Thomas Jefferson signed legislation that prohibited American ships from exporting products to other nations. Initially "Mr. Jefferson's Embargo" applied just to American ships that engaged in foreign trade. A supplementary embargo act of March 12, 1808, prohibited the export of any goods by any means. During Jefferson's years as president (1801–09), Americans engaged in a flourishing sale of agricultural and forest products such as flour and lumber to customers in Europe, the West Indies, and the Canadian maritime provinces. Most of these commodities were shipped in American vessels. A substantial fraction of Americans made their living as seamen, merchants and shippers, and shipbuilders. Because ships and the sea were critical to the livelihood of many Americans, Jefferson's embargo placed a harsh burden on his own people. Why did he do it?

The United States had become locked in a dispute with Great Britain and France over foreign trade and the protection of American shipping. President Jefferson saw his options to this dilemma as either economic coercion or war. He chose economic pressure for two reasons. First, the president's first instinct was to seek a nonviolent solution to a diplomatic impasse. In principle, Jefferson was a pacifist, although in practice he sometimes relented, as in the instance of sending the U.S. Navy to face down the Barbary states in northern Africa. Second, Jefferson knew that war with Britain would pit his country against the strongest naval power in the world. There was no way that the United States could take on the British navy. War against France made little sense, either, as Napoléon's army and allies dominated the European continent. Thus, avoiding war seemed a more prudent strategy. Furthermore, Jefferson envisioned that the embargo would be effective within months.

The embargo was fairly successful in limiting foreign trade, although it failed to change English or French policy. That the embargo worked at all is surprising, in that it was denying an economic livelihood to thousands of Americans, and given the weakness of government. The central government had few of the tools for enforcement that national officials now possess. The federal bureaucracy, including the army and navy, were minuscule in the new republic. There were no FBI or national police agencies, such as drug enforcement officials or secret service agents. No aircraft for surveillance or radar to detect smugglers and nighttime evaders existed. Communications were limited to face-to-face verbal exchanges and written letters. In addition to Jefferson's own personal attention, enforcement of the embargo was delegated to Secretary of the Treasury Albert Gallatin and the customs agents in his department. As complaints and violations of the embargo mounted, especially in Massachusetts, treasury agents received sweeping powers to prevent the illegal departure of vessels. Customs agents could deny a permit to leave port to any vessel if its captain was suspected of intending to violate the law. Violators lost their cargo and were subject to a $10,000 fine for each offense, a huge penalty at the time.

The embargo lasted until March 1, 1809, when Jefferson signed repeal legislation, three days before he left the presidency. Opposition to the embargo grew during 1808 and early 1809, putting Jefferson's Republican Party in Congress under pressure to remove the ban or perhaps face a political insurrection at home. Jefferson made no effort to stop the repeal effort, but he never lost faith in the embargo. Shortly after the War of 1812 concluded, he wrote that "a continuance of the embargo for two months longer would have prevented our war."

Was Jefferson engaging in self-delusion? Can embargos actually work? Under the right conditions, they can. For an embargo to be effective, imports or exports must be critical to a nation's economic viability. In 1973, the members of the Organization of Oil Exporting Countries (OPEC) prohibited the sale of petroleum to the United States. Even though the United States got most of its petroleum from domestic wells, gasoline prices tripled in the country within months, triggering a serious economic recession in 1974 and 1975. In this instance, the critical element was oil, a commodity on which industrial economies and the United States in particular had become dependent. A total embargo on exports from Japan, whose economic lifeline depends heavily on foreign sales, would wreak havoc on the country. On the other hand, an embargo on sales to or purchases from lesser-developed nations would be far less likely to leverage the desired diplomatic effects. The economies of many of these nonindustrialized countries revolve around agriculture for internal use.

James Madison, a Virginian and the fourth president of the United States, led the nation into the War of 1812. (© Niday Picture Library/Alamy)

(continued from page 45)

relax their orders in council. English ships continued to seize American vessels. The rising anger against British "aggression" was manifested in the election of a large number of new representatives to Congress in 1810, a group that some older historical accounts somewhat misleadingly labeled the "War Hawks." These new additions swelled the Republican delegation in the 12th Congress (which was seated in December 1811) to a three-to-one majority in the House and a five-to-one majority in the Senate. And most Republicans were poised to face down Great Britain over affronts to American national sovereignty.

Pressure from Congress put Madison in a difficult position. By philosophic disposition, he opposed war. This conviction, which derived partially from his preferences for low taxes, had helped to cement his long-time political collaboration with Thomas Jefferson. While not a forceful leader, Madison was, however, a realist. He heard the demands from Republicans in Congress to stand up to British affronts. Plus, Madison kept his eye on 1812, when he hoped for reelection as president. In his third annual message to Congress on November 5, 1811, Madison reported on the failure of diplomacy to resolve the issues related to neutrality and urged military preparations. He expressed his pessimism that the "crisis" could be resolved easily. At some point over the six months, Madison decided that war was the only viable solution.

Madison summarized his thoughts on the matter in a special message to Congress on June 1, 1812. He charged the British government with perpetrating "a series of acts hostile to the United States as an independent and neutral nation." Claiming that a state of war with Great Britain, in fact, existed, the president asked Congress whether the United States should remain "passive under these progressive usurpations and these accumulating wrongs" or exercise force "in defense of their national rights." Lawmakers debated Madison's proposal for the next two weeks and on June 18 approved a declaration of war against Britain. The House voted 79 to 49 for the declaration; the Senate vote was closer, 19 to 13. Representatives from New York, Massachusetts, Connecticut, and New Jersey cast the largest bloc of opposition votes. The proponents of war were most numerous in districts in Pennsylvania and Virginia. All the votes cast by House members from Ohio, Kentucky, Tennessee, South Carolina, and Georgia favored the declaration. This sectional division in Congress was an omen of the dissent that emerged as "Mr. Madison's War" proceeded.

Why did Congress vote to go to war? No single or certain answer exists, although the debates in Congress offer numerous clues. Clearly, the British had seized American ships, impressed some American sailors, and claimed to have installed a blockade of American ports. But Napoléon, too, had taken American ships, even after issuing the Cadore Letter. Indian attacks on the frontiers around the Great Lakes and along the border area with Spain in the Gulf Coast region generated anger as well. Partisan politics came into play, too, with congressional Republicans showing a willingness to support their president and fend off

Federalist sniping at administration policy. There is also the possibility that Britain miscalculated, believing that Americans would not, or, perhaps, could not, fight. The evidence suggests that British officials took a hard line toward Americans in part because they overvalued communications from American Federalists, who predicted public repudiation of Madison's war policy.

All of these considerations probably played a role in pushing Congress to war. Another likely cause, in the opinion of the historian Roger Brown, was a feeling among Americans that their "republican experiment" was in jeopardy from Britain, whose real intent was to dominate American trade and to recolonize North America. This, at least, was the gist of some charges made against Great Britain. If even only partly true, such intentions put the nation's very survival at stake. Defense of American honor and independence thus may have induced some members of Congress, backed up by some of their constituents, to make a manly stand against their diabolical tormentor.

THE DEBATE

The Argument for War Against Britain

As the foreign "crisis" deepened, Madison anticipated the possibility of military conflict, for which the United States was poorly prepared. The president used his Third Annual Message to Congress in November 1811 to recommend improvements in the army and navy. The question of enlarging the country's military establishment and whether to use it against Britain set off an extended debate in Congress. Lawmakers discussed the issue for weeks and rehearsed all the arguments that proponents of war later cited.

Representative Richard Johnson (R-KY) argued that British "encroachments" at sea threatened American independence and justified war. He called the British interference with American commerce a "piratical system of paper blockade" and urged liberation of "our captured seamen" on British ships. (See "Representative Richard M. Johnson Favors War Against Britain, 1811," on page 62 in the Primary Sources section.) Impressments should be stopped, he argued, and the orders in council repealed, steps necessary to afford proper respect for America's "neutral rights" and its status "as an independent people."

Felix Grundy (Library of Congress)

Adding injury to insult, Johnson accused the British of whipping up the hostility of Indians on the northern frontier. If these practices were not stopped and U.S. sovereignty not shown respect, it was within the rights of the United States to drive Britain from North America.

Representative Felix Grundy (R-TN) added support and embellishment to Johnson's observation. The debate, he claimed, was about "whether we will resist by force the attempt . . . to subject our maritime rights to the arbitrary and capricious rule" of Britain. (See "Representative Felix Grundy Urges an Invasion of Canada, 1811," on page 63 in the Primary Sources section.) Answering his own question, he stated, "I prefer war to submission." War would allow the United States to "drive the British from our continent." Not only would this step stop Britain from stirring up the Indians, but also the annexation of Canada would have "beneficial political effects." He argued that the likely admission of Louisiana as a new state and the probability that the United States would acquire Florida from Spain, with more southern states to follow, would diminish the political power of the northern states. The annexation of Canada (and presumably its incorporation into the Union as one or more states) would preserve the sectional balance of the country. The geo-political visions presented in Johnson's and Grundy's remarks were predictions of the so-called manifest destiny of America to spread its institutions across North America, a theme that became popular in the 1840s.

More immediately, however, Canada represented a practical military target. Canada remained a colony of Great Britain, which stationed troops at strategic locations and anchored naval vessels in Canadian ports, such as Halifax. Despite the proximity of the British vessels, Congress balked at creating a navy capable of offering real resistance to the British fleet. Lawmakers did, however, authorize an increase in the regular army from 6,700 to 35,000, allowed a call for volunteers, and approved a larger militia. Despite approving the plan to enlarge American forces, Congress hoped that military action would not be necessary.

In view of Congress's half-hearted reform of the nation's defenses, President Madison concluded that Britain would not repeal its orders in council nor offer real concessions on the other maritime issues. Reporting on his administration's futile negotiations to redress these grievances in his June 1, 1812, message to Congress, Madison reminded lawmakers that under the British blockade "our commerce has been plundered in every sea, the great staples of our country have been cut off from their legitimate markets, and a destructive blow aimed at our agricultural and maritime interests." British cruisers "hover over and harassed our . . . commerce" and "wantonly spilt American Blood within the sanctuary of our territorial jurisdiction." (See "President James Madison, War Message, 1812," on page 64 in the Primary Sources section.) The president charged the English with using the European war as a pretext for perpetuating its "monopoly" over world commerce. Madison asked Congress to decide whether to use force to uphold American honor. The president made only passing mention of the Indian issue or France's recent confiscation of American ships in European ports. In effect, Madison had asked for a declaration of war against Great Britain.

Ironically, Britain indicated its willingness to suspend its orders in council on June 23, 1812. However, this news did not reach the United

States until after Congress had declared war. Britain's willingness to relent on its blockade was considered in Congress in January 1813. One lawmaker suggested legislation that would bar British subjects from serving as crew members on American ships as a way to prevent the impressments of Americans. Speaker of the House Henry Clay (R-KY), an ardent proponent of a hard line against the British, doubted that the proposed restriction would prove successful. (See "Speaker of the House Henry Clay Supports the War, 1813," on page 66 in the Primary Sources section.) Clay saw impressments as part of a larger British scheme to regulate commerce in their own interest, pursued through aggressive actions on the high seas. He concluded that "An honorable peace is attainable only by an efficient war," which might entail military incursions into Canada. Referring to the war against Great Britain that led to "independence," Clay stated that America had once triumphed over "haughty" England when its liberties were in jeopardy, and it would do so again. Although Clay was right about his prediction on the outcome of the war, he was wrong about how Canada figured in the result.

The Argument Against War with Britain

As events unfolded in the years leading up to the congressional vote for war, Republicans gradually coalesced behind military action to force a settlement with Great Britain, but not all members of Madison's party fell into line. One such critic was Representative John Randolph (R-VA), whose acerbic criticism of the Madison administration bedeviled the president. Randolph took aim at Grundy's charge that the British were behind the Indian uprisings around the Great Lakes. (See "Representative John Randolph Opposes War with Britain, 1811," on page 67 in the Primary Sources section.) Where, asked Randolph, was the evidence? Grundy's "insinuation," he charged, was "a presumption the most rash." Further, Randolph questioned the truth in the claim that the United States would go to war over the defense of its maritime rights. The driving motive, he thought, was articulated in a "monotonous tone—Canada! Canada! Canada!" Randolph reminded fellow Republicans that they stood on the brink of abandoning party promises of reducing taxes and the national debt. War meant standing armies, loans, taxes, and navies.

Josiah Quincy (F, MA) was more pointed in his criticism of the president's war. He charged that Madison's decision for war was predicated to help his re-election in 1812. He agreed with Randolph that the plan to conquer Canada made no sense. Canadians are our neighbors, he said, and they have done no harm to Americans. Randolph extended this motif, regretting that his countrymen might fight a people—the English— whose "blood runs in our veins," who shared a great tradition, and "whose form of government is the freest on earth, our own only excepted."

With war declared and the initial Canadian campaign unsuccessful, Madison asked Congress to expand the militia. Lawmakers in the House of Representatives debated the measure for two weeks in January 1813. By this time, it had become known that Britain had suspended its orders in council, a decision that Representative Joseph Pearson (R-NC) thought negated the reasons for war, save the issue of impressments. (See "Representative Joseph Pearson Proposes an End to the War, 1813," on page 68 in the Primary Sources section.) And the matter of impressments, Pearson suggested, could be solved by passing legislation that excluded British subjects from serving on American ocean vessels. By doing this, Pearson claimed, "I venture to predict you will obtain a peace and secure your just rights more speedily, more effectually, and more satisfactorily to the people of this country than by all the military operations in the compass of your power."

Federalists, the small minority party in Congress, rejected Republicans' arguments for war. Mainly representing New England, Federalist leaders understood that shipping and overseas commerce were a lifeblood of northern coastal states. Ocean shipping was inherently a risky business. British trade restrictions were just one more hazard in a dangerous trade. Even with a British blockade, which in actuality was more formidable on paper than in practice, there was money to be made in trans-Atlantic commerce. Moreover, many New Englanders shared a kinship feeling with Protestant Britain and supported its struggle against Catholic France. Massachusetts governor Caleb Strong, a Federalist, agreed with these views. He urged his constituents to condemn the war "against the nation from which we are descended and which for many generations has been the bulwark of the religion we profess." As the historian Samuel Eliot Morison wrote in 1970, Federalists thought "it seemed wicked and unchristian . . . to attack England when she was 'the world's last hope' against tyrant Napoleon."

New England's opposition to the war reached a climax with the Hartford Convention, which met between December 1814 and early January 1815. Delegates from Massachusetts, Connecticut, Rhode Island, Vermont, and New Hampshire attended the meeting in Hartford,

Connecticut. John Quincy Adams, a New Englander himself, charged that the convention was part of a secession plot that envisioned break-away New England making a separate peace with Britain. While some delegates at Hartford may have entertained thoughts of secession, the main business of the convention was to prepare resolutions for submission to Congress. Delegates at the convention articulated long-standing political grievances, such as the three-fifths clause in the Constitution of the United States, which allowed southern states to count slaves in apportioning congressional districts and electoral votes for the presidency. The delegates made plain their dissatisfaction with the succession of Virginia presidents, which stemmed from "a combination among certain states . . . to control public affairs." The desire for "party power," the convention report and resolutions declared, was the real reason behind hostility to Britain. (See "Report and Resolutions of the Hartford Convention, 1815," on page 68 in the Primary Sources section.)

To remedy this sectional favoritism, the convention proposed a series of amendments to the Constitution. Delegates recommended a two-thirds vote of both houses of Congress to admit new states to the union, to "interdict" commerce with the United States, and to authorize declarations of war. Another amendment barred presidents from a second term. The convention also recommended that Congress legislate to afford states more control over their own defense, a provision that reflected unhappiness with the use of state militias beyond their own borders and outside the United States during the War of 1812. The three delegates dispatched to deliver these resolutions arrived in the national capital just as the news of Andrew Jackson's stunning victory over the British army and of the treaty ending the war arrived, in January 1815. These successes took the wind out of the sails of the Hartford delegates, who pocketed their petition and returned home.

OUTCOME AND IMPACT

Despite the bravado of some members of Congress, who boasted that a small band of Kentucky riflemen could easily conquer Canada, the odds that the United States could defeat Great Britain looked bleak in 1812. The United States had only a token navy. While American frigates scored several victories over individual enemy ships, the Britain navy blockaded the American coast during the war. The regular army of the United States was woefully small, had no general staff, and lacked sufficient trained junior officers. The nation depended heavily on state militias to shoulder much of the fighting, but reluctance of some state officials to allow their militias to maneuver beyond state borders hampered logistical operations. And when militias were employed, conflicts over who should command it—the ranking regular army officer or the leader of the militia—caused disorder. Of greater relevance, poorly trained militiamen were no match against seasoned professionals.

These liabilities were borne out early, as the American effort to dislodge the British at the western end of Lake Erie resulted in the surrender of the U.S. fort at Detroit in September 1812. Subsequent efforts to penetrate Canada failed as well. At sea, the British blockade offered protection for foraging attacks on coastal communities. Britain extended its blockade to the New England coast in 1814, using its naval presence to burn Yankee ships at anchor.

The combination of these strategies took its most ignominious turn in the burning of Washington, D.C., on August 24, 1814. A British naval force containing marines pushed up Chesapeake Bay, raiding coastal communities en route and giving rise to the prospect of capturing the president of the United States. Largely because American military intelligence was so poor (nearly nonexistent is a better description), Madison discounted rumors that a sizeable British force might attack the nation's capital. Not only was the president misinformed, he barely escaped the city as the British entered, virtually unimpeded. Just hours earlier, Dolly Madison, the president's wife, had loaded a wagon

Drawing of the U.S. Capitol after it was burned by the British (Library of Congress)

with valuables from the White House, including Gilbert Stuart's precious portrait of George Washington, and escaped across the Potomac River into Virginia. British marines torched public buildings in the city, including the White House and the Capitol, supposedly in retaliation for Americans setting York, Canada, ablaze. Private structures in Washington were left unharmed. The British withdrew from the capital within days after their arrival. Humiliating as the attack on Washington was, it reaped no strategic advantage for Britain. The same British force was foiled in its attempt to capture the port city of Baltimore several weeks later. The British bombardment of Fort McHenry there provided the setting for Francis Scott Key's immortal poem about the attack, lines that eventually became the nation's national anthem.

Baltimore was one of the bright spots in America's second war against the British. The United States also scored surprising successes on the Great Lakes and Lake Champlain, where Americans built freshwater fleets from scratch and then defeated rival warships. These victories gave the United States control of the northern waters and thwarted Britain's attempt to invade the United States from Canada. The greatest American military triumph occurred under the leadership of General Andrew Jackson at New Orleans. The British landed a force of 10,000 troops 60 miles west of the strategic port located on the Gulf of Mexico. The British operation was poorly planned, both for the transit from their transport ships to New Orleans and then to the field for the encounter with the Americans. On a narrow plain outside the city, British regulars met Jackson's forces on January 8, 1815. Jackson's army was a rag-tag assemblage, but it was well entrenched and prepared. Line upon line of Redcoats were mowed down and their commanding officers killed, while the Americans suffered minimal casualties. It was an extraordinary victory and made Jackson an instant national hero. It mattered little that negotiators had already signed a peace agreement in Ghent, Belgium; the news of this event had not yet reached the United States.

An American team of negotiators that included John Quincy Adams and Henry Clay had parlayed with British counterparts for months in 1814 until the British recognized that they had little to gain from continuing the war. A turn in the European situation played a key role in British policy. Napoléon had abdicated, ending the European war. This development removed many of the British concerns about maritime trade. (Napoléon returned for 100 days in 1815, before his final defeat.)

The peace agreement was little more than an armistice, as few of the issues that had brought on the conflict were addressed in the Treaty of Ghent, but it set the tone for future Anglo-American discussions. Lingering issues such as naval strength on the Great Lakes, boundary disputes, and determination of fishing rights were amicably negotiated in subsequent years. The Senate ratified the peace treaty unanimously on February 17, 1815. It is an exaggeration to say that the United States won the War of 1812. More accurately put, Americans could take pride that they had held off the world's strongest military power long enough not to lose.

Historians commonly point to several significant consequences that flowed from the War of 1812. Economically, the British blockade, which reduced imports of goods into the United States, stimulated American manufacturing. Military victories over Native Americans in Indiana (Battle of Tippecanoe, 1811) and in the South (Andrew Jackson at Horseshoe Bend, 1814) had crushed Indian resistance to western migrants in these regions. The Federalist Party lost creditability by its opposition to the war and soon faded from view. With Britain neutralized and Spain unable to prevent American encroachment in Florida, the United States was left the dominant power on the North American continent. And finally, 1812 fanned the flames of American nationalism. Americans were proud that they had sustained their rights and their republic. The citizens of Baltimore expressed this sentiment in an address forwarded to President Madison in 1815, proclaiming that the war "has tried and vindicated our republican institutions: it has given us that moral strength, which consists in the well-earned respect of the world, and in the just respect for ourselves. It has raised up and consolidated national character, dear to the hearts of the people, as an object of honest pride and a pledge of future union, tranquility, and greatness."

WHAT IF?

While the Americans certainly did not extract a surrender from Great Britain, they did score a resounding victory over a British army in New Orleans. Without taking credit away from Andrew Jackson, who cobbled together a force that included pirates and slaves on loan, the British defeat was partially, if not largely, due to their strategic and tactical mistakes. For one, the British army had to slosh through 60 miles of swamp, bayous, and mud from where they disembarked from their oceangoing ships to reach the outskirts on New Orleans. For another, the British used a classic

18th-century style frontal assault along a narrow strip of land, marching directly into American fire, including artillery. The Redcoats were sitting ducks, which explains why Britain suffered almost 2,000 casualties, versus only 50 for the Americans.

But what if the British had planned better and at least salvaged a stalemate at New Orleans? Or perhaps they might have cobbled together a victory, permitting the British to occupy the Crescent City. Such possibilities could have altered the peace settlement. In 1814, British negotiators in Ghent entertained aspirations of recovering territories lost to the United States as a result of the American Revolution. British soldiers occupied portions of Maine in 1814; the region's boundary with Canada had been disputed since the Treaty of Paris (1783). It is conceivable that the British military would have remained entrenched around the Great Lakes. Perhaps gaining a foothold in New Orleans would have supported Spain's contention that the Louisiana Purchase had been illegal. A British presence in New Orleans certainly could have disrupted commerce along the Mississippi River, which developed into a vital north-south artery in the interior of the country after 1815.

While these conjectures have elements of plausibility, they suggest several counterspeculations. First, Britain did not want to fight a long and hard war with the United States. Britain's primary objective in 1812–14 was the defeat of Napoléon in Europe. The British did not throw their full force against America, but the strategic situation changed when Napoléon attacked Russia in 1812. Clearly, Napoléon's turn against his erstwhile Russian ally increased England's military prospects against France. Madison is reputed to have written after the war that he would not have asked for war had he known of Napoléon's defeat in Russia. Timing plays a major role in diplomatic decision making. News traveled slowing in the early 19th century. The British concession on its orders in council was made before Congress had declared war, but the news did not arrive in America until after Congress had voted for war. Congress might have voted differently had the British decision reached Washington sooner.

A second consideration suggests that the British would be evicted from the heartland of North America even if they had done better on the battlefield at New Orleans. Americans had been streaming into the region west of the Appalachian Mountains before the war of 1812. The volume of migrants accelerated after 1815, populating Indiana, Illinois, Missouri, Mississippi, and Alabama sufficiently to admit them to the union between 1816 and 1821. The total American population grew from 7 million people in 1810 to nearly 13 million in 1830. By 1850, Americans outnumbered the residents of England, Wales, and Scotland combined. It is highly unlikely that Britain could have withstood this flood of Americans into the interior of the United States. In fact, the course of diplomatic events suggests the English officials had no burning desire to do so. Excepting

Maine, Britain amicably agreed to a transcontinental border between the United States and Canada in 1818. The Americans were lucky to have held off the British during the War of 1812. And even if they had lost at New Orleans, Americans appeared destined by demography, geography, and economics to control the interior of North America.

CHRONOLOGY

1803   War resumes between England and France.

1805   Battle of Trafalgar

1806   *April 6:* Non-importation Act
November 21: Berlin Decree

1807   *June 22:* Clash between USS *Chesapeake* and HMS *Leopard*
November 11: Orders in Council
December 17: Milan Decree
December 22: Embargo Act

1808   *December:* James Madison is elected president.

1809   *March 1:* Embargo Act is repealed.
Non-intercourse Act replaces Embargo Act.
May: British ministry rejects a commercial treaty with the United States.

1810   *May 1:* Macon's Bill No. 2
August 5: Napoléon issues the Cadore Letter.

1811   *November 7:* Battle of Tippecanoe

1812   *April 4:* Britain embargoes American Trade.
June 1: President Madison's "war" message
June 18: United States declares war on Great Britain.
June 23: Repeal of the Orders in Council
June 24: Napoléon invades Russia.

1813   *September 10:* Battle of Lake Erie (Put-in Bay)

1814   *August 24:* British soldiers burn Washington, D.C.
September 11: Battle of Plattsburgh Bay, Lake Champlain
December 15: Hartford Convention begins; adjourned January 5, 1815.
December 24: Treaty of Ghent is negotiated.

1815   *January 8:* Americans win the Battle of New Orleans.
February 17: U.S. Senate approves the Treaty of Ghent.

DISCUSSION QUESTIONS

1. Who represented a greater threat to American interests—Great Britain or France's Napoléon?
2. How valid is the claim that a country not officially engaged in a war has the right to trade with whomever or wherever it chooses?
3. Could the United States have overcome its military and naval weaknesses sufficiently before June 1812 to pressure Great Britain into reducing or suspending its restrictions on American maritime commerce?
4. Some Americans argued it would be easy to drive the British from Canada. Was this a realistic prediction? Could it have been achieved?
5. Was President James Madison too anxious to go to war?

WEB SITES

Battle of New Orleans at Chalmette. Website of the National Park Service, Historical Preserve and Battlefield Site. Available at http://www.nps.gov/jela/chalmette-battlefield.htm.

James Madison. An Online Reference Resource of the Miller Center of Public Affairs, University of Virginia. Available at http://millercenter.org/academic/americanpresident/madison.

James Monroe. An Online Reference Resource of the Miller Center of Public Affairs, University of Virginia. Available at http://millercenter.org/academic/americanpresident/monroe.

War of 1812. Web Sources for Military History. Richard Jensen. Available at http://tigger.uic.edu/~rjensen/military.html#H.

BIBLIOGRAPHY

Banner, James. *To the Hartford Convention: The Federalists and the Origins of Party Politics in Massachusetts, 1789–1815.* New York: Knopf, 1970.

Brown, Roger H. *The Republic in Peril: 1812.* New York: Columbia University Press, 1964.

Coles, Harry L. *The War of 1812.* Chicago: University of Chicago Press, 1965.

Morison, Samuel Eliot, Frederick Merk, and Frank Freidel. *Dissent in Three American Wars.* Cambridge, Mass.: Harvard University Press, 1970.

Rutland, Robert A. *The Presidency of James Madison.* Lawrence: University Press of Kansas, 1990.

Smelser, Marshall. *The Democratic Republic, 1801–1815.* New York: Harper and Row, 1968.

Stagg, J. C. A. *Mr. Madison's War.* Princeton, N.J.: Princeton University Press, 1983.

PRIMARY SOURCES

1. Representative Richard M. Johnson Favors War Against Britain, 1811

On December 11, 1811, Representative Richard M. Johnson (R-KY) gave numerous reasons for going to war against Great Britain during a debate over President Madison's proposal to increase the army and the navy. Johnson pointed to British impressments of American sailors, the restrictions on trade through their orders in council, and British instigation of northern Indians to go to war.

[W]e must now oppose the farther encroachments of Great Britain by war, or formally annul the Declaration of our Independence, and acknowledge ourselves her devoted colonies. The people who I represent will not hesitate which of the courses to choose; and, if we are involved in war, to maintain our dearest rights, and to preserve our independence, I pledge myself to this House, and my constitutions to this nation, that they will not be wanting in valor, nor in their proportion of men and money to prosecute the war with effect. Before we relinquish the conflict, I wish to see Great Britain renounce the piratical system of paper blockage, to liberate our captured seamen on board her ships of war, relinquish the practice of impression on board our merchant vessels; to repeal her Orders in Council; to cease, in every other respect, to violate our neutral rights; to treat us as an independent people.

Therefore, I can have no doubt of the influence British-agents in keeping up Indian hostility to the people of the United States, independent of the strong proofs on this occasion; and I hope it will not be pretended that these agents are too moral or too religious to do the infamous deed. So much for the expulsion of Great Britain from her dominions in North America, and their incorporation into the United States of America.

For God's sake let us not again be told of the ties of religion, of laws, of blood, and of customs, which bind the two nations together, with a view to extort our love for the English Government. . . . Let us not be told of the freedom of that corrupt Government whose hands are washed alike in the blood of her own illustrious statesmen for mainly opposition to tyranny. . . . It has been said that Great Britain was fighting the battles of the world—that she stands against universal dominion. . . . If, however she would act the part of a friendly Power towards the United States, I would never wish to deprive her of power. . . . But if her energies are to be directed against the liberties of this free and happy people, against my native country, I should not drop a tear if the fast-anchored isle would sink into the waves. . . .

Source: Annals of Congress, December 11, 1811, 457–459.

—⁊⁊⁊—

2. Representative Felix Grundy Urges an Invasion of Canada, 1811

On December 9, 1811, in the debate over increasing the military, Representative Felix Grundy (R-TN) charged the British with stirring up Native Americans in "the West" (in the southern Great Lakes region). He argued that the invasion of Canada and its annexation to the United States would solve this issue.

What, Mr. Speaker, are we now called on to decide? It is, whether we will resist by force the attempt made by that Government, to subject our maritime rights to the arbitrary and capricious rule of her will; for my part I am not prepared to say that this country shall submit to have her commerce interdicted or regulated by any foreign nation. Sir, I prefer war to submission.

This war, if carried on successfully, will have its advantages. We shall drive the British from our Continent—they will no longer have an opportunity of intriguing with our Indian neighbors, and setting on the ruthless savage to tomahawk our women and children. That nation will lose her Canadian trade, and by having no resting place in this country, her means of annoying us will be diminished. The idea I am now about to advance is at war, I know, with sentiments of the gentleman from Virginia; I am willing to receive the Canadians as adopted brethren; it will have beneficial political effects; it will preserve the equilibrium of the Government. When Louisiana shall be fully peopled, the Northern states will lose their power; they will be at the discretion of others; they can be depressed at pleasure, and then this Union might be endangered—I therefore feel anxious not only to add the Floridas to the South, but the Canadas to the North of this empire. . . .

Source: Annals of Congress, December 9, 1811, 427–429.

—⚬—

3. President James Madison, War Message, 1812

President James Madison sent a special message to Congress on June 1, 1812, that recited the major complaints that the United States had against Great Britain. Called his "War Message" by historians, Madison did not explicitly ask lawmakers to declare war, but rather let Congress decide the appropriate course of action.

British cruisers have been in the continued practice of violating the American flag on the great highway of nations, and of seizing and carrying off persons sailing under it, not in the exercise of a belligerent right founded on the law of nations against an enemy, but of a municipal prerogative over British subjects. British jurisdiction is thus extended to neutral vessels in a situation where no laws can operate but the law of nations and the laws of the country to which the vessels belong. British cruisers have been in the practice also of violating the rights and the peace of our coasts. They hover over and harass our entering and departing commerce. To the most insulting pretensions they have added the most lawless proceedings in our very harbors, and have wantonly spilt American blood within the sanctuary of our territorial jurisdiction. The principles and rules enforced by that nation, when a neutral nation, against armed vessels of belligerents hovering near her coasts and disturbing her commerce are well known. When called on, nevertheless, by the United States to punish the greater offenses committed by her own vessels, her Government has bestowed on their commanders additional marks of honor and confidence.

The practice, hence, is so far from affecting British subjects alone that, under the pretext of searching for these, thousands of American citizens, under the safeguard of public law and of their national flag, have been torn from their country and from everything dear to them; have been dragged on board ships of war of a foreign nation and exposed, under the severities of their discipline, to be exiled to the most distant and deadly climes, to risk their lives in the battles of their oppressors, and to be the melancholy instruments of taking away those of their own brethren.

Under pretended blockades, without the presence of an adequate force and sometimes without the practicability of applying one, our commerce has been plundered in every sea, the great staples of our country have been cut off from their legitimate markets, and a destructive blow aimed at our agricultural and maritime interests.

Not content with these occasional expedients for laying waste our neutral trade, the cabinet of Britain resorted at length to the sweeping system of blockades, under the name of orders in council, which has been molded and managed as might best suit its political views, its commercial jealousies, or the avidity of British cruisers.

It has become, indeed, sufficiently certain that the commerce of the United States is to be sacrificed, not as interfering with the belligerent rights of Great Britain; not as supplying the wants of her enemies, which she herself supplies; but as interfering with the monopoly which she covets for her own commerce and navigation. She carries on a war against the lawful commerce of a friend that she may the better carry on a commerce with an enemy—a commerce polluted by the forgeries and perjuries which are for the most part the only passports by which it can succeed.

In reviewing the conduct of Great Britain toward the United States our attention is necessarily drawn to the warfare just renewed by the savages on one of our extensive frontiers—a warfare which is known to spare neither age nor sex and to be distinguished by features peculiarly shocking to humanity. It is difficult to account for the activity and combinations which have for some time been developing themselves among tribes in constant intercourse with British traders and garrisons without connecting their hostility with that influence and without recollecting the authenticated examples of such interpositions heretofore furnished by the officers and agents of that Government.

Such is the spectacle of injuries and indignities which have been heaped on our country, and such the crisis which its unexampled forbearance and conciliatory efforts have not been able to avert.

Our moderation and conciliation have had no other effect than to encourage perseverance and to enlarge pretensions. We behold our seafaring citizens still the daily victims of lawless violence, committed on the great common and highway of nations, even within sight of the country which owes them protection.

Whether the United States shall continue passive under these progressive usurpations and these accumulating wrongs, or, opposing force to force in defense of their national rights, . . . is a solemn question which the Constitution wisely confides to the legislative department of the Government.

Source: James D. Richardson, comp. *Messages and Papers of the Presidents.* Vol. I. Washington, D.C.: Bureau of National Literature and Art, 1897. 484–490.

—⁂—

4. Speaker of the House Henry Clay Supports the War, 1813

Speaker of the House of Representatives Henry Clay (R-KY) took the floor on January 8, 1813, to support the war effort in the debate over a proposal to enlarge the militia. "Haughty" Britain was to blame for causing the war, the Speaker claimed, and its officials could not be trusted. Clay favored continuation of the war rather than try negotiations over issues such as impressments.

The war was declared because Great Britain arrogated to herself the pretension of regulating foreign trade, under the delusive name of retaliatory Orders in Council—a pretension by which she undertook to proclaim to American enterprise, "Thus far shalt thou go, and no farther." Orders which she refused to revoke after the alleged cause of their enactment had ceased; because she persisted in the act of impressing American seamen; because she had instigated the Indians to commit hostilities against us; and because she refused indemnity for her past injuries upon our commerce. . . . The war in fact was announced, on our part, to meet the war which she was waging on her part.

The founders of our liberties saw, however, that there was no security short of independence and they achieved our independence. When nations are engaged in war those rights in controversy, which are acknowledged by the treaty of peace, are abandoned. And who is prepared to say that American seamen shall be surrendered, the victims to the British principle of impressments? . . . Now, I deny that she has any right, without her jurisdiction, to come on board our vessels on the high seas, for any other purpose but in pursuit of enemies, or their goods, . . . But she further contends that her subject cannot renounce their allegiance to her and contract a new obligation to other sovereigns.

We are told that England is a proud and lofty nation. . . . Haughty as she is, we once triumphed over her, and if we do not listen to the counsels of timidity and despair we shall again prevail.

Source: Annals of Congress, January 8, 1813, 667–670.

—⁊⁊⁊—

5. Representative John Randolph Opposes War with Britain, 1811

On December 10, 1811, in the debate in Congress over increasing the military, Representative John Randolph (R-VA) rebutted Representative Felix Grundy's allegation that the British were behind the Indian troubles around the Great Lakes. Randolph saw no evidence to support the charge. Further, he wondered why Americans wanted war with a nation with which they shared so much in common.

An insinuation had fallen from the gentleman from Tennessee (Mr. Grundy) that the late massacre of our brethren on the Wabash had been instigated by the British Government. Has the President given any such information? Has the gentleman received any such, even informally, from any officer of this Government? Is it so believed by the Administration? He had cause to think the contrary to be the fact; that such was not their opinion. This insinuation was of the grossest kind—a presumption the most rash, the most unjustifiable. Show but good ground for it. . . . It was indeed well calculated to excite the feelings of the Western people particularly, who were not quite so tenderly attached to our red brethren as some modern philosophers.

He called upon those professing to be Republicans to make good the promises held out by the Republican predecessors when they came into power—promises, which for years afterwards they had honestly, faithfully fulfilled. We had vaunted of paying off the national debt, of retrenching useless establishments; and yet had now becomes as infatuated with standing armies, loans, taxes, navies, and war, as ever were the Essex Junto. What Republicanism is this?

Source: Annals of Congress, December 12, 1811, 445, 454–455.

—∿—

6. Representative Joseph Pearson Proposes an End to the War, 1813

Representative Joseph Pearson (R-NC) argued during the debate over the bill to enlarge the militia on January 2, 1813, that in light of the apparent British retraction of its orders in council, impressments remained the only important disagreement between Great Britain and the United States. He thought that legislation barring British subjects from serving on American ships would solve this issue, which would render further prosecution of the war unnecessary.

Whatever may have been the original causes for the declaration of this war, we are now taught to believe that the question in contest is reduced to a single point. The British Orders in Council were repealed on the 21st of June, three days after our declaration of war. . . . The sole avowed cause, therefore remaining and for which the war is now carried, is the practice of impressment from on board our merchant vessels. . . . This is what I ask you now to do—pass a law effectually to exclude all British subjects from the public and private maritime service of the United States. . . . I venture to predict you will obtain a peace and secure your just rights more speedily, more effectually, and more satisfactorily to the people of this country than by all the military operations in the compass of your power.

Source: Annals of Congress, January 2, 1813, 501–502.

—∿—

7. Report and Resolutions of the Hartford Convention, 1815

New England Federalists expressed their disagreement with the war with Britain by meeting in Hartford, Connecticut, in December 1814. The report of the Hartford Convention, issued January 4, 1815, summarized their complaints and recommended a series of amendments to the Constitution.

First.—A deliberate and extensive system for effecting a combination among certain states, by exciting local jealousies and ambition, so as to secure to popular leaders in our section of the Union, the control of public in perpetual succession. . . .

Eighthly.—Hostility to Great Britain and partiality to the late government of France, adopted as coincident with popular prejudice, and subservient to the main object, party power.

Resolved, That the following amendments of the constitution of the United States be recommended. . . .

Fourth. Congress shall not have power without the concurrence of two thirds of both houses, to interdict the commercial intercourse between the United States and any foreign nation, or the dependencies thereof.

Fifth. Congress shall not make or declare war, or authorize acts of hostility against any foreign nation, without the concurrence of two thirds of both houses. . . .

Seventh. The Same person shall not be elected president of the United States a second time; nor shall the president be elected from the same state two terms in succession.

Source: Theodore Dwight, *History of the Hartford Convention.* New York: N. and J. White, 1833, 368–371, 376–378.

3

THE MEXICAN WAR:
Should the United States Have Avoided War with Mexico?

—⁂—

THE CONTROVERSY

The Issue

On May 11, 1846, President James Polk informed Congress that "war exists" between the United States and Mexico. The next day Congress approved a Declaration of War against Mexico and began deliberations to bolster American military forces. Instead of a brief war, as the president had envisioned, the conflict dragged on for nearly two years. The fighting continued until General Winfield Scott led American troops into Mexico City, in the heart of the enemy's territory, in September 1847. The treaty ending the war in February 1848 gave the United States a huge expanse of territory in the southwest.

- ◆ *Arguments in favor of war with Mexico:* Notwithstanding America's military successes, the Mexican War engendered criticism from its start. Debate centered over which nation started the war, whether it was justified, and what the implications of an American victory would be. The president and his supporters argued that the Mexican army had "invaded our territory and shed American blood upon the American soil." The president stated that it was his duty to "vindicate . . . the honor, the rights, and the interests of our country." After the fighting began, Polk revealed his desire to take territory from Mexico as an indemnity for going to war against the United States.
- ◆ *Arguments in opposition to war with Mexico:* Opponents challenged the president's rendition of the facts and questioned his motives. They charged that Polk had deliberately moved American troops into a disputed area of Texas north of the Rio Grande, provoking hostilities. Mexico not only denied that the region belonged to Texas but also considered the annexation of the province to the United States in 1845 illegal. The most outspoken opponents of the war contended that Polk, a Tennessee

Democrat, was acting as a front for slave-owners, who sought to widen their empire of bondage. These Whig critics and some northern Democrats supported the Wilmot Proviso, a congressional measure that would have blocked the expansion of slavery into lands taken from Mexico.

———⁕———

INTRODUCTION

In September 1847, General Winfield Scott and a small force of American troops overwhelmed Mexican defenders of Mexico City and triumphantly entered the Mexican capital. Scott had won a stunning victory over the country's neighbor to the south and its enigmatic military leader, General Antonio López de Santa Anna. The U.S. expedition had begun on March 9, 1847, with an amphibious landing on the beaches south of Veracruz, Mexico. The Americans then traveled 300 miles overland into the heart of enemy territory, with the goal of capturing the capital. After a nine-month military occupation of their chief city, Mexican officials consented to a treaty that transferred to the United States a vast expanse of territory that extended from Texas to the Pacific Ocean and included the future states of Arizona, Nevada, California, and Utah and parts of New Mexico, Colorado, and Wyoming. Included in the "Mexican Cession" was the prized harbor at San Francisco. The United States was now positioned to become a Pacific power. These were breathtaking achievements. They become even more amazing when one realizes that the United States did not possess a large army or navy when war with Mexico

General Winfield Scott led the American expedition from the port city of Veracruz on the Gulf of Mexico to the occupation of Mexico City in 1847. (Library of Congress)

commenced in 1846. To some, the military victory and the territory it gained represented confirmation of the nation's "destiny" to build a continental empire.

President James Polk claimed that the United States had been provoked by a military attack into an unwanted war with Mexico. He asserted that the Mexican army had crossed the Rio Grande onto American soil in Texas, which the United States had annexed in 1845. Most Democrats in Congress sided with the president, supporting his defense of American territory and honor.

Critics saw the unfolding of events in a much different light. The volume and persistence of these dissents made the war with Mexico one of the most contentious conflicts in American history, notwithstanding the battlefield triumphs and the acquisition of a massive expanse of territory. Critics charged that the president had acted unconstitutionally and unnecessarily, manipulating Mexico into striking at the United States. By this reasoning, the war was the product of deliberate presidential aggression. An equally damning charge was that the war was in reality an attempt by slave-owners to spread their institution into new lands. They predicted that this strategy would backfire, resulting in the destruction of the nation. The prophecy was fulfilled in 1860–61, when South Carolina and neighboring southern slave states seceded from the union. Although numerous causes led to the ensuing Civil War, the Mexican War played a pivotal role in causing the nation's sectional conflict. Was the Mexican War worth this terrible legacy? Could have—should have—the war been avoided?

BACKGROUND

The Annexation of Texas and Conflict with Mexico

The origins of the Mexican War are linked to the history of Texas. Shortly before Mexico gained its independence from Spain in 1821, Spanish officials invited Americans to settle its northern province, which now includes the state of Texas. Requiring that immigrants swear allegiance to Spain (and to Mexico after its independence), Spanish officials hoped that Texas would provide a buffer against further encroachment of the United States. Within a decade, 20,000 Americans had relocated to the rich soils of the Texas delta region along the Gulf coast, but American tempers rose over Mexican regulations, including a prohibition against slavery and conversion to Catholicism.

The imposition of more centralized political control by General Santa Anna, who became Mexico's ruler in 1834, was the final straw. Eager for independence, Texans established their own provisional government in 1835 and created an army. Santa Anna responded by leading a large force northward, where he met and annihilated Texas defenders at the Battle of the Alamo in San Antonio in 1836. Three weeks later, Santa Anna captured the city of Goliad and ordered the execution of Texans who had surrendered there. These atrocities produced a rush of new recruits for the Texas army, which routed Mexicans in the Battle of San Jacinto. In the process, they captured a surprised Santa Anna, who consented to a treaty that granted Texas independence, with territory that extended southward to the Rio Grande. However, the Mexican congress repudiated the treaty, refused to recognize Texas's independence, and maintained that the southern boundary of the rebellious province remained the Nueces River 150 hundred miles to the north.

Texans desired incorporation into the United States, but President Andrew Jackson (1829–37) sidestepped the request, as did his successor, President Martin Van Buren (1837–41). Both men also realized that the addition of another slave state to the union would unleash a hornet's nest of protest in the United States. But John Tyler, a southerner and slave owner, who had succeeded to the presidency on the death of William Henry Harrison in 1841, saw an opportunity to aid his bid for reelection in 1844. He negotiated an annexation treaty with Texas and submitted it to the Senate, which rejected it in June 1844. Although the possible expansion of slavery caused the treaty to fail, the issue of Texas arose in the election of 1844. James Polk of Tennessee, the Democratic Party's unlikely nominee for the presidency, fully supported the acquisition of Texas as well as undisputed possession of the Oregon Territory (which Britain jointly claimed). His opponent was not Tyler, whom the Whig Party disowned, but the former Kentucky senator Henry Clay, who opposed the immediate annexation of Texas, a step that he knew would provoke Mexico. Polk won the election by a whisker. The key to the outcome may have been antislavery voters who chose the recently founded Liberty Party over Clay in New York, which provided a slim margin for Polk and thereby won the election for the Democrats. In one of the oddest decisions in American presidential history, Tyler interpreted the election as a national mandate for territorial expansion. Early in 1845, during the last days of his administration, Tyler submitted to Congress a resolution that offered annexation to Texas. The measure passed on a close partisan vote.

The stage was now set for a showdown with Mexico, and Polk was ready for it. Like most of his southern and western Democratic colleagues, President Polk was fully committed to the territorial growth of the nation. He restated his campaign pledge of the "reannexation of Texas" and the "reoccupation" of Oregon in his inaugural address on March 4, 1845, echoing language used in the press to champion the nation's territorial expansion. The idea that Providence willed the United States to spread its institutions and culture across the continent was termed name "manifest destiny." (See the sidebar "Manifest Destiny" on page 76.) The president asserted that America's claim to all of the Oregon country was "clear and unquestionable." Referring to the Americans who had migrated to the region, which Britain and the United States had jointly controlled since 1818, Polk stated that the nation had a duty to extend "the benefits of our republican institutions" to the pioneers in "our territory which lies beyond the Rocky Mountains." (See "President James Polk on Texas and Oregon in His Inaugural Address, 1845," on page 91 in the Primary Sources section.) During his first year in office, the president demanded that Britain agree to unilateral U.S. control of Oregon, hinting that he would support a claim as far north as the "54-40" parallel (located near the southern border of present-day Alaska). Although they had moved warships to the disputed area, the British saw little value in fighting for Oregon and proposed a compromise solution—dividing it at the 49th parallel—which Polk accepted in June 1846. But the president had coyly kept the news of this settlement private until after the Mexican War had begun in March.

California, in Polk's opinion, was the crown jewel of the west, and San Francisco harbor was its brightest gem. Polk was determined to secure this prize by negotiation and purchase if possible and perhaps by war if other options failed. Texas was a key to his strategy, but the president had to tread cautiously, lest he embroil the country in two wars simultaneously—with Britain over Oregon and with Mexico over Texas. In late 1845, Polk sent a special envoy, John Slidell, to Mexico in an effort to purchase California and to trade monetary claims that Mexico owed to Americans for the recognition of the Rio Grande as Texas's

President James Polk welcomed a war with Mexico, which resulted in the transfer of nearly half of Mexico's territory to the United States. (© Archive Pics/Alamy)

southern border as well as the remaining portion of the New Mexico region. Although its treasury was empty and its government in turmoil, the Mexicans refused to negotiate with Slidell. Mexico would not part with its northern empire, including the disputed region between the Nueces River and Rio Grande that Texas claimed—a position Polk backed up in his annual message to Congress in December 1845.

MANIFEST DESTINY

In summer 1845, an anonymous author in the *Democratic Review,* a New York periodical, urged Texans to approve the agreement that would annex their country to the United States. John L. O'Sullivan, reputed by historians to have authored the article, argued that it was "the fulfillment [sic] of our manifest destiny to overspread the continent allotted by Providence for the free development of our yearly multiplying millions." By coining the term *manifest destiny,* O'Sullivan added one of the most memorable phrases to the dictionary of American history. Still, the idea that the United States was preordained to spread across the continent was not new in the 1840s. The notion matured as the nation expanded territorially. The Louisiana Purchase of 1803 and the agreement with Great Britain in 1818 to occupy the Oregon Territory jointly had pushed the United States across the continent, giving it a foothold on the Pacific. The Texas declaration of independence in 1836 offered the prospect of further acquisition, which Congress fulfilled with a joint resolution and treaty of annexation in 1845. O'Sullivan's construction of *manifest destiny* was as much a recognition of these developments as it was a cause of expansion.

The most emboldened "continentalists" envisioned the rise of a benevolent empire set between the Atlantic shoreline and the Pacific coast, reaching as far north as the Bering Straits in Alaska and as far south as the Yucatan peninsula in Mexico, if not to the Isthmus of Panama in Central America. Supporters of manifest destiny saw powerful forces propelling the growth of America's continental empire. It began with American migrants who were anxious to carve new homes out of the wilderness and who then

Slidell's mission failed in early 1846. When Polk received news of this, he ordered the U.S. Navy to blockade the port of Veracruz and General Zachary Taylor to move U.S. Army troops into the disputed territory. Taylor trained American cannon on the Mexican army across the Rio Grande in the town of Matamoros and blockaded the mouth of the river at the Gulf of Mexico, a step that Mexico interpreted as an act of war. Polk waited for an incident to spark a war. When the provocation planted their cultures as well as crops. Inevitably, these settlers recreated the self-governing political arrangements they had left behind in the east. It was this penchant for democratic "freedom," enlarging within a federal union of semisovereign and equal states, that differentiated American expansion from European colonialism, with its centralized rule. As O'Sullivan put the notion in 1845, America's empire was special because of "the beneficence of our institutions." Eventually, these new, democratically formed sister republics would be invited to join the "Temple of Freedom," as some called the confederation of American states. President James Polk saw expansion following this path, claiming in his inaugural address on March 4, 1845, that both Texans and Oregonians were models of democratic aspirations. Less fortunate peoples, especially Native Americans and Mexicans, expansionists argued, would benefit from the advance of American civilization by their eventual amalgamation into Anglo-Saxon, Protestant culture.

Manifest destiny became the rage in many urban daily newspapers during the mid-1840s. The appearance of the inexpensive "penny press" in the nation's largest cities during the 1840s was part of a technological revolution that vastly increased the spread of information and transportation. The emergence of steam power and the invention of the telegraph in 1844 keynoted these developments. By the middle 1840s, advocates were calling for the construction of a transcontinental railroad. The lingering effects of the economic depression of the early 1840s boosted the appeal of manifest destiny. Although many Americans, members of the Whig Party in particular, saw dangers lurking in the enthusiasm to expand, manifest destiny was a powerful companion to the general democratization of popular politics that characterized the era.

failed to materialize, he drafted a war message on May 9, 1846, that cited Mexico's failure to pay indemnities to Americans and other minor diplomatic infractions as a cause for hostilities. Later that day, the president received news that the Mexican army had engaged an American patrol north of the Rio Grande—land claimed by Texas and thus the United States. Now the president could charge that Mexico had "invaded our territory and shed blood on American soil." Two days later, Congress

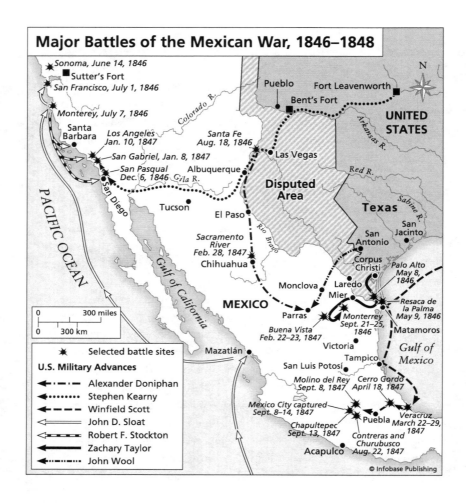

Major Battles of the Mexican War, 1846–1848

Sonoma, June 14, 1846
Sutter's Fort
San Francisco, July 1, 1846
Monterey, July 7, 1846
Santa Barbara
Los Angeles Jan. 10, 1847
San Gabriel, Jan. 8, 1847
San Pasqual Dec. 6, 1846
San Diego

Pueblo   Fort Leavenworth
Bent's Fort

UNITED STATES

Colorado R.
Santa Fe Aug. 18, 1846
Albuquerque
Gila R.
Las Vegas

Arkansas R.
Red R.

Disputed Area

Texas

Sabine R.
San Jacinto

Tucson
El Paso
Rio Bravo
San Antonio
Corpus Christi
Palo Alto May 8, 1846

Sacramento River Feb. 28, 1847
Chihuahua

PACIFIC OCEAN

Gulf of California

Monclova
Laredo
Mier
Resaca de la Palma May 9, 1846

MEXICO
Parras
Monterrey Sept. 21–25, 1846
Matamoros

0   300 miles
0   300 km

Buena Vista Feb. 22–23, 1847

Mazatlán
Victoria
Gulf of Mexico

Selected battle sites

U.S. Military Advances

San Luis Potosí
Tampico

◄—·—·— Alexander Doniphan
◄········ Stephen Kearny
◄— — — Winfield Scott
◄═════ John D. Sloat
◄▬▬▬ Robert F. Stockton
◄▬▬▬ Zachary Taylor
◄—··—··— John Wool

Molino del Rey Sept. 8, 1847
Cerro Gordo April 18, 1847

Mexico City captured Sept. 8–14, 1847
Chapultepec Sept. 13, 1847
Puebla
Contreras and Churubusco
Acapulco Aug. 22, 1847
Veracruz March 22–29, 1847

© Infobase Publishing

received the president's war message, which lawmakers approved with minimal debate and by overwhelming margins on May 12.

The one-sided vote for war—174-14 in the House of Representatives and 40-2 in the Senate—hid significant misgivings among most Whigs and some Democratic legislators. Whig reluctance to oppose what many considered an unnecessary and aggressive war seemed to be partially due to fears of political backlash from a patriotic public, which would punish a party that failed to support their country in time of crisis. Horace Greeley, editor of the *New York Tribune*, saw the vote in Congress "as a normal public response to an attack on the flag."

The Course of the War

Neither country was ready for a long war in 1846. Mexico had a professional army that looked good on paper and was well-regarded in Europe. The Mexicans also believed—erroneously as it turned out—that they would receive assistance from England or France. On the basis of these presumptions, Mexican authorities doubted that the Americans had the stomach to fight for Texas. North of the border, the dominant sentiment expressed disdain for Spanish culture and the political instability that had characterized Mexico since its independence. Mexico did not possess a navy, and its treasury was empty, further weakening its military potential. Polk and most Americans thought Mexico would not last past the first decisive battle. Even though the United States had an army in name only, as barely 7,500 regulars were available in 1846, Americans thought that their volunteer force, recruited when military necessity dictated, would easily and quickly win the war. (See the sidebar "General Winfield Scott and the U.S. Army" on page 80.) Congress did authorize a volunteer force of 50,000 men in 1846, yet both sides came to realize the folly of their miscalculations for a short war.

After the altercation at the Rio Grande near Matamoros in April 1846, General Taylor crossed the river and drove southward with his small army, numbering a little more than 6,000. The Americans defeated Mexican forces at Monterrey and others spots, putting northeastern Mexico largely in U.S. control by the end of 1846. Nonetheless, Mexico refused to be bullied to the bargaining table, which prompted President Polk to adopt a more ambitious strategy whereby American forces would penetrate to the heart of Mexico. In the meantime, Americans attacked Mexico's northern periphery. A force of 1,500 under the command of Colonel Stephen W. Kearny marched westward from Fort Leavenworth (in what later became eastern Kansas) and occupied Santa Fe, New Mexico, on August 16, 1846, without firing a shot. Leaving the bulk of his force in New Mexico and dispatching a unit under Alexander Doniphan southward toward the Mexican town of Chihuahua, Kearny set out with a small detachment for California.

Prior to the outbreak of hostilities, the American Pacific Squadron had been instructed to occupy key locations along the California coast if war with Mexico occurred. The American navy raised the flag in Monterey, California, on July 7, 1846, when news of the war was received,

GENERAL WINFIELD SCOTT AND THE U.S. ARMY

General Winfield Scott's triumphant entry into the Grand Plaza of Mexico City on September 14, 1847, occurred in an era when America's highest-ranking officer was in the field with his troops. A professional soldier, Scott's victory over General Antonio Lopez de Santa Anna, Mexico's top commander and sometime president and political strongman, was the crowning achievement of a long career. Scott was born on a farm in Petersburg, Virginia, in 1786 of parents of Scottish descent. He attended the College of William and Mary, where he studied law but instead chose army life in 1808. He served in the War of 1812, emerging as a brigadier general, and took part in the Black Hawk and Seminole Wars against Native Americans during the 1830s. In 1841, he was appointed major general and head of the army, a position he held until his retirement 20 years later. Despite his southern birth, Scott remained loyal to the Union when the Civil War erupted in 1861. "Old Fuss 'n Feathers" (referring to the feathered plumes on a general's hat), as he was affectionately nicknamed, was a favorite among his troops, who recognized the value of his insistence on military order and careful planning.

Scott was a professional soldier, but the force he commanded can be called "professional" only figuratively. The U.S. Army numbered barely 7,500 soldiers when the Mexican War began in 1846. Scattered primarily in frontier outposts, the army was badly supplied and poorly coordinated. This minuscule force fit America's political tastes in the years before the Civil War. Taking note of the tendency of monarchs to rely on military force to preserve royal power, Americans regarded large standing armies as incompatible with liberty. They also insisted on keeping taxes low and expenditures to a minimum, a financial situation that further constrained the creation of a professionalized military. America's geographic isolation from potential foreign adversaries complemented these convictions. The country's leaders

and in San Francisco three days later. Weeks earlier, the army explorer John C. Frémont had trekked over the mountains into California with a small party that supported local residents, whom Frémont encouraged to declare an independent republic. The American conquest of California proceeded in fits and starts until navy commodore Robert F. Stockton suppressed a revolt in Los Angeles early in 1847.

were content to rely on local militias and "volunteer" armies when substantial military force was required.

Congress and President James Polk honored these dictums when the war with Mexico began. Congress doubled the size of the regular army, called up several state militia units, and authorized the formation of a volunteer force recruited under the auspices of state governments. Mixing regular and militia units provided no end of problems, largely because the citizen-soldiers were unfamiliar with the routines of military life; the regulars looked down their noses at their amateur colleagues. Yet volunteers comported themselves well on the battlefield. Some of this success was due to leadership by junior officers who were West Point graduates. Although small and under-funded, West Point had produced a series of qualified military graduates since the academy's founding in 1802. Captain Robert E. Lee, on Scott's staff, was one of several West Pointers who gained battlefield experience in the Mexican War and went on to lead armies in the Civil War.

President Polk reluctantly selected Scott to lead the attack on Mexico City. Both Scott and General Zachary Taylor were Whigs, and each harbored presidential aspirations. A Democrat, Polk hoped not to inflate the popularity of an army general who could be a potential electoral rival in 1848. The Whigs had won the presidency in 1840 behind William Henry Harrison, a military hero. George Washington and Andrew Jackson also were war hero presidents. Partisan bickering plagued the execution of the Mexican War, culminating in Polk's relieving Scott of command of the American occupation force in Mexico City. Accused of trumped-up charges, Scott faced court-martial proceedings in 1848. Although commissioners found the general guiltless of the charges, Polk had successfully maneuvered him out of the presidential race. The Whigs went on to nominate Taylor, who won the presidency in 1848. Scott's turn to run came in 1852, when he lost a close race to Democrat Franklin Pierce.

In the meantime, Polk's plan to conquer the heart of Mexico proceeded under the leadership of General Winfield Scott, the commander in chief of the army, whom the president appointed to lead the expedition. Partnering with the U.S. Navy, which blocked Mexico's gulf ports, Scott coordinated an amphibious landing of 10,000 soldiers on the beach three miles south of the city of Veracruz on

March 9, 1847. After capturing the city, Scott headed inland, hurrying to escape the onset of the yellow fever season along the low-land coast. Scott paused en route to Mexico City until replacements arrived for the one-year volunteers, who decided to go home at the expiration of their enlistment. With troop strength rebuilt, Scott moved within sight of Mexico City by late August 1847. After several hard-fought victories around the capital, such as the valiant storming of the castle at Chapultepec, Scott's forces drove the redoubtable General Santa Anna and his much larger army from Mexico City. The Americans occupied the city for nine months, with Scott in residence at the palace known as the Halls of Montezumas.

Facing a hopeless situation, Mexican leaders consented to peace talks. At the start of Scott's expedition into Mexico, Polk had appointed Nicholas Trist to negotiate a treaty with Mexico. The president's instructions were to secure undisputed title to Texas, the northern region of Mexico, and California up to the Oregon border (known as Alta California). As Scott's victories mounted, Polk upped his territorial demands and recalled Trist, whom the president believed (correctly) had failed to press Mexico hard enough for a satisfactory deal. But Trist ignored the president's recall order and offered treaty terms at the Mexican town of Guadalupe Hidalgo that he believed the Mexicans would accept. Polk was outraged at this insubordination and failure to secure a larger chunk of Mexico. Nonetheless, Polk submitted the Treaty of Guadalupe Hidalgo, as Trist's treaty came to be called, to the Senate for ratification. Helping the president to overcome his reservation were the 1846 congressional elections, which gave Whigs a majority in the House of Representatives. The Senate ratified the treaty on May 30, 1848. Mexico lost nearly half of its territory from the agreement. The war cost the United States 12,876 military deaths, 86 percent of which were due to disease.

THE DEBATE

The Case for War with Mexico

President Polk had already drafted a war message, which his cabinet had approved, when he received word of the Mexican attack on the detachment of American soldiers. This new development became the centerpiece of the president's message to Congress on May 11, 1846. He asked Congress to recognize that a state of war existed between Mexico and the United States and "to place at the disposition of the Executive the means of prosecuting the war with vigor." (See "President James Polk, War Message, 1846," on page 93 in the Primary Sources section.) Polk reminded lawmakers that he had ordered General Zachary Taylor to take up a defensive position near the Rio Grande, in the disputed region south of the Nueces River. The Republic of Texas had considered this territory part of its domain since its independence, the president continued, and Congress had accepted this interpretation when it invited Texas to join the Union. But "Mexican forces assumed a belligerent attitude," Polk argued, and demanded Taylor "to retire beyond the Nueces River." The next day, Mexico "invaded our territory and shed American blood upon the American soil." The president concluded that "we are called upon by every consideration of duty and patriotism" to vindicate "the honor, the rights, the interests of our country."

Most Democrats in Congress saw events through the same lens as the president. Senator Lewis Cass of Michigan defended Polk's request for war, observing that "A Mexican army invades our territory." (See "Senator Lewis Cass Defends the Mexican War, 1846," on page 94 in the Primary Sources section.) If Mexico was not willing to come to a reasonable settlement over the boundary dispute, he argued, then the United State should take possession of its capital and "dictate our own conditions." The basis of the claim by Texas that its boundary extended to the Rio Grande was debated in the House during consideration of the war resolution. Massachusetts representative John Quincy Adams, the former president, was among the critics of the president's interpretation of the legal border, while future presidential candidate Representative Stephen A. Douglas, Democrat of Illinois, upheld President Polk's claim of the area extending to the Rio Grande. The debate turned on whether the treaty that general Santa Anna had signed with Texas in April 1836, following the general's defeat at San Jacinto, had been ratified by Mexico. Douglas acknowledged that it had not been ratified by the Mexican congress yet was valid. He argued that Santa Anna had usurped control of the government of Mexico, abolished the constitution, and taken power into his own hands. (See "Representative Stephen Douglas on Santa Anna and Texas, 1846," on page 95 in the Primary Sources section.) Douglas admitted that Santa Anna was a prisoner of war when the treaty was signed, but claimed the Mexican general was the de facto government at the time. Thus, he upheld Polk's position that the Rio Grande River was rightly and legally the southern boundary of Texas.

The Case Against War with Mexico

Opponents of the war challenged Polk's interpretation of the facts and his method of handling the affair with Mexico. These criticisms began when Congress considered Polk's War Message. Denunciation of Polk's policy continued during the course of the war, even as Taylor and Scott won victories on the battlefield. Polk's requests to Congress to pass appropriation bills to fund the war—measures that passed by large majorities—offered further occasions to denounce the conflict. These criticisms followed two lines of argument. One stream of dissent, often articulated by more conservative politicians, claimed that the president

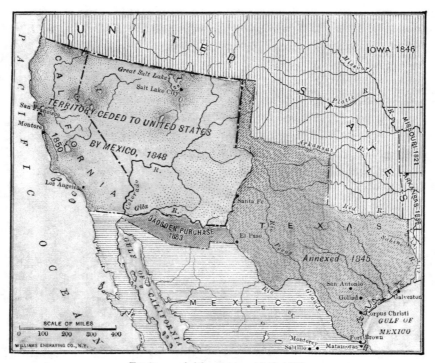

Territory ceded by Mexico, 1848–1853

The Mexican War confirmed U.S. possession of Texas and resulted in the cession of a huge portion of Mexican territory that extended to the Pacific coast. (© North Wind Picture Archives/Alamy)

had misstated the facts concerning which side had been the aggressor. Some asserted that it was Polk, not the Mexicans, who had initiated the confrontation. Daniel Webster, a moderate Whig senator from Massachusetts, expanded this analysis. He claimed that the president had acted unconstitutionally by placing American troops in harm's way and then asked Congress to recognize that war currently existed. The president had usurped a power that only the Congress could exercise.

The second critique plumbed a deeper and more sinister motivation for the war. These critics, centered among the antislavery "radicals" in the Whig Party, alleged that the war was a plot by slaveowners to protect and extend the institution of slavery. The addition of new territory would mean the likelihood of creating additional slave states. Representative Joshua Giddings, an Ohio Whig, expressed this opinion in debate in the House over the army appropriation bill in May 1846, contending that the purpose of this "aggressive, unholy, and unjust war" was to protect slave owners, who had foisted the annexation of Texas onto the United States. (See "Representative Joshua Giddings Calls the Mexican War 'Unjust,' 1846," on page 96 in the Primary Sources section.) Now they were using war and murder as the lever to advance their interests. The Massachusetts legislature seconded this thesis in resolutions voted in April 1847 that denounced the effort of, at most, 300,000 slaveholders to harness the authority of the national government "to strengthen the Slave Power." (See "The Massachusetts Legislature Condemns the War with Mexico, 1847," on page 98 in the Primary Sources section.) Based in part on a report written by the Boston attorney Charles Sumner, later a U.S. senator from Massachusetts, the resolution condemned the "war of conquest" as "wanton, unjust, and unconstitutional."

Polk had not revealed his interest in using the war for territorial gain in his War Message. This objective was not publicly disclosed until August 1846, when the president asked Congress to approve a $2 million appropriation that could be used as partial payment to Mexico for territory—or perhaps for a bribe to Santa Anna. Polk's interest in wresting lands from Mexico via the muzzle of a gun stirred resentments, particularly in the northern states. Representative David Wilmot, a Pennsylvania Democrat, attached an amendment to the appropriation bill that became known as the Wilmot Proviso. The measure stated that slavery would be barred from any territory secured with the appropriation. Adopted in the House with the votes of Whigs and northern Democrats, the proviso was rejected in the Senate. The Wilmot Proviso was attached to subsequent war appropriation measures in 1847 and 1848. Each time, the proviso met a similar fate: passed in the House and defeated in the Senate, where slave state legislators held half the seats. While many abolitionists saw the proviso as a step toward emancipating slaves, Wilmot and kindred northern Democrats argued that his amendment would keep blacks out of the territories. White racism played a formidable role in the support for this attack on the "Slave Power."

Opposition to the war was centered among members of the Whig Party, especially residents of the nonslave states. Whigs were dubious of the merits of territorial expansion, especially via war, and questioned the costs of waging it. In debate over a bill to provide further war funding, Senator Tomas Corwin, an Ohio Whig, lampooned the notion that "destiny" willed the United States to wrench lands from Mexico. (See "Senator Thomas Corwin Criticizes Expenditures for the War with Mexico, 1847," on page 99 in the Primary Sources section.) Greedy nations inevitably experienced a downfall, observed Corwin. The $100 million asked for in the legislation could be better spent on building a transcontinental railroad, which would put Washington within 30 or 40 days' travel "of every point on the map of the civilized world."

OUTCOME AND IMPACT

Despite their opposition to the war, most Whigs supported military appropriation measures through 1847. Fear of the political consequences of being labeled disloyal overrode their feelings about the war. The party praised the Whig military men, such as Generals Taylor and Scott, but castigated the president for his aggressiveness and mismanagement of the war. The Whigs did score a major upset in the congressional elections of 1846, partially on account of antiwar sentiments. They won enough seats to regain a majority in the House of Representatives, while Democrats retained control of the Senate. Under the operation of the Constitution at the time, however, the new (30th) Congress did not convene until 13 months later, in December 1847, by which time the American army had scored its battlefield victories and General Scott was encamped in Mexico City.

The Whig midterm election victory, nonetheless, did influence subsequent relations with Mexico. Polk's aspiration for Mexican territory had grown as the U.S. Army triumphed. His appetite no doubt was whetted by the "All Mexico" chant that appeared in various newspapers, offering the possibility of securing a route for a canal across Mexico between Bahía de Campeche and the Gulf of Tehuantepec and Baja California, deep in southern Mexico. But the All Mexico movement failed to generate wide public support, perhaps due to Whig opposition, which gravitated toward a "No Territory" from Mexico position. Furthermore, Whig control of the House reduced Polk's prospects of securing more funds for the military and thus reduced his ability to apply pressure on Mexico as negotiations pended. These reasons apparently convinced the president to accept the Treaty of Guadalupe Hidalgo in early 1848, which failed to gain as much territory as Polk had hoped. For their part, Whigs joined Democrats in accepting the treaty. The prospect of ending the war—and the divisiveness that it had brought—apparently trumped reservations that lawmakers and the public had about waging war on Mexico.

Yet the war continued to reverberate in American politics, and 1848 was a presidential election year. As Polk had feared and tried to prevent, the war had produced several Whig military heroes. The Whig Party turned to General Zachary Taylor for their presidential nominee in 1848. Taylor was a military man, not a politician. Even though he was a slave owner, his prior disengagement from politics made him a fitting choice in an atmosphere rent with conflict over war, expansion, and slavery. Taylor won the election, collecting 47 percent of the popular vote to 42.5 percent for the Democrat Lewis Cass. Martin Van Buren, the former president and a Democrat angry with the Polk administration, accepted the nomination of the Free Soil Party, which endorsed the principles embodied in the Wilmot Proviso. Van Buren took 10 percent of the vote nationally but captured more than a quarter of the ballots cast in four northern states.

WHAT IF?

What if Henry Clay, the Whig candidate for president in 1844, had been the victor rather than James Polk?
Would history have turned out differently? Quite possibly. Clay was opposed to the annexation of Texas if the decision met resistance from Mexico. His later equivocation on this point near the end of the election campaign perhaps influenced some potential supporters to vote for the Liberty Party in New York,

allowing Polk to take the state and the election. Confirmation of this speculation may never be established definitively. Yet Whig opposition to territorial expansion, especially if it threatened to bring war, was clear. A Whig in the White House probably would have averted a war with Mexico in 1846. Certainly, Clay would not have acted as belligerently as Polk toward Mexico. The likelihood of political party influence to temper policy is given further credence by the Whig victories in the 1846 congressional elections. The new Whig majority in the House of the Representatives probably dissuaded President Polk from holding out for a larger territorial concession from Mexico than Trist secured in his treaty.

Would Clay's election have meant that the United States would not have obtained California? Here the future is a little clearer to see. One word tells much of the story—gold. On January 24, 1848, James Marshall discovered gold in the mill race of Johann Sutter's sawmill in northern California. Word of the find found its way to San Francisco in May, stimulating a rush of prospectors from the Pacific Rim region into the foothills of the Sierra Nevada. President James Polk announced the discovery in his final Annual Message to Congress in December 1848. This news lured a flock of people from around the world to California.

California's population swelled as a result of the Gold Rush. In 1848, before the rush, California held perhaps 14,000 people, a little more than half of them Spanish speakers. By 1850, when U.S. census takers counted heads, California hosted 93,000 people. This influx of Americans, lured initially by the prospect of easy riches and then by a wider array of enticements, including excellent harbors in San Francisco and San Diego, drew California closer to life in the eastern half of the United States. As early as 1845, talk of sponsoring a transcontinental railroad already was in the air. The prospect of gaining a concession from Mexico for an interocean canal and sectional conflict in the United States over the location of a western route delayed the rail project until the Civil War, when Congress incorporated the Union Pacific and Central Pacific Railroads. The railroad link between California and the eastern United States was completed in 1869.

These growing connections between east and west, coupled with Mexico's weak administrative control of its northernmost province, stacks the odds against the maintenance of the status quo. The trek of Americans to the Pacific coast suggests that California would have fallen under the control of the United States one way or the other—by diplomacy, purchase, or annexation backed up by force. The Mexican War may have been the writing on the wall for policy makers in America's weaker neighbor to the south so far as California was concerned.

Notwithstanding the ways that California and the Southwest might have come into American possession—via the Treaty of Guadalupe Hidalgo of 1848 or by some other method—history suggests what the outcome of the acquisition would be. The surge of people to California during the gold rush immediately launched the region's bid for statehood. Californians sought to join the union as a free state, a position that President Taylor supported. This proposal and how slavery would be handled in the New Mexico territory (which included present-day Arizona) caused a crisis in Congress. Taylor's untimely death in 1850 and the adroit leadership of Henry Clay and Stephen Douglas fashioned compromise legislation that papered over the sectional dispute. This Compromise of 1850 brought California into the Union.

The Whigs were not anxious to rouse these sectional tensions. This was a principal reason they turned to their second Mexican War hero, Winfield Scott, to head their presidential ticket in 1852. Although the general lost decisively to Democrat Franklin Pierce in 1852, the times had changed measurably since Taylor's presidency just two years earlier. Americans wanted to distance themselves from sectional conflict, but this was not to be. The issue of slavery in the territory burst into politics with renewed ferocity in 1854 following passage of the Kansas Nebraska Act. Thereafter, the conflict between north and south festered, until war erupted between the states in 1861. The Mexican War had put in place a critical cause of the Civil War.

CHRONOLOGY

1819 United States relinquishes claim to Texas in the Adams-Onís Treaty.

1821 Mexico secures its independence from Spain.

1820s Americans begin settling in Texas under the leadership of Stephen Austin.

1835 Americans in Texas revolt against Mexican rule.

1836 *March 2:* Texas declares independence.
March 6: Battle of the Alamo in Texas

1845 *March 1:* President John Tyler signs the resolution to annex Texas.
August 23: General Zachary Taylor orders to regard any Mexican army movement north across the Rio Grande as a hostile action.
December 28: Texas is admitted as the 28th and last slave state.

1846 *April 25:* Mexican army captures American dragoons on the north bank of the Rio Grande.
May 9: Polk receives news that Mexico has attacked American forces.

May 12: Congress votes for war against Mexico.

Fall: Whigs win a narrow majority in elections to the House of Representatives.

1847   *January 10:* Commodore Robert Stockton occupies Los Angeles, securing California for the United States.

February 23: General Zachary Taylor wins the Battle of Buena Vista.

March 9: American amphibious landing at Veracruz, Mexico

September 14: General Winfield Scott occupies Mexico City.

1848   *January 24:* Gold is discovered at Sutter's Mill in California.

February 2: Treaty of Guadalupe Hidalgo with Mexico is signed.

May 30: Senate ratifies Treaty of Guadalupe Hidalgo.

Fall: Election of president Zachary Taylor, a Whig.

December 5: President Polk announces the discovery of gold in California in his annual message.

1850   *September:* Congress passes the Compromise of 1850.

DISCUSSION QUESTIONS

1. How would the interests of the United States have been assisted by avoiding war with Mexico?
2. Was President James Polk's strategy for acquiring California and the Southwest justified? What alternative tactics might have been better?
3. Assess the performance of the Whig Party in Congress regarding the president's policy toward Mexico.
4. How realistic was the hope of Mexican leaders for retaining the lands subsequently lost to the United States?
5. Evaluate the role of the Mexican War in igniting disagreements over slavery.

WEB SITES

Jensen, Richard. Web Sources for Military History. Available at http://tigger.uic.edu/~rjensen/military.html. See H. 19th Century: Texas/Mexico/US.

The Mexican War, 1846–1848. PBS. Available at http://www.pbs.org/ kera/usmexicanwar/index_flash.html.

The Mexican War. Descendants of Mexican War Veterans. Available at http://www.dmwv.org/mexwar/mexwar1.htm.

BIBLIOGRAPHY

Bergeron, Paul H. *The Presidency of James Polk.* Lawrence: University Press of Kansas, 1987.

Holt, Michael. *The Rise and Fall of the Whig Party: Jacksonian Politics and the Onset of the Civil War.* New York: Oxford University Press, 1999.

Johannsen, Robert W. *To the Halls of the Montezumas: The Mexican War in the American Imagination.* New York: Oxford University Press, 1985.

Merk, Frederick. *Manifest Destiny and Mission in American History.* New York: Knopf, 1963.

Peskin, Allan. *Winfield Scott and the Profession of Arms.* Kent, Ohio: Kent State University Press, 2003.

Sellers, Charles G. *James K. Polk.* Princeton, N.J.: Princeton University Press, 1957.

Singletary, Otis A. *The Mexican War.* Chicago: University of Chicago Press, 1960.

PRIMARY SOURCES

1. President James Polk on Texas and Oregon in His Inaugural Address, 1845

President James Polk argued in his Inaugural Address on March 4, 1845, that an "independent" Texas had every right to join with the United States and that Oregon also was properly part of the United States. The themes that he articulated in the address became central elements of the slogan known as "manifest destiny."

The Republic of Texas has made known her desire to come into our Union, to form a part of our Confederacy and enjoy with us the blessings of liberty secured and guaranteed by our Constitution. Texas was once a part of our country—was unwisely ceded away to a foreign power—is now independent, and possesses an undoubted right to dispose of a part or the whole of her territory and to merge her sovereignty as a separate and independent state in ours. I congratulate my country that by an act of the late Congress of the United States the assent of this Government has been given to the reunion, and it only remains for the two countries to agree upon the terms to consummate an object so important to both.

I regard the question of annexation as belonging exclusively to the United States and Texas. They are independent powers competent to contract, and foreign nations have no right to interfere with them or to take exceptions to their reunion.

To Texas the reunion is important, because the strong protecting arm of our Government would be extended over her, and the vast resources of her fertile soil and genial climate would be speedily developed, while the safety of New Orleans and of our whole southwestern frontier against hostile aggression, as well as the interests of the whole Union, would be promoted by it.

Nor will it become in a less degree my duty to assert and maintain by all Constitutional means the right of the United States to that portion of our territory which lies beyond the Rocky Mountains. Our title to the country of the Oregon is "clear and unquestionable," and already are our people preparing to perfect that title by occupying it with their wives and children. But eighty years ago our population was confined on the west by the ridge of the Alleghanies. Within that period—within the lifetime, I might say, of some of my hearers—our people, increasing to many millions, have filled the eastern valley of the Mississippi, adventurously ascended the Missouri to its headsprings, and are already engaged in establishing the blessings of self-government in valleys of which the rivers flow to the Pacific.

As our population has expanded, the Union has been cemented and strengthened. As our boundaries have been enlarged and our agricultural population has been spread over a large surface, our federative system has acquired additional strength and security. It may well be doubted whether it would not be in greater danger of overthrow if our present population were confined to the comparatively narrow limits of the original thirteen States than it is now that they are sparsely settled over a more expanded territory. It is confidently believed that our system may be safely extended to the utmost bounds of our territorial limits, and that as it shall be extended the bonds of our Union, so far from being weakened, will become stronger.

The world beholds the peaceful triumphs of the industry of our emigrants. To us belongs the duty of protecting them adequately wherever they may be upon our soil. The jurisdiction of our laws and the benefits of our republican institutions should be extended over them in the distant regions which they have selected for their homes.

Source: James D. Richardson, comp. *Messages and Papers of the Presidents.* Washington, D.C.: Bureau of National Literature and Art, 1897, vol. III, 2229–2231.

—⁓—

2. President James Polk, War Message, 1846

President James Polk claimed that Mexico had attacked American forces on U.S. soil. On May 11, 1846, he asked Congress to recognize that a state of war existed between the United States and Mexico.

In my message at the commencement of the present session I informed you that upon the earnest appeal both of the Congress and convention of Texas I had ordered an efficient military force to take a position between the Nueces and the Del Norte. This had become necessary to meet a threatened invasion of Texas by the Mexican forces, for which extensive military preparations had been made. The invasion was threatened solely because Texas had determined, in accordance with a solemn resolution of the Congress of the United States, to annex herself to our Union, and under these circumstances it was plainly our duty to extend our protection over her citizens and soil.

This force was concentrated at Corpus Christi, and remained there until after I had received such information from Mexico as rendered it probable, if not certain, that the Mexican Government would refuse to receive our envoy.

Meantime Texas, by the final action of our Congress, had become an integral part of our Union. The Congress of Texas, by its act of December 19, 1836, had declared the Rio del Norte to be the boundary of that Republic. Its jurisdiction had been extended and exercised beyond the Nueces. The country between that river and the Del Norte had been represented in the Congress and in the convention of Texas, had thus taken part in the act of annexation itself, and is now included within one of our Congressional districts. Our own Congress had, moreover, with great unanimity, by the act approved December 31, 1845, recognized the country beyond the Nueces as a part of our territory by including it within our own revenue system, and a revenue officer to reside within that district has been appointed by and with the advice and consent of the Senate. It became, therefore, of urgent necessity to provide for the defense of that portion of our country. Accordingly, on the I3th of January last instructions were issued to the general in command of these troops to occupy the left bank of the Del Norte. This river, which is the southwestern boundary of the State of Texas, is an exposed frontier.

The Mexican forces at Matamoras assumed a belligerent attitude, and on the 12th of April General Ampudia, then in command, notified General Taylor to break up his camp within twenty-four hours and to retire beyond the Nueces River, and in the event of his failure to comply with these demands announced that arms, and arms alone, must decide the question. But no open act of hostility was committed until the 14th of April. On that day General Arista, who had succeeded to the command of the Mexican forces, communicated to General Taylor that he considered hostilities commenced and should prosecute them. A party of dragoons of 63 men and officers were on the same day dispatched from the American camp up the Rio del Norte, on its left bank, to ascertain whether the Mexican troops had crossed or were preparing to cross the river, became engaged with a large body of these troops, and after a short affair, in which some 16 were killed and wounded, appear to have been surrounded and compelled to surrender.

The cup of forbearance had been exhausted even before the recent information from the frontier of the Del Norte. But now, after reiterated menaces, Mexico has passed the boundary of the United States, has invaded our territory and shed American blood upon the American soil. She has proclaimed that hostilities have commenced, and that the two nations are now at war.

As war exists, and, notwithstanding all our efforts to avoid it, exists by the act of Mexico herself, we are called upon by every consideration of duty and patriotism to vindicate with decision the honor, the rights, and the interests of our country.

Source: James D. Richardson, comp. *Messages and Papers of the Presidents.* Washington, D.C.: Bureau of National Literature and Art, 1897, vol. III, pp. 2287–2293.

—⚭—

3. Senator Lewis Cass Defends the Mexican War, 1846

Senator Lewis Cass (D-MI), who would be the Democratic presidential candidate in 1848, defended the Mexican War in a speech he gave in Congress on May 12, 1846. Cass asserted that the state of Texas reached the Rio Grande, rather than the Nueces River, which Mexico recognized as its border.

A hostile army is in our country; our frontier has been penetrated; a foreign banner floats over the soil of the Republic; our citizens have been killed while defending their country; a great blow has been aimed at us; and, while we are talking and asking for evidence, it may have been struck and our army been annihilated. And what then? The triumphant Mexicans will march onward till they reach the frontiers of Louisiana, or till we receive such a formal certificate of the intentions of the Mexican Government as will unite us in a determination to recognize the existence of the war, and to take the necessary measures to prosecute it with vigor. I have no doubt the boundary of Texas goes to the Rio 'del Norte. But I do not place the justification of our Government upon any question of title. Granting that the Mexicans have a claim to that country as well as we, still the nature of the aggression is not changed. We were in the possession of the country—a possession obtained without conflict. And we could not be divested of this possession but by our own consent or by an act of war. The ultimate claim to the country was a question for diplomatic adjustment. Till that took place the possessive right was in us; and any attempt to dislodge us was a clear act of war.

Source: Marion Mills Miller, ed. *Great Debates in American History.* New York: Current Literature Publication Co., 1913, vol. 2, 348.

—◇◇—

4. Representative Stephen Douglas on Santa Anna and Texas, 1846

Representative Stephen Douglas (D-IL), who would be the Democratic presidential candidate in 1860, asserted that when Mexican general Santa Anna had agreed to a treaty with Texas he had the power to concede to Texas the territory extending southward to the Rio Grande. In the debate in the House of Representatives in mid-May 1846, Douglas upheld President Polk's interpretation of Texas's territorial claim.

Immediately after the battle of San Jacinto, Santa Anna made a proposition to the commander of the Texan army to make a treaty of peace, by which Mexico would recognize the independence of Texas, with the Rio del Norte as the boundary. In May, 1836, such a treaty was made between the government of Texas and Santa Anna, in which the independence of the republic of Texas was acknowledged, and the Rio del Norte recognized as the boundary. In pursuance of this treaty, the remnant of the Mexican army were ordered by Santa Anna to retire beyond the confines of the Republic of Texas, and take their position on the west side of the Rio del Norte, which they did in conformity with the treaty of peace.

Mr. J. W. Houston: I wish to ask of the gentleman from Illinois was that treaty ever ratified by the Government of Mexico?

Mr. Douglas: That treaty was never ratified on the part of Mexico by anybody except Santa Anna, for the very good reason that, in the year previous, Santa Anna had usurped the Government of Mexico, had abolished the constitution and the regularly established government, and taken all the powers of government into his own hands. This treaty was entered into by the Government of Mexico de facto, Santa Anna combining in his own person at the time all the powers of the government, and as such was binding on the Mexican nation.

Mr. Adams: I desire to inquire of the gentleman from Illinois if Santa Anna was not a prisoner of war at the time, and in duress, when he executed that treaty?

Mr. Douglas: Santa Anna was a prisoner of war at the time, and so was the entire Government of Mexico, he being the government de facto, and clothed with all the powers of government, civil and military. The government was a prisoner at the time, and in duress. . . . How is a conquered nation ever to make peace if the gentleman's doctrine is to prevail? They refuse to make peace before they are conquered, because they hope for victory. They are incompetent to do so afterward, because they are in duress! I fear that, if this doctrine shall prevail, these gentlemen will soon find their Mexican friends in a most pitiable condition. . . . Our crude notions of things may teach us that the city of Mexico would be the most suitable place to form a treaty of peace.

Source: Marion Mills Miller, ed. *Great Debates in American History.* New York: Current Literature Publication Co., 1913, vol. 2, 362–363.

—⚏—

5. Representative Joshua Giddings Calls the Mexican War "Unjust," 1846

Representative Joshua Giddings (W-OH) charged that the U.S. annexation of Texas was another effort by the slave states to extend their institution of bondage over additional territory. In the House debates of mid-May 1846, Giddings called the Mexican War "unjust" and claimed that the president had violated the Constitution in pursuing it.

The President in his message, as a pretext for sending our army to invade and conquer the country upon the Rio Grande, says: "Texas, by its act of December 19, 1836, had declared the Rio del Norte to be the boundary of that republic."

This mere declaration on paper by the legislature of Texas could not change or alter the facts. They were entered upon the page of history, as well as upon the records of eternal truth; and no flagrant falsehood by that body, indorsed by a dignitary of this Government, can change or alter them. The truth is that Texas had agreed upon the Nueces as her boundary.

I regard the message as having been put forth to divert public attention from the outrage committed by the President upon our own Constitution, and the exercise of usurped powers, of which he has been guilty in ordering our army to invade a country with which we are at peace, and of provoking and bringing on this war. I am led to this inevitable conclusion from the fact that he dare not rest his justification upon truth. He reminds us of the grievous wrongs perpetrated (as he says) by Mexico upon our people in former years, and alludes to the delay of that government in the payment of debts due our people, and mourns over the loss of our commerce with Mexico; all for the purpose of justifying himself in sending the army to the Rio Grande, and commencing the work of human butchery!

Sir, no man regards this war as just. We know, the country knows, and the civilized world are conscious, that it has resulted from a desire to extend and sustain an institution on which the curse of the Almighty most visibly rests. Mexico has long since abolished slavery. She has purified herself from its crimes and its guilt. That institution is now circumscribed on the southwest by Mexico, where the slaves of Texas find an asylum. . . . Experience has shown that they cannot be held in servitude in the vicinity of a free government. It has therefore become necessary to extend our dominions into Mexico in order to render slavery secure in Texas. Without this, the great objects of annexation will not be attained. We sought to extend and perpetuate slavery in a peaceful manner by the annexation of Texas.

Tomorrow this nation will probably be in a state of war with Mexico. It will be an aggressive, unholy, and unjust war. . . . while the war continues efforts will probably be made to conquer Mexico, and we shall be called on to appropriate money and raise troops to go there and slay her people and rob her of territory. But the crime of murdering her inhabitants and of taking possession of her territory will be as great to-morrow, after war shall have been declared, as it would have been yesterday.

Source: Miller, Marion Mills, ed., *Great Debates in American History.* New York: Current Literature Publication Co., 1913), vol. 2, pp. 353–354, 356–373.

—⁓—

6. The Massachusetts Legislature Condemns the War with Mexico, 1847

The Massachusetts legislature approved a resolution on April 26, 1847, that called the conflict with Mexico "a war to strengthen the 'Slave Power.'" The statement was based largely on a report written by Boston attorney Charles Sumner, who would later be an influential Republican senator from Massachusetts.

It is a War Against the Free States. Regarding it as a war to strengthen the "Slave Power," we are conducted to a natural conclusion, that it is virtually, and in its consequences, a war against the free States of the Union. Conquest and robbery are attempted in order to obtain a political control at home; and distant battles are fought, less with a special view of subjugating Mexico than with the design of overcoming the power of the free States, under the Constitution.

Resolved, That the present war with Mexico has its primary origin in the unconstitutional annexation to the United States of the foreign State of Texas, while the same was still at war with Mexico; that it was unconstitutionally commenced by the order of the President, to General Taylor, to take military possession of territory in dispute between the United States and Mexico, and in the occupation of *Mexico; and that it is now waged ingloriously,—by a powerful nation against a weak neighbor,—unnecessarily* and without just cause, at immense cost of treasure and life, for the dismemberment of Mexico, and for the conquest of a portion of her territory, from which slavery has already been excluded, with the triple object of extending slavery, of strengthening the "Slave Power," and of obtaining the control of the Free States, under the Constitution of the United States.

Source: Acts and Resolves of Massachusetts, 1846–48, 541–542.

—⁓—

7. Senator Thomas Corwin Criticizes Expenditures for the War with Mexico, 1847

Senator Thomas Corwin (W-OH) lampooned the idea that "destiny" made American expansion inevitable, noting the downfall of other great nations. In a speech delivered in the Senate on February 11, 1847, he argued that money devoted to the war would be better spent on constructing a transcontinental railroad.

Mr. President, this uneasy desire to augment our territory has depraved the moral sense, and blunted the otherwise keen sagacity of our people. What has been the fate of all nations who have acted upon the idea that they must advance? Our young orators cherish this notion with a fervid, but fatally mistaken zeal. They call it the mysterious name of "destiny." "Our destiny," they say, is "onward." . . .

Rome thought, as you now think, that it was her destiny to conquer provinces and nations, and no doubt she sometimes said as you say, "I will conquer a peace." And where now is she, the Mistress of the World? . . . Sad, very sad, are' the lessons which time has written for us. Through and in them all I see nothing but the inflexible execution of that old law, which ordains as eternal that cardinal rule, "Thou shalt not covet thy neighbor's goods, nor *anything* which is his."

One hundred millions of dollars will be wasted in this fruitless war. Had this money of the people been expended in making a railroad from your northern lakes to the Pacific, as one of your citizens has begged of you in vain, you would have made a highway for the world between Asia and Europe. Your Capitol then would be within thirty or forty days' travel of any and every point on the map of the civilized world. Through this great artery of trade you would have carried through the heart of your own country the teas of China, and the spices of India, to the markets of England and France.

Source: Marion Mills Miller, ed. *Great Debates in American History.* New York: Current Literature Publication Co., 1913, vol. 2, pp. 369, 371.

4

THE CIVIL WAR:
Should Lincoln Issue an Emancipation Proclamation?

—⁄⁄⁄—

THE CONTROVERSY

The Issue

President Abraham Lincoln issued the Emancipation Proclamation on New Year's Day, 1863, in the midst of the Civil War. Although the proclamation applied only to places still under Confederate control and did not free slaves throughout the United States, Lincoln's order ranks among the most important presidential decisions in American history. Announced when the Union's attempt to suppress the Confederate rebellion was stalled, the president called the proclamation a military necessity. Did Lincoln make the right decision?

♦ *Arguments that Lincoln made the right decision:* Numerous Northerners urged Lincoln to strike down slavery. Abolitionists had urged this step for years, largely for moral reasons. During the war, "radical" and moderate Republicans, the party that nominated Lincoln for president, supported emancipation, in part as a way to reduce the ability of the Confederacy to wage war. Lincoln never fully revealed his private thinking about the proclamation, but he left suggestions that he thought emancipation was morally appropriate. Yet he also stuck by his justification that emancipation was a military measure. Diplomatic considerations, too, appear to have entered into his decision.

♦ *Arguments that Lincoln did not make the right decision:* Lincoln's proclamation took political courage because he faced considerable opposition to a presidential fiat that emancipated slaves. Members of Congress from the border states and Democrats generally in the North, including high-ranking officers in the Union military, denounced the idea, as did some conservative members of Lincoln's own party. Some argued that emancipation would spur the South on rather than speed the end of the war.

—⁄⁄⁄—

INTRODUCTION

Abraham Lincoln arrived in Washington, D.C., in the dead of night on February 23, 1861, after making a 12-day rail trip from his home in Springfield, Illinois. The capital was a-buzz with anticipation, not only to hear what the incoming president would say about the seven states that had seceded from the Union since his election in 1860, but also because of assassination rumors that circulated in the city. Because of this danger, 600 U.S. Army troops assisted by 2,000 volunteers lined the parade route that took the president-elect to the inaugural platform on the Capitol steps on March 4.

Devoted entirely to the secession crisis then confronting the nation, Lincoln's inaugural address offered an olive branch in one hand and an iron fist in the other. Secession, Lincoln said, was "legally void" and "anarchy." He contended that "the Union of these States is perpetual" and that no state could break away on its own. Because his responsibility was to administer the union intact, he pledged to stand firm against "insurrection." Turning to the Confederacy's demand that Fort Sumter in Charleston harbor surrender, Lincoln said he would "hold, occupy, and possess" federal property. But Lincoln also disclaimed any intent or authority to interfere with slavery "in the states where it exists" as a legal institution. The "rights of the states," he said, were "inviolate" on this matter. In short, the president had made plain that he would not attempt to overturn slavery in the South.

Despite these assurances, Confederates fired on Fort Sumter on April 12, 1861, inaugurating the Civil War. A year and a half later, on September 22, 1862, Lincoln announced a preliminary Emancipation Proclamation. It gave Southern rebels 100 days to cease hostilities toward the Union or suffer the loss of their slaves. When the South refused to lay down its arms, the president made good on his threat by issuing the Emancipation Proclamation on New Year's Day, 1863. Why had Lincoln reversed his position on slavery? Was his decision to free slaves the appropriate decision?

BACKGROUND

Coming of the Civil War

The roots of the crisis that Lincoln confronted as he took office reach back to earlier generations of Americans. The causes of the Civil War have generated endless debate, but most observers agree that three fundamental trends played central roles in the breakdown of the national union. The first of these three developments was the territorial expansion of the United States. From its original enclave east of the Mississippi River after independence was secured in 1783, the United States tripled in size between the Louisiana Purchase in 1803 and the Gadsden Purchase in 1853. Behind each acquisition of territory stood countless land-hungry Americans who journeyed to these frontier regions in quest of new homes and greater wealth. As settlers flooded into the territories, segments of the new domains were organized into states. From the 13 original states in 1787, 32 existed in 1859, 15 of which allowed slavery.

Slavery was the second of the driving forces in the coming of the Civil War. Rather than a static institution, slavery expanded in rough approximation to the growth of the territory and population as the United States evolved in the first half of the 19th century. The growth of cotton production and increased use of slave labor in the South went hand in hand. Many Southerners, in fact, saw the expansion of slavery as critical to the survival of the institution, but the failure of slave territory to advance in the 1850s was taken by some supporters of slavery as ominous for its future. Equally worrisome to slave owners was the rise of abolitionism, the third of three juggernauts that brought on the Civil War. The sustained crusade against slavery is traditionally dated with the appearance of William Lloyd Garrison's *The Liberator* in 1831, an abolitionist newspaper that ran until 1865. (See the sidebar "William Lloyd Garrison" on page 104.) Although despised and often physically harassed in much of the North as well as the South, Garrison and other outspoken abolitionists disseminated a stream of Christian-based criticism of human bondage. More pragmatically minded antislavery advocates turned to electoral politics, first with the Liberty Party (1840, 1844) and then through the Free Soil Party (1848, 1852). The small numbers of voters that supported abolitionist politics appears to have reflected public opinion generally about militant antislavery activity before the Civil War. Many Northerners as well as slaveholders saw Garrison's movement as a fuse that if lit, could consume the Union in flames.

The Mexican War (1846–48) engaged all three of these incendiary elements. A fateful legacy of this conflict was the Mexican Cession, which transferred the Southwest and California to American jurisdiction but which also raised anew the question of the expansion of slavery into federal territories. The Compromise of 1850 broke up the logjam in Congress over how to handle slavery in the newly acquired lands. Comparative political harmony reigned until the Kansas-Nebraska Act of 1854 opened up the possibility of slavery gaining a foothold in northern areas. A whirlwind of criticism in the North over the 1854 act and fighting between pro- and antislavery advocates in the Kansas territory gave birth to the Republican Party, whose principal position was opposition to the extension of slavery in federal territories. Abraham Lincoln, a lawyer and one-time Whig congressman from Illinois, signed on with the new party. Like most others who found their way to the Republicans, Lincoln endorsed the party's "free soil" position of barring slavery from territories but was willing to allow existing states to determine the fate of slavery within their own borders.

Lincoln's moderate position on slavery played a key role in his nomination as the Republican candidate for president in 1860. Although not a frontrunner when the party's convention began, his middling way on slavery, the tinderbox of American politics in 1860, raised his appeal as Republican operatives sized up the varying shades of opinion among available presidential aspirants. One feature of the new political party was clear: The vast bulk of its voter support lay in the North, in states that prohibited slavery. The emerging sectional crisis over slavery destroyed the old Whig Party and gave an advantage to Democrats in the South. Fearful of what the future might bring, southern Democrats wanted an ironclad guarantee that would secure slavery's future. This was too self-serving for northern Democrats, who nominated Senator Stephen A. Douglas of Illinois, who favored popular sovereignty, allowing white settlers in the territories to allow or ban slavery. Southern Democrats rallied around Vice President John C. Breckinridge of Kentucky, who strongly supported slavery. Remnants of the Whig Party, principally in the "border" states (such as Kentucky, Tennessee, and Missouri), nominated Senator John Bell on a newly founded Constitutional Union ticket, which essentially avoided the issue of slavery. The four-way presidential election of 1860 set the stage for a fateful verdict on the matter of slavery and nationhood.

Lincoln received only 40 percent of the popular vote, virtually all from free states, yet garnered the majority of electoral votes, all in the North, which delivered the presidency to the Republicans. Within a

WILLIAM LLOYD GARRISON

William Lloyd Garrison (1805–79) was the most famous abolitionist in the United States. Garrison was born in 1805 in Newburyport, Massachusetts, where he launched a career as a newspaper publisher when he was 21. Soon after, he found his main calling in a crusade against slavery, which he began in Boston in 1831 with the publication of a newspaper called *The Liberator*. The active, organized campaign for abolition is usually dated from the appearance of Garrison's publication. For the next 34 years, Garrison worked tirelessly, even frantically, to convert all who would listen to his Christian-based message of the immorality of slavery. His appeals were directed as much at his New England neighbors as to slave owners in the South. Nonetheless, his reception in the North was often less than cordial, as Garrison's close brush with a mob bent on lynching him in 1835 in Boston testifies. Other abolitionists endured similarly hostile treatment in the years before the attack on Fort Sumter.

Garrison survived his harrowing experience, yet he continued to generate controversy over his long career as a reformer. Many of his battles were fought with other abolitionists, many of whom opposed the public participation of women in antislave activities. Garrison supported gender and racial equality in abolitionist ventures. Other abolitionists favored politics and elections as avenues by which to attack slavery. Garrison saw political

month of the news of Lincoln's election, delegates meeting at a convention in South Carolina voted to secede from the Union. By the end of January 1861, six other slave states followed South Carolina. The seven slave states proceeded to form a new nation, the Confederate States of America, in early February. Rebel state militias seized federal property, including all but two U.S. forts—Fort Pickens in Pensacola, Florida, and Fort Sumter in Charleston, South Carolina. Outgoing president James Buchanan viewed these developments passively, although he did not succumb to Confederate demands to surrender Fort Sumter. Meanwhile, a flurry of activity went on in Congress and elsewhere to find a compromise that could stop the deepening sectional crisis.

The president-elect prepared his inaugural address as the secession crisis unfolded. Lincoln pondered his options carefully, ever mindful activity as contaminated by callousness and immorality. He called the Constitution "a covenant with death, and an agreement with hell" because it embraced a union with slaveholders. To make his point, Garrison publicly burned a copy of the Constitution in Framingham, Massachusetts, during a July 4 antislavery rally in 1854. In his writing as well as his public theatrics, Garrison was outspoken and often abusive. Even Abraham Lincoln was an object of his literary virulence. In 1861, Garrison called the new president "nothing better than a wet rag" and characterized him as a "man of very small caliber."

However, the Civil War caused Garrison to change his mind about government's role in the crusade against slavery. He supported the Union effort to suppress the Southern rebellion, and he was a leading figure among abolitionists who petitioned Lincoln to emancipate slaves and enlist blacks in the Union Army in 1861 and 1862. Garrison worried publicly about Lincoln's commitment to follow through on the preliminary emancipation proclamation, issued on September 22, 1862, writing that "a man so manifestly without moral vision . . . cannot be safely relied upon in any emergency." Yet Garrison hailed the final proclamation, issued on January 1, 1863, and expressed joy at the adoption of the Thirteenth Amendment two years later, a step he had advocated. He mourned Lincoln's death and paid great tribute to the slain president in the *Liberator*, which published its last issue in 1865.

of two fundamental considerations. First, he wished to retain the eight slave states that still remained in the Union. Second, Lincoln did not intend to abandon his party, which had carried him to victory in 1860. Republicans remained firm in their insistence to block slavery from federal territories.

The War: 1861–1862

The secession crisis took on urgency when Lincoln learned that Major Robert Anderson's 200 federal troops at Fort Sumter, situated on a small island in Charleston Harbor, were running low on supplies. Determined to demonstrate firmness on the preservation of the Union by holding Fort Sumter, and yet unwilling to fire the first shot of war,

Lincoln sought a middle way out of the dilemma. He informed the Confederate government of his decision to send a humanitarian relief convoy to Anderson's garrison. But the fate of Fort Sumter was as much a symbol to the Confederacy as to the Union. Faced with the prospect of appearing weak, Confederate president Jefferson Davis and his cabinet ordered General Pierre G. T. Beauregard on April 12 to bombard Sumter with the cannon placed around Charleston Harbor. Some 33 hours later, Anderson surrendered. Although no Union soldier was killed by hostile fire, the bloodiest war in American history had begun.

President Lincoln responded swiftly to the attack on Fort Sumter. He proclaimed that an "insurrection" existed and called on the governors to provide 75,000 "90-day" volunteers to suppress "combinations" in the secession states. Two days later, Virginia voters reversed their earlier decision to reject a secession resolution and approved withdrawal from the Union. Symbolically, the Confederacy moved its capital northward, to Richmond. North Carolina, Tennessee, and Arkansas followed Virginia's lead, bringing the Confederacy to a total of 11 states. Lincoln and his supporters managed to keep the four other slaves states—Maryland, Kentucky, Missouri, and Delaware—in the Union. West Virginia, split from Virginia in 1863, became a fifth "border" state that remained with the Union. On April 19, Lincoln ordered a naval blockade of the South. In early May, the president called for recruits to expand the Union (regular) army. By July, roughly 35,000 Union soldiers were encamped around Washington, D.C., looking forward to extinguishing the rebellion with one swift, decisive blow.

Yankee expectations for a brief war were shattered at the Battle of Bull Run on July 21, 1861. General Irvin McDowell attacked General Beauregard's Confederate forces in Manassas, Virginia, only hours distant by horse and buggy from the nation's capital. The Union suffered an ignominious defeat that sent panicked Yankee soldiers retreating toward Washington. The shock of the disaster at Bull Run Creek spurred Congress to authorize a volunteer federal army of half a million. Lincoln turned to a new general, George McClellan, to command the Army of the Potomac. McClellan assembled a huge force under the watchful eyes of rebel pickets who were stationed across the Potomac river.

Virginia was not the only theater of the war. Fierce conflict raged in Missouri, whose population included both pro- and anti-Unionists. A year elapsed before Union troops drove Confederate troops out of the state. But rebels continued to ravage Union supporters in Missouri, where vicious guerrilla warfare flared at the hands of terrorists such as William Quantrill and Frank and Jesse James. A more concerted military thrust at secession occurred in Kentucky and Tennessee, and later, southward along the lower Mississippi River. In what was known as the Anaconda Plan, Union strategists hoped to split the Confederacy in two by controlling the Mississippi. Union forces overran southern forts on the Tennessee River, winning a major victory at Fort Donelson on February 16, 1862. Even so, the war in the West was tough going, as General Ulysses S. Grant learned at Shiloh, a spot along the Tennessee River a few miles from the Mississippi border. There, Confederate forces surprised Union troops on April 6 in the largest battle of the war to this point. Grant's men held out, but at tremendous cost. Shiloh resulted in 24,000 killed and wounded, equally split between both sides. The slaughter at Shiloh signaled that the war had turned an ominous corner. Grant recollected in his memoirs that before Shiloh he thought one more Union victory would win the war; after it, he "gave up all idea of saving the Union except by complete conquest." Better news came from downriver, where Admiral David G. Farragut captured New Orleans by steaming up from the Gulf in April 1862. However, the Union did not secure full control of the Mississippi until Grant took Vicksburg on July 4, 1863.

Meanwhile, Lincoln prodded and cajoled the ever-cautious McClellan to launch an offensive against the Confederates. As the casualties mounted and the cost of the military operations skyrocketed, the president worried about sustaining public support for an all-out war. In April, McClellan was ready. He sent 100,000 troops via the sea to landfall southeast of Richmond, with the intention of putting the rebel capital under siege. McClellan fought his way to the outskirts of the city, where Confederate troops, ensconced in a series of trenches, held off their attackers. Moreover, the South gained a new commander for its Virginia army, Robert E. Lee. In late June, the daring Lee, arguably the most brilliant military strategist of the Civil War, pushed McClellan back down the York Peninsula in the Seven Days Battle (June 25–July 1, 1862). A total of 16,000 Union troops were killed, wounded, or captured. In *Battle Cry of Freedom* (1983), the eminent Civil War historian James McPherson observed that "After the Seven Days, Union policy took a decisive turn toward total war" (page 490). As McClellan retreated back

This photograph of President Abraham Lincoln was taken on November 3, 1863. (Library of Congress)

to Washington, Lincoln called for more volunteers, signed legislation to federalize the state militia, and fretted about how to save the Union.

Pressures on Lincoln to Strike Against Slavery

The Confederate army was not Lincoln's only worry. He faced serious political opposition in the North, both from Democrats and from members of his own party. The scale and intensity of the fighting and accelerating casualty lists during the first year of the war shocked most Americans, including many soldiers and their commanders. Despite making these sacrifices, the North's war effort had stalled. Lincoln's management of the war elicited criticism from all directions. Among the loudest critics were abolitionists. Most abolitionists, Garrison included, silently supported the president's approach when the war began, but after Bull Run in summer 1861, some abolitionists called on Lincoln to use his presidential powers as commander in chief of the army to strip Southerners of their slaves, whose labor helped the Confederate cause. As the war dragged on and its brutality magnified over the following year, sectional resentment increased, creating a more receptive audience for proposals to strike at slavery. Once dismissed as a fanatical fringe group, abolitionist ideas won widespread support by mid-1862. Antislavery advocates amplified these sentiments by flooding Congress with petitions demanding that the government end slavery.

Advocates of emancipation found receptive lawmakers in Congress. Republicans held a commanding majority in both houses as a result of the 1860 election, which prompted legislators from the Confederate states to relinquish their seats. "Radical" Republicans, the wing of the party that favored emancipation, pressured the president for action. Senator Charles Sumner, the Massachusetts lawmaker who had been sidelined for three years following the assault by South Carolinian Preston Brooks in 1856, was a leading member of this faction. Speaking to his colleagues in Massachusetts in October 1861, Sumner rallied Republicans to attack the "peculiar institution." (See "Senator Charles Sumner Addresses Republicans in Massachusetts, October 1, 1861," on page 124 in the Primary Sources section.) Sumner delivered this message personally to the president on several visits to the White House. Increasingly, opinion in the North viewed slavery as a critical element in the South's ability to wage war. Horace Greeley, editor of the influential *New York Tribune,* summed up this reasoning in an editorial entitled "The Prayer of Twenty Millions," which he addressed to the president. (See "Horace Greeley, 'The Prayer of Twenty Millions,' August 19, 1862," on page 125 in the Primary Sources section.)

Political reality disposed Lincoln to listen to, if not accept, advice from the Radicals. But he also had to acknowledge the "Moderates" among Republicans, who represented about half the party. Moderates supported Lincoln's objective of suppressing the rebellion but possessed conservative views about slavery. Despite their factional differences, congressional Republicans unified sufficiently to enact a set of antislavery laws in 1862. Congress abolished slavery in Washington, D.C. (April), prohibited slavery in the territories (June), and adopted a Confiscation Act (July 17), which declared that individuals in rebellion against the United States forfeited their property, including slaves. Lincoln reluctantly signed the Confiscation Act, despite his criticism of some provisions, such as reliance on federal courts to determine whether individual slave owners were guilty of treason.

Besides picking his way through the divided counsels within his own party, Lincoln faced other pressures. The Democratic party saw an opportunity to recoup its losses of 1860 in the upcoming congressional elections of 1862. Democratic officials and editors pounced on every Republican action that advanced emancipation and threatened white supremacy. They painted Lincoln as a tool of radical abolitionists, whose crusade against slavery would open up a cauldron of mayhem and murder as liberated slaves flowed northward. Lincoln was aware of the pervasiveness of white racist feelings in the country, made quite evident by antiblack riots that erupted in summer 1862. The president viewed the coming election with apprehension. Complicating this partisan dilemma, Lincoln's leading general, George McClellan, a Democrat, endorsed his party's critique of the Lincoln administration.

Democrats predominated among a third political group that Lincoln hoped to placate—the border-state lawmakers from Missouri, Maryland, Delaware, and Kentucky. Lincoln saw their support as pivotal to Union success, especially the Kentuckians. The border-state representatives supported the suppression of the rebellion, but they also stood by slavery, which was legal in their states. Lincoln made a personal appeal to them at a White House meeting on July 12, arguing the logic of a plan of gradual, compensated emancipation. Five days later, Congress passed the Confiscation Bill. On July 20, the border-state lawmakers rejected Lincoln's plan. Two days later, on July 22, Lincoln told his cabinet that he intended to issue a proclamation that would strip rebels of their slaves unless they ceased armed resistance to the Union. At the suggestion of Secretary of State William Seward, a trusted adviser, Lincoln agreed to pocket the announcement until the administration had some promising war news, so as not to give the impression

The Battle of Antietam on September 17, 1862, produced the deadliest single day of fighting during the Civil War. (© Pictorial Press Ltd./Alamy)

that emancipation was retribution for military failure or to be seen as a sign of weakness.

The Battle of Antietam on September 17 offered an opportune moment for Lincoln. (See the sidebar "Antietam" on page 112.) Antietam was not the overwhelming victory that Lincoln wanted. In fact, the battle produced the deadliest day of fighting in the war, taking a tremendous toll of Yankee lives. But McClellan had stopped Lee's foray into Maryland, which allowed the North to claim victory. Five days later, Lincoln announced the preliminary Emancipation Proclamation. It gave Confederates 100 days to lay down their arms or lose their slaves. Linked ambiguously to the Confiscation Act, Lincoln implied that his authority for issuing the edict rested on his power as commander in chief of the army and navy. He stated this authority more explicitly in the formal Emancipation Proclamation, issued on New Year's Day 1863. The president called his decision "a fit and necessary war measure," derived from his powers as commander in chief "in time of actual armed rebellion against the authority and government of the United States." (See "President Abraham Lincoln, Emancipation Proclamation, January 1, 1863," on page 126 in the Primary Sources section.)

ANTIETAM

In early September 1862, General Robert E. Lee led 50,000 Confederate troops across the Potomac River from Virginia into Maryland. Lee, the South's most revered military leader and a daring strategist, had decided to take the Civil War to the Yankees. Lee reasoned that a Southern military success in Maryland, a slave state that remained in the Union during the Civil War, would weaken Northern resolution to continue the conflict and perhaps also win British recognition of the Confederacy, an objective it desperately sought. These outcomes, the hope went, might pressure the Lincoln administration to negotiate a settlement with the Confederacy that left slavery intact. Opposing Lee's gambit was General George B. McClellan, commander of the Union's Army of the Potomac. McClellan brought 80,000 bluecoats from Washington, D.C., and other theaters of the war to Antietam Creek, a tributary of the Potomac situated near the village of Sharpsburg in western Maryland, roughly 65 miles northwest of Washington. Popular with his men, McClellan had dogged Lincoln for months with his hesitancy and indecisiveness in combat. Now, he was itching for a return engagement with Lee, who had foiled his campaign to capture Richmond, the Confederate capital, during the summer.

The two generals maneuvered their forces into position on September 17, 1862. Yankee units, led by Joseph Hooker, Edwin Sumner, and Ambrose E.

THE DEBATE

The Argument that Lincoln Should Issue an Emancipation Proclamation

Did Lincoln make the right decision? And why did he call the Emancipation Proclamation a military measure? The president claimed that the Emancipation Proclamation was undertaken as a measure to suppress the Southern rebellion, yet many of Lincoln's contemporaries regarded the proclamation as a great moral victory that ended the injustice of legal bondage. Later generations have understood the proclamation as part of a sweeping social revolution fomented by the Civil War. Lincoln

Burnside, attacked at separate points across Antietam Creek, engaging rebel troops commanded by Thomas J. "Stonewall" Jackson, James Longstreet, and Ambrose P. Hill. McClellan had envisioned a coordinated attack all along a three-mile front, but his cautious indecisiveness undermined his plan, a failure that allowed Lee to reposition his forces as the battle unfolded. Still, McClellan's forces dealt Lee a staggering blow on September 17. True to form, McClellan failed to follow up with further attacks the next day, permitting Lee to avoid total annihilation by withdrawing the remnants of his shattered army back to Virginia.

McClellan had stopped Lee on the doorstep of the North's territory, but at a terrible cost. Both sides suffered a total of 6,000 killed and another 17,000 wounded. Bloody Lane, a sunken road that snaked through parts of the battlefield, was the site of furious fighting, documented by layers of dead bodies. Antietam claimed four times the number of casualties that the United States would suffer in the storming of the beaches at Normandy in 1944. The Battle of Antietam was one of the turning points of the Civil War. The North had withstood the best the rebel nation could throw at them, allowing McClellan to claim a victory of sorts. Lincoln seized on this strained interpretation as the opportune moment to announce his Preliminary Emancipation Proclamation. His decision expanded the purpose of the Civil War from an effort to preserve the Union to include the liberation of 4 million individuals from a life of bondage.

may have agreed with these sentiments, yet he never fully revealed his reasoning for issuing the Emancipation Proclamation, nor how much weight he gave to supplicants on various sides of the question. By disposition and deliberate political strategy, Lincoln kept his thinking to himself. Historians must tease the motivation for Lincoln's decision from fragments of information.

A place to begin is with Lincoln's own views on slavery. Lincoln personally opposed slavery. He told a group of blacks at the White House in 1862 that slavery was "the greatest wrong inflicted on any people." Nonetheless, he was not an abolitionist. His nomination in 1860 stemmed, in part, from his moderation on slavery. Lincoln supported the Republican Party position that slavery should not be expanded into the federal territories, but he was willing to accept its legality in states that permitted it. This reliance on state determination of slavery's legality was consistent with the widely accepted understanding of how the Constitution worked at the time. This view held that decisions on certain subjects, slavery in particular, resided with the people within each state. Lincoln did, however, endorse gradual, compensated emancipation. This plan would have allowed emancipation to unfold over time, with payment to slaveholders for their loss of their property. This is the plan Lincoln urged on the border-state lawmakers in July 1862. He reiterated the idea in his annual message to Congress in December 1862, arguing that it was cheaper to pay slaveholders for their property than to finance the cost of war. (See "President Abraham Lincoln, Plan of Compensated Emancipation, December 1, 1862," on page 127 in the Primary Sources section.) The constitutional amendment he proposed gave states until 1900 to abolish slavery in order to receive federal payments for emancipation. His plan also would have authorized appropriations to relocate "free colored persons with their own consent" outside the United States, presumably in Africa or the Caribbean. Lincoln expressed doubt on several occasions that a racially integrated society could exist. Neither the border-state representatives nor most Republicans supported compensated emancipation, although their opposition rested on different reasoning.

Lincoln was confronted with the nascent rebellion when he assumed office in March 1861. His position as president was that secession was illegal and that the restoration of the Union was his chief objective. Throughout 1861, he reiterated his pledge not to interfere with slavery in the states where it existed. The goal of the Civil War, Lincoln contended, was to preserve the Union, not to emancipate the slaves. Perhaps his most famous articulation of this position was his reply to Greeley's "Prayer of Twenty Millions." In a letter to the *New York Tribune* on August 22, 1862, Lincoln wrote that "If I could save the Union without freeing any slave, I would do it, and if I could save it by freeing all the slaves, I would do it; and if I could do it by freeing some and leaving others alone, I would also do that." (See "President Abraham Lincoln, Reply to Greeley's Editorial, August 22, 1862," on page 128 in the Primary Sources section.) The president, it must be remembered, wrote his statement after he had decided to issue the Emancipation Proclamation but before its public announcement. Lincoln customarily chose his words carefully. In this instance, he was waiting for the right moment to go public with his decision. Nevertheless, the president drew a distinction between his "view of official duty" and his "personal wish that all men everywhere, could be free." As was so often the case in his presidency, Lincoln's message contained something for various audiences.

Part of the difficulty in pinning Lincoln down on where stood on issues was the fact that the political and military situation remained volatile throughout 1862. The Union war effort had stalled, with General Lee's Army of Virginia threatening the national capital. Criticism of the administration by both Republicans and Democrats accelerated, notably in relation to the lengthening list of war deaths. Northerners increasingly agreed with abolitionists that slaves were providing vital help to the Confederate war effort. Lincoln seemed inclined to accept this conclusion. He told several cabinet members in July that emancipation was "a military necessity to preserve the union" and that his administration must "strike at the heart of the rebellion."

As the body count rose, many Northerners sought revenge. They wondered why soldiers were sacrificing their lives for a war that sought to reunite the slave section with the free states. In this way of thinking, justice meant striking at Southerners where it hurt most—by confiscating their property, including slaves. Even this step was not enough for Representative Thomas Eliot (R-MA), who had introduced the Confiscation Bill in the House. The penalty for treason, Eliot argued, was hanging. (See "Representative Thomas Eliot, Speech Supporting the Confiscation Bill, May 26, 1862," on page 129 in the Primary Sources section.) Sentiments such as these cast emancipation as a measure of retribution, as punishment, for the crime of armed rebellion against the nation. Whatever the motive for its initial conception, the Emancipation Proclamation did give satisfaction to Unionists who sought retribution against Southern traitors.

In fact, slaves were flocking to Union lines, creating a situation that demanded a clear policy. During the course of the war, 700,000 "contrabands," as escaping slaves came to be called, fled to the Yankee side. Some Union generals began to employ them as laborers; some military leaders enlisted them as soldiers. Several Union generals actually proclaimed freedom for slaves in their military region, edicts that Lincoln overrode or modified. Roundly criticizing Lincoln for these countermanding orders, Republicans in Congress supported the use of black troops. In July 1862, Lincoln signed the Militia Act, which allowed blacks to be enrolled in state military units, a precedent-breaking step. The combination of the Confiscation Act and the use of black troops gained increased support by mid-1862, when the Lincoln administration concluded that the Union Army required far more military enlistments. Advocates of emancipation argued that the president possessed unique powers as commander in chief during time of war or rebellion.

In addition to managing the operations on the battlefield, Lincoln gave careful consideration to foreign relations, especially with Great Britain. The South sought aid from European countries and had contracted with British firms to construct military vessels. Great Britain's wavering position on the Confederacy provided an on-going concern for Lincoln, who worried that Britain might recognize Southern rebels as an independent nation. This decision would have opened numerous doors to the Confederacy for trade and loans with numerous foreign jurisdictions. Until the North clearly demonstrated that it had the rebellion in hand, British officials played a coy waiting game. The British public, workers in particular, wondered why the administration failed to strike at slavery. Doing so would put public pressure on British officials to side with the North and end the possibility of British support for the Confederacy. Lincoln breathed a sigh of relief when the proclamation had the diplomatic impact he sought. Britain did not recognize the Confederacy, which failed to make good on its claim as a sovereign entity.

Yet military and diplomatic reasons for Lincoln's emancipation order may not tell the whole story. Lincoln's personal views about slavery and its relationship to the future of the United States may have altered as the rebellion progressed. Suggestive of this possibility is the way that Lincoln phrased the Emancipation Proclamation. Toward the conclusion of the document, he inserted the statement that "And upon this act, sincerely believed to be an act of justice, warranted by the Constitution upon military necessity. . . ." Was Lincoln deferring to the sentiments of abolitionists and Radical Republicans in inserting this line, or did the remark reflect his own outlook? While this point remains unresolved, the president is alleged to have stated on signing the proclamation that "I never in my life, felt more certain that I was doing right than I do in signing this paper." As the war unfolded in 1863 and 1864, Lincoln stood by his emancipation decision, raising it to a goal alongside restoration of the Union. And he went beyond the proclamation, which affected slavery only in areas still under Confederate control, by urging Congress to adopt a Constitutional amendment that would end slavery everywhere in the United States. By so doing, Lincoln demonstrated that he was a friend of freedom.

Whatever prejudices he may have had about African Americans, Lincoln regarded slavery as incompatible with the development of

American democracy. Freedom and the federal union were intimately connected for Lincoln, as they were for many American citizens. The war seemed to have pushed Lincoln toward a public acknowledgement of this ideological principle. In so doing, Lincoln overcame some of his earlier constitutional conservatism concerning slavery. If Lincoln did change his mind, he was not the only famous person to do so during the war. William Lloyd Garrison switched his views dramatically about the use of government to strike a blow against slavery. Before the war began, Garrison rejected politics as a strategy for eradicating slavery, but once the war began, he supported the Union effort to suppress the rebellion and applauded Lincoln's Emancipation Proclamation.

The Argument that Lincoln Should Not Issue an Emancipation Proclamation

Without denying that Lincoln probably allowed his own feelings to influence his decision about slavery, it is also true that the president faced pressures from various quarters about how to proceed. In broad terms, these pressures concerned issues of social justice, political strategy, the constitutionality of private property, desires for revenge, and foreign relations. Lincoln certainly was aware of each of these lines of persuasion. In fact, his skill as a political leader drew considerably on his ability to placate divergent political interests.

Lincoln's relationship with the Republican Party was central to these political calculations. On the one hand, he needed the support of his own party. On the other, he realized that close identification with the outspoken Radical wing of the Republicans would benefit the Democrats and could drive border-state leaders out of the Union. Moreover, some Republicans opposed the inclusion of abolition as a purpose for fighting the war. Senator Edgar Cowan of Pennsylvania, one of the most conservative Republicans in Congress, made this point during consideration of the Confiscation Bill in March 1862. Cowan argued that the measure violated the Fifth Amendment of the Constitution, which prohibited the taking of property without due process of law. Rather than hastening the end of the war, confiscation of slaves would prolong it by increasing Southern hatred of the North. (See "Senator Edgar Cowan, Speech Opposing the Confiscation Bill, March 2, 1862," on page 130 in the Primary Sources section.)

Democrats went well beyond Cowan's misgivings and slammed Republican attacks on slavery as legally unconstitutional and socially revolutionary. In the House, Representative John Law of Indiana used vitriolic racial imagery to condemn the Confiscation Bill. (See "Representative John Law, Speech Denouncing the Confiscation Bill, May 1862," on page 131 in the Primary Sources section.) Referring to American slaves as "human gorillas," Law drew on White supremacist rhetoric that was common among Democratic politicians. The party's spokesmen argued that the United States was a white man's country, which now was endangered by social revolution, fomented by abolitionists and radicals, who had captured Lincoln's ear. Democrats—as well as some Republicans—claimed that Union soldiers would desert in droves if the war were transformed into an abolitionist crusade. Lincoln is on record as sharing this worry. Democrats and Conservatives further argued that emancipation would stiffen "the spirit of resistance in the South" and make reunion impossible. Adding injury to insult, Democrats in the House introduced a resolution that branded the preliminary Emancipation Proclamation of September 22, 1862, "a high crime against the Constitution." The legislature of Illinois, Lincoln's home state, denounced the proclamation. (See "The Illinois Legislature Condemns the Emancipation Proclamation, January 7, 1863," on page 132 in the Primary Sources section.) Besides its unconstitutionality, the Democratic-controlled body called the president's decision "a revolution in social organization of the Southern States" that promised the "dismal foreboding of horror and dismay."

Lincoln was rightly concerned about the impact of such opinions on the congressional elections of 1862. Democrats, in fact, did spring back in these polls, gaining 38 seats in the House of Representatives and winning several governors' chairs, including in New York. Republicans, however, retained their majority in Congress and of the governorships of the Northern states. Still, Democratic denunciation of "Black Republicans" was a source of concern for Lincoln and many Republicans. Lincoln bent over backward to accommodate the border states. However, when they turned down his proposal for gradual, compensated emancipation, the president threw in his lot with Republicans.

OUTCOME AND IMPACT

Lincoln gave Confederates 100 days to lay down their arms before confiscation of their property under a presidential edict would commence.

Some of the deadliest fighting occurred during these remaining days of 1862, with engagements in the lower Mississippi region and in Kentucky, Tennessee, and Virginia. Despite firing McClellan and elevating Ambrose Burnside to command the Northern Army, Lincoln still had not found the right general. On December 13 at the Battle of Fredericksburg, 52 miles south of Washington, Lee blocked Burnside's effort to push into Confederate territory. Another 13,000 Yankees lay dead or wounded. The mood turned somber in Washington. Angry Republicans in the Senate voted in party caucus to urge a reorganization of Lincoln's cabinet. Besieged with bad news, the president said to a friend: "We are on the brink of destruction."

Antislavery advocates were worried that Lincoln would renege on issuing the Emancipation Proclamation on New Year's Day. They were kept wondering when Lincoln made his pitch for gradual, compensated emancipation once again in his annual message of December 1, 1862, setting a 1900 target date to eradicate slavery completely. But Lincoln did keep his word and issued the final proclamation on January 1, 1863. The following December, the president stated in his annual message of 1863 that he would not send any freed slave back into bondage. Lincoln won reelection in 1864 on a Republican platform that endorsed a constitutional amendment abolishing slavery nationwide. Lincoln interpreted his victory as an endorsement of the amendment, and he played a key role in getting the lame duck Congress to adopt it on January 31, 1865. The Thirteenth Amendment was ratified on December 18, 1865, overriding the Emancipation Proclamation.

The survival of slavery was also linked to Union military fortunes, which improved in 1863. In July, General Grant took Vicksburg, the last major Confederate stronghold on the Mississippi River. That same month, Yankee soldiers stopped Lee's attempt to penetrate Northern territory at Gettysburg, Pennsylvania. General William T. Sherman began his famed march through Georgia in March 1864. The war dragged on for another 13 bloody months until Lee surrendered to Grant at Appomattox Court House in Virginia on April 9, 1865. The North's celebration of this long and hard-fought victory was short-lived. Five days later, John Wilkes Booth shot Abraham Lincoln, who was attending a play at Ford's Theater in Washington, D.C. Lincoln died on April 15.

Lincoln's death heightened rather than reduced political conflict over the slave South, as congressional Republicans fought with

The surrender of General Lee to General Grant at Appomattox Court House,
Virginia, April 9, 1865 (Library of Congress)

President Andrew Johnson, who was elevated from the vice presidency
by Lincoln's assassination. A Democrat from Tennessee, Johnson had
accepted the second position on the national ticket in a Republican
effort to present a unified front to voters in 1864. Johnson accepted
emancipation but also adhered to the Democratic belief in white
supremacy. He took no effective action to block the attempt of former slave owners to recreate a world that looked much like slavery.

Republicans countered Johnson's policy with a plan for Reconstruction that lawmakers enacted over the president's veto. The president had no direct role in congressional adoption of the Fourteenth Amendment in 1866 (ratified 1868), which held states to national standards concerning the due process of law and equal treatment of all citizens under the law, and Fifteenth Amendment in 1869 (ratified 1870), which prohibited the denial of suffrage on account of race, color, or previous condition of servitude. Union troops offered blacks some protection from white intimidation in the South during Johnson's presidency, which ended in March 1869, and during Ulysses S. Grant's first term, when Republicans regained control of the White House. By the early 1870s, however, northern support for federal intervention in southern political affairs collapsed. Reconstruction officially ended in 1877. By then, conservative factions, many laden with former Confederates and slave owners, had taken control of southern state governments and began to systematically strip African Americans of civil, political, and economic rights.

WHAT IF?

Did the Emancipation Proclamation make a difference? What if Lincoln had decided not to issue it?

The adoption of the Thirteenth Amendment to the Constitution, which forbade slavery, suggests a plausible scenario. In light of the improvement of Union military fortunes after 1862 and the enlargement of Republican majorities in Congress following the election of 1864, the likelihood is that Republicans would have ended slavery via constitutional amendment. The party's commitment to civil liberties remained strong during the years of Johnson's presidency, animated in part by the memory of the martyred Lincoln. How much Lincoln's Emancipation Proclamation furthered these events is difficult to determine. Arguably, his leadership served as a morale booster during a bleak period of the Civil War. Lincoln had not taken the lead in the abolitionist movement, but he was an effective leader as president in fusing the themes of liberty with union.

There is a second and less optimistic scenario. This line of reasoning begins with the reality of deep racial cleavages in America. Even with the Thirteenth, Fourteenth, and Fifteenth Amendments and several broad civil rights laws adopted during Reconstruction, conditions for African Americans deteriorated during the late 19th century. By 1900, blacks lived in a world framed by violence, economic marginalization and poverty, and exclusion from the political process.

The Progressive Era reform period of American history paid little attention to these injustices. Nor did the New Deal of the 1930s take forceful action against racial inequalities, such as denial of the right to vote. The armed forces remained segregated during both World War I and World War II. A century elapsed after the Thirteenth Amendment before effective national legislation outlawed blatant forms of segregation and forged a commitment to equal voting rights. This failure to address racism in America suggests that slavery may have survived until the 1930s, when the mechanical cotton picker replaced black field hands.

CHRONOLOGY

1860   *November 10:* News reaches South Carolina that Lincoln was elected president.

December 20: South Carolina secedes from the Union.

1861   *March 4:* Lincoln is inaugurated president.

April 12: Confederacy attacks Fort Sumter.

July 21: Battle of Bull Run

August: Lincoln countermands General John C. Frémont's emancipation order.

1862   *April 6–7:* Battle of Shiloh (Tennessee)

April 16: Act abolishing slavery in Washington, D.C.

June 19: Act prohibiting slavery in the territories

June 25: Seven Days Battle (June 25–July 1)

July 12: Lincoln meets with border-state congressmen at the White House.

July 17: Confiscation Act

July 22: Lincoln tells his cabinet of his intention to issue an emancipation proclamation.

August: Confederate troops advance into Kentucky.

September 17: Battle of Antietam

September 22: Lincoln issues the Preliminary Emancipation Proclamation.

Fall: Congressional elections; Democrats gain 34 seats in U.S. House of Representatives.

December 1: Lincoln proposes a plan of compensated emancipation in his annual message to Congress.

December 13: Battle of Fredericksburg

1863   *January 1:* Lincoln issues the Emancipation Proclamation.

July 1–3: Battle of Gettysburg, which stops General Robert E. Lee's northward advance

July 4: Ulysses S. Grant captures Vicksburg.

1864   *September 2:* General William T. Sherman captures Atlanta.

1865   *February 1:* Congress passes Thirteenth Amendment.

April 9: Robert E. Lee surrenders to Ulysses S. Grant at Appomattox Court House, Virginia.

April 15: Lincoln dies of wounds by an assassin.

December 18: Thirteenth Amendment is ratified, abolishing slavery.

DISCUSSION QUESTIONS

1. Should Lincoln have included moral reasons for freeing slaves in the Emancipation Proclamation?
2. Evaluate the role of political pressures in Lincoln's decision to issue the Emancipation Proclamation.
3. Discuss how war can significantly change political opinions and the context in which public officials make public policy decisions.
4. Would the abolitionists have succeeded if the Civil War had not taken place?

WEB SITES

American President. An Online Reference Resource. Miller Center of Public Affairs, University of Virginia. Available at http://millercenter.org/academic/americanpresident.

"The End of Slavery: The Creation of the 13th Amendment" from *Harper's Weekly* magazine. Includes Lincoln's decisions on emancipation. Available at http://13thamendment.harpweek.com/.

Jensen, Richard. Guide to Political Research On-line. Available at http://tigger.uic.edu/~rjensen/political.htm#Hist:US.

BIBLIOGRAPHY

Bogue, Alan G. *The Earnest Men: Republicans of the Civil War Senate.* Ithaca, N.Y.: Cornell University Press, 1981.

Donald, David. *Lincoln.* New York: Touchstone, 1995.

Franklin, John Hope. *The Emancipation Proclamation.* Garden City, N.Y.: Doubleday and Company, 1963.

McPherson, James M. *Battle Cry of Freedom: The Civil War Era.* New York: Oxford University Press, 1988.

———. *The Struggle for Equality: Abolitionists and the Negro in the Civil War and Reconstruction.* Princeton, N.J.: Princeton University Press, 1964.

Paludan, Phillip S. *The Presidency of Abraham Lincoln.* Lawrence: University Press of Kansas, 1994.

Silbey, Joel R. *A Respectable Minority: The Democratic Party in the Civil War Era, 1860–1868.* New York: W. W. Norton, 1977.

PRIMARY SOURCES

1. Senator Charles Sumner Addresses Republicans in Massachusetts, October 1, 1861

Senator Charles Sumner (R-MA) addressed the state Republican Convention in Worcester, Massachusetts, on October 1, 1861. Sumner urged President Lincoln to use his war powers to emancipate the slaves, a step that Sumner predicted would hasten the end of the war.

The Government is assailed by a rebellion without precedent. Never, since Satan warred upon the Almighty, has rebellion assumed such a front *[applause]*, and never before has it begun in such a cause. The Rebels are numerous and powerful, and their cause is Slavery. *[Sensation]*

A simple declaration that all men within the lines of the United States troops are freemen, will be in strict conformity with the Constitution, and also with precedent. The Constitution knows no man as slave. It treats all within its jurisdiction as *persons,* while the exceptional provision for the rendition of persons held to service or labor, you will observe, is carefully confined to such has escaped into another State,— so that in Virginia it cannot require the surrender of a Virginia slave. . . . It is clear, therefore, that there is no sanction under the Constitution for turning a national camp into a slave-pen, or for turning military officers into slave-hunters. Let his plain construction be adopted, and then, as our lines advance, Freedom will be established everywhere. . . .

There is a higher agency that may be invoked, which is at the same time under the Constitution and above the Constitution: I mean Martial Law in its plenitude and declared by solemn Proclamation. It is under the Constitution, because the War Power to which it belongs is positively recognized by the Constitution. It is above the Constitution, because, when set in motion, like necessity, it knows no other law.

That this law might be employed against Slavery, with impediment from State Rights, was first proclaimed in the House of Representatives by a Massachusetts statesman, who was a champion of Freedom, John Quincy Adams *[Applause]*.

"So many enemies as slaves!" Unless this ancient proverb has ceased to be true, there are now four million of enemies intermingled with the Rebels, toiling in their fields, digging in their camps, and sitting at their firesides, constituting four millions of allies to the National Government.

Source: Charles Sumner. *The Works of Charles Sumner.* Vol. 6. Boston: Lee and Shepard, 1872, 7–29.

—⚏—

2. Horace Greeley, "The Prayer of Twenty Millions," August 19, 1862

In his editorial entitled "The Prayer of Twenty Millions," on August 19, 1862, Horace Greeley, the influential editor of the New York Tribune, *offered a variety of reasons why Lincoln should emancipate the slaves of Southern rebels immediately.*

To Abraham Lincoln, President of the United States:

Dear Sir: I do not intrude to tell you—for you must know already—that a great portion of those who triumphed in your election, and of all who desire the qualified suppression of the rebellion now desolating our country, are sorely disappointed and deeply pained by the policy you seem to be pursuing with regard to the slaves of rebels.

II. We think you are strangely and disastrously remiss in the discharge of your official and imperative duty with regard to the emancipating provisions of the new Confiscation Act. Those provisions were designed to fight Slavery with Liberty. They prescribe that men loyal to the Union, and willing to shed their blood in her behalf, shall no longer be held, with the nation's consent, in bondage to persistent, malignant traitors, who for twenty years have been plotting and for sixteen months have been fighting to divide and destroy our country. Why these traitors should be treated with tenderness by you, to the prejudice of the dearest rights of loyal men, we cannot conceive. . . .

III. We think you are unduly influenced by the councils, the presentations, the menaces, of certain fossil politicians from the Border Slave States. . . .

V. We complain that the Union cause has suffered, and is now suffering immensely, from mistaken deference to rebel Slavery. . . .

VI. We complain that the Confiscation Act which you approved is habitually disregarded by your Generals, and that no word of rebuke for them from you has yet reached the public ear. Fremont's Proclamation and Hunter's Order favoring Emancipation were promptly annulled by you; while Halleck's Number Three, forbidding fugitives from slavery to rebels to come within this lines . . . have never provoked even your remonstrance. . . .

VIII. On the face of this wide earth, Mr. President, there is not one disinterested, determined, intelligent champion of the Union cause who does not feel that . . . every hour of deference to Slavery is an hour of added and deepened peril to the Union.

Source: New York Tribune, August 19, 1862.

—⁂—

3. President Abraham Lincoln, Emancipation Proclamation, January 1, 1863

President Abraham Lincoln issued the Emancipation Proclamation on January 1, 1863. Lincoln cited his powers as commander in chief as the legal authority for the decision.

Now, therefore I, Abraham Lincoln, President of the United States, by virtue of the power in me vested as Commander-in-Chief, of the Army and Navy of the United States in time of actual armed rebellion against the authority and government of the United States, and as a fit and necessary war measure for suppressing said rebellion, do, on this first day of January, in the year of our Lord one thousand eight hundred and sixty-three, and in accordance with my purpose so to do publicly proclaimed for the full period of one hundred days, from the day first above mentioned, order and designate as the States and parts of States wherein the people thereof respectively, are this day in rebellion against the United States, the following, to wit: Arkansas, Texas, Louisiana, (except the Parishes of St. Bernard, Plaquemines, Jefferson, St. John, St. Charles, St. James Ascension, Assumption, Terrebonne, Lafourche, St. Mary, St. Martin, and Orleans, including the City of New Orleans) Mississippi, Alabama, Florida, Georgia, South Carolina, North Carolina, and Virginia, (except the forty-eight counties designated as West Virginia, and also the counties of Berkley, Accomac, Northampton, Elizabeth City, York, Princess Ann, and Norfolk, including the cities of Norfolk and Portsmouth), and which excepted parts, are for the present, left precisely as if this proclamation were not issued. And by virtue of the power, and for the purpose aforesaid, I do order and declare that all persons held as slaves within said designated States, and parts of States, are, and henceforward shall be free; and that the Executive government of the United States, including the military and naval authorities thereof, will recognize and maintain the freedom of said persons.

And I further declare and make known, that such persons of suitable condition, will be received into the armed service of the United States to garrison forts, positions, stations, and other places, and to man vessels of all sorts in said service.

Source: James D. Richardson, comp. *Messages and Papers of the Presidents.* Vol. 5. Washington, D.C.: Bureau of National Literature and Art, 1897, 3359.

—∞—

4. President Abraham Lincoln, Plan of Compensated Emancipation, December 1, 1862

President Lincoln proposed a plan of compensated emancipation in his annual message to Congress on December 1, 1862. Lincoln had proposed this solution for resolving the controversy over slavery on previous occasions.

I recommend the adoption of the following resolution and articles amendatory to the Constitution of the United States:

ART.—. Every State wherein slavery now exists which shall abolish the same therein at any time or times before the 1st day of January, A.D. 1900, shall receive compensation from the United States as follows, to wit:

The President of the United States shall deliver to every such State bonds of the United States bearing interest at the rate of ___ per cent per annum to an amount equal to the aggregate sum of ___ for each slave shown to have been therein by the Eighth Census of the United States, said bonds to be delivered to such State by installments or in one parcel at the completion of the abolishment, accordingly as the same shall have been gradual or at one time within such State; and interest shall begin to run upon any such bond only from the proper time of its delivery as aforesaid.

ART.—. All slaves who shall have enjoyed actual freedom by the chances of the war at any time before the end of the rebellion shall be forever free; but all owners of such who shall not have been disloyal shall be compensated for them at the same rates as is provided for States adopting abolishment of slavery, but in such way that no slave shall be twice accounted for.

Among the friends of the Union there is great diversity of sentiment and of policy in regard to slavery and the African race amongst us. Some would perpetuate slavery; some would abolish it suddenly and without compensation; some would abolish it gradually and with compensation: some would remove the freed people from us, and some would retain them with us; and there are yet other minor diversities. Because of these diversities we waste much strength in struggles among ourselves. By mutual concession we should harmonize and act together. This would be compromise, but it would be compromise among the friends and not with the enemies of the Union. These articles are intended to embody a plan of such mutual concessions. If the plan shall be adopted, it is assumed that emancipation will follow, at least in several of the States.

Source: James D. Richardson, comp. *Messages and Papers of the Presidents.* Washington, D.C.: Bureau of National Literature and Art, 1897, vol. 5, 3337–3338.

—⁓—

5. President Abraham Lincoln, Reply to Greeley's Editorial, August 22, 1862

President Lincoln replied to Horace Greeley's August 19, 1862, editorial, "The Prayer of Twenty Millions," on August 22, 1862. The president said that his primary goal in the war was to restore the Union, not to liberate the slaves.

> Dear Sir: I have just read yours of the 19th, addressed to myself through the New York Tribune. . . .
>
> As to the policy I "seem to be pursuing," as you say, I have not meant to leave anyone in doubt.
>
> I would save the Union. I would save it the shortest way under the Constitution. The sooner the National authority can be restored, the nearer the Union will be "the Union as it was."
>
> If there be those" who would not save the Union unless they could at the same time save Slavery, I do not agree with them. If there be those who would not save the Union unless they could at the same time destroy Slavery, I do not agree with them. My paramount object in this struggle is to save the Union, and is not either to save or destroy Slavery.
>
> If I could save the Union without freeing any slave, I would do it; and if I could save it by freeing all the slaves, I would do it; and if I could do it by freeing some and leaving others alone, I would also do that. What I do about Slavery and the colored race, I do because I believe it helps to save this Union; and what I forbear, I forbear because I do not believe it would help to save the Union.

Source: http://showcase.netins.net/web/creative/lincoln/speeches/greeley.htm.

—⁓—

6. Representative Thomas Eliot, Speech Supporting the Confiscation Bill, May 26, 1862

Representative Thomas Eliot (R-MA) advocated the adoption of the Confiscation Bill in the House of Representatives on May 26, 1862. The desire for revenge against Southern traitors appears to be one of his motives.

> This bill seeks to condemn the property of the leading rebels, and to place the proceeds in the treasury for the purpose of helping to defray the expenses of the war, and also in aid of those who have been robbed by the Confederate Government. All laws of this kind, gentlemen must be aware, must be in their terms severe. The rebels began to confiscate a year ago. They passed confiscation laws, and under those laws there is but little property of loyal men left in their States. We are slow in

following their example. I am surprised that, after a year's experience of the effects of their confiscation schemes, and after they have used the property taken from loyal citizens against the Government of the United States, gentlemen should come here and speak of this bill as being too severe. There is not a rebel of the classes mentioned in the bill who does not deserve to be hanged by the neck until he is dead.

I believe, Mr. Speaker, that this bill will accomplish good in the border States. It will strengthen the hands and hearts of loyal men. If made effectual, it will deprive the enemy of his means of carrying on the war. It will help to weaken and subdue him. It will increase our strength. It will, in part, indemnify us against the cost of this rebellion. It will give the property of rebels, first, to their creditors in loyal States; and, secondly, it will provide a means of indemnity for loyal men whose property, owned in rebellious States, has been taken from them.

Source: Marion Mills Miller, ed. *Great Debates in American History.* New York: Current Literature Publication Co., 1913, vol. 6, 207–208.

———

7. Senator Edgar Cowan, Speech Opposing the Confiscation Bill, March 2, 1862

Senator Edgar Cowan (R-PA) raised political and constitutional objections to emancipation in the debate over the Confiscation Bill on March 2, 1862. Cowan said that stripping Southerners of their property would make them more hostile to the Union and thus would prolong the war.

We are standing now squarely face to face with questions of most pregnant significance. Shall we stand or fall by the Constitution, or shall we leave it and adventure ourselves upon the wide sea of revolution? Shall we attempt to liberate the slaves of the people of the rebellious States, or shall we leave them to regulate their domestic institutions the same as before the rebellion? Shall we go back to the doctrine of forfeitures which marked the middle ages, and introduce feuds which intervening centuries have not yet sufficed to quiet? These are great questions, and they are in this bill, everyone of them. This bill proposes, at a single stroke, to strip four millions of people of all their property, real, personal, and mixed, of every kind whatsoever, and reduce them at once to absolute poverty; and that, too, at a time when four hundred thousand of them are in the field opposing us desperately.

Pass this bill, sir, and all that is left of the Constitution is not worth much. Certainly it is not worth a terrible and destructive war, such as we now wage for it. And it must be remembered that that war is waged solely for the Constitution, and for the ends, aims, and purposes sanctioned by it, and for no others.

As a Republican, standing upon the Constitution as construed by that party, I protest against this bill as being a total and entire departure from the principles of that instrument, most mischievous at this time, because it uselessly distracts, divides, and weakens the friends of the country when they ought to be united and of one accord in action, if ever such were needed before. In addition to this, it would make us do of all things in the world that which would most gratify and strengthen our enemies everywhere—worth to-day more than a hundred thousand armed men to the traitors of the South, and worth more than five hundred thousand votes to the would-be traitors of the North; thus enabling the latter again to get control of the Government, to wield it as they have wielded it before. No, sir; pass that bill by this Congress and every falsehood uttered and every design charged upon us in six years of desperate struggle is verified by our deliberate act, an act as useless to the country and to the cause in which we are engaged (apart from other objections) as would be a law against serfdom in Russia passed here.

Source: Marion Mills Miller, ed. *Great Debates in American History.* New York: Current Literature Publication Co., 1913, vol. 6, 192–202.

―――

8. Representative John Law, Speech Denouncing the Confiscation Bill, May 1862

Representative John Law (D-IN) denounced the Confiscation Bill in the House debate during May 1862. Law used racist themes that Democrats articulated frequently during the era.

The man who dreams of closing the present unhappy contest by reconstructing this Union upon any other basis than that prescribed by our fathers, in the compact formed by- them, is a madman—aye, worse, a traitor—and should be hung as high as Haman. Sir, pass these acts, confiscate under these bills the property of these men, emancipate their negroes, place arms in the hands of these human gorillas, to murder their masters and violate their wives and daughters, and you will have a war such as was never witnessed in the worst days of the French Revolution, and horrors never exceeded in St. Domingo, for the balance of this century at least.

Source: Marion Mills Miller, ed. *Great Debates in American History.* New York: Current Literature Publication Co., 1913, vol. 6, 207.

—⚊⚊—

9. The Illinois Legislature Condemns the Emancipation Proclamation, January 7, 1863

The Illinois state legislature adopted a resolution on January 7, 1863, that condemned the Emancipation Proclamation as inviting a social revolution, which promised "the most dismal foreboding of horror and dismay."

Resolved: That the emancipation proclamation of the President of the United States is as unwarrantable in military as in civil law; a gigantic usurpation, at once converting the war, professedly commenced by the administration for the vindication of the authority of the constitution, into the crusade for the sudden, unconditional and violent liberation of 3,000,000 negro slaves; a result which would not only be a total subversion of the Federal Union but a revolution in the social organization of the Southern States, the immediate and remote, the present and far-reaching consequences of which to both races cannot be contemplated without the most dismal foreboding of horror and dismay. The proclamation invites servile insurrection as an element in this emancipation crusade—a means of warfare, the inhumanity and diabolism of which are without example in civilized warfare, and which we denounce and which the civilized world will denounce as an uneffaceable disgrace to the American people.

Source: *Illinois State Register,* January 7, 1863.

5

THE SPANISH-AMERICAN WAR:
Should the United States Free Cuba?

—⚹—

THE CONTROVERSY

The Issue

On April 20, 1898, Congress proclaimed the independence of Cuba and authorized the president to use military force to end the Spanish effort to suppress an anticolonial rebellion on the island. The brief, successful war against Spain led to an American protectorate over Cuba and the acquisition of the Philippine Islands and Puerto Rico as American colonies.

- ◆ **Arguments in favor of military force:** President William McKinley argued that considerations of humanitarian compassion, the preservation of commercial relations, and the dangers of political instability in Cuba justified American intervention, but he asked Congress to decide whether to use force against Spain. Most lawmakers agreed with the president, although some thought that the explosion of the USS *Maine* in Havana Harbor was sufficient in itself to warrant retaliation against Spain, which they held responsible for the attack.

- ◆ **Arguments against military force:** Opponents warned that intervention in Cuba would lead to American acquisition of Spanish colonies in the Caribbean and the Pacific, steps that contradicted the nation's ideological principles and its political history. Most critics of intervention denounced Spanish cruelties in Cuba yet held that the end (stop the suffering) did not justify the means (military intervention in Cuba). Another line of opposition saw the war as benefiting generals and speculators, not the working man.

—⚹—

INTRODUCTION

On February 15, 1898, an explosion ripped the forward section of the USS *Maine*, which had been anchored in Havana Harbor, Cuba. The explosion killed 266 seamen and naval officers aboard the ship, which sank almost immediately following the blast. The *Maine* had been ordered to Cuba to offer protection to American residents of the island, where a bloody insurrection between local inhabitants and their Spanish colonial rulers raged. Many observers in the United States charged the Spanish with culpability for the disaster. Theodore Roosevelt, the assistant secretary of the U.S. Navy, had no doubt that Spanish saboteurs had mined the vessel. Across America during the weeks that followed, citizens repeated the *New York Journal* headline "Remember the *Maine*, to hell with Spain." For Roosevelt and many other Americans, the attack on the *Maine* constituted an affront to American honor that justified war against Cuba's Spanish overlords.

Spanish control of Cuba had become contentious in the last decades of the 19th century. The depression of the 1890s triggered renewed conflict on the island between anticolonial insurgents, who rebelled in 1895, and Spanish loyalists. Americans gave only passing notice to the disturbance until the sinking of the *Maine*. More than any other event, the *Maine* disaster raised the visibility of the rebellion in Cuba and gave credibility to charges of cruelty by the Spanish military. Public pressure mounted on Congress and on President William McKinley to persuade Spain to resolve the dispute with its Cuban subjects. Frustrated by Spain's indecision and faced with increasingly insistent demands for action, McKinley asked Congress to give him authority to use force to create a stable government in Cuba. On April 19, 1898, Congress approved the president's request and went a step further by declaring Cuba to be independent. Did Congress act appropriately?

Most members of Congress and probably the majority of American voters said yes. A revulsion swept across the United States over Spain's "reconcentration" policy, whereby its army herded rural populations into fortified towns,

The wrecked battleship USS *Maine* in Havana Harbor, Cuba, 1898 (Library of Congress)

which were not prepared to accommodate hordes of refugees. Thousands of deaths among civilians resulted. Many Americans approved intervention to stop this holocaust on humane and moral grounds. Others pointed to the sinking of the *Maine* as a warlike act that warranted military retaliation. There were Americans who anticipated and perhaps even hoped for an event that would provide a justification to eject the last Old World colonial power from the Western hemisphere. Some among this group urged the United States to annex islands in the Caribbean and the Pacific for naval bases and commercial contacts. In addition, leaders of the Republican Party worried that if the McKinley administration did not display forceful resolve toward Cuba, American voters would penalize them in the fall elections.

None of these reasons satisfied a minority of individuals who opposed the use of force against Spain. Their opposition to military intervention usually was coupled with the presumption that the United States would annex Cuba and perhaps other Spanish possessions after the war. Such a step, they argued, violated fundamental American principles of self-determination and the respect for liberty. A few critics saw American annexation of distant lands as threatening to open up the country to "inassimilable" peoples, notably those with dark skins. A small contingent of cynics labeled a war with Spain as good for business but bad for workers. The voices of opposition to American imperialism coalesced into an Anti-Imperialism League after the United States defeated Spain, opening up the question of what to do with the Philippine Islands. Expansionists won the day. McKinley approved the annexation of the Philippines, where the U.S. Army, in a long, bloody war, crushed an insurgency campaign for independence.

BACKGROUND

Spain was the first European nation to colonize the Americas and among the last to relinquish a major colonial possession in the Western Hemisphere. Christopher Columbus sailed into the Caribbean in 1492 and claimed the island of Cuba for Spain, the sponsor of his voyage across the Atlantic. Although most other Spanish colonies gained their independence in the early 19th century, Cuba and Puerto Rico remained Spanish colonies for 400 years. Cuba developed a thriving sugarcane production, undertaken largely by slave labor until 1888. The 750-mile-long island lies roughly 90 miles south of Key West, Florida, the southernmost city of the United States. This close proximity to the United States and Cuba's slave-based plantation culture made the island appealing to southern annexationists before the Civil War. Even after slavery was eliminated from the United States, Cuba remained a perennial issue in American foreign relations.

North Americans, especially New Englanders, had established commercial ties with the Caribbean islands early in their history. These connections acquired greater political significance in the decades after U.S. independence, when Americans applauded the anticolonial revolts in Central and South America. The Monroe Doctrine, enunciated by President James Monroe in 1823, formalized this diplomatic interest by warning European powers not to reestablish imperial footholds in the Americas. American leaders reiterated this position in the last third of the 19th century, when European powers embarked on a new round of colonization, principally in Africa and Asia. Europe's new imperialism and the military power that facilitated it played an instrumental role in persuading the national government to modernize the U.S. Navy, which had become obsolete in comparison with other large nations. Congress began to rectify America's naval impotence in 1882. Within a few years, lawmakers had authorized funds to construct steel-hulled, steam-driven vessels for the American fleet. (See the sidebar "Battleships and America's New Navy" on page 138.) By the late 1890s, the U.S. Navy had grown into a formidable force, considerably stronger than Spain's fleet.

Theodore Roosevelt, naval historian, politician, and Assistant Secretary of the Navy beginning in 1897, loudly and proudly championed the transformation of the modern navy. Since publishing his 1882 book, *The Naval War of 1812*, "TR," as Roosevelt was affectionately known, urged a strong, combat-ready navy, built around battleships. When he became second in command of the navy department in the administration of William McKinley, who became president in March 1897, Roosevelt had a highly visible platform for disseminating his views. His address to the Naval War College in Newport, Rhode Island, in June 1897 emphasized his conviction that the surest way of achieving peace was by maintaining a world-class navy. (See "Theodore Roosevelt, Address to the Naval War College, 1897," on page 156 in the Primary Sources section.) "It is necessary," he stated, "to have a fleet of great battle-ships if we intend to live up to the Monroe Doctrine." Roosevelt believed that the United States had strategic interests in the Pacific region, too, although he did not advocate an active imperialist program along the lines of the European colonization of Africa. Still, the assistant secretary was convinced that national character was formed through martial activities. If war with Spain was to come, TR was ready for it.

Spain, in fact, had an intractable problem in Cuba. The Panic of 1893 and the depression it spawned had induced Congress in 1894 to withdraw tariff concessions on sugarcane imported from Cuba. Faced with a high tax on sugar, Cubans watched sugar exports to the United States, which purchased the bulk of the island's cane, plunge. The island's economy tailspun into depression, which in turn triggered animosity among native-born Cubans toward Spanish colonialism and the *peninsulares* (Spanish-born Cubans), who held most economic and political power on the island. A full-scale rebellion was underway in 1895.

Spain's response to resistance in Cuba was military suppression. Spanish officials appointed General Valeriano Weyler to crush the rebels. A key to Weylar's strategy was reconcentracion, a policy that relocated rural residents to fortified towns, as a way of smothering the capacity of insurgents to sustain their fight. Reconcentracion towns were ill-prepared to handle the thousands of refugees, largely women and children, who had been forcibly ejected from their homes. Thousands died under "Butcher" Weyler's program.

President Grover Cleveland initially took a neutral stance on the insurgency in Cuba but later urged Spain to grant autonomy to the island. The Spanish government showed no interest in the idea, yet was unable to quell the violence in Cuba, where discontented residents called for American intervention. Their appeals whetted the appetite of individuals in the United States who had long sought the annexation of Cuba. American citizens had already begun sending humanitarian aid to the dispossessed in Cuba, where a scorched earth policy by both rebels and the Spanish army devastated the island and its economy. Here the matter rested in the fall of 1896, when William McKinley, the Republican candidate for president, triumphed over William Jennings Bryan, his Democratic opponent.

McKinley inherited the Cuban dilemma when he assumed the presidency in March 1897. The president's strategy was to say little about the issue in public and work behind the scenes diplomatically, urging Spain to declare an armistice and cease its reconcentracion policy in Cuba. McKinley's reticence to go public about his negotiations with Spanish officials was interpreted by some observers at the time

BATTLESHIPS AND AMERICA'S NEW NAVY

The U.S. Navy changed course in the 1880s. Following its extensive deployment during the Civil War, the navy languished for nearly two decades. The navy failed to create a viable organization that could guide the service to the next era. Recruiting and retaining qualified crew was a perennial problem, as was a surplus of aging, mediocre officers. Navy shipyard facilities were notorious for corruption and patronage. The most glaring deficiency to its critics, however, was the navy's aging fleet. American ships were still made largely of wood in 1880, with most fighting vessels powered by a combination of steam and sail. Compared with the more technologically advanced ships of Europe, America's navy was barely third-rate. According to Secretary of the Navy Benjamin F. Tracy in his 1889 annual report, the United States ranked 12th, behind Turkey, China, and Austria-Hungary, among the navies of the world.

Tracy became a forceful advocate of a battleship navy. Modern battleships had hulls of steel, with plenty of armor to deflect enemy shells and rifled guns on turrets that swiveled by electrically driven hydraulics. In 1889, Great Britain possessed 37 of these high-tech fighting ships. France had 33, Russia had seven, but the United States had none. Military strategists lamented the inability of the United States to confront a modern naval adversary on the high seas.

Convincing skeptics in Congress to pony up funds for building a modern navy was another matter. America had a long history of diplomatic isolation from the powerhouses of Europe and an aversion to keeping a large peacetime army and navy. Devotees of this outlook pointed to the Atlantic and Pacific Oceans as protective shields for the nation from potentially hostile nations. Rebuilding the navy would cost public money, lots of it. In addition to this obstacle, some opponents of naval reform believed that the creation of a modernized navy would lead to foreign adventurism and unwanted international conflicts.

Theodore Roosevelt, the future president of the United States, scoffed at these arguments. In his well-received 1882 book, *The Naval War of 1812*, and later as a reflection of indecision and vacillation. However, these charges were largely the product of unrealistic expectations created by talk in Congress, the press, and among public figures and by deliberate

the 24-year-old Roosevelt argued that the lack of naval preparation in the years before the War of 1812 had left the United States at the mercy of British intrigue. Admiral Alfred Thayer Mahan, a professor at the Naval War College (established in 1884), seconded Roosevelt's recommendation in his widely read work *The Influence of Sea Power Upon History, 1680–1783*. Mahan contended that great powers achieved their international stature largely by maintaining strong navies. Mahan, Roosevelt, and other advocates of a new navy pointed to Europe's rapid colonization of Africa and Asia in the 1880s, warning that these countries were likely to meddle in waters closer to home, especially if America lacked a navy. Technology, they argued, made the age of sail obsolete. Building a modern navy would allow the United States to play a larger role in global affairs. A rising nationalist pride, drummed up by the military marches of John Philip Sousa, the marine's chief band leader; the Grand Army of the Republic (an organization of Civil War veterans); and other patriotic impulses helped to popularize these ideas.

President Chester Arthur and his secretary of the navy persuaded Congress in 1883 to fund the construction of three steel-hulled cruisers armed with modern guns. These ships still mixed sail with steam and were restricted to American coastal waters, but it was a start. In 1890, during the administration of Benjamin Harrison, Congress authorized the construction of three battleships, although it restricted their cruising radius to 1,000 miles. Two years later, when Congress authorized the battleship *Iowa*, this limitation was lifted. By the mid-1890s, the U.S. Navy had jettisoned its older strategy of coastal defense and commerce raiding in favor of an offensive outlook based on state-of-the-art vessels that could steam 5,000 miles from home before refueling. Among the first of these showcase vessels was the USS *Indiana*, authorized in 1890 and commissioned for service in 1895. The vessel carried guns of 13-and eight-inch sizes, each mounted on swirling turrets. The ship weighed 10,288 tons, it was 350 feet in length, and its armor was as thick as 18 inches in places. The *Indiana* was part of the American flotilla that defeated the Spanish fleet in Cuba in 1898. For the United States, the age of the battleship had arrived.

foot-dragging by Spanish officials. McKinley wanted to find a peaceful solution to Cuba, but his options were limited, especially by the dynamics of Spanish politics.

Central to the Spanish mentality was its unwillingness to relinquish control of Cuba and Puerto Rico, which represented the last vestiges of its empire in the Americas. No Spanish politician could advocate Cuban independence and hope to remain in office. Retention of Cuba was an axiom in Spanish politics, akin to the sanctity of individualism in American culture. No regime in Spain could survive without the support of the army, which was committed to retaining the empire. Cuban loyalists to Spanish colonialism, who by and large represented the economically successful and the politically powerful on the island, lobbied key politicians in Spain to reinforce this maxim. Compounding these political and ideological factors was the widespread understanding that Spain was ill-prepared for a war with the United States. The country's naval officers offered a gloomy but rational appraisal of their capacity to win against the Americans. Even so, dictates of Spanish political life meant that it was more acceptable for Spain to lose a war honorably than to deal away a national treasure by diplomacy. Hence, Spanish officials equivocated and delayed, hoping for a military miracle in Cuba or an offer from a major European power to become an ally. Neither option materialized.

So events limped along through most of 1897 until a flurry of provocations over the next several months reordered the political situation. The first incident began with a change in the composition of the government in Spain following the assassination of the prime minister in August 1897. The queen turned to the Liberal Party for a new prime minister, who suggested a grant of autonomy to Cuba (something short of independence, along the lines of Canada's relationship to Great Britain after the American Revolution). This news provoked an antiautonomy riot in Havana. The outbreak showed that the struggle in Cuba was not just between insurrectionists seeking independence from Spain, but a civil war within Cuba. Worried about violence, President McKinley ordered the battleship USS *Maine* to Havana in January 1898, in part to protect American citizens. Then, on February 9, a purloined letter written by Spain's minister to the United States, Enrique Dupuy de Lôme, was printed in American newspapers. De Lome characterized President McKinley as "weak and a bidder for the admiration of the crowd." In addition, de Lôme inferred that Spanish negotiations with the United

States over Cuba were disingenuous, a sham. The scandal resulted in de Lôme's recall. Six days later, on February 15, news flashed across the United States that the *Maine* had exploded and sank in Havana. Patriotic sentiment welled up across the nation, where most citizens were prepared to believe that the explosion had been the work of Spanish agents. A court of inquiry was established in the United States to get to the bottom of the disaster.

The de Lôme letter and *Maine* explosion riveted public attention on Cuba. Richard Olney, attorney general of the United States in the Cleveland administration, wrote to his former boss that these two events had furnished "more material for the inflammation of popular passion against Spain" than all that had happened in the previous three years. The historian H. Wayne Morgan saw these events and the January riots as changing American demands for Cuba from autonomy to independence. Events in March fanned the flames of public outrage over the Cuba affair. On March 17, Senator Redfield Proctor (R-VT) reported to fellow U.S. senators on his recent trip to Cuba. (See "Senator Redfield Proctor, Report on Cuba, 1898," on page 158 in the Primary Sources section.) He went to Cuba, he said, "with a strong conviction that the picture had been overdrawn." However, seeing conditions with his own eyes, he admitted, confirmed the "desolation and distress, misery and starvation" conveyed in newspaper stories. "I could not believe that out of a population of one million six hundred thousand, 200,000 had died within these Spanish forts, practically prison walls, within a few months past, from actual starvation and disease caused by insufficient and improper food." Known for his conservatism, Proctor's report tugged at the conscience of moderates who had been willing to allow Spain to find a solution to its Cuba problem.

Moderates received a second shock days later when they read the U.S. Naval Court of Inquiry findings on the sinking of the *Maine*. Released on March 21, the navy's report concluded that the explosion was of external origin, implying Spanish treachery. (Modern research contradicts this finding, holding that an internal blast, perhaps ignited by spontaneous combustion in the coal bunker or in the ammunition magazine, had doomed the vessel.) Newspaper headlines had already anticipated the commission's verdict. When the official news was released, the *New York Journal* headline read "Remember the Maine, to hell with Spain."

Rising public animosity toward Spanish brutality in Cuba pressured President McKinley to confront Spain with an ultimatum: Seek an armistice that would halt the fighting, cease the reconcentracion policy, and adopt a plan to settle the Cuban dispute by October. The subtext of the communication was that the solution must provide for eventual Cuban independence. Predictably, Spain equivocated. Facing pressure from Congress, including by members of his own party, and from the public and the press, the president delivered a message to Congress on April 11 asking for authority to intervene in Cuba, with military force if necessary, to create a stable government on the island. Expectations that American intervention would come via military force was a foregone conclusion in Congress. Debate in the national legislature over the issue hinged on whether the United States should recognize the insurgents as the legitimate government of Cuba. McKinley explicitly opposed this overture in his April 11 message, but the Senate forged ahead with a vote that recognized the Republic of Cuba. The majority in the House of Representatives blocked Democratic support for recognition and then approved the joint congressional resolution on April 19 that declared Cuba independent and authorized a military solution to achieve it. The final resolution included an amendment offered by Senator Henry Teller of Colorado, known as the "Teller Amendment," that disclaimed any American intention of annexing the island. Spain declared war against the United States on April 24. Congress responded with its own declaration of war on April 25, postdating the statement to April 21, when the U.S. Navy had commenced a blockade of Cuba.

THE DEBATE

The Argument in Favor of Using Military Force to Free Cuba

From the vantage point of the 21st century, an American declaration that a colony of a sovereign nation ought to be free and that the United States could use military force to enforce this decree might seem to be a bold expression of national arrogance. President McKinley was aware of the complicated diplomatic and legal issues that surrounded America's relations to Cuba and Spain. Consequently, he phrased his April 11 message to Congress carefully. Rather than ask for a declaration of war against Spain, the president requested that Congress authorize him to terminate the war in Cuba, to establish a "stable government" on the island, and to use military force if "necessary for these purposes." (See "President William McKinley, War Message to Congress, 1898," on page 159 in the Primary Sources section.) The president recounted the brutality of the Cuban conflict, characterizing the reconcentracion policy as uncivilized and a plan of "extermination." McKinley offered four justifications for intervention in Cuba. First, his proposal was a humane step to "put an end to the barbarities, bloodshed, starvation, and horrible miseries" in Cuba. Second, he claimed that it was the obligation of the United States to afford the Cubans a government that could protect their lives and property. Third, the Cuban affair threatened American commerce, trade, and business. Finally, McKinley stated that "The present condition . . . in Cuba is a constant menace to our peace" and saddled the United States with "an enormous expense."

Perhaps 90 percent of Congress agreed with the president that the United States was acting in the name of morality and humanity. This sentiment is what gave Senator Teller's amendment to foreswear imperial desires in Cuba such emotional force. The United States did not intend to derive direct material benefit from its intervention, Teller stated, but rather "we go out to make battle for the liberty and freedom of Cuban patriots." Citing the Monroe Doctrine for justification to remove European colonizers from the Western Hemisphere, Teller urged the application of "Anglo-Saxon vigor" to drive Spain out of the Americas. Besides upholding American values of self-determination and liberty, honor was at stake as well. Roosevelt spoke for numerous Americans who thought that the sinking of the *Maine* was sufficient reason to wrench Cuba from Spain. Roosevelt admitted in a letter on April 5 that he had badgered McKinley so much with this "doctrine" that the president refused to talk to him about Cuba. (See "Theodore Roosevelt, Letter to William Tudor, 1898," on page 161 in the Primary Sources section.) McKinley dutifully mentioned in his April 11 message the conclusion of the Navy Court of Inquiry about the cause of the *Maine* explosion and noted that the Spanish government could not ensure the safety of American vessels in its waters.

More than the honor of the nation was at stake, in the opinion of Albert Beveridge, an attorney from Indiana. On April 17, as Congress debated McKinley's message on Cuba, Beveridge told a convention of Republicans in Indianapolis that "At last God's hour has struck. The American people go forth in a warfare holier than liberty—holy as humanity." Beveridge was considering a bid for a seat in the Senate when he uttered the remark, but it sprang from more than a cynical attempt to use patriotism to curry favor with Republicans. Beveridge believed that it was the destiny of the United States to expand around the world. Speaking to the Middlesex Club of Massachusetts on April 27, he announced that the "Almighty's infinite plan" was for the United States to gain an empire. (See "Albert Beveridge, Speech to the Middlesex Club in Massachusetts, 1898," on page 162 in the Primary Sources section.) War offered the opportunity to wrest Cuba and the Philippines from Spain. He also wanted Hawaii and control of the isthmus in Central America, too, neither of which were Spanish colonies. Beveridge gave two justifications for this aggressive posture. First, he welcomed the creation of "an English-speaking people's league of God for the permanent peace of this war-worn world." Second, colonies would serve as "trading-posts throughout the world." These overseas footholds would facilitate the marketing of factory surpluses to foreign customers. In early 1898, the United States was emerging from a devastating economic depression. A sentiment widespread among American entrepreneurs at the time was that foreign markets were critical to the continuation of high levels of industrial production. Business gained an international cheerleader when Beveridge took his seat in the Senate in 1899.

Beveridge's confident prediction of American's destiny made good newspaper copy. Others may have held similar views, but it is likely that the push to free Cuba was moved along by one additional factor: party politics. Roosevelt's letter of April 5 reveals a fear that some Republicans had about the Cuban issue, which could cost their party seats in Congress in the 1898 elections. Democrats pushed for intervention more vociferously than did Republicans, most of whom were willing to give McKinley's private diplomacy a chance to succeed. Democrats led the drive in Congress to recognize the insurgents in Cuba as the legal government.

William Randolph Heart's *New York Journal,* a newspaper aligned with the Democrats, was a staunch advocate of Cuban independence. Heart's *Journal* and Joseph Pulitzer's *New York World* were the centerpieces of so-called yellow journalism, the term used to identify New York newspapers that featured tantalizing but exaggerated—if not fanciful—exposès of the rebellion in Cuba. Some histories of the conflict with Spain have claimed that yellow journalism stampeded the public into a demand for war, a wave of anger that carried Congress and the president with it. The journalism scholar W. Joseph Campbell finds this claim

This propaganda drawing, published in *Judge* on April 30, 1898, shows Spain as a bloody, brutal figure trampling on an emaciated Cuban child and a dead USS *Maine* sailor. (Library of Congress)

unsubstantiated, stating that it rests on an "unsupported assumption." His careful analysis of the press in New York and around the country reveals no universal clamor for war from editors, including the *Journal*, even after the *Maine* explosion. The *Journal* urged Cuban independence, not an American invasion. Campbell's conclusion fits comfortably with the dictum that the public generally follows the lead of the president in diplomatic relations, especially in going to war. Even so, there is no denying that the Cuban crisis was widely discussed in public and in private.

The Argument Against Using Military Force to Free Cuba

The large majority of Americans probably supported the decision of the president and Congress to use military force to free Cuba from Spanish control. How opinions precisely split on the question remains unknown, as public opinion polls were not regularly taken at the time. Nonetheless, some Americans opposed military intervention in Cuba. One of these opponents was Thomas Reed (R-ME), the Speaker of the House of Representatives, where his Republican Party held the majority. Reed said little about the impending war and imperial annexation in public, but he used his powers as Speaker to block an anti-Spanish resolution in the House. America was abandoning the spirit of its own Declaration of Independence and "the foundation principles of our government," he wrote in 1898. Yet Reed voted with his party for the war resolutions in April. In all likelihood, other congressional Republicans were similarly conflicted over going to war. Reed had no stomach for annexation of the Philippines (which the United States obtained in the peace treaty with Spain after the war) or imperialism in general. Unwilling to battle the president on these issues, Reed resigned from Congress following his reelection in 1898.

Well-respected intellectuals echoed Reed's complaint that the United States was straying from its fundamental principles. Charles Eliot Norton, a professor of literature and history at Harvard College in Massachusetts, held this view. By replacing Spain in Cuba by force, America was abandoning its ideals, he told the men's club in Cambridge in June. (See "Charles Eliot Norton, Criticism of Intervention in Cuba, 1898," on page 163 in the Primary Sources section.) The end did not justify the means, he said. Similar sentiments were contained in William Graham Sumner's complaint about America's turn toward military action. In an 1899 essay entitled "The Conquest of the United States by Spain," Sumner saw partisan politics as the cause of the war. A professor of political economy at Yale and a well-known essayist, Sumner bitterly resented that "the war with Spain was precipitated upon us headlong without reflection or deliberation." (See "William Graham Sumner, Rejection of Imperial Conquest, 1899," on page 164 in the Primary Sources section.) "Patriotism is being prostituted," he wrote, while rational discussion of the Cuban affair was "howled down in a storm of vituperation and cant."

Charles Eliot Norton (Library of Congress)

Sumner may have exaggerated a bit; Congress had debated the McKinley war message and previously had considered resolutions concerning Cuba. Still, Sumner may have had a point about the public being in a fog about Spain and its colonies. The humorist Finley Peter Dunne's fictional protagonist Mr. Dooley joked that "Americans did not know whether the Philippines were islands or canned goods."

The war with Spain also disturbed E. L. Godkin, editor of the *Nation,* an influential public affairs magazine published in New York. Godkin was a staunch anti-imperialist and commanded an arsenal of arguments to defend his position. For one, America was betraying its heritage of national self-determination. For another, the acquisition of colonies brought with it the responsibility for their defense, which meant expansion of the military, new taxes to pay for the build-up, and a bureaucracy of colonial officials. Moreover, Godkin took a racist view of the peoples that came with annexations. Referring to Hawaii, which Congress annexed in 1898 in a decision unrelated to the quarrel with Spain, he wrote that the acquisition allowed "the admission of alien, inferior, and mongrel races to our nationality." Further imperialism, he added, would bring "dependencies inhabited by ignorant and inferior races." American soldiers in Cuba, Puerto Rico, and the Philippines during the Spanish-American War commonly displayed racist attitudes toward dark-skinned residents they encountered on the islands.

Who would benefit from the war? Not workers, in the opinion of Bolton Hall, the treasurer of the American Longshoremen's Union. Speaking to union members on April 17, 1898, in New York, Hall said that working men "will furnish the corpses and the taxes, and others will get all the glory. Speculators will make money out of it—that is, out of you." (See "Bolton Hall, The Effect of the War on Workingmen, 1898," on page 165 in the Primary Sources section.) Hall admitted that Spain had treated Cubans badly, but he also offered the classic bromide that rich men make wars and the poor fight them. Hall may have taken his cue, in part, from one member of Congress who articulated this truism in the debate over the McKinley message. Senator George Frisbie Hoar (R-MA) stated plaintively on the Senate floor on April 14 that "Every modern war is an additional burden on the poor man, the laboring man, the plain man, while the glory is reaped by a few officers, and the profits by a few stock jobbers and contractors." Cubans, too, would suffer, as workers on the island would be drafted and homes would be destroyed. To compound these evils, war piled up a great national debt. Despite these reservations about the use of military force, Hoar stood by his president and his party, voting for the resolution to free Cuba.

OUTCOME AND IMPACT

The "splendid little war," as Secretary of State John Hay called it, thrust the U.S. Army and Navy into a conflict on two sides of the globe—in the Caribbean and in the Philippine Islands in the Pacific. Theodore Roosevelt was second in command at the Department of the Navy but, in fact, was often in charge, given the frequent vacations of his boss, Secretary John D. Long. Such was the case on the day Roosevelt learned of the *Maine* explosion. TR immediately cabled Admiral George Dewey, whose appointment as commander of the U.S. Pacific fleet he had engineered, to prepare for an attack on the Spanish fleet in the Philippines in the event of war. Roosevelt also contacted other naval units, ordering them to be ready for action. Virtually moments after war was declared in April, Roosevelt instructed Dewey to steam toward Manila. Spain's wooden warships in the region were no match for Dewey's steel-hulled and better-gunned fleet. The United States sank or disabled the Spanish vessels easily on April 30. The U.S. Army steamed for the Philippines in July and occupied the island of Guam en route. The army and Admiral Dewey extracted a surrender from the Spanish defenders in Manila in August. American land forces subsequently faced a far lengthier and bloodier campaign against Filipino insurrectionists, led by Emilio Aguinaldo, who sought to expel the new colonizers.

Ready for deployment in the Caribbean, the U.S. Navy blockaded Cuba after Congress voted independence for the island. American vessels subsequently bottled up the small Spanish Caribbean fleet in

Theodore Roosevelt gained national fame for his role in the Battle of San Juan Hill in Cuba during the Spanish-American War. (Library of Congress)

Santiago Harbor in Cuba. Capturing the fort in the city of Santiago that defended the harbor required American land forces. The U.S. Army's paper strength numbered less than 28,000 men prior to the war. The army's generals had no plans for a sustained land campaign against the Spanish in the Caribbean. President McKinley surprised army leaders when he asked for 125,000 volunteers in April and another 75,000 in

SAN JUAN HILL

Gasping for breath after his rush to the top of San Juan Hill, Theodore Roosevelt nonetheless felt euphoric. From the summit of the ground he had just captured, "TR" watched in pride as Spanish soldiers scurried to safety in the direction of Santiago. Moments earlier, Roosevelt had led his Rough Riders on a charge up Kettle Hill. Then he regrouped his regiment for the final assault at Spanish defenses dug in on the crest of San Juan Hill. On the way, he miraculously had dodged enemy bullets, although his horse was mortally wounded, and had killed an enemy soldier with a revolver that had been retrieved from the wreck of the battleship *Maine.* July 1, 1898, was "the great day of my life," he later recorded. He had demonstrated his manliness, he effectively fulfilled the duties of his command, and he and his comrades had "driven the Spaniard from the New World."

Roosevelt had yearned for this opportunity for years. He had urged that the United States expand into the Caribbean and the Pacific islands. He lobbied vociferously for a stronger navy, one that complemented the nation's industrial might. And he demanded that Old World powers relinquish their colonial holdings in the Americas. His appointment as Assistant Secretary of the Navy in 1897 put the 38 year old in a unique position to fulfill these aspirations. Exercising authority to the point of insubordination during the lackadaisical tenure of Navy Secretary John D. Long, Roosevelt badgered President McKinley to free the Cubans of their Spanish overlords as he ordered the navy to battle readiness. He had handpicked Commodore (later Admiral) George Dewey to command the navy's Asiatic Station, passing over a less bellicose officer. The ink was barely dry on the congressional resolution authorizing the president to use force to free Cuba when the impetuous assistant secretary ordered Dewey to attack Spain's fleet in the Philippines.

Even before Congress declared war against Spain in April 1898, Roosevelt was angling for a commission in the army. He was itching to trade a desk job in

May. The influx of recruits nearly overwhelmed the logistical capacity of the army, which faced confusion and near chaos in Tampa, Florida, the jumping-off spot for the land campaign on Cuba.

McKinley's initial call for troops included a provision for raising three regiments of sharp-shooting horsemen. Roosevelt, who was denied a request to obtain a commission in the army, resigned as Assistant

Washington for the opportunity to demonstrate his manhood on the battlefield in Cuba. He got his opportunity on April 23, when McKinley called for volunteers to the army, a plan that included provisions for three regiments of sharp-shooting horsemen. Initially offered the command of a regiment, Roosevelt cited his inexperience but indicated that he would serve as deputy to Leonard Wood, his friend and President McKinley's assistant surgeon. Within days, TR and Wood had vetted 23,000 applications from leathery cowboys, Harvard graduates, and others to join the regiment. By May 15, inductees assembled at Camp Wood in San Antonio, Texas. Two weeks later, the "Roosevelt Rough Riders" set out for Tampa, Florida. There, chaos reigned over the sleepy Gulf-port town, creating logistical snarls for the army. Roosevelt's timely action was required to commandeer a berth on a transport vessel, which had room for only a third of his corps, but not their horses. He did find space for several reporters, who escorted him during his Cuban adventure. Their reports made "Teddy" a national hero literally days after the Spanish had surrendered San Juan Hill. Though saddened by the battlefield deaths of his comrades, Roosevelt recalled his time in Cuba as "beautiful days."

Letters reaching Roosevelt in Cuba urged him to run for governor of New York in the fall election. Following a tumultuous welcome on his arrival home in Long Island, Roosevelt accepted the Republican bid to head their ticket. When the race tightened, Roosevelt took matters into his own hands. He organized a whistle-stop campaign tour around New York State and took along several Rough Riders dressed in military garb to accentuate his military exploits. Roosevelt's customary frenetic activity probably helped to coax out a narrow victory. TR's new notoriety worried the Republican leadership, who concocted a scheme to get him into a less visible position—the vice presidency of the United States. Roosevelt accepted the opportunity and assumed his position as second to the president with McKinley's reelection in 1900. Six months after the inauguration, McKinley was assassinated, thrusting the 42-year-old Roosevelt into the presidency.

Secretary of the Navy and formed a volunteer unit of horsemen. TR and his volunteers, nicknamed the Rough Riders, performed brilliantly on the hills surrounding Santiago, Cuba, although without their horses because of a logistical tangle in Tampa. (See the sidebar "San Juan Hill" on page 150.) The Spanish surrender of Santiago effectively ended enemy resistance in Cuba; by mid-July fighting had ceased in Cuba. American troops also made an amphibious landing on the south coast of Puerto Rico and marched across the island, intent on taking San Juan, the capital city. An armistice on August 12 prevented this assault. A peace treaty was signed between Spain and the United States on December 10, 1898. The Treaty of Paris included formal cession of the Philippine Islands, Guam, and Puerto Rico to the United States. The Senate ratified the treaty on February 6, 1899. Fearing an insurrection in Cuba similar to the unrest in the Philippines, the administration persuaded Congress to enact the Platt Amendment in 1901 (attached to an army appropriations bill) that asserted the authority of the United States to intervene in Cuba if civil disorder or foreign powers threatened its political stability. Without directly denying the island's independence, the Platt Amendment essentially made Cuba a protectorate of the United States, governed under the watchful eyes of American officials.

The Spanish-American War constitutes an important turning point in the diplomatic history of the United States. Seldom has such a small war had such large consequences for a nation's subsequent affairs. The defeat of Spain had transferred the Philippines to American control. McKinley mulled over what to do about the islands and decided that "There was nothing left for us to do but to take them all [that is, the Philippines, Guam, and Puerto Rico] and to educate the Filipinos, and uplift and civilize and Christianize them." An Anti-Imperialist League, which included articulate intellectuals and wealthy businessmen, such as Mark Twain, William James, and Andrew Carnegie, and former president Grover Cleveland, formed to protest the retention of the Spanish holdings, but their protest fell short. McKinley was elected to a second term as president in 1900, beating William Jennings Bryan, who opposed imperialism. The United States mounted a three-year campaign to defeat the Filipino insurrectionists, in which 4,165 Americans and perhaps 200,000 Filipinos died.

The war against Spain was crucial in vaulting Theodore Roosevelt into the presidency. Publicity from his brave dash up San Juan Hill was instrumental in his nomination as the Republican vice presidential candidate in 1900. McKinley's assassination in 1901 put TR in the White House. Roosevelt used his new position to project American power in the Caribbean and the Pacific. One bold step in this direction was Roosevelt's role in fomenting a revolution on the Isthmus of Panama in 1903 that led to American control of the Panama Canal Zone. Roosevelt was pivotal in the expansion of the navy and reform of the army. The regular army was enlarged, greater federal control over state militias was adopted, and a general staff was created to provide more overall military planning. Naval expenditures increased by a factor of 3.5 between 1897 and 1909, vaulting the U.S. Navy to second or third rank in the world, depending on the criteria used to make comparisons. The *Washington Post*'s assertion in 1898 that "the policy of isolation" is dead was overstated, yet it contained much truth. At the dawn of the 20th century, the new American state now was willing and able to project its power around the world.

WHAT IF?

What if Spain had acceded to American demands concerning Cuba?

Actually, the Spanish came close to doing so. Spain ended its reconcentracion policy, recalled General Weyler from Cuba, and indicated a willingness to consider autonomy for residents of the island. Perhaps the combination of a Spanish unilateral cease-fire in Cuba, a firm commitment to discuss self-rule on the island, and a pledge of aid for the victims of war would have persuaded President McKinley and Congress to delay, if not table, a decision to free Cuba by force. Instead of moving decisively toward compromise positions, however, Spanish officials allowed their internal politics to trump the potential loss of their American colonies. They could have played their hand more deftly. Concessions could have allowed it to retain control of Cuba, perhaps under a commonwealth arrangement similar to Canada. Some Caribbean islands, such as Jamaica and Trinidad, remained under European control until the late 20th century; others, such as Aruba, Montserrat, and Martinique, continue as colonial possessions.

Accommodation with Spain also would have forestalled America's annexation of the Philippines, an unplanned development arising out of military operations. This course would have spared the United States the bloody military campaign to suppress the Filipino rebels. Further, the absence of an American presence in the Philippines perhaps would have altered Japanese plans in World War II. Japan struck American military installations in the Philippines the day after it attacked Pearl Harbor on December 7, 1941.

While conceivable, these conjectures confront formidable realities. Two dominant facts probably doomed Spanish control of Cuba in the long run. First, independence movements had swept through Latin America since the early 19th century and probably would eventually have succeeded in Cuba, if not in 1898, then in the 20th century. Second, American economic and diplomatic interest in the Caribbean region and a military capacity to assert these aspirations was growing. Theodore Roosevelt (whose elevation to the presidency rested considerably on his military exploits during the Spanish-American War) orchestrated the revolution in Panama in 1903, the first step toward building the American canal across the isthmus. The United States purchased the Danish Virgin Islands in 1917, which supplemented ports in Puerto Rico and Cuba (Guantánamo Bay) as strategic sites for the navy's defense of the canal. American armed forces occupied Haiti, the Dominican Republic, Nicaragua, Honduras, and Cuba in the early 20th century, indicating American willingness and ability to intervene in Caribbean affairs. This hegemonic control suggests that the existence of a Spanish colony 90 miles south of Florida was doomed in the long run.

CHRONOLOGY

1894   Congress passes the Wilson-Gorman tariff that raises duties on Cuban sugarcane.

1895   Conflict with Britain over Venezuela

Revolt in Cuba against Spanish colonial rule

1896   William McKinley is elected president.

1898   *February 9:* De Lome letter appears in the *New York Journal.*

February 15: Explosion sinks the USS *Maine* in Havana Harbor.

March 17: Senator Redfield Proctor reports on his trip to Cuba.

March 27: McKinley issues ultimatum to Spain.

April 11: McKinley transmits war message to Congress.

April 20: Congress proclaims Cuban independence and authorizes the president to use force to achieve it.

April 25: Congress votes a declaration of war against Spain.

April 30: Commodore George Dewey defeats the Spanish fleet in the Philippines.

July 7: Congress annexes the Hawaii Islands.

July 17: Spanish surrender to Americans in Cuba.

August 12: Spain agrees to a cease-fire.

August 16: Battle of Manila ends.
December 10: Treaty of Paris between Spain and the United States is signed.

1899   *February 6:* Senate ratifies Treaty of Paris.

DISCUSSION QUESTIONS

1. Was the revolt in Cuba during the 1890s unusual or predictable?
2. Some opponents of intervention in Cuba contended that the end does not justify the means. How valid is this argument regarding Cuba? Does the end ever justify the means in diplomacy or in war?
3. Does/should the proximity of a place (such as Havana, 90 miles from Key West) to the United States have an effect on how the country should conduct its foreign policy?
4. Did Theodore Roosevelt act irresponsibly when he was assistant secretary of the Department of the Navy in 1898?
5. How realistic is it to argue that decisive leadership by President McKinley could have prevented American military intervention in Cuba?

WEB SITES

Library of Congress. The Spanish American War. Available at http://www.loc.gov/rr/hispanic/1898/.

PBS. The Crucible of Empire: The Spanish American War (1999). Available at http://www.pbs.org/crucible/.

The Spanish American War Centennial Website! Available at http://www.spanamwar.com/.

BIBLIOGRAPHY

Beisner, Robert L. *Twelve against Empire: The Anti-Imperialists, 1898–1900.* New York: McGraw-Hill, 1968.

Campbell, W. Joseph. *Yellow Journalism: Puncturing the Myths, Defining the Legacies.* Westport, Conn.: Praeger, 2001.

Gould, Lewis. *The Presidency of William McKinley.* Lawrence: University Press of Kansas, 1980.

Morgan, H. Wayne. *America's Road to Empire: The War with Spain and Overseas Expansion.* New York: John Wiley and Sons, 1965.

Morris, Edmund. *The Rise of Theodore Roosevelt.* New York: Ballantine, 1979.

Perez, Louis A., Jr. *Cuba: Between Reform and Revolution.* New York: Oxford University Press, 1995.

Schoonover, Thomas. *Uncle Sam's War of 1898 and the Origins of Globalization.* Lexington: University of Kentucky Press, 2003.

Trask, David F. *The War with Spain in 1898.* New York: Macmillan, 1981.

PRIMARY SOURCES

1. Theodore Roosevelt, Address to the Naval War College, 1897

When serving as assistant secretary of the navy, Theodore Roosevelt spoke to the Naval War College in June 1897. Calling his address "Washington's Forgotten Maxim," Roosevelt recommended that the United States build a 20-battleship navy. He argued that military preparedness prevents war, but that if war did come, a strong navy will uphold the nation's character.

A CENTURY has passed since Washington wrote "To be prepared for war is the most effectual means to promote peace."

If we forget that in the last resort we can only secure peace by being ready and willing to fight for it, we may some day have bitter cause to realize that a rich nation which is slothful, timid, or unwieldy is an easy prey for any people which still retains those most valuable of all qualities, the soldierly virtues. We but keep to the traditions of Washington, to the traditions of all the great Americans who struggled for the real greatness of America, when we strive to build up those fighting qualities for the lack of which in a nation, as in an individual, no refinement, no culture, no wealth, no material prosperity, can atone.

Preparation for war is the surest guaranty for peace. Arbitration is an excellent thing, but ultimately those who wish to see this country at peace with foreign nations will be wise if they place reliance upon a first-class fleet of first-class battleships rather than on any arbitration treaty which the wit of man can devise.

A really great people, proud and high-spirited, would face all the disasters of war rather than purchase that base prosperity which is bought at the price of national honor. All the great masterful races have been fighting races. . . .

No triumph of peace is quite so great as the supreme triumphs of war. The courage of the soldier, the courage of the statesman who has to meet storms which can be quelled only by soldierly qualities—this stands higher than any quality called out merely in time of peace.

The men of Bunker Hill and Trenton, Saratoga and Yorktown, the men of New Orleans and Mobile Bay, Gettysburg and Appomattox are those to whom we owe most. None of our heroes of peace save a few great constructive statesmen can rank with our heroes of war. The Americans who stand highest on the list of the world's worthies are Washington, who fought to found the country which he afterward governed, and Lincoln, who saved it through the blood of the best and bravest in the land;

No battle-ship can be built inside of two years under no matter what stress of circumstances, for we have not in this country the plant to enable us to work faster. Cruisers would take almost as long.

If this point needs any emphasis surely the history of the War of 1812 applies to it. For twelve years before that war broke out even the blindest could see that we were almost certain to be drawn into hostilities with one or the other of the pair of combatants whose battle royal ended at Waterloo. Yet we made not the slightest preparation for war.

The enemies we may have to face will come from over the sea; they may come from Europe, or they may come from Asia. Events move fast in the West; but this generation has been forced to see that they move even faster in the oldest East. Our interests are as great in the Pacific as in the Atlantic, in the Hawaiian Islands as in the West Indies. Merely for the protection of our own shores we need a great navy; and what is more, we need it to protect our interests in the islands from which it is possible to command our shores and to protect our commerce on the high seas.

Still more is it necessary to have a fleet of great battle-ships if we intend to live up to the Monroe Doctrine, and to insist upon its observance in the two Americas and the islands on either side of them. If a foreign power, whether in Europe or Asia, should determine to assert its position in those lands wherein we feel that our influence should be supreme, there is but one way in which we can effectively interfere.

Diplomacy is utterly useless where there is no force behind it; the diplomat is the servant, not the master, of the soldier.

Source: Roosevelt, Theodore. "Washington's Forgotten Maxim." In *American
Ideals and Other Essays.* Vol. 2, 66–91. New York: Putnam, 1907.

—⚹—

2. Senator Redfield Proctor, Report on Cuba, 1898

*On March 17, 1898, Senator Redfield Proctor (R-VT) reported to the
U.S. Senate on the "desolation and distress" in Cuba that he had witnessed during a trip to the island early in 1898. Proctor made no policy
recommendation, but his poignant description of conditions reputedly
influenced how some senators viewed American military intervention.*

My observations were confined to the four western provinces, which
constitute about one-half the island. The two eastern ones are practically in the hands of the insurgents, except a few fortified towns. These
two large provinces are spoken of today as "Cuba Libre." Havana, the
great city and capital of the island, is, in the eyes of the Spaniards and
many Cubans, all Cuba, as much as Paris in France.

Everything seems to go on much as usual in Havana. Quiet prevails
and except for the frequent squads of soldiers marching to guard and
police duty and their abounding presence in all public places, one sees
little signs of war. Outside Havana all is changed. It is not peace, nor is it
war. It is desolation and distress, misery and starvation. Every town and
village is surrounded by a trocha, a sort of rifle pit, but constructed on
a plan new to me, the dirt being thrown up on the inside and a barbed
wire fence on the outer side of the trench.

The purpose of these trochas is to keep reconcentrados in as well as
to keep the insurgents out.

From all the surrounding country the people have been driven into
these fortified towns and held there to subsist as they can. They are virtually prison yards and not unlike one in general appearance, except that
the walls are not so-high and strong, but they suffice, where every point
is in range of a soldier's rifle, to keep in the poor *reconcentrado* women
and children.

I saw no house or hut in the 400 miles of railroad rides from Pinar del
Rio Province in the west across the full width of Havana and Matanzas
Provinces, and to Sagua La Grando on the north shore and to Cienfuegos

on the south shore of Santa Clara, except within the Spanish trochas. There are no domestic animals or crops on the rich fields and pastures except such as are under guard in the immediate vicinity of the towns. It is concentration and desolation. This is the "pacified" condition of the four western provinces.

I could not believe that out of a population of one million six hundred thousand, 200,000 had died within these Spanish forts, practically prison walls, within a few months past, from actual starvation and disease caused by insufficient and improper food.

Source: "Cuban Reconcentration Policy and its Effects," Proctor speech in the U.S. Senate March 17, 1898. *Congressional Record,* reprinted in Clara Barton. *The Red Cross.* Washington D.C.: American National Red Cross, 1899, 534–539.

—⁂—

3. President William McKinley, War Message to Congress, 1898

President William McKinley sent a message to Congress on April 11, 1898, in which he asked for authority to intervene in Cuba in order to halt the fighting and establish a "stable government." The president explicitly opposed recognizing "the so-called Cuban Republic."

The present revolution is but the successor of other similar insurrections which have occurred in Cuba against the dominion of Spain, extending over a period of nearly half a century, each of which during its progress has subjected the United States to great effort and expense in enforcing its neutrality laws, caused enormous losses to American trade and commerce, caused irritation, annoyance, and disturbance among our citizens, and, by the exercise of cruel, barbarous, and uncivilized practices of warfare, shocked the sensibilities and offended the humane sympathies of our people.

Our trade has suffered, the capital invested by our citizens in Cuba has been largely lost. . . .

The efforts of Spain were increased both by the dispatch of fresh levies to Cuba and by the addition to the horrors of the strife of a new and inhuman phase happily unprecedented in the modern history of civilized Christian peoples. The policy of devastation and concentration, inaugurated by the Captain-General's *bando* of October 21, 1896, in the Province of Pinar del Rio was thence extended to embrace all of the island to which the power of the Spanish arms was able to reach by occupation or by military operations.

The war in Cuba is of such a nature that, short of subjugation or extermination, a final military victory for either side seems impracticable. The alternative lies in the physical exhaustion of the one or the other party, or perhaps of both.

The forcible intervention of the United States as a neutral to stop the war, according to the large dictates of humanity and following many historical precedents where neighboring states have interfered to check the hopeless sacrifices of life by internecine conflicts beyond their borders, is justifiable on rational grounds.

The grounds for such intervention may be briefly summarized as follows:

First. In the cause of humanity and to put an end to the barbarities, bloodshed, starvation, and horrible miseries now existing there, and which the parties to the conflict are either unable or unwilling to stop or mitigate. It is no answer to say this is all in another country, belonging to another nation, and is therefore none of our business. It is specially our duty, for it is right at our door.

Second. We owe it to our citizens in Cuba to afford them that protection and indemnity for life and property which no government there can or will afford, and to that end to terminate the conditions that deprive them of legal protection.

Third. The right to intervene may be justified by the very serious injury to the commerce, trade, and business of our people and by the wanton destruction of property and devastation of the island.

Fourth, and which is of the utmost importance. The present condition of affairs in Cuba is a constant menace to our peace and entails upon this Government an enormous expense. With such a conflict waged for years in an island so near us and with which our people have such trade and business relations; when the lives and liberty of our citizens are in constant danger and their property destroyed and themselves ruined; where our trading vessels are liable to seizure and are seized at our very door by war ships of a foreign nation; the expeditions of filibustering that we are powerless to prevent altogether, and the irritating questions and entanglements thus arising—all these and others that I need not mention, with the resulting strained relations, are a constant menace to our peace and compel us to keep on a semi war footing with a nation with which we are at peace.

Source: James D. Richardson, comp. *Messages and Papers of the Presidents*, vol. 9. New York: Bureau of National Literature, 1911, 6282–6292.

—⟶—

4. Theodore Roosevelt, Letter to William Tudor, 1898

Assistant Secretary of the Navy Theodore Roosevelt revealed his war-hawkishness in this letter to his friend William Tudor on April 5, 1898. Roosevelt mounted a lobbying effort to persuade President McKinley to intervene in Cuba, which he argued would uphold the nation's "honor."

Not only do I want to thank you for your letter to me, but especially your letter to [Senator Henry Cabot] Lodge. For a week past he has been receiving twenty or thirty letters and telegrams a day from men who consider themselves to be the best and most representative citizens of Boston—its leading bankers, merchants and lawyers; and these letters and telegrams, almost without exception, are couched in terms of abject fear, and the abject anger that comes from that fear. Lodge stands firm, but his colleague has been turned over by these letters, and Lodge realizes that if the President and Hoar stand one way and he another, his own republican party will throw him out of the Senate next year. Nevertheless, as I say, he is playing, and will play, the part of a patriot; but I do think that all the men who feel as you and I do in Boston should begin to send in telegrams entreating him to put the honor of the nation above the desire for that sordid peace which is begotten of fear and greed. During the last few days, however, I am happy to say that the pressure from the honest men of the country who are not careless of the nation's honor has been such that I believe the President will be forced to intervene. I have preached the doctrine to him in such plain language that he will no longer see me! If we will not fight for the blowing up of the *Maine* (and personally I believe we should have fought long ago because of the atrocities in Cuba) we are no longer fit to hold up our heads among the nations of the earth. It is one of the greatest crises in our history.

Source: Reprinted by Permission of the publisher from *The Letters of Theodore Roosevelt*. Vol. 2, *The Years of Preparation, 1898–1900*, selected and edited by Elting E. Morison, p. 812, Cambridge, Mass.: Harvard University Press. Copyright © 1951 by the President and Fellows of Harvard College. Copyright © renewed 1979 by Elting Elmore Morison.

—⟶—

5. Albert Beveridge, Speech to the Middlesex Club in Massachusetts, 1898

Albert Beveridge stated that it was the "Almighty's infinite plan" for the United States to expand and acquire an empire. In his speech to the Middlesex Club in Massachusetts on April 27, 1898, the future Republican senator from Indiana argued that economic necessity and political responsibilities destined these steps.

"He [Grant] never forgot that we are a conquering race, and that we must obey our blood and occupy new markets, and, if necessary, new lands."

He had the prophet's seer-like sight which beheld, as a part of the Almighty's infinite plan, the disappearance of debased civilizations and decaying races before the higher civilization of the nobler and more virile types of men.

American factories are making more than the American people can use; American soil is producing more than they can consume. Fate has written our policy for us; the trade of the world must and shall be ours. And we will get it as our mother [England] has told us how. We will establish trading-posts throughout the world as distributing-points for American products. We will cover the ocean with our merchant marine. We will build a navy to the measure of our greatness. Great colonies governing themselves, flying our flag and trading with us, will grow about our posts of trade. Our institutions will follow our flag on the wings of our commerce. And American law, American order, American civilization, and the American flag will plant themselves on shores hitherto bloody and benighted, but by those agencies of God henceforth to be made beautiful and bright.

If this means the Stars and Stripes over an Isthmian canal . . . over Hawaii . . . over Cuba and the southern seas . . . then let us meet that meaning with a mighty joy and make that meaning good, no matter what barbarism and all our foes may do or say.

—ᵐ—

6. Charles Eliot Norton, Criticism of Intervention in Cuba, 1898

Charles Eliot Norton, a professor of history and literature at Harvard College, told the Men's Club in Cambridge, Massachusetts, on June 7, 1898, that America was abandoning its historic ideals by intervening in Cuba. While Spanish cruelty in suppressing the rebellion on the island was despicable, the ends—Cuban independence—did not justify the means—U.S. military operations against Spain.

Every genuine American holds to the ideal of justice for all men, of independence, including free speech and free action within the limits of law, of obedience to law, of universal education, of material well-being for all the well-behaving and industrious, of peace and good-will among men. These, however far short the nation may fall in expressing them in its actual life, are, no one will deny it, the ideals of our American democracy. And it is because America represents these ideals that the deepest love for his country glows in the heart of the American, and inspires him with that patriotism which counts no cost, which esteems no sacrifice too great to maintain and to increase the influence of these principles which embody themselves in the fair shape of his native land, and have their expressive symbol in her flag.

There are, indeed, many among us who find justification of the present war in the plea that its motive is to give independence to the people of Cuba, long burdened by the oppressive and corrupt rule of Spain, and especially to relieve the suffering of multitudes deprived of their homes and of means of subsistence by the cruel policy of the general who exercised for a time a practical dictatorship over the island. The plea so far as it is genuine deserves the respect due to every humane sentiment. But independence secured for Cuba by forcible overthrow of the Spanish rule means either practical anarchy or the substitution of the authority of the United States for that of Spain. Either alternative might well give us pause. And as for the relief of suffering, surely it is a strange procedure to begin by inflicting worse suffering still. It is fighting the devil with his own arms. That the end justifies the means is a dangerous doctrine, and no wise man will advise doing evil for the sake of an uncertain good. But the plea that the better government of Cuba and the relief of the reconcentrados could only be secured by war is the plea either of ignorance or of hypocrisy.

So confused are men by false teaching in regard to national honour and the duty of the citizen that it is easy to fall into the error of holding a declaration of war, however brought about, as a sacred decision of the national will, and to fancy that a call to arms from the Administration has the force of a call from the lips of the country, of the America to whom all her sons are ready to pay the full measure of devotion. This is indeed a natural and for many a youth not a discreditable error. But if the nominal, though authorized, representatives of the country have brought us into a war that might and should have been avoided, and which consequently is an unrighteous war, then, so long as the safety of the State is not at risk, the duty of the good citizen is plain. He is to help to provide the Administration responsible for the conduct of the war with every means that may serve to bring it to the speediest end.

Source: Sara Norton and M. A. DeWolfe, eds. *Letters of Charles Eliot Norton,* vol. 2. Boston: Houghton Mifflin Co., 1913, 261–269.

—∞—

7. William Graham Sumner, Rejection of Imperial Conquest, 1899

William Graham Sumner, a Yale professor, noted essayist, and defender of laissez-faire, rejected the idea that the United States should replace Spain in Cuba and the Philippines as a colonizing power. He thought the decision for war had been rammed through Congress without full consideration of its contradiction with American traditions.

During the last year the public has been familiarized with descriptions of Spain and of Spanish methods of doing things until the name of Spain has become a symbol for a certain well-defined set of notions and policies. . . . I intend to show that, by the line of action now proposed to us, which we call expansion and imperialism, we are throwing away some of the most important elements of the American symbol and are adopting some of the most important elements of the Spanish symbol. We have beaten Spain in a military conflict, but we are submitting to be conquered by her on the field of ideas and policies.

The war with Spain was precipitated upon us headlong, without reflection or deliberation, and without any due formulation of public opinion. Whenever a voice was raised in behalf of deliberation and the recognized maxims of statesmanship, it was howled down in a storm of vituperation and cant. . . . Patriotism is being prostituted into a nervous intoxication which is fatal to an apprehension of truth.

Source: Summer, William Graham. "The Conquest of the United States by Spain," *Yale Law Journal* 8 (1899): 168–193.

—⟶⟵—

8. Bolton Hall, The Effect of the War on Workingmen, 1898

Bolton Hall, treasurer of the American Longshoreman's Union, argued that the intervention of the U.S. military in Cuba worked against the interests of American workingmen. In his address to the Central Labor Union of New York on April 17, 1898, Hall noted that charges of Spanish cruelty toward Cubans had a ring of hypocrisy in light of similar injustices suffered by African Americans in the United States.

The inhuman conditions which exist in Cuba have been primarily produced by that greed which gets in its work wherever man has the power to oppress his fellows. The cruelty exhibited in Cuba is no peculiarity of the Spanish race; within the last few week instances of cruelty to negroes has occurred in this country which equal, if they do not surpass, anything has occurred in Cuba. . . . We see every day the vast injustice prevailing in our own land, the hopeless toil, the wretched poverty, the armies of unemployed. . . .

If it is true that some thousands of Spanish speculators and office-holders have oppressed the Cubans, how in the name of common sense can that justify American workmen in shooting down Spanish workmen? . . . If there is a war, you will furnish the corpses and the taxes, and others will get all the glory. Speculators will make money out of its—that is, out of you. . . . Men will get high prices for inferior supplies . . . and the only satisfaction you will get is the privilege of hating your Spanish fellow-workmen, who are really your brothers and who have had as little to do with the wrongs of Cuba as you have.

Source: Speech reprinted in Murray Polner and Thomas E. Woods, Jr., eds. *We Who Say No to War: American Antiwar Writing from 1812 to Now.* New York: Basic Books, 2008, 89–91, from Bolton Hall Papers, New York Public Library.

6

WORLD WAR I:
Should the United States Enter World War I Against Germany?

—⟨⟩—

THE CONTROVERSY ————————————————

The Issue

President Woodrow Wilson declared American neutrality when World War I began in August 1914 and tried to keep the United States out of the conflict for two and a half years. However, in Wilson's view, Germany's use of submarines to prevent cargoes from reaching Britain interfered with American rights as a neutral. After Germany sank several American ships, the president asked Congress on April 2, 1917, to declare war against Germany. Did the President make the proper decision?

- ◆ *Arguments for declaring war on Germany:* Most Americans supported Wilson's condemnation of German submarine warfare, agreeing that it violated the nation's rights as a neutral. This side of the debate saw Germany as an autocratic society that was out of step with modern democracy and civilized conduct. Morality and honor demanded that the United States stand up for its rights against "Prussian" militarism.

- ◆ *Arguments against declaring war on Germany:* A minority in the United States saw intervention as a mistake, largely due to the president's one-sided policy of favoring England but condemning Germany. They argued that Wilson could have followed a less belligerent course toward Germany, perhaps by avoiding the war zone altogether. Some skeptics contended that war enriched bankers and manufacturers at the expense of the working class, while other opponents saw this as a "foreign conflict" that was producing horrific losses of life.

—⟨⟩—

INTRODUCTION

Without warning, a German submarine torpedoed the British Cunard liner *Lusitania* on May 7, 1915, off the coast of Ireland. (See the sidebar

"Lusitania" on page 174.) Among the 1,198 people aboard the vessel who perished were 128 Americans. The public in the United States expressed outrage at Germany's brazen assault against civilians aboard a passenger liner. True, Britain and Germany were at war, and Germany had announced that its navy would sink all enemy vessels that entered a war zone around the British isles. They had printed a warning to this effect in New York newspapers just prior to the *Lusitania*'s departure for England. Still, unrestricted submarine warfare against civilians constituted barbarous behavior in the eyes of most American and British citizens. The most incensed critics demanded that the United

President Woodrow Wilson led the United States during World War I. (© Archive Pics/Alamy)

States retaliate in kind against the "autocratic Prussian" (that is, German) regime that authorized such behavior.

President Woodrow Wilson had declared U.S. neutrality when World War I began in August 1914, pitting Germany, Austria-Hungary, and later the Ottoman Empire against Britain, France, and Russia. The president also announced that he would hold Germany "strictly accountable" for unlawful acts against American lives and property. Now the unthinkable had occurred, and Wilson was obligated to respond. The president turned to his secretary of state, William Jennings Bryan, for advice. Bryan recommended that the United States request monetary damages, but nothing more. Bryan knew that the *Lusitania* had carried Canadian-made ammunition (which was an article of war, known as contraband) destined for England. The secretary argued that "A ship carrying contraband should not rely upon passengers to protect her from attack—it would be like putting women and children in front of an army."

Bryan's advice was directly counter to the objections that hard-liners made to Germany's use of its submarines. Robert Lansing, the chief legal counsel of the State Department and its second-ranking official, urged Wilson to reiterate his intention to hold Germany accountable for its actions. Bryan wanted the president to denounce Britain's harassment of American and other neutral maritime traffic as well. Lansing, who strongly favored the "Allies" (especially Britain and France) over "autocratic" Germany, dissented. When Germany's response to the first Wilson protest proved unsatisfactory, the president drafted a stronger second note. It was too critical for Bryan, who resigned in protest as Secretary of State. Wilson appointed Lansing in his place. The president now had a head of the State Department who believed that "the design of the German Government" was to "become overlord of the world."

The disagreement between Bryan and Lansing represents a microcosm of the debate that went on in the nation after the outbreak of World War I. Wilson tried to keep the United States out of military involvement in the conflict, but both Britain and Germany instituted blockades that compromised U.S. neutrality. American trade with Europe and with Great Britain in particular was a lifeline for the nation's economy. Germany's use of submarines to interdict merchant ships headed for England threatened this economic connection. However, Germany's fragile *Unterseebooten* (undersea boats, often called U-boats) had to strike first and ask questions later, for to surface put a submarine at risk of destruction by a vessel armed with deck guns. Germany chose to unleash its submarines without restrictions, even against U.S. merchant vessels that entered European waters. Wilson and many Americans saw such attacks as violations of American neutral rights. The question that became pressing for the president and the nation as World War I dragged on into 1917 was: Should the United States declare war against Germany?

Americans who agreed with Wilson and Lansing's condemnation of German submarine warfare said yes. This side of the debate held a sympathetic view of the "Allies" from the start of the war. They saw Germany as an autocratic society that conducted war in a barbarous manner and was out of step with modern democracy. Morality and honor demanded that the United States punish the "Prussians" for their uncivilized behavior and protect the rights of a neutral nation.

A minority in the United States asserted that intervention in the war was a mistake. They argued that the president had not conducted a strict policy of neutrality during the war but had favored Britain by excusing its interference with American ships, including confiscation of their cargoes. They noted further that the United States allowed large loans to the British for the purchase of war materials. The president, they argued, could have followed a less belligerent course toward Germany and perhaps kept American ships out of the war zone altogether. These skeptics predicted that a congressional vote for war would put money in the pockets of bankers and manufacturers and bring death and economic hardship to working families.

BACKGROUND

World War I developed out of series of decisions by European nations. On June 28, 1914, a Serbian nationalist assassinated Archduke Francis Ferdinand, heir to the throne of the Austro-Hungarian Empire, in Sarajevo, Serbia, a province of Austria-Hungary. Believing Serbia to be responsible for the attack, Austria-Hungary declared war on the rebellious province on July 28. After Russia began mobilizing its army to aid its ally, Serbia, Germany (allied to Austria-Hungary) declared war on Russia, which had rejected a demand to reverse its military preparations. These declarations of war brought Britain and France into war against Germany, the Austro-Hungarian Empire, and later the Ottoman Empire (which primarily was Turkey), which entered the war in October 1914 as a partner with Germany. World War I was on. In 1915, Italy joined the Allies.

Historians continue to debate the causes of the "Great War." Most agree that its overt spark was the assassination in Sarajevo and a treaty system among European powers that formally committed various nations to aid their allies. The deeper historical forces that produced the conflict come into focus less clearly. Nonetheless, scholars point to three trends that seem to be central to decisions for war. First, for some decades the major countries of Europe had been engaged in an arms buildup involving global competition for territory and trade. Weaponry production was spurred on by relentless advances in military technology (as manifested in battleships, machine guns, and airplanes). Germany's naval buildup that commenced in 1897, a result of its desire to broaden the country's role in international affairs, played a key role in this competition. Second, waves of nationalism swept across Europe.

Nationalism is a sociopolitical phenomenon that emphasizes the culture and glory of one's country and its traditions. Emotional swells of patriotism, fanned by nationalist appeals, were critical in allowing European nations to field armies that numbered millions of men between 1914 and 1918. Finally, domestic politics in each country became entangled in the decisions to commit the nation to military action.

Referring to the conflict as a "World War" warrants some explanation. Most of the fighting during the war (1914–18), also known as the Great War, occurred among the large nations of Europe (including Russia) on European soil, including the western region of Russia, known as the eastern front, and France and Belgium, known as the western front. The war settled into a stalemate on both the eastern and western fronts. On the western front, both sides defended fortified lines of "trenches" that stretched across much of France and Belgium and remained largely stationary. Occasional thrusts over the top of a defensive line across "no man's land" to attack the enemy in its entrenched position produced mass slaughters that numbered tens of thousands of dead. Larger offensives cost hundreds of thousands of casualties. Rapid-firing weapons such as the machine gun and the use of poison gas dramatized how technology had permitted new and more deadly ways of killing. The need to overcome the strength of defensive warfare led to the development, later in the war, of tanks and military aircraft.

Calling this conflict a "world war" is partly a consequence of European imperialism. In 1914, nearly all of Africa and much of Asia were colonial possessions of a European country. China was a weak state that was dominated by Western interests and faced with growing pressure from Japan. Canada, Australia, and New Zealand—all former British "settler" colonies—maintained "Commonwealth" attachments to Britain and sent soldiers to help. Britain also drew troops from its imperial holdings in India and Africa. France recruited soldiers from its African possessions. Turkey (the heart of the declining Ottoman Empire) joined Germany and attempted to rally Muslims in the Middle East against the Allies. Japan declared war on Germany but did not send troops to Europe; it did occupy German holdings in China. The United States entered the war in April 1917, substantially bolstering a North American military presence in Europe. Central and South America took no active part in the war, although several South American nations declared war against Germany. Most residents of Latin America, Africa, Asia, and the Middle East had little direct involvement in World War I.

On August 4, 1914, the day after Germany declared war on France, President Woodrow Wilson announced that the United States would remain neutral. Historians have estimated that nearly all Americans initially supported this position (there were no regular public opinion polls at the time), since neutrality was the traditional posture of the United States toward European conflicts. Although most Americans favored neutrality and opposed U.S. participation in the conflict, they did have some preferences about the war and its contestants. A majority of the nation's population were pro-British, reflecting their ancestral connections or the nation's cultural-political affinity with England, but a substantial group felt differently. Most individuals of German birth or heritage, a group that constituted a sizable segment of the population of the United States, favored the German "Fatherland." Scandinavians were also sympathetic toward Germany or at least opposed American participation in the war. Long-standing hostility of most Irish toward Britain prompted their pro-German position. However, as the European war continued, a battle was waged for American public opinion, and Allied supporters generally had the upper hand.

While most Americans recoiled at the thought of joining the war directly, they sensed that the conflict could help the economy. The American economy had been shaky for much of the time since the panic of 1907 and had slipped back into recession in 1914. Unemployment had shot upward, and worker incomes dropped sharply. However, the prospect of increased trade with Europe's powerhouses, all of whom were engaged in war, offered hope to American farmers, manufacturers, and workers. Most understood that Wilson's proclamation of neutrality was closely tied to increased trade with the Europeans, a sentiment considered normal and appropriate. American financiers offered to lend money, which would allow Britain and France to continue purchases of American goods. Secretary of State William Jennings Bryan initially blocked the loans, arguing that "Money is the worst of contrabands—it commands all other things." President Wilson overruled these objections, following the advice of Secretary of the Treasury William McAdoo and others, who warned that failure to aid Britain financially would prolong the recession.

Under international law, neutral nations had the right to trade with belligerents (nations at war), which were permitted to confiscate contraband but not goods destined for civilian usage or neutral nations. However, there was a practical difficulty with this legal theorem: Britain, long the world's dominant naval power, had command of the open ocean. Its navy had driven the German fleet into harbor to sit out the war, which opened the seaways across the Atlantic to British ships. Moreover, Britain prevented neutral ships from reaching Germany, a blockade that included indirect passage through neutral nations on the Continent. Britain pushed this advantage aggressively during the early phase of the war, placing mines in the North Sea and seizing American merchant ships, some of which the British impounded.

Germany fought back by turning to a new instrument of war—the submarine. On February 4, 1915, Germany announced it would sink all enemy vessels in a war zone around Britain. Wilson responded that he would hold Germany "strictly accountable" for violations of the rights of neutral nations on the seas. Germany's *Unterseebooten* presented a new problem for international law. Submarines worked best by stealth attacks on ships. Subs were easily sunk by deck guns mounted on freighters when they surfaced. Attacking while submerged limited a sub captain's ability to ascertain the nature of the cargo aboard a vessel or even to determine its country of origin. Britain armed its merchant vessels and sometimes flew foreign flags.

On May 7 the inevitable happened: A German sub torpedoed the *Lusitania*. Wilson, like most Americans, was shocked that Germany would use deadly force on civilians. Submarine warfare was an entirely new form of military conflict, which did not fit older rules of warfare and the rights of neutrals. Britain violated American neutral rights repeatedly during World War I, but, unlike Germany, the British blockage did not kill civilians.

One casualty of the *Lusitania* disaster was the resignation of the secretary of state, William Jennings Bryan, who objected to Wilson's reproachful notes to Germany. A second consequence was stimulation of a military preparedness movement in the United States. Wilson used his Annual Message to Congress in December 1915 to urge expansion of the army and navy. The proposal irritated numerous "progressives," who philosophically opposed militarization and in some cases were pacifists. Bryan led a movement to block military expansion. Ferocious battles in Congress produced compromise measures that doubled the size of the regular army and began funding for a navy "second to none." Political leaders in Germany, especially Chancellor Theobald Bethmann Hollweg, civilian head of the government, watched this development closely. The German military was divided over how to treat the Americans. Bethmann Hollweg took a cautious stand, realizing that despite America's small army and traditional isolationism, the United States was a sleeping tiger. In terms of its population size, its extraordinary economic growth since the Civil War, and its recent expansion into the Caribbean and the Pacific, the United States would be a formidable opponent should it enter the war against Germany. But Bethmann Hollweg was fighting a losing battle against German naval leaders, who argued that daring use of submarines could tip the balance of the stalemated land war toward Germany.

In February 1916, Germany announced it would sink all armed merchant ships in the war zone without warning. A submarine torpedoed the unarmed French ship *Sussex* on March 24, which led Wilson to issue an ultimatum to Germany: Cease unrestricted submarine warfare against all ships or the United States would break off diplomatic relations. Chancellor Bethmann Hollweg convinced German military leaders, including Kaiser Wilhelm, that it was imprudent to defy the United States. Germany agreed to the Wilson demand, known as the Sussex Pledge, for a time. In the meantime, Wilson campaigned for reelection in 1916 and narrowly won a victory for a second term. Although he was aware that maintaining neutrality depended largely on the actions of other nations, Wilson held his tongue while his Democratic Party campaigned on the slogan, "He Kept Us Out of War."

Flush from his reelection and harboring a desire to broker a settlement to the war, Wilson offered some bold ideas to the Senate in January 1917. In his "peace without victory" speech, the president called on the warring parties to join a negotiated settlement of the war, which would be maintained by an organization of the world powers. The latter proposal became Wilson's quest to create a League of Nations. German leaders showed little interest in the plan. Their goal was to break out of the military stalemate, a deadlock that increasingly became a political liability at home. Their much enlarged arsenal of U-boats induced German military leaders to urge resumption of unrestricted submarine war. They argued that Germany could starve Britain into submission before

LUSITANIA

On May 7, 1915, the British Cunard liner *Lusitania* was torpedoed by a German submarine off the coast of Ireland. The ship sank in 18 minutes, causing 1,198 deaths, 128 of them American citizens. About a third of the passengers and crew escaped the stricken vessel. The next day the *New York Times* ran a headline on page one: "Washington Believes that a Grave Crisis Is at Hand."

The *Lusitania* was a 790-foot-long vessel that some described as a palace afloat. This queen of the British transatlantic crossing ferried passengers and cargo on regular sailings between New York and Liverpool. On May 7, the vessel had entered waters around the British isles, which Germany had designated as a war zone. Enemy vessels within its perimeters would be subject to attack. Germany had published a warning to this effect in New York newspapers on the day the *Lusitania* departed from the United States. Some private vessels that entered the war zone were armed with deck guns, which could sink a submarine that had surfaced. The *Lusitania* was unarmed, but it did carry 4,200 cases of Canadian-made ammunition, although the captain of the German submarine did not know this. He followed orders to sink ships of belligerents (such as Great Britain). His torpedo struck midship, causing a secondary explosion and tearing a huge hole in the vessel's starboard side. Fifteen minutes later the ship began to sink. Many lifeboats were swamped or became tangled because of the ship's severe listing to starboard. Then the ship plunged downward. Its bow lodged in the mud on the sea floor, leaving the upper portion of the vessel above water on a vertical axis until it crashed into the water.

The surprise attack on the *Lusitania* produced outrage in the United States and Britain. Former president Theodore Roosevelt, never one to

the United States could mount an effective military retaliation. On February 1, Kaiser Wilhelm gave permission to the navy to use its submarines without restrictions. Two days later, the United States broke diplomatic relations with Germany.

Three weeks later, an extraordinary revelation rocked the United States. President Wilson released a telegraphed message from German foreign minister Arthur Zimmermann to Mexico that proposed a military partnership between Germany and Mexico. The so-called mince words, called the attack "piracy on a vaster scale of murder than old-time pirates ever practiced." He and other Americans called for military retaliation. President Woodrow Wilson tried to keep a calmer demeanor. In his first public response to disaster, issued on May 10, Wilson said, "There is such a thing as a man being too proud to fight. There is such a thing as a nation being so right that it does not need to convince others by force that it is right." Roosevelt countered that Wilson was "an abject coward." The ex-president added for good measure that only "flubdubs and the mollycoddles" stood behind Wilson. These words are outdated now, but people got the message in 1915.

Wilson's official reprimand to Germany on May 13 did have more backbone to it. The president demanded reparations and a promise that such an attack would not be launched again. He also asserted the right of Americans to travel on belligerent passenger lines and merchant ships. When Germany essentially ignored the note, Wilson put the American position more forcefully in a series of notes in July, urging Germany to cease use of surprise attacks, which would have required surfacing and inspecting vessels. While these letters did not constitute an American ultimatum, their implications were too strong for Secretary of State William Jennings Bryan, who resigned. Bryan was a committed devotee of peace. Furthermore, he argued that Germany had a right to prevent contraband from reaching its enemy. Wilson disagreed. The president had regularly ignored Bryan's advice. The president selected Robert Lansing, an official in the State Department, as his replacement. Lansing took a much more bellicose position on German submarine warfare and urged the president to condemn the German "menace" on the high seas.

Zimmermann Telegram informed Mexican authorities that Germany would soon resume unrestricted submarine warfare and that this step was likely to provoke war with the United States. If this occurred, the German minister offered to help Mexico regain territory lost in the Mexican-American War (1846–48). British intelligence had intercepted the cable message and handed it over to Wilson, who released the news to the press. Newspaper editors spewed venom on Germany for hatching such a bold scheme. Frank Cobb, editor of the *New York World*,

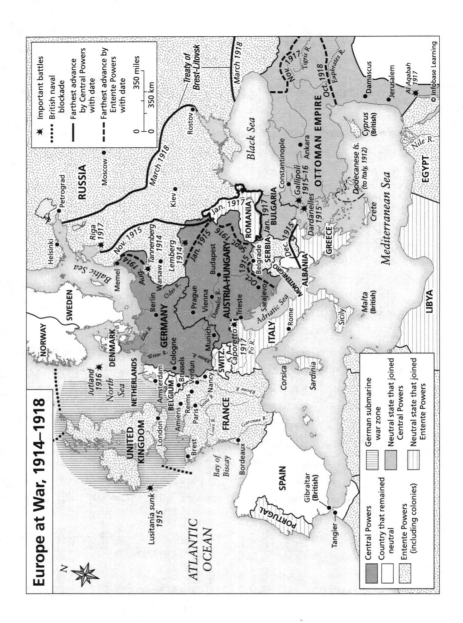

Europe at War, 1914–1918

Legend:
- ★ Important battles
- •••• British naval blockade
- ─── Farthest advance by Central Powers with date
- - - - Farthest advance by Entente Powers with date

350 miles
350 km
0

- Central Powers
- Country that remained neutral
- Entente Powers (including colonies)
- German submarine war zone
- Neutral state that joined Central Powers
- Neutral state that joined Entente Powers

© Infobase Learning

called for war, arguing that "Germany has been making war upon the United States for more than two years." The "welfare and safety" of the nation were at stake, he wrote, because "Germany under a desperate and criminal autocracy has made itself the enemy of mankind."

President Wilson responded to these provocations by proposing to arm American merchant ships with deck guns and give orders to "shoot on sight" at submarines. When Senator Robert M. La Follette (R-WI) blocked by filibuster the administration's bill, the president took the extraordinary step of imposing his policy by use of executive authority. In March 1917, German subs sank three U.S. merchant ships.

The German submarine attacks presented the Wilson administration with a crisis. On March 20, Wilson summoned his cabinet to the White House and solicited the advice of each department secretary. Their opinion unanimously supported a declaration of war against Germany; even several previously antiwar secretaries had changed their minds and fallen in line. Although Wilson did not reveal his reaction to their verdict, the president apparently decided on war within the next 24 hours. On March 21, the president issued a call for a special session of Congress. In the days ahead, the president prepared his war message while staffers readied the necessary supporting legislation. On April 2, the president stood before a cheering body of lawmakers, many of whom were waving American flags, and asked Congress to declare war. After brief debates in each body, the Senate approved the declaration of war on April 4 by a vote of 82 to 6, and the House concurred two days later by a vote of 373 to 50.

THE DEBATE

The Argument in Favor of War with Germany

President Woodrow Wilson had called his full cabinet together on March 20, 1917, to discuss the situation with Germany. Secretary of State Robert Lansing made lengthy entries in his diary of these discussions. The president opened the proceedings by stating that he did not see what more he could do to safeguard American vessels "unless we declare war." He went on to review political developments in the countries at war, "particularly in Russia, where the revolution against autocracy had been successful." Then the president asked each member to state his opinion of the matter.

The diary entry for Lansing's remarks was detailed, in part because the secretary's comments paraphrased a letter on the crisis that he had given to Wilson the previous day. (See "Secretary of State Robert Lansing Recommends War Against Germany, March 20, 1917," on page 191 in the Primary Sources section.) Germany and the United States were already in "an actual state of war," Lansing observed, in all but official acknowledgement of this fact. He recommended no delay in calling Congress to consider the question. Taking note of the movement to oust the czar, he suggested to the president that "the revolution in Russia, which appeared to be successful, had removed one objection to affirming that the European war was a war between Democracy and Absolutism." Wilson repeated these basic ideas in his April 2 message to Congress. Lansing also noted that entering the war would "put an end to the charges of vacillation and hesitation," implying that the administration was under increasing political pressure to take decisive action on the German crisis. Lansing went on to suggest at the March 20 meeting that world peace would be advanced by the creation of a League of Peace and that achieving this goal would be facilitated if no "powerful autocracy" was a member of the founding nations. In other words, creation of a league was more likely if the United States joined the Allies to crush Germany. Wilson, it appears in retrospect, shared these sentiments.

Wilson's war message to Congress on April 2 was long and filled with moralistic homilies characteristic of the president, who had been a professor of history and a popular writer prior to his political career. This famous document contained three principal arguments asking for Congress to declare war. (See "President Woodrow Wilson's War Message to Congress, April 2, 1917," on page 193 in the Primary Sources section.) First, Wilson charged Germany with violating the rights of the United States as a neutral nation to ply the open seas. The president contended that the Germans' resumption of unrestricted submarine warfare went "beyond the pale of law." More than just ignoring long-standing rules of international law, Wilson indicted Germany for wantonly disregarding "the humane practices of civilized nations." Generalizing further, Wilson claimed that "German submarine warfare against commerce is a warfare against mankind."

Wilson amplified the tenor of this indictment in his second charge against Germany, which he claimed challenged the honor of the United States. The United States could not submit to Germany's unethical use of submarines, which the president said were rogue "outlaws." The United States had a "duty" to uphold "the most sacred rights of our nation." Wilson's third theme went beyond international law and national honor to address the matter of government globally. He charged that the German government was a "natural foe to liberty." Along with its allies, a set of "autocratic governments backed by organized force" denied the popular aspirations of their peoples. America's entrance into the war would remove these "little groups of ambitious men," allowing citizens of autocracies "to choose their way of life." The president concluded this lofty expression of purpose for war with the message's most famous phrase: "The World must be made safe for Democracy."

Most of the ideas in Wilson's message had been aired previously in the public debate over America's relationship with the European belligerents. The editors of *The New Republic*, a public affairs magazine, touched on some of them in their comment on Wilson's break of diplomatic relations with the kaiser's government. They argued in "Justification" that Wilson's policy of "benevolent neutrality" had been sound and appropriate. (See "Editors of *The New Republic* Support President Wilson, Febrary 10, 1917," on page 194 in the Primary Sources section.) Historically, keeping open the avenues of travel by sea had been critical to the development of the United States. Heretofore, "Great Britain has policed the world's highways," benefiting American trade. Now, German subs threatened to overthrow Britain's "empire of the seas." The United States was wholly justified in waging war against Germany's "barbarous sub warfare." The editors noted, too, that American entrance into the war would assist Wilson's objective of creating a League of Nations.

The importance of American trade with Europe had been on the minds of leaders in business and government since the outbreak of the war. They realized that the European belligerents had increased their purchase of American goods and that these orders were pulling the United States out of its economic recession. Secretary of the Treasury William McAdoo made these points on several occasions to the president, including in a confidential letter dated August 21, 1915. (See "Secretary of the Treasury William McAdoo Explains the International Financial System, August 21, 1915," on page 195 in the Primary Sources section.) Referring to American exports, McAdoo observed that "Great Britain is, and always has been, our best customer." Now, with the war on, higher prices "have brought great prosperity to our farmers, while the purchases of war munitions have stimulated and have set factories going to full capacity. . . . Our prosperity is dependent on our continued and enlarged foreign trade." But Britain was running short of funds with which to buy American goods. Since it was legal to sell munitions to nations at war, it was illogical to prohibit loans. McAdoo urged the president to allow banks to extend "credit" to the Allies. This the president did and removed all restrictions on loans to Britain once the United States entered the war. McAdoo's appeal to the president accentuated the extent to which America's conflict with Germany rested on economic realities.

The Argument Against War with Germany

The arguments for going to war against Germany failed to convince opponents of intervention. One of the most articulate of these naysayers was Senator George W. Norris (R-NE). Norris contended that the United States should have adopted a policy that would have both preserved its neutrality and still traded with nations at war. (See "Senator George Norris Opposes the War, April 4, 1917," on page 196 in the Primary Sources section.) He charged that this course was not followed because of the ever-tightening financial bond that had formed between economic interests in the United States and Britain. American bankers had loaned money to the British, and now, Norris charged, American citizens are being used "as insurance policies to guarantee the delivery of munitions of war to belligerent nations." This was a war for the sake of Wall Street, not Main Street. "War brings prosperity to the stock gambler on Wall Street," he said, while average citizens are saddled with a higher cost of living of a war-time economy. "We are going into war upon the command of gold," which ran the "risk of sacrificing millions of our countrymen's lives." Despite his denunciation of Wall Street and the bankers, Norris's indictment persuaded few members of the Senate.

Senator Robert M. La Follette (R-WI), however, needed no coaxing to oppose Wilson's call to war. La Follette had pointed out the contradictions in American neutrality policy on several occasions and had single-handedly blocked Wilson's legislation to arm American merchant ships. He condemned entrance into the war on April 6 during the Senate debate and remained a critic of war policy afterward. Wilson had not acted neutrally, La Follette charged, but had aided Britain. (See "Senator Robert M. La Follette Opposes the War, April 4, 1917," on page 197 in the Primary Sources section.) He faulted the president for not acknowledging the British mining of the North Sea in his war message. La Follette condemned the president's speech for presenting a one-sided view of so-called Prussian autocracy. The Allies, including Britain, were hardly democracies in La Follette's view. Britain had its hereditary House of Lords, a system of limited voting rights, and a worldwide colonial empire that subjugated indigenous inhabitants. La Follette contended, probably erroneously, that the majority of the American population opposed the war. Nevertheless, the senator had raised the interesting point that the people had not been consulted about the decision for war, which put lives at risk. The Constitution, of course, places the authority to declare war with Congress and does not provide for a popular referendum on these questions. For his troubles in offering this lesson in political science, La Follette was depicted in a cartoon as a friend of Kaiser Wilhelm of Germany.

The American Socialist Party echoed La Follette's contention that most Americans were against the war, but Socialists were less concerned with how the public divided over the issue than with the underlying reality as they saw it. (See "American Socialist Party Condemns United States' Entry into War, April 7, 1917," on page 199 in the Primary Sources section.) "Our entrance into the European war was instigated by the predatory capitalists in the United States who boast of the enormous profit of $7,000,000,000 from the manufacture and sale of munitions and war supplies." Socialists saw this motive to profit from war as a general characteristic of modern industrial societies, in which war flowed from "commercial and financial rivalry and intrigues of the capitalist interests in the different countries." The Socialists urged working-class solidarity to oppose a "war of contending national groups of capitalists," which would bring "suffering, death and demoralization to the workers." American Socialists continued their denunciation of the war after April 1917 and paid a heavy price for their opposition. So did Americans who objected to entering the war on moral and religious grounds. Some who publicly aired their criticism of the war were arrested and thrown in jail. There was little freedom of speech or tolerance for war opponents at home when American doughboys fought in France.

OUTCOME AND IMPACT

Like so many other wars, misconceptions among contemporaries about the likely course of World War I abounded. Europeans initially thought the war would be over in weeks. The British thought their island was prepared to fight a land war in Europe in 1914. It was not. The German military did not think the United States would be much of a factor in the outcome of the war, but it proved decisive. Many members of Congress and presumably segments of the American public did not realize that war meant sending combat troops to Europe, as opposed to confronting Germany on the high seas. Moreover, few anticipated that the Russian Revolution would have a second and more radical phase, in which Vladimir Lenin and the Bolsheviks would seize power and withdraw Russia from the war. (See the sidebar "The Russian Revolution" below.) This development allowed Germany to transfer troops from the eastern to the western front. American troops proved critical to

THE RUSSIAN REVOLUTION

On March 8, 1917, riots in the capital city of Petrograd (formerly St. Petersburg) signaled the start of the Russian Revolution. Russia was a highly stratified society, dominated by aristocratic land barons and ruled by Czar Nicholas II, a descendant of a line of Romanov monarchs. A parliament had been established following the Revolution of 1905, but it was weak and ineffective. In consort with Russian aristocrats, Czar Nicholas retained his grip over the working of an inefficient Russian government. His police used deadly force to put down riots and uprisings among dissident groups. The most radical opponents of the absolutist regime, such as Vladimir Lenin, had been exiled.

World War I posed tremendous challenges for a country that had only recently begun to industrialize, lacked a tradition of administrative government, and faced a formidable German enemy on the eastern front. The Russian military was plagued with poor leadership and inadequate supplies, while residents on the home front suffered through hyperinflation and food shortages by 1916. The czar personally took command of Russia's army, taking up quarters at the front lines. His wife, Alexandra, secluded in Petrograd and prompted by her personal adviser, the mystic monk Rasputin, urged the czar to clamp down on his critics. The assassination of Rasputin by Russian aristocrats in December 1916 symbolized the political chaos that gripped Petrograd. The frigid winter of 1917 coupled with transportation breakdowns sparked food riots in the capital and other cities. Unable to extinguish the political uprising, the czar abdicated on March 15. Liberal opposition groups formed a Provisional government, which pledged to revitalize the country's flagging war effort.

On March 17, President Woodrow Wilson received confirmation that a parliamentary government had formed in Russia. Wilson's initial reaction to counter this German buildup. But the United States did not have an army ready to man the trenches on the western front in April 1917. American military leaders had to create this expeditionary force.

It took both the army and the navy a year to reach full mobilization. When the United States declared war in April 1917, the regular army counted 133,000 men. Eventually, 4.8 million were put in uniform,

---

the news is not known, but no doubt the president shared the jubilation that the American press showered on the new "democratic" Russia. The overthrow of absolutism in aristocratic Russia met the approval of most Americans. For Wilson and Secretary of State Robert Lansing, the Russian Revolution occurred at a pivotal moment in deciding how to deal with Germany. On March 20, the president assembled his cabinet to solicit opinions about the recent German sinking of American merchant ships. All 10 members present agreed that the United States should use force to protect American ships from German submarine attacks. Lansing argued that the overthrow of the czar permitted the president to frame the entrance of the United States into the war in terms of democracy versus German ("Prussian") autocracy. Wilson incorporated the suggestion into his War Message to Congress on April 2, 1917. He noted in the speech that Americans had been heartened by the news from Russia, whose citizens would now be "fighting for freedom in the world." Russia, Wilson observed, was "a fit partner for a league of honour."

The news from Russia was militarily as well as ideologically welcome. Administration officials thought that the new Russia would pose a more formidable opponent for Germany, Austria-Hungary, and Turkey. They were wrong. The new regime did not mount a more effective front against Germany. The Russian Revolution had a second phase, in which the radical Bolshevik segment of anticzarist socialists launched a coup d'état against the parliamentary regime. Germany helped Lenin return to Russia from his exile in Switzerland. Under Lenin's leadership, the Bolsheviks consolidated their control and in December 1917 brokered an armistice with Germany. Russia signed the Treaty of Brest-Litovsk on March 3, 1918, which formally ended its war with Germany. The conclusion of the fighting on the eastern front allowed Germany to transfer forces to the western front. Here they confronted the Allies now bolstered by the United States, whose Expeditionary Force in France was just building up strength.

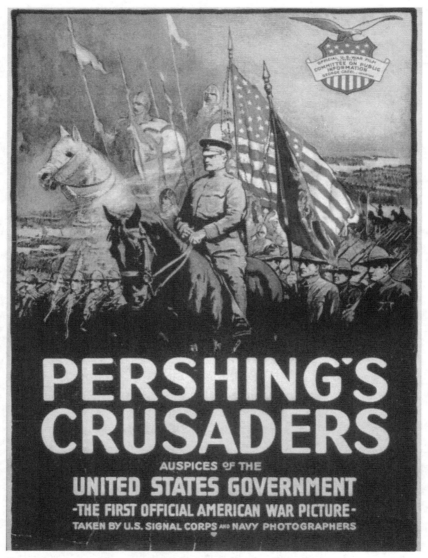

This propaganda poster shows General John Pershing leading his troops, with the spirits of crusaders floating above. (Library of Congress)

counting the navy. Half of this number was raised by a draft, authorized by the Selective Service Act of May 18, 1917. A total of 2 million Americans, including 200,000 African Americans, were sent overseas, and 1.3 million were sent into combat; 48,909 were killed in action, and 56,000 died of disease. War-time service was an eye-opener for many new recruits, even if they were not sent to France. Some 60 percent of war-time draftees were introduced to indoor plumbing. Many took up the use of toothbrushes for the first time. Members of the American Expeditionary Force—most of whom had never been out of the country—traveled to France on troop ships. The innovative convoying techniques implemented by Admiral William Sims of the U.S. Navy worked almost flawlessly; not one U.S. soldier was lost to enemy fire on an American ship in these transatlantic voyages.

The American Expeditionary Force to France was placed under the command of General John Pershing. The first American troops reached the front in Europe in October 1917, but it was not until April of the following year that a large contingent of Americans flowed into the trenches. Pershing insisted that the Americans operate within their own units and be deployed only after they had sufficient training. British and French generals wanted the Americans to be integrated with European units as fast as possible. The timetable for the insertion of Americans into combat was hastened by the Bolshevik Revolution, which resulted in the withdrawal of the Russian army from the war in March 1918. At the time, there were only 300,000 Americans on the western front, which Germany was reinforcing with soldiers transferred from the eastern sector. Americans were rushed into service to block a German attack in spring 1918. By this time, a quarter of a million Americans were arriving in France each month, a buildup that was critical in stemming the German thrust. An Allied counterattack (the Meuse-Argonne Offensive) in September 1918 included 600,000 American troops. Pershing pushed his troops to the limit, driving the Germans back to their border. Rather than fight on their own territory, the Germans sought an armistice. A cease-fire was signed on November 11, 1918. American troops had been in combat for 200 days.

The major nations engaged in the war, minus Russia, sent delegations to Versailles, France, outside Paris, to negotiate a peace treaty. In a fateful decision, President Woodrow Wilson decided to head the American delegation. The president's entourage excluded his Republican critics in the U.S. Senate, which under the Constitution had the authority to ratify or reject treaties to which the United States was a signatory. Wilson's trip to Versailles was largely motivated by his desire to secure a League of Nations organization as part of the peace treaty. The president achieved his goal, but at the cost of conceding much to European leaders—especially those of Britain, France, and Italy, whose main objective was revenge against Germany and protection of their empires. Instead of a "peace without victory" and "peace among equals," as Wilson had envisioned in his January 1917 speech, the Versailles Treaty saddled Germany with the responsibility for starting World War I. The agreement imposed on Germany a large financial obligation, called reparations, payable to the European Allies.

The Versailles Treaty redrew the map of Europe and the Middle East. Germany lost considerable territory, including a slice of land that gave the resurrected nation of Poland an outlet to the ocean. The Polish Corridor isolated East Prussia from the bulk of Germany, which also lost its African and Asian colonies. The peace settlement created the countries of Czechoslovakia and Yugoslavia and enlarged Romania and Bulgaria by taking land from the old Austro-Hungarian Empire. The treaty also led to the final dismantling of the Ottoman Empire. Portions of its former holdings were placed in "mandates" under League of Nations supervision. Iraq was administered by Britain until it became independent in 1932. Egypt gained its independence in 1922, and the state of Palestine was created.

Most of these events had little immediate relevance for most Americans. Their attention was riveted on the League of Nations proposal that was contained in the Versailles Treaty. Wilson urged the Senate to ratify the document, which disturbed many Republican senators. Opponents saw the league as a threat to American freedom of action in the Caribbean and as potentially entangling the United States in future wars. Many Republican critics of the league were "reservationists," which meant they were willing to approve an amended agreement. Wilson however, pushed relentlessly in Paris to secure "his" league proposal. He refused to budge one iota afterward on its provisions. The president placed the league issue before the public in the congressional elections of 1918, with disappointing results. The Republican Party picked up six seats in the Senate and a thumping 54 seats in the House. Although as many as 80 senators may have favored a league in some form (with or without amendments), the measure never mustered enough votes (two-thirds) to win approval.

The United States never ratified the Versailles Treaty, nor did it ever join the League of Nations. The United States signed a separate peace treaty with Germany in 1921. By then, the league idea was dead as a doornail in the United States. The Republican presidential candidate in 1920, Warren G. Harding, and the leaders of his party adamantly opposed the league. Harding won the election by a landslide. The league limped along until it was absorbed by the United Nations in 1946.

WHAT IF?

Some observers have seen the American entrance into World War I against Germany as inevitable, given the way events unfolded. Such a conclusion may be accurate, although statements about inevitability carry with them absolute certainty about how circumstances would develop. Some alternate scenarios for the United States and World War I have plausibility. Consider several "ifs." If German leaders had mellowed their aggressive use of submarines a bit, if the German ambassador Arthur Zimmermann had not sent his infamous telegram (or the British had not intercepted it), and if Americans leaders had tried one more round of negotiations, perhaps backed up with threats of military intervention (and a sufficient military buildup), then perhaps the United States would have avoided intervention. Such a turn of events perhaps would have led to a genuine armistice between the western Allies and the Central Powers. Both sides were clearly exhausted by early 1918, when the first American troops arrived in France.

The implications of these altered decisions are immense in light of what subsequently did happen. Of foremost significance, World War II might have been avoided. The Versailles Treaty, which designated Germany the loser in the war, imposed heavy financial reparations on it, and stripped the country of territory, were potent factors in Hitler's rise to power in 1933. Germany's hyperinflation of the 1920s, followed by deep depression in the early 1930s, had linkages to World War I and contributed to Hitler's political successes. A soldier in the German army during World War I, Hitler carried with him through the 1920s a burning anger at his country's humiliation in 1918 and 1919. Redressing this defeat was fundamental to Hitler's decisions to renew German military aggression.

America's participation in World War I afforded Woodrow Wilson an opportunity to leverage the western Allies into support of the League of Nations. Some historians have seen the league as an accomplice in the coming of World War II, as Western Europeans may have put too much faith in its capacity to resolve international crises. The league had no means of enforcing negotiated settlements among nations. At Versailles, Wilson had forced the incorporation of the league into the peace treaty but then botched the job of convincing skeptics in the United States to accept American participation in the organization. Republicans put up a furious battle against the league, and in the process the GOP developed a firm commitment to diplomatic nonentanglement with Europe, a policy called isolationism. Had the

United States avoided war in 1917, perhaps the Republican Party would not have battled President Franklin Roosevelt's effort to aid Britain during the opening years of World War II, when the United States was technically neutral. Not all Republicans opposed assistance to Britain, after it went to war with Germany in September 1939. Admittedly, some Democrats were isolationists during these years. Yet, the GOP was more committed to noninvolvement than were Democrats.

World War I was responsible for turning a flu virus that appeared in the United States into a worldwide health disaster. The flu pandemic (a disease epidemic on a global scale) erupted in 1918 and 1919. From its first major outbreak in army training camps in the eastern United States, the flu traveled first on troop ships and then other vessels back and forth across the Atlantic and throughout much of the world, reaching the west coast of the United States, including Alaska, and on to India, China, and the Pacific islands and southerly into the Caribbean and South America. Perhaps a fourth of all Americans caught the flu during fall 1918 and the winter that followed. The disease had no cure at the time, and 600,000 Americans died from it. The scourge may have taken 60 million lives globally, making it the deadliest pandemic in world history. Strangely, President Woodrow Wilson did not publicly acknowledge the pandemic. His priorities in 1918 were the defeat of Germany and imposition of the peace settlement afterward.

World War I had several additional consequences. Most historians acknowledge that the war unleashed a destructive attack on civil liberties in the United States. The Wilson administration made a concerted effort to clamp down on dissenters to the war and to demand acceptance of administration objectives. German-Americans in particular suffered mightily during this reign of intolerance, largely because of their German ancestry. The state of Iowa, for instance, banned the public use of the German language. Wartime intolerance developed into an attack on suspected political radicals in 1919, which ranks as one of the worst violation of civil liberties in American history. Hundreds of residents, most of whom were immigrants, were rounded up on charges of subversion and deported without full judicial hearings.

On the other side of the coin, female suffrage won approval largely because of America's role in World War I. Women had battled long and hard for the right to vote and had made substantial progress toward this goal in various states by 1914, but opposition to a constitutional amendment that would make female suffrage a national right met stubborn opposition in Congress. Suffrage advocates made a point of supporting the war effort rather than continue their voting rights campaign during the war. The Senate approved the woman suffrage amendment in February 1919 by one vote. Would female suffrage have happened without World War I? Probably, but not as soon.

Counterfactual speculations must be understood as conjectured possibilities. There is no way of proving how likely any alternate historical pathway would have materialized had circumstances been different. World War I occurred because leaders made critical decisions on specific issues. Perhaps slight alternations of one or more of these calls may have kept the United States out of World War I and charted a different historical course for the world.

CHRONOLOGY

1914 *August 3:* Germany declares war on France; World War I begins.
August 4: Wilson proclaims American neutrality.

1915 *February 4:* Germany announces it will sink all enemy vessels in the British war zone.
February 10: Wilson holds Germany to "strict accountability" for unlawful use of submarines.
May 7: A German submarine torpedoes and sinks the *Lusitania.*
June 8: Bryan resigns as Secretary of State.
August 19: A submarine sinks the *Arabic.*
September 1: Arabic Pledge: Germans will not sink passenger liners without warning.
September 15: United States lifts loan ban to Allies.

1916 *February 10:* Germany announces intentions to sink armed merchantmen without warning.
March 24: Germany sinks the unarmed channel packet *Sussex.*
May 4: Germans acquiesce to U.S. demands in the Sussex Pledge.
November 7: Woodrow Wilson is reelected president.

1917 *January 18:* Wilson gives "Peace without victory" speech.
February 1: Germany resumes unrestricted sub warfare.
February 3: United States breaks diplomatic relations with Germany.
March 1: Zimmermann note appears in American newspapers.
March 9: Wilson arms merchantmen by executive authority.
March 15: Czar Nicholas abdicates in Russia.
March 18: Germany sinks three American merchant ships.
April 2: Wilson submits War Message to Congress.
April 6: Congress votes for war against Germany.
July 4: First American troops land in Europe.
December 7: Germany and Russia agree on an armistice.

1918　*January 8:* President Wilson presents his Fourteen Points.
March 3: Treaty of Brest-Litovsk formalizes Russia's withdrawal from the war.
September–November: Meuse-Argonne offensive in France
November: Republicans win control of Congress in mid-term elections.
November 11: Armistice ends the fighting on the western front.

1919　*May:* Versailles Treaty between Germany and the Allies
July 19: Wilson presents the Versailles Treaty with League of Nations proposal to Senate.

1920　*March 19:* U.S. Senate rejects the Versailles Treaty.
November: Republican Warren G. Harding is elected president.

DISCUSSION QUESTIONS

1. In the 1930s, the United States enacted legislation that prohibited loans to belligerents and kept American ships out of the war zone. Should Congress have adopted similar laws in 1914–16?
2. Was President Woodrow Wilson too pro-British and anti-German in the way he conducted neutrality policy during World War I? What explains his sympathies?
3. Is the maintenance of commercial trading contacts under any circumstances a reasonable diplomatic policy?
4. Robert La Follette and others questioned whether the majority of American citizens were in favor of war with Germany. Should the Constitution be revised to require a popular vote (referendum) on all declarations of war? Should a referendum be required for any military action undertaken by the U.S. government?
5. How did technological advances and traditional definitions of law collide in the period of American neutrality during World War I?
6. Would a German victory in World War I have threatened American national security? How?

WEB SITES

"Hell in the Trenches." Available at http://www.youtube.com/watch?v=FsBUXTgt-YE&NR=1.

The Sinking of the *Lusitania* [historical dramatization]. Available at http://www.youtube.com/watch?v=sURi21sJsWc.

Trench Warfare in Europe. Available at http://www.youtube.com/watch?v=uXX9DNN2aHM.

BIBLIOGRAPHY

Freidel, Frank. *Over There: The Story of America's First Great Overseas Crusade.* New York: McGraw-Hill, 1990.

Gregory, Ross. *The Origins of American Intervention in the First World War.* New York: W. W. Norton, 1971.

Joll, James. *The Origins of the First World War,* 2d ed. New York: Longman, 1992.

Kennedy, David M. *Over Here: The First World War and American Society.* New York: Oxford University Press, 1980.

Lansing, Robert. *War Memoirs of Robert Lansing, Secretary of State.* Indianapolis: Bobbs-Merrill Company, 1935.

Link, Arthur S. Wilson: *Campaigns for Progressivism and Peace, 1916–1917.* Princeton, N.J.: Princeton University Press, 1965.

Peterson, H. C., and Gilbert C. Fite. *Opponents of War, 1917–1918.* Madison: University of Wisconsin Press, 1957.

Preston, Diana. *Lusitania: An Epic Tragedy.* New York: Berkley, 2002.

Smith, Daniel M. *The Great Departure: The United State and World War I, 1914–1920.* New York: John Wiley, 1965.

Zieger, Robert. *America's Great War.* Lanham, Md.: Rowman and Littlefield, 2000.

PRIMARY SOURCES

1. Secretary of State Robert Lansing Recommends War Against Germany, March 20, 1917

Secretary of State Robert Lansing took comprehensive notes at the meeting on March 20, 1917, when President Woodrow Wilson asked his cabinet officers to give their opinions about the conflict with Germany. Lansing stated that he thought war with Germany already existed and that the Russian Revolution opened up the opportunity to describe American participation as an effort by democracies to oppose autocratic Germany.

I followed Baker and can very naturally remember what I said better and more fully than I can the remarks of others.

I began with the statement that in my opinion an actual state of war existed today between this country and Germany, but that, as the acknowledgement of such a state officially amounted to a declaration of war, I doubted the wisdom as well as the constitutional power of the President to announce such fact or to act upon it; that I thought that the facts should be laid before Congress and that they should be asked to declare the existence of a state of war and to enact the laws necessary to meet the exigencies of the case. I pointed out that many things could be done under our present statutes which seriously menaced our national safety and that the Executive was powerless to prevent their being done. I referred in some detail to the exodus of Germans from this country to Mexico and Cuba since we severed diplomatic relations, to the activities of German agents here, to the transference of funds by Germans to Latin American countries, to the uncensored use of the telegraph and the mails, etc.

For the foregoing reasons I said that I felt that there should be no delay in calling Congress together and securing these necessary powers.

In addition to these reasons which so vitally affected our domestic situation I said that the revolution in Russia, which appeared to be successful, had removed the one objection to affirming that the European war was a war between Democracy and Absolutism; that the only hope of a permanent peace between all nations depended upon the establishment of democratic institutions throughout the world; that no League of Peace would be of value if a powerful autocracy was a member, and that no League of Peace would be necessary if all nations were democratic; and that in going into the war at this time we could do more to advance the cause of Democracy than if we failed to show sympathy with the democratic powers in their struggle against the autocratic government of Germany.

The President said that he did not see how he could speak of a war for Democracy or of Russia's revolution in addressing Congress. I replied that I did not perceive any objection but in any event I was sure that he could do so indirectly by attacking the character of the autocratic government of Germany as manifested by its deeds of inhumanity, by its broken promises, and by its plots and conspiracies against this country.

Source: Arthur S. Link, *Wilson: Campaigns for Progressivism and Peace 1916–1917.* Princeton N.J.: Princeton University Press, 1965, 401–408, reproducing the Lansing Diary.

—⁓—

2. President Woodrow Wilson's War Message to Congress, April 2, 1917

President Woodrow Wilson's War Message to Congress on April 2, 1917, is one of the most famous documents in American history. Wilson condemned Germany's violation of American neutral rights by its use of submarines. The speech is perhaps most remembered for Wilson's plea that "The world must be made safe for democracy."

On the 3d of February last I officially laid before you the extraordinary announcement of the Imperial German Government that on and after the 1st day of February it was its purpose to put aside all restraints of law or of humanity and use its submarines to sink every vessel that sought to approach either the ports of Great Britain and Ireland or the western coasts of Europe or any of the ports controlled by the enemies of Germany within the Mediterranean.

The new policy has swept every restriction aside. Vessels of every kind, whatever their flag, their character, their cargo, their destination, their errand, have been ruthlessly sent to the bottom without warning.

The present German submarine warfare against commerce is a warfare against mankind. It is a war against all nations. American ships have been sunk, American lives taken, in ways which it has stirred us very deeply to learn of, but the ships and people of other neutral and friendly nations have been sunk and overwhelmed in the waters in the same way. There has been no discrimination. The challenge is to all mankind. . . . Our motive will not be revenge or the victorious assertion of the physical might of the nation, but only the vindication of right, of human right, of which we are only a single champion.

There is one choice we can not make, we are incapable of making: we will not choose the path of submission and suffer the most sacred rights of our nation and our people to be ignored or violated. The wrongs against which we now array ourselves are no common wrongs; they cut to the very roots of human life.

We have no quarrel with the German people. We have no feeling towards them but one of sympathy and friendship. It was not upon their impulse that their Government acted in entering this war. It was not with their previous knowledge or approval. It was a war determined upon as wars used to be determined upon in the old, unhappy days when peoples were nowhere consulted by their rulers and wars were provoked and waged in the interest of dynasties or of little groups of ambitious men who were accustomed to use their fellow men as pawns and tools.

We are glad, now that we see the facts with no veil of false pretence about them, to fight thus for the ultimate peace of the world and for the liberation of its peoples, the German peoples included: for the rights of nations great and small and the privilege of men everywhere to choose their way of life and of obedience. The world must be made safe for democracy.

We desire no conquest, no dominion. We seek no indemnities for ourselves, no material compensation for the sacrifices we shall freely make. We are but one of the champions of the rights of mankind.

Source: U.S. 65th Congress, 1st sess. Senate Document 5.

—⁓—

3. Editors of *The New Republic* Support President Wilson, February 10, 1917

The editors of The New Republic, *a magazine of opinion on public affairs, applauded President Wilson's policy of "benevolent neutrality" in their editorial of February 10, 1917. They acknowledged that both Britain and Germany had interfered with American commerce, yet held that Germany was more of a threat to American interests, especially world trade, than was Great Britain.*

The American nation will be entering the war ostensibly as the defender of the law of nations against the onslaught of an unscrupulous Germany, which in the pursuit of her military advantages refused to recognize the rights of neutrals and the claims of humanity. . . . We are being drawn into the war as a consequence of Mr. Wilson's policy of benevolent neutrality towards the Allies. Both groups of belligerents have been ignoring and violating the body of ambiguous precedents which composed the law of nations at the outbreak of the war.

The policy of benevolent neutrality, even though it has resulted in war, is not one for which any apology needs to be made. It was dictated by a sound and just estimate of the issue of the great war and of the proper relation of American national purposes to those issues. It would have been inconceivable for a nation with the ideals of the United States to have assisted the violator [Germany] of Belgium in reaping any benefit from the outrage.

The settlement of the American continent and the building up of the American nation are a part of the same historical process and have been determined by the same fundamental conditions as the making of the British Empire. It has all depended upon the emancipation of travel by sea from the obstacles of a rudimentary technique, of adverse political claims and theories and from outbreaks of sporadic or organized violence. In the work of emancipation Great Britain has always played the major part. She has given security to the world's highway and to those nations which could only be approached by the world's highway; and under the shadow of this security not only has the British Empire carried free British institutions to many parts of the world, but the American nation has been allowed to grow unvexed and unretarded by any by its own domestic difficulties. . . . In spite of the fact that the United States has protested against British maritime police power, the American people has been one of its chief beneficiaries.

Source: The New Republic 119 (February 10, 1917), 36–38.

—⁓—

4. Secretary of the Treasury William McAdoo Explains the International Financial Situation, August 21, 1915

In a memo for President Wilson dated August 21, 1915, Secretary of the Treasury William McAdoo explained the financial implications of the war in Europe. American loans not only helped Great Britain, but also its purchases were critical to sustaining the economy of the United States.

The high prices for food products have brought great prosperity to our farmers, while the purchases of war munitions have stimulated industry and have set factories going to full capacity throughout the great manufacturing districts, while the reduction of imports and their actual cessation in some cases, have caused new industries to spring up and others to be enlarged. Great prosperity is coming. . . . Our prosperity is dependent on our continued and enlarged foreign trade. To preserve that we must do everything we can to assist our customers to buy.

We have repeatedly declared that it is lawful for our citizens to manufacture and sell to belligerents munitions of war. It is lawful commerce and being lawful is entitled to the same treatment at the hands of our bankers, in financing it, as any other part of our lawful commerce. Acceptances based upon such exportations of goods are just as properly the subject of legitimate bank transactions as if based on non-contraband.

It is imperative for England to establish a large credit in this country. She will need at least $500,000,000. She can't get this in any way, at the moment, that seems feasible, except by sale of short time Government notes. Here she encounters the obstacle presented by Mr. Bryans letter of Jany [January] 20, 1915 to Senator Stone in which it is stated that "war loans in this country were disapproved because inconsistent with the spirit of neutrality" &c and "this Government has not been advised that any general loans have been made by Foreign Governments in this country since *the President expressed his wish that loans of this character* should not be made." . . . Large banking houses here which have the ability to finance a large loan, will not do so or even attempt to do so, in the face of this declaration.

In fact England & her allies will have great difficulty in getting the amount of credit they need here even if our Government is openly friendly. I wish you would think about this so we may discuss it when I see you. To maintain our prosperity, we must finance it. Otherwise it may stop and that would be disastrous.

Source: Arthur S. Link, ed. *The Papers of Woodrow Wilson*, vol. 34. Princeton, N.J.: Princeton University Press, 275–279.

—∞—

5. Senator George Norris Opposes the War, April 4, 1917

In a speech in Congress on April 4, 1917, Senator George W. Norris (R-NE) opposed a war with Germany. Norris argued that the United States could have chosen several options to preserve its neutrality. The war, he said, would enrich "the stock gambler on Wall Street" and bring misery to average families.

To my mind, what we ought to have maintained from the beginning was the strictest neutrality. If we had done this I do not believe we would have been on the verge of war at the present time. We had a right as a nation, if we desired, to cease at any time to be neutral. We had a technical right to respect the English war zone and to disregard the German war zone, but we could not do that and be neutral. I have no quarrel to find with the man who does not desire our country to remain neutral.

I think such people err in judgment and to a great extent have been misled as to the real history and the true facts by the almost unanimous demand of the great combination of wealth that has a direct financial interest in our participation in the war. We have loaned many hundreds of millions of dollars to the allies in this controversy. While such action was legal and countenanced by international law, there is no doubt in my mind but the enormous amount of money loaned to the allies in this country has been instrumental in bringing about a public sentiment in favor of our country taking a course that would make every bond worth a hundred cents on the dollar and making the payment of every debt certain and sure. . . .

It is now demanded that the American citizens shall be used as insurance policies to guarantee the safe delivery of munitions of war to belligerent nations. The enormous profits of munition manufacturers, stockbrokers, and bond dealers must be still further increased by our entrance into the war.

To whom does the war bring prosperity? Not to the soldier who for the munificent compensation of $16 per month shoulders his musket and goes into the trench, there to shed his blood and to die if necessary; not to the broken-hearted widow who waits for the return of the mangled body of her husband; not to the mother who weeps at the death of her brave boy; not to the little children who shiver with cold; not to the babe who suffers from hunger; nor to the millions of mothers and daughters who carry broken hearts to their graves. War brings no prosperity to the great mass of common and patriotic citizens. It increases the cost of living of those who toil and those who already must strain every effort to keep soul and body together. War brings prosperity to the stock gambler on Wall Street—to those who are already in possession of more wealth than can be realized or enjoyed.

Source: Congressional Record, 65th Cong., 1st sess., April 4, 1917.

—⚹—

6. Senator Robert M. La Follette Opposes the War, April 4, 1917

In a speech in the U.S. Senate on April 4, 1917, Senator Robert M. La Follette (R-WI) criticized President Wilson for coddling the British and taking a one-sided approach to neutrality. Britain's possession of its global empire, he stated, made a mockery of Wilson's contention that the democracies were standing together.

It is idle to talk of a war upon a government only. We are leagued in this war, or it is the President's proposition that we shall be so leagued, with the hereditary enemies of Germany. Any war with Germany, or any other country for that matter, would be bad enough, but there are not words strong enough to voice my protest against the proposed combination with the Entente Allies.

When we cooperate with those governments, we endorse their methods; we endorse the violations of international law by Great Britain; we endorse the shameful methods of warfare against which we have again and again protested in this war; we endorse her purpose to wreak upon the German people the animosities which for years her people have been taught to cherish against Germany; finally, when the end comes, whatever it may be, we find ourselves in cooperation with our ally, Great Britain, and if we cannot resist now the pressure she is exerting to carry us into the war, how can we hope to resist, then, the thousandfold greater pressure she will exert to bend us to her purposes and compel compliance with her demands?

In the sense that this war is being forced upon our people without their knowing why and without their approval, and that wars are usually forced upon all peoples in the same way, there is some truth in the statement; but I venture to say that the response which the German people have made to the demands of this war shows that it has a degree of popular support which the war upon which we are entering has not and never will have among our people. The espionage bills, the conscription bills, and other forcible military measures which we understand are being ground out of the war machine in this country is the complete proof that those responsible for this war fear that it has no popular support and that armies sufficient to satisfy the demand of the Entente Allies cannot be recruited by voluntary enlistments. . . .

The only reason why we have not suffered the sacrifice of just as many ships and just as many lives from the violation of our rights by the war zone and the submarine mines of Great Britain as we have through the unlawful acts of Germany in making her war zone in violation of our neutral rights is simply because we have submitted to Great Britain's dictation. If our ships had been sent into her forbidden high-sea war zone as they have into the proscribed area Germany marked out on the high seas as a war zone, we would have had the same loss of life and property in the one case as in the other; but because we avoided doing that, in the case of England, and acquiesced in her violation of law, we have not only a legal but a moral responsibility for the position in which Germany has been placed by our collusion and cooperation with Great Britain. By suspending the rule with respect to neutral rights in Great Britain's case, we have been actively aiding her in starving the civil population of Germany. We have helped to drive Germany into a corner, her back to the wall to fight with what weapons she can lay her hands on to prevent the starving of her women and children, her old men and babes.

Source: Congressional Record, 65th Cong., 1st sess., April 4, 1917.

—⚬⚬—

7. American Socialist Party Condemns United States' Entry into War, April 7, 1917

The American Socialist Party adopted a resolution on April 7, 1917, that condemned the United States' entry into World War I. The resolution charged that the war brought "more wealth and power to the ruling classes" and "suffering, death, and demoralization to the workers."

Modern wars as a rule have been caused by the commercial and financial rivalry and intrigues of the capitalist interests in the different countries. Whether they have been frankly waged as wars of aggression or have been hypocritically represented as wars of "defense," they have always been made by the classes and fought by the masses. War brings wealth and power to the ruling classes and suffering, death, and demoralization to the workers.

They breed a sinister spirit of passion, unreason, race hatred, and false patriotism. They obscure the struggles of the workers for life, liberty, and social justice. They tend to sever the vital bonds of solidarity between them and their brothers in other countries, to destroy their organizations, and to curtail their civil and political rights and liberties.

The Socialist Party of the United States is unalterably opposed to the system of exploitation and class rule which is upheld and strengthened by military power and sham national patriotism. We, therefore, call upon the workers of all countries to refuse to support their governments in their wars. The wars of the contending national groups of capitalists are not the concern of the workers. The only struggle which would justify the workers in taking up arms is the great struggle of the working class of the world to free itself from economic exploitation and political oppression. As against the false doctrine of national patriotism we uphold the ideal of international working-class solidarity. . . .

The mad orgy of death and destruction which is now convulsing unfortunate Europe was caused by the conflict of capitalist interests in the European countries.

Source: American Socialist, April 21, 1917.

7

WORLD WAR II:

Did Germany Threaten the United States in 1941?

—ɯ—

The Issue

President Franklin D. Roosevelt declared American neutrality when World War II erupted in September 1939. For the next 26 months, Roosevelt kept the United States out of active combat, yet his administration provided increasing levels of support for Great Britain. The adoption of the Lend-Lease program in 1941 permitted the president to send billions of dollars of assistance to the "Allies" that opposed Germany. By the fall of 1941, the United States engaged Germany in an undeclared naval war in an effort to ensure the safe arrival of this aid overseas. Did Roosevelt assess the German threat to American security accurately?

♦ **Arguments that Germany threatened the United States:** President Roosevelt argued that Germany was a threat to the security of the Western Hemisphere. He charged that Hitler had acted in concert with the Italian dictator Benito Mussolini and the leaders of Japan, who aimed to dominate the world and suppress freedoms that the Western democracies valued. Roosevelt maintained that the "survival" of Britain from German aggression was the key to American security.

♦ **Arguments that Germany did not threaten the United States:** Opponents of Roosevelt's movement toward an outright alliance with Great Britain challenged the president's premises. The critics contended that Britain's survival was not critical to American security. America would fare better by bolstering its defenses at home. The famed airman Charles Lindbergh was the most prominent spokesperson for this "noninterventionist" position. Lindbergh's expertise with flight gave his rebuttal of Germany's capacity to invade the United States particular credence.

—ɯ—

INTRODUCTION

On July 9, 1933, Charles Lindbergh set off in a single-engine aircraft on a journey that would cover 29,781 miles over the next five and a half months. It was the kind of daring trip the public had come to expect of the *The Spirit of St. Louis* navigator, who had flown the Atlantic alone in 1927. On this odyssey, he took along his wife, Anne Morrow Lindbergh, and plotted an elaborate course, in part to explore air routes for Pan Am Airlines. Taking off from La Guardia Airport in New York City, the couple flew north to Halifax, Nova Scotia, and Newfoundland, then to Greenland, Iceland, and Britain. The next leg of the trip took them to Copenhagen, Stockholm, and other points in Europe, including Russia. At every stop, the Lindberghs were entertained by luminaries and royalty and mobbed by a public fascinated by the flying couple. Their trip home began from Bathurst on the west coast of Africa, where they set course for the Pan Am barge (to accommodate Lindbergh's amphibious plane) at Natal, Brazil, 1,875 miles away westward. From South America, the couple island hopped the Caribbean to Florida and then back to New York. Soon after touching down on American soil, Franklin Roosevelt, the president of the United States, telegrammed his "Congratulations upon the successful completion of this, another flight made by you in the interest and for the promotion of American aviation."

Already a celebrity in America and across the globe, Lindbergh's 1933 trip further enhanced his reputation. By the end of the 1930s, however, this luster had faded. To some, Lindbergh became an object of vilification, and to others, a Nazi sympathizer. The reason for the animosity was Lindbergh's failure to oppose publicly Adolf Hitler, the German dictator whose actions caused the outbreak of World War II. As Hitler had become more aggressive in incorporating neighboring countries into Germany in the late 1930s, Roosevelt became more alarmed. The German conquest of France in June 1940 and the threatened invasion of Britain in the following months persuaded Roosevelt to find ways of assisting Great Britain, but without formally submitting a declaration of war. By 1941, the United States was providing Britain many millions of dollars worth of assistance and offering U.S. naval protection for its safe passage from German submarines in the North Atlantic. Roosevelt told the nation that Hitler's U-boats threatened the safety of freedom-loving people everywhere.

Did Germany threaten the United States? Roosevelt thought so. He claimed that Germany was a global menace, a threat that included people in North and South America. "Internationalists," as individuals of FDR's outlook were known, saw Hitler as a ruthless dictator who would stop at nothing to gain control of Europe and, eventually, the world. The last remaining stronghold that blocked Hitler's ambition in Europe after his conquest of France in June 1941 was the United Kingdom. Roosevelt put Britain's survival at the center of American security policy. Political pressures in the United States deterred Roosevelt from recommending direct American military intervention in the war. To surmount this obstacle, Roosevelt supported Britain "short of war" by sending war supplies. By late 1941, the president had ordered the U.S. Navy to aid Britain in countering German submarine attacks on Allied shipping across the Atlantic.

Lindbergh emerged as the star critic of Roosevelt's pro-British policy. "Lindy" and like-minded Americans saw the war in Europe as a foreign affair, of no immediate threat to the security of the United States. While many of these critics were Republicans who opposed an administration headed by a Democrat, they also were patriots. These opponents of internationalism saw the security of the United States rooted in its geographic separation from Europe and in adequate military preparation. In 1940, they formed the America First Committee, which became the largest organization lobbying for this "isolationist" position. Lindbergh became its star speaker. He doubted that Germany posed a risk to the United States. During 1940 and 1941, Lindy and FDR fought a bitter fight over how the United States should deal with Germany.

BACKGROUND

Adolf Hitler was born in Austria in 1889 and moved to Munich, Germany, in 1913. Following service in the German army in World War I, he gravitated toward politics and was instrumental in the rise of the National Socialist Party (or Nazi Party) in Germany. Despite Hitler's captivating oratory, his party languished until the Great Depression, which began in 1930 and cast millions of workers out of jobs. The hard times in Germany proved fertile ground for Hitler's strident nationalism.

The Versailles Treaty (1919) that ended World War I had demilitarized Germany, stripped it of territory, and tarnished its national pride. Hitler and Nazi propagandists cleverly manipulated this anger into support for their party's candidates. Germany's multiparty democracy became stalemated by late 1930, resulting in chancellors governing by decree. Exploiting this chaos, Hitler leveraged his appointment as chancellor in January 1933 following an inconclusive general election. Aided by his paramilitary Storm Troopers, Hitler used the office to consolidate his power, picking off opposition parties and pressure groups one by one. Within a year and a half, he became a powerful dictator—known as der Fuhrer, or the leader—brutally suppressing all opposition. His vision of a fascist Third Reich glorified the state and emphasized the duty of Germans to further this objective. Central to the new Germany was the integration of German-speaking peoples in neighboring countries into a greater German Fatherland.

Prior to September 1939, England and France had done little to thwart Hitler's ambitions. Their timidity was partially explained by a preoccupation to preserve their colonial empires. Second, some Europeans saw communism in Russia as more objectionable than fascism in Germany, a country that embraced Christianity and private property. Third, neither Britain nor France was militarily prepared to take on Germany. In the United States, President Roosevelt was largely a bystander to Hitler's intrigues, although he personally detested fascist values and was alarmed at Hitler's attacks on Jews. First, the Fuhrer stripped German Jews of citizenship. Then, in 1938, he inspired a night of terror known as Kristallnacht in which Nazi rioters killed 91 Jews and broke windows in 7,500 Jewish shops. A shocked Franklin Roosevelt said he "could scarcely believe that such things could occur in a twentieth-century civilization." Privately, Roosevelt grew increasingly uneasy about Germany's remilitarization and aggressiveness. Publicly, he claimed noninvolvement with Europe's diplomatic problems. The economic depression, the New Deal, and politics in the United States kept him from giving close attention to foreign matters through the mid-1930s, a time when many Americans saw little reason to meddle in European affairs. Isolationist sentiment in the United States had a long and deep history. Senator Gerald Nye (R-ND) invoked this tradition by spearheading legislation that sought to block the nation by law from entering another foreign war. The Neutrality Act of 1935 prohibited the sales of arms manufactured in the United States to nations at war. A 1936 amendment added loans and financial credits to these prohibitions, and a revision in 1937 required that belligerents pay cash and furnish transportation ("cash and carry") for nonmilitary goods purchased during a military conflict.

While hoping to avoid war, Roosevelt became increasingly concerned about the actions of the powerful dictators (Hitler, Mussolini in Italy, and the military clique that had gained control in Japan). In an address in Chicago in 1937, he condemned Japan's invasion of China earlier in the year as part of "the epidemic of world lawlessness." Although Roosevelt warned that "there is no escape through mere isolation or neutrality," he took no forceful steps to stop Germany or Japan before 1940. After seizing all of Czechoslovakia in early 1939, Hitler secured a nonaggression treaty with Russia in August. While Roosevelt lacked a clear plan on how to contain Germany or Japan, Hitler knew his next move. Secure against Russian retaliation, der Fuhrer sent his army on a lightning drive into Poland on September 1, 1939. The attack prompted Britain and France to declare war against Germany on September 3. World War II had begun.

American Neutrality, 1939–1940

Most Americans detested the Nazi dictatorship, yet they favored neutrality over intervention in the war. Knowing that Congress would not declare war against Germany, Roosevelt saw the provision of material assistance to Hitler's foes as his next best option. In late September 1939, he asked Congress to revise the Neutrality Act to allow the sale of weapons to nations at war on a "cash and carry" basis. On November 4, after six weeks of intense lobbying, the administration got its bill enacted. Allied purchases and the release of "surplus" American weapons to England and France constituted the core of Roosevelt's "aid short of war" strategy to keep the western democracies afloat.

The fierce battle to enact the "cash and carry" amendment to the Neutrality Act highlighted the political dilemma that dogged the president for next two years. Because of the vociferous opposition to American intervention in a "foreign war," Roosevelt painted the danger he perceived in vivid, even hyperbolic, language. Late in 1939, he told the Senate that Germany and its allies were bent on "world domination"

President Franklin D. Roosevelt, pictured here in 1940, was adamant in his support of Great Britain as it fought to hold off Germany. (Hulton Archive/Getty Images)

and that the "survival" of Britain was critical to American security. This assessment became the bedrock of Roosevelt's response to Hitler's threat to American security.

Most Americans hoped that the Allies (Britain and France) would defeat Germany. Yet nearly as many Americans opposed joining the war. Isolationists were particularly strong in the midwestern states and probably over-represented in Congress, given division among the public. Between September 1939 and October 1941, Roosevelt carefully calculated how far he could go in support of Britain's battle against Hitler in light of congressional and public resistance to full-scale military intervention. The president seized on opportunities when altercations with Germany arose and employed his great rhetorical abilities to fuse a closer military partnership with Britain.

In fall and winter 1939–40, FDR's concern seemed overblown, for Germany made no advance to the west. Then, in April 1940, Hitler unleashed his blitzkrieg (lightning war), first into Denmark and Norway and then into France through the Netherlands and Belgium. Astonished Americans watched France capitulate in June and a pro-Nazi regime established at Vichy in southern France. The day Hitler launched his invasion into western Europe, Parliament replaced Neville Chamberlain with Winston Churchill as Britain's prime minister. The pugnacious Churchill defiantly proclaimed "we will never surrender." He continued his fierce resolve when German airplanes began bombing Britain in July. Great Britain's ability to hold off the Nazis, who planned a cross-channel invasion, depended heavily on help from the United States. Roosevelt refused Churchill's plea to enter the war, but he did accelerate a U.S. military buildup. The president asked Congress in June 1940 for money to build a "two-ocean navy," 50,000 planes a year, and an enlarged army. A keen student of developments in aviation, Roosevelt argued that the Atlantic Ocean no longer provided an adequate defense barrier, drawing attention to the comparatively short flying time from Europe and Africa to the Americas. Congress granted much of the request. In September, lawmakers also agreed to enact a selective service program, which limited military service to one year, although the law prohibited sending draftees beyond the Western Hemisphere. Critics of the presidential defense preparedness nonetheless saw the program as a step toward war. Out of this opposition arose the America First Committee, which advocated nonintervention in European affairs.

The fall of France allowed Germany to move submarines to bases in western France, which put U-boats closer to their prey in the North Atlantic. As U-boat torpedoes sank an increasing number of British vessels, and as a German invasion of England appeared imminent, Churchill pleaded with Roosevelt to provide Britain with 50 surplus destroyers in exchange for eight British bases in the Western Hemisphere. The trade was a big gamble for Roosevelt, not only because his military leaders thought that Britain was doomed, but also because the exchange was likely to trigger new isolationist protests, which it did. Although Roosevelt's move provoked criticism, polls showed the public largely behind the president's cautious policy of "aid short of war." This fact, coupled with the fall of France in June, convinced FDR to run for an unprecedented third consecutive term for president. He won a convincing victory over Republican Wendell Willkie in November 1940. During the last days of the campaign, Willkie goaded the president to pledge not to send American "boys" into "foreign wars." Roosevelt's pledges to avoid military engagement in Europe and to increase defense spending, which helped the economy, were instrumental in his reelection.

1941

The November 1939 revision of the Neutrality Act opened up a critical supply line between the United States and Great Britain. Initially, Britain paid for its purchases, but in December 1940, Churchill informed the president that his country would soon be unable to pay cash for the materials. Roosevelt's solution was the Lend-Lease program, a plan that he announced publicly in a "fireside chat" radio address. Citing the importance of Britain's survival and the desire to keep the United States out of combat, the president said, "We must be the great arsenal of democracy." Over spirited opposition by isolationists, Congress adopted the Lend Lease Act in March 1941. The law allowed the President to dispose of—or "lend"—war materials in whatever way he thought served the national interest. Congress appropriated $7 billion to implement the act; over the life of the program, the United States distributed $54 billion of aid, more than half of which went to Great Britain. "Lend-Lease" was a euphemism; the United States gave away most of the materials supplied.

The Lend-Lease Act prohibited the U.S. Navy from convoying vessels across the North Atlantic, where German submarines lurked. This legislative restriction put Roosevelt in a delicate position. On the one hand, he wanted to ensure the safe arrival of war materials to Britain; on the other hand, he was sensitive to charges that he was deliberately leading the United States into war. Some of the president's aides thought that FDR overreacted to isolationist criticism. Nonetheless, the president remained adamant against direct intervention in the war, telling his cabinet in May that "I am unwilling to fire the first shot." But he did look for "incidents" that would provide justification to take more aggressive action toward Nazi submarines. Clutching at straws, as it were, Roosevelt "flipflopped, dodged, waffled, and dissembled," in the words of the historian David Kennedy, as he wove a zigzagged course that moved the United States closer to naval escorts for American and then British merchant ships.

In April 1941, he secured permission from the Danish government to build bases in Greenland, from which U.S. naval vessels patrolled (which Roosevelt said was not the same as "convoying") well out into the North Atlantic. In May, the Germans sank the *Robin Moor*, an American merchant ship, in the South Atlantic. FDR seized on the incident to declare an "Unlimited National Emergency," in which he graphically outlined Germany's threat to American security. He used the occasion to order the navy to "extend our patrol in north and south Atlantic waters." In June, Iceland was brought into the navy's patrolling radius, which now overlapped with Germany's "combat zone." In mid-August, Roosevelt and Churchill met in Newfoundland, where their military staffs conferred. The two leaders released a statement of common principles known as the Atlantic Charter. (See the sidebar "Friends: FDR and Churchill" on page 210.) In September, FDR ordered naval escorts of all Allied shipping as far as Iceland, with orders to "shoot on sight" at enemy raiders. For all intents and purposes, the United States had entered an undeclared naval war against Germany in the North Atlantic.

By then the military context in Europe had changed dramatically. In June 1941, Hitler launched a massive invasion of Russia. The attack sprang from various motives, including Hitler's decision not to (and probably, inability to) invade England. Russia, a potential British ally, seemed a more tempting target, in part because of its oil fields in the region around the Caspian Sea.

On the other side of the globe, Japan's threat loomed larger as 1940 gave way to 1941. Japan's immediate problem was its stalled invasion of China, a campaign that had become a symbolic national commitment to the Japanese. In June 1940, the Japanese occupied northern Indochina (a French colony, then administered by the Vichy French regime), in part to cut off supplies destined for the Chinese.

FRIENDS: FDR AND CHURCHILL

On August 8, 1941, President Franklin D. Roosevelt welcomed Winston Churchill, prime minister of Great Britain, aboard the USS *Augusta*, which was anchored in Placentia Bay in Newfoundland. Both the president and the prime minister had looked forward to their first meeting since they had begun corresponding in September 1939, when World War II began. At that time, Churchill was First Lord of the Admiralty (head of the British navy), his second stint at the post. The correspondence flowed more frequently after Churchill became head of the British government in June 1940. By the time FDR died in 1945, Churchill had received 800 messages from Roosevelt and sent him 1,200, most signed "former naval person." Churchill knew of Roosevelt's keen interest in naval matters, an outlook the president had cultivated when he served as assistant secretary of the U.S. Navy during World War I, and from his recreational sailing.

Churchill was anxious about how he would get along with the president at their first meeting. The conference in Newfoundland was hardly a social call. Cultivating FDR's friendship and support was vital to the survival of Britain, in Churchill's view. He had badgered the president for aid virtually from the moment he became head of the British government, which at the time faced imminent invasion from Germany. It was Churchill's frantic pleas to Roosevelt that motivated the trade of 50 aging American destroyers to Britain in exchange for the use of naval installations in the Americas, including Argentia on Placentia Bay, Newfoundland, in September 1940. As Britain's crisis worsened from Nazi submarine and air attacks, Churchill became relentless in requesting American help, both of materials and, if he could get it, active American participation in the fight against Hitler. FDR was determined to provide the war supplies, despite loud political opposition at home to entering the war. Roosevelt's push for the Lend Lease Act (March 1941) testifies to his commitment to Britain's survival. Nonetheless,

In September, Japan signed a mutual defense pact with Germany and Italy. Many Americans, prompted by the administration, interpreted the agreement as confirmation of a fascist plan to dominate the globe. Once Russia entered the war against Germany, Roosevelt and Churchill committed aid to the Chinese resistance, in part to he turned down Churchill's request for a joint military venture against Hitler. The president said he "would wage war, but not declare it."

But the meeting in Newfoundland did produce important results. Roosevelt and Churchill issued a statement known as the Atlantic Charter, which articulated broad mutual goals, including "the final destruction of the Nazi tyranny" and the establishment of an international organization in the postwar world. Second, the military chiefs of both countries conferred, which began a personal relationship between the army and naval leaders of each nation. Perhaps most significant for the successful prosecution of the war, Roosevelt and Churchill began a friendship that lasted until the president's death in 1945. On his return to Washington, Roosevelt told his cabinet that he liked Churchill, and the prime minister sent a cable to the king of England, writing, "I have established with the President the most cordial personal relations."

Roosevelt and Churchill met 10 more times during the course of the war, including the prime minister's visit to the United States during the Christmas season of 1941. The president and the prime minister were together at five wartime conferences overseas. The first took place at Casablanca in January 1943. They met again at Cairo in November and once more in December 1943, sandwiched around a conference with Joseph Stalin, Russia's leader, in Tehran, Iran. Their final meeting took place at Yalta in February 1945, where Stalin was also present. While friends, Roosevelt and Churchill did not agree on all matters concerning the war. Roosevelt's decision to launch a frontal attack on Germany, the plan pushed by his chief military adviser, George C. Marshall, and demanded by Joseph Stalin, came over Churchill's objection. They did not see eye-to-eye on the details of strategy and war administration, but they both were fully committed to the defeat of Adolf Hitler. This shared vision coupled with their mutual fondness formed the foundation of a fruitful partnership that was critical to winning World War II.

block a possible Japanese thrust at Russia. The United States began to embargo critical materials, especially oil, to Japan in June 1940 and intensified this economic pressure when Japan refused to withdraw its forces from China. Prior to the embargo, 80 percent of Japan's oil came from the United States.

Faced with the prospect of a war without end and a diminishing supply of fuel for its military, the Japanese set their sights on capturing oil-rich islands in the Dutch East Indies (present-day Indonesia). Calculating that the United States would aid the British and Dutch if their Pacific colonies were attacked, Japan launched a preemptive strike at the American Pacific naval fleet anchored at Pearl Harbor, Hawaii, on December 7, 1941. The Japanese knew that they could not survive a long war with the United States and gambled that the United States would soon be fighting Germany. Reasoning that the Americans would be preoccupied with war in Europe, the Japanese hoped to hold out until they could negotiate an armistice with the Allies. It was an act of desperation, without much consideration of the long-run consequences. The day after the Pearl Harbor attack, the United States declared war on Japan. Germany declared war on the United States three days later; Hitler's action arose in part from his hope that the Japanese would come to his aid by attacking Russia. They did not.

THE DEBATE

The Argument that Germany Threatened the United States

At the Munich Conference in 1938, the British and French had agreed to Hitler's demand to annex a portion of Czechoslovakia. The concession was called "appeasement." The concession—and Hitler's broken pledge not to grab more territory—convinced President Roosevelt that Germany posed a threat to the United States. Even if Hitler did not actually attack the Western Hemisphere, FDR viewed the prospect of a German-dominated Europe as detrimental to American interests. In the president's opinion, the "Axis Powers [Germany, Italy, Japan] constituted a threat to democratic nations everywhere." But it was only in 1940 that the president began to articulate this conviction publicly. His message encountered numerous skeptics in Congress and among the general public.

The president's first priority after war broke out in September 1939 was to revise the Neutrality Acts in order to allow the sale of arms and munitions to friendly countries at war. The intent was to aid Britain and France, although Roosevelt did not say this publicly at the time. Rather, he encouraged groups of citizen lobbyists to argue the soundness of the policy. William Allen White, a well-respected newspaper editor from Kansas, rallied supporters with a publicity blitz to combat isolationist opposition to Roosevelt's "cash and carry" amendment to the Neutrality Act, adopted in November 1939. White continued his support of the president after the enactment by spearheading the formation of the Committee to Defend America by Aiding the Allies (CDAAA) in May 1940. Leaders of the organization consulted officials in the White House and composed their messages to closely mirror the administration's line. The CDAAA's statement of November 20, 1940, claimed that the defeat of Britain would leave the United States exposed to "the forces of despotism which seek to dominate the world." (See "Statement of the Committee to Defend America by Aiding the Allies, November 20, 1940," on page 227 in the Primary Sources section.) "Sooner or later . . . war inevitably would come to this hemisphere." The CDAAA called the struggle against European fascists a moral issue; Hitler and his minions threatened "the fate of human freedom, the freedom of thought, of religion, of individual initiative."

The CDAAA's program emphasized increased arms production. So did the president, who proposed a major increase of military expenditures on May 16, 1940. The imbalance between the United States' military capability compared with that of Germany and Japan was enormous. Germany possessed an army of 2.75 million in mid-1939, while the United States had only nine divisions numbering about 130,000 men. Germany greatly out-produced American aircraft output. Fascinated by aeronautics and the possibilities of flight, Roosevelt called for the manufacture of 50,000 airplanes a year, with special priority given to long-range bombers. The figure stunned observers, given that only 2,141 aircraft had been built in the United States the previous year. Roosevelt justified his proposal by arguing that "New powers of destruction, incredibly swift and deadly, have been developed; and those who wield them are ruthless and daring." He noted that the oceans were no longer adequate barriers of defense. To accentuate the point, Roosevelt stated that the flying time from Greenland to Newfoundland was four hours; six hours more put a plane over New England. Only 2,000 miles separated the Azores off the coast of Africa from the eastern coast of South America; an additional 200 minutes of flight would take a plane from a base in the West Indies to Florida.

The president's concern about the capabilities of long-range aircraft was based on first-hand knowledge. Roosevelt was keenly aware of developments in aviation and particularly in transatlantic flight. (See the sidebar "Pan Am and Overseas Flight" below.) In summer 1939, the U.S. Army Air Force began secret discussions about developing a four-engine airplane capable of carrying a 20,000-pound load of

PAN AM AND OVERSEAS FLIGHT

Pan American World Airways made its first international flight on October 19, 1927, flying from Key West, Florida, to Havana, Cuba. Juan Tripp (1899–1981) organized the company early in the year, in part to take advantage of a government contract to carry U.S. mail. Encouraged by the U.S. Post Office, which sought to promote commercial aviation and stimulate scheduled flights to the Caribbean, and engaging the expertise of the famed aviator Charles Lindbergh, who joined the company as a technical adviser, Tripp made Pan Am into the first international air carrier. Shortly after Lindbergh flew a twin-engine plane to Panama in 1929, Pan Am won the postal service contracts to carry mail to South America. In 1932, the company signed a deal with the Sikorsky Company to build a four-engine "flying boat," an amphibious aircraft capable of transoceanic flight. The following year, a flying boat crossed the Pacific to the Philippine Islands, stopping at Hawaii, Wake Island, and Guam. In 1933, Tripp visited President Franklin Roosevelt, who was fascinated by the Pam Am chairman's maps and charts. The company initiated regular service to Asia in 1935.

Most of Pam Am's flying boats took off for the Caribbean and Latin America during the 1930s, when Pan Am was the world's biggest airline. Lindbergh scouted out routes and landing fields for the company and recommended plane designs, including proposals from manufacturers in 1936 for aircraft that could carry 100 people at 200 miles per hour for 5,000 miles or more. Aircraft of these dimensions could fly to Europe, the next destination on Tripp's agenda. The Europeans led the establishment of transatlantic flight. In 1936, the Germans investigated the possibility of flying from Europe and Africa to South America and initiated commercial flights to the United States with a dirigible (blimp), the *Hindenburg*. The disastrous explosion of the hydrogen-filled airship in 1937 as it approached the landing field in New Jersey destroyed the industry. Tripp contracted with Boeing to build a huge bombs 6,000 miles. These plans developed into the B-29, which flew a test flight in September 1942. Less than a year later, the first production model rolled out of a factory in Wichita, Kansas. On August 6, 1945, a B-29 "Superfortress" made a six-and-one-half hour trip from the island of Tinian in the South Pacific to Hiroshima, Japan, where the flight crew dropped an atomic bomb. Hitler possessed no similar

flying boat, complete with toilets and sleeping berths, to make transatlantic flights.

Pan Am commenced scheduled transatlantic passenger service in June 1939. A round-trip ticket to Europe via the Azores aboard the "Dixie Clipper" cost $675. Later in the year, Pan Am began flying a "Yankee Clipper" along the northern "great-circle" route via Newfoundland and Iceland to England. The United States' Neutrality Act, which prohibited flights to countries at war, stopped commercial flights to Europe in September 1939. The war was not, however, the principle reason that the days of the flying boats were numbered. They could not take off in choppy seas, and they could not fly above bad weather. Clippers soon gave way to aircraft with pressurized cabins, which could fly over storms and land on firm ground. In 1940, Pan Am contracted with Lockheed for 40 four-engine aircraft designed for high-altitude flight and runway landings. America's entrance into World War II forced cancellation of the contract.

The war, nonetheless, stimulated transatlantic air travel. Pan-Am built airfields in Africa to help get supplies to the British and in South America. The company flew war supplies to the Sudanese city of Khartoum. British prime minister Winston Churchill returned from his visit with President Roosevelt in January 1942 on a Boeing flying boat that stopped in Bermuda before completing the trip to England. All told, Pan-Am made 15,000 crossings during the war, some of them commercial. New companies emerged, including Trans World Airlines (TWA) and American Airlines. TWA flew a Douglas DC-4 aircraft across the Atlantic in 1942; American Airlines logged many transatlantic flights during the war. Americans piloted thousands of U.S.-built bombers to England during the war. The postwar era saw transatlantic flight blossom, with Pan Am among the leaders. The deregulation of air traffic in the 1970s put Pan Am under severe competitive pressure. The company went out of business in 1991, 10 years after Tripp's death.

long-range bomber capability in 1940 (although whether American officials fully understood this limitation is questionable). But Germany was a leader in industrial technology, so it does not take much imagination to presume that Hitler's war machine could have developed aircraft capable of intercontinental flight.

A second factor prompted the president to weigh the security threat posed by long-range aircraft. Hitler's conquests of Denmark and France opened up the possibility that Germany could use the colonies of the conquered nations, particularly Denmark's Greenland and French West Africa, as staging areas to attack the Americas. Enemy occupation of Greenland could put bombers within striking distance of the northeastern United States. The Africa-to-Brazil route especially worried military leaders, such as General George Marshall, chief of staff of the U.S. Army. The flying distance from Dakar (in Senegal) in French West Africa (under Vichy French control) to Natal on the coast of Brazil was 1,875 miles. Marshall worried that a weak Brazilian leader would partner with Germany or be overrun by German and Italian settlers in Brazil and neighboring Argentina. France also had Caribbean colonies. A German foothold in South America would put the Panama Canal in danger.

Operational in late 1943, B-29 bombers pounded Japan and were used to drop two atomic weapons on the island nation. (Keystone/Getty Images)

As Britain's position became more desperate, Roosevelt resolved to increase American aid to the embattled island, proposing a Lend-Lease program to manage the transfer. Because the proposal to assist a country at war was guaranteed to raise protests, the president carefully laid out a game plan to generate support. One step was to encourage William Allen White to form the CDAAA. A second step was to speak directly to Americans on the radio in a "fireside chat," a forum in which the president excelled. (See "President Franklin D. Roosevelt, 'Arsenal of Democracy' Fireside Chat, December 29, 1940," on page 229 in the Primary Sources section.) "The Nazi masters of Germany," he intoned on December 29, 1940, seek to "enslave the whole of Europe and then . . . to dominate the rest of the world." If this was Hitler's intention and if he had the capacity to pull it off, Americans should understandably be frightened. The linchpin of this process would be the defeat of Great Britain, which would allow the Axis to control Europe and thus much of Asia, Africa, Australia, and the oceans. Then Hitler would look to America. "It is no exaggeration to say that all of us," the president continued, "would be living at the point of a gun." The United States must become "the great arsenal of democracy" to keep Great Britain afloat.

Lend-Lease passed, but not before a knock-down, drag-out fight in Congress. A concession to its enactment was a provision that forbade the use of the U.S. Navy to convoy cargo vessels. This restriction irritated Roosevelt, who chafed when German submarines sent American aid aboard British ships to the bottom of the North Atlantic. He looked for "incidents" to ratchet up American protection of American goods. The sinking of the *Robin Moor*, an American merchant ship, in the South Atlantic in May 1941 afforded FDR an excuse to declare an Unlimited National Emergency. In his radio address explaining his action, the president went further in his warning about the safety of Americans from the Axis Powers. (See "President Franklin D. Roosevelt, Proclamation of Unlimited National Emergency, May 27, 1941," on page 230 in the Primary Sources section.) He repeated his belief that the Axis sought "world domination" and that only Britain stood in the way of Nazi invasion of the Americas. "Nobody can foretell tonight just when the acts of the dictators will ripen into attack on this hemisphere," but "it would be suicide," Roosevelt added, "to wait until they are in our front yard." He repeated his belief that new technologies of warfare had pushed America's defense perimeters further beyond America's shorelines. In view of the "sudden striking force of modern war," FDR named Nova Scotia, Brazil, and Trinidad as locations that now took on strategic importance to America's security. These places were a hop, skip, and jump—by air—from the United States. Soon after the radio talk, he stationed American troops in Iceland.

Roosevelt wanted the U.S. Navy to offer active protection for British merchant ships. He used an incident in September 1941, when a German submarine allegedly fired on the U.S. destroyer *Greer* "without warning," as the occasion to order American naval vessels to "shoot-on-sight" at German raiders. (In reality, the *Greer* had been tracking a German sub and had dropped a depth charge on it.) "This attack on the *Greer*," Roosevelt said, was "one determined step toward a permanent world system based on force, on terror, and on murder." When you see a rattlesnake poised to strike, he warned, you do not wait for it to bite but you crush it first. "These Nazi submarines . . . are the rattlesnakes of the Atlantic." Another "incident" at sea in October spurred FDR to request authority to arm American merchant ships and send them into the war zone. Congress complied in November, permitting American cargo vessels to sail all the way to England.

The Argument that Germany Did Not Threaten the United States

Critics claimed that Roosevelt exaggerated the danger Germany posed to the United States. Opponents of Roosevelt's foreign policy sometimes are lumped together as "isolationists," but, in fact, they were a diverse group of people. Not all isolationists supported American disengagement from all foreign relations. A more apt term for FDR's critics during the Great Debate of 1940 and 1941 over Germany is *noninterventionists*. The point on which most agreed was that the United States should not intervene militarily in the war in Europe. Disagreements also existed over whether the United States should provide aid to Britain and how to do it. There was no disagreement over who was the star noninterventionist. It was Colonel Charles A. Lindbergh.

Lindbergh rivaled the president, movie stars, and famous athletes as an American idol in the 1930s. In the years between his historic transatlantic flight in 1927 and the outbreak of World War II, he was America's most revered hero. The tragic kidnapping of his first son in 1932 and the highly publicized trial of the alleged murderer accentuated his public persona. Along with his wife and the best-selling author, Anne Morrow, the couple's round-the-world flights were media sensations. Lindbergh abandoned the United States to live in Europe in the mid-1930s, largely to escape incessant media attention, or, more aptly put, prying gossip columnists and photographers. At the request of the U.S. Army, which respected his expertise as an aeronautics specialist and recognized his broad range of contacts in Europe, Lindbergh was asked to inspect the German Air Force in 1936 and 1937. He reported that Germany was ahead of other European nations in air capacity and would soon rival the United States if it failed to accelerate its aviation buildup. Lindbergh returned to the United States in early 1939. At the request of General Henry Arnold, commander of the U.S. Air Force (than part of the U.S. Army), Lindbergh returned to active duty as a colonel.

The outbreak of war in Europe stirred Lindbergh to enter the lime-light as an advocate of nonintervention. His first public statement on the war occurred in a radio address from Washington, D.C., on September

Charles Lindbergh, the famed aviator, became President Roosevelt's chief nemesis in the debate over aid to Great Britain in 1940 and 1941. (AFP/AFP/Getty Images)

15, 1939. For the next two years, Lindbergh was the top-billed opponent of involvement in the European war. In this two-year span, Lindbergh essentially made two arguments, one political in nature and one
concerning the technology of aviation and its link to military capacity.
Most listeners agreed that Lindbergh knew a lot about airplanes.

Delivering a radio address from Chicago in May 1940, Lindbergh
indicated that Germany was ahead in air power in Europe and that it
was possible to construct aircraft capable of crossing the Atlantic and
returning. (See "Charles Lindbergh, 'The Air Defense of America,' May
19, 1940," on page 232 in the Primary Sources section.) Yet neither factor
constituted an imminent threat to the United States, he argued, because
Germany currently had no long-range bombers, and they would be costly
to build. He also doubted that "great armies" could be flown across the
Atlantic—a project that exceeded Germany's capacity. Adequate defense
preparedness in the United States—a buildup of the army, navy, and air
units—would protect against an invading foe. In testimony to Congress
against Lend-Lease in January 1941, Lindbergh noted that Germany
could not even launch an invasion of England, which was only 21 miles
distant from the closest point in France. Lindbergh opposed Lend-Lease
because he thought it would weaken American defenses and might compromise America's neutrality. "No one wishes to attack us, and no one is
in a position to do so," he said in his May 1940 radio address. Lindbergh
was not thinking about Japan when he made this remark, in part because
Roosevelt worked assiduously to keep policy toward Japan out of public view. The debate between the noninterventionists and Roosevelt was
over an alliance with Great Britain.

The America First Committee opposed a partnership with Great
Britain. This organization formed in September 1940 in the wake of
the president's destroyer-base deal with Churchill and as Congress
debated the Selective Service bill. By December 1941, the group had
450 chapters and nearly a million members. Its statement of principles
was short and direct: Stay out of the "foreign wars." (See "America First
Committee, Principles, 1941," on page 233 in the Primary Sources section.) The United States should keep its navy and merchant ships out
of the war zone, build up defenses at home, and hold a national referendum on the question of peace or war. The America First Committee
made several invitations to Lindbergh, the nation's most recognized
noninterventionist, to join the group. In April 1941, Lindbergh

accepted, becoming the committee's headline speaker. Lindbergh saw the European war as a power struggle among traditional enemies that should be ended by a negotiated settlement. Neither Britain nor Germany has "a monopoly of right," he said. Continuation of the war in Europe threatened to weaken Western civilization and possibly could lead to "racial suicide." He was referring to Europeans, who needed to join collectively, including a strong Germany, to counter emerging threats from the "Asiatic hordes" and "the Mongol, Persian and Moor." Communism, he charged, constituted an even greater danger. The European quarrel would divert attention from opposing the Leninist-Stalinist regime in Russia, which Lindbergh considered a more serious peril than Nazi Germany.

As Roosevelt edged the United States closer to outright military partnership with Britain, Lindbergh became less restrained in his remarks. In a speech in September 1941, Lindbergh named three groups leading the chorus for intervention in the war: the Roosevelt administration, the British, and American Jews. Pointing to the last group was widely viewed as anti-Semitic. The remark brought such a tidal wave of repudiation that Lindbergh resigned from the America First Committee. Lindbergh had already lost a good deal of credibility because of administration charges that he was the "No. 1 Nazi fellow traveler."

Some advocates of nonintervention argued from premises quite different from Lindbergh's position. Robert M. Hutchins, president of the University of Chicago, criticized Roosevelt's course of action in an NBC radio address in January 1941, as Congress was debating the Lend-Lease bill. Hutchins questioned a string of assumptions that the president attached to the adoption of Lend-Lease: that Britain would be defeated without U.S. aid, that the totalitarian rulers would survive, that their regimes would attack the United States, and that they had the capacity to do so. (See "Robert M. Hutchins, 'America and the War,' January 23, 1941," on page 233 in the Primary Sources section.) In a devastating critique of Roosevelt's Wilsonian appeal to defend democracy around the world, Hutchins contended that the freedom of speech and worship and from want and fear were not adequately honored at home. He pointed to the harassment of labor radicals and black sharecroppers, the denial of the franchise to African Americans, the widespread poverty of American families, and corruption in government. In short, Hutchins saw more pressing problems right here at home.

OUTCOME AND IMPACT

The debate over intervention was a bitter, no-holds-barred political brawl that lasted two years. Roosevelt was infuriated by Lindbergh's antiintervention radio talks. The president permitted his officials, especially Secretary of the Interior Harold Ickes, to attack Lindbergh's credibility. Ickes charged that Lindbergh failed to condemn Hitler's suppression of free speech and brutality toward dissenters and Jews. FDR ordered the Federal Communications Commission to track how much time radio stations extended to America First activities. During the presidential campaign of 1940, the FBI investigated German support for isolationist activities in the United States. In turn, Lindbergh took the president to task for allegedly using the war as a justification to restrict congressional power and seize dictatorial procedures.

In the end, Roosevelt triumphed over Lindbergh. As the debate unfolded from 1940 into 1941, the interventionists grew stronger, and isolationist support eroded. Polls showed that a majority of the public supported the president's "aid short-of-war" position in 1941, despite opposition to full intervention in the war. After December 7, 1941, the day the Japanese attacked the United States at Pearl Harbor, virtually the entire nation stood behind the president, who asked Congress to declare war on Germany and Italy as well as Japan. Lindbergh had resigned from the air force when he launched his speaking campaign against intervention. With the war on, he wanted to rejoin the force, but FDR blocked his reinstatement. Lindbergh did see combat against Japan in the Pacific as a civilian in an auxiliary role with the air force.

Two major decisions guided American strategy during the war. The first gave Europe priority over Japan, and the second was to launch a frontal attack on Germany on the European continent. Mindful of the slaughter in the trenches during World War I, Churchill opposed a direct assault on Germany. Soviet leader Joseph Stalin pressed the western Allies to open a major second front in western Europe to divert some of the German fury being unleashed on Russia. George Marshall and Dwight D. Eisenhower, who was given command of Allied forces in Europe, grudgingly supported Churchill's plan to force the Germans from North Africa in 1942 and then invade Italy, but both generals resisted a premature assault on Germany. The United States was not ready to launch a land invasion in France until spring 1944. On June 6, 1944, D-Day, the Allies stormed the beaches of France. Then they closed in on Germany from the west, while the Russian army advanced from the east, eventually entering Berlin in 1945. Eisenhower wisely kept Allied troops out of the final assault on the Nazi capital, where house-to-house fighting took place.

Although the Pacific theater was a secondary priority, the United States mounted a military effort that pushed Japan to near defeat by May 1945, when Germany surrendered. The combination of naval, air, and marine forces methodically reduced the Japanese defense perimeter on the islands of the South Pacific. U.S. air and submarine attacks had virtually shut off oil to Japan by 1945, leaving the island largely defenseless against relentless American firebombing of its cities. Japan surrendered after the United States dropped a second atomic bomb on August 9, 1945.

The two atomic bomb explosions that nearly eradicated two major Japanese cities symbolized the scale of death and destruction of World War II. Perhaps 50 million died from war activity, more than half of them civilians. Axis forces slaughtered much of the European Jewish population and millions of Slavs, gypsies, communists, and anti-German "partisans." The United States mounted no direct effort to intercede in these atrocities, nor did FDR criticize Stalin's ruthlessness toward his political opponents in Russia. The war left most of the industrial world in ruins, with the United States a fortunate exception. General Eisenhower could hardly find words to describe the severity of destruction when he flew over Germany immediately after the war ended. In the Pacific, U.S. bombers had ignited infernos in all major Japanese cities, deliberately causing civilian casualties.

Nevertheless, World War II is remembered in the United States as the "good war." Most Americans in the 1940s saw World War II as a necessary conflict, thrust upon the nation by brutal, bloodthirsty foes. It was a war fought for noble objectives, successfully pursued. Roosevelt was instrumental in cultivating the "good war" motif, in part by exaggerating the unity among the Axis Powers and overstating their sinister intentions. No evidence has surfaced that Hitler had planned to invade the Western Hemisphere. The defense pact between Germany, Italy, and Japan was not a plan to "control" the world. Nevertheless, these nations were indeed led by dictators who were unpredictable and who had quashed civil liberties. With Allied support, the United States vanquished all three. In the process, the mobilization of industry and agriculture to fight the war had accelerated the American economy back to health. In addition, Roosevelt took the lead in setting up the United Nations, designed in hopes that a world forum could lessen international tensions. All in all, most Americans viewed the war as a noble enterprise.

WHAT IF?

The story of World War II is extremely complex, involving six major nations and many smaller countries engaged in a conflict spread over four continents fighting an air, navy, land, and diplomatic war that also included various civil "partisan" fighters. The European phase of the conflict lasted nearly six years. Numerous crucial decisions influenced the way this saga unfolded. One key call was Hitler's decision to declare war on the United States after the attack on Pearl Harbor. The terms of Germany's defense pact with Japan did not require Hitler's intervention. The dictator gambled that Japan would return the favor by attacking Russia, thereby contributing to the German effort to defeat Russia. Japan, however, did not join the war against Russia. Nor did Russia, America's erstwhile ally in the fight against Germany, attack Japan (although Stalin did declare war on the island nation after the first atomic explosion). What if Hitler had not declared war on the United States?

Had Hitler exercised greater restraint, the possibility of a negotiated settlement to the war exists, perhaps along the lines that Lindbergh envisioned. This outcome requires that Russia would have survived the German attack without an Allied invasion of France. There is evidence this would have been the case. A second requirement for this scenario to unfold is the survival of Britain. Great Britain was able to hold on, of course, partially on the strength of American aid. Hitler had been cautious not to become too aggressive in the naval war in the North Atlantic. Perhaps a continuation of this undeclared conflict at sea, a stalemate of sorts, would have disposed Hitler to seek an armistice. This counterfactual speculation hinges in part on Hitler's drive into Russia. Had he foregone this route and struck at the Middle East—and British control of Arabian oil concessions—the story could have been much different.

Had Hitler kept his army out of Russia, Japan may not have acted as aggressively as it did. But Hitler did attack Russia, and Japan did expand its invasion of China and move into Indo-China. What if the Roosevelt administration had not demanded that Japan abandon its military campaign in China? Even more pertinent, what if Roosevelt had not embargoed oil to Japan? The Roosevelt administration knew that placing a stranglehold on petroleum products to Japan was liable to cause war. It was this pressure that led critics to charge that Roosevelt deliberately maneuvered Japan into attacking the United States. The evidence does not support this accusation, yet Roosevelt's heavy-handedness toward Japan is hard to explain. Needless to say, the actions of the dictators played into the hands of the administration. Roosevelt wanted to contain the dictators but felt politically unable to extract a war decision from Congress unless the United States was attacked first. The dictators in Japan and Germany had acted in decisive ways that settled the great debate in favor of the interventionists.

CHRONOLOGY

1933   *March:* Franklin Roosevelt is inaugurated president.
Adolf Hitler takes power in Germany.

1935   Congress passes Neutrality Act.
Congress passes second Neutrality Act.
Japan invades China.

1938   *March:* Germany annexes Austria.
September: Munich Conference

1939   *March:* Hitler invades Czechoslovakia.
August: Germany and Russia sign nonaggression pact.
September 1: Germany invades Poland.
September 3: Britain and France declare war against Germany.
November 4: Congress passes "Cash and Carry" revision of the Neutrality Act.

1940   *May 10:* Winston Churchill becomes British prime minister.
June: Germany invades France.
September 3: United States and Britain agree to destroyer-base deal.
September 4: America First Committee forms.
September 27: Germany and Japan form mutual defense pact.
November 6: Roosevelt wins reelection as president.

1941   *March 11:* Congress passes Lend Lease Act.
May 27: Roosevelt declares Unlimited National Emergency.
June 22: Germany invades Russia.
July: Japan invades Indochina.
August 14: Roosevelt and Churchill issue the Atlantic Charter.
September 11: Roosevelt issues "shoot-on-sight" orders for enemy raiders.
December 7: Japanese attack Pearl Harbor.

1942   Allies attack Germans in North Africa.

1944   *June 6:* D-Day Allies invade France.
1945   *April 12:* Roosevelt dies; Truman becomes president.
         May 7: Germany surrenders.
         August 6: United States drops atomic bomb on Hiroshima, Japan.
         August 14: Japan surrenders.

DISCUSSION QUESTIONS

1. To what extent did technological advances contribute to the debate over German threats to American security?
2. President Franklin Roosevelt never encouraged a broad and general debate in American society about how the war in Europe represented a threat to the national interests of the United States. Was he wrong in stifling this discussion?
3. Did the Roosevelt administration overact in its attempt to discredit Charles Lindbergh during the debate over intervention in the war?
4. One could argue that the very complexity of the international situation from 1939 to 1941, in which numerous players existed and conditions changed over time, contributed to the Great Debate in America on policy toward the world and whether the United States should openly ally with Great Britain. Discuss the reasoning and circumstances that support such a thesis.

WEB SITES

"America from the Great Depression to World War II: Photographs from the FSA and OWI" [images from the Farm Security Administration and the Office of War Information]. Available at http://memory.loc.gov/ammem/fsowhome.html.

"American Political History On-Line." See FDR-Lindbergh and America First; World War II Resources. Available at http://tigger.uic.edu/~jensen/pol-gl.htm.

"A People at War" [National Archive exhibit of Americans' contributions to the war effort]. Available at http://www.archives.gov/exhibit_hall/a_people_at_war/a_people_at_war.html.

"World War II on the Web." See 1941; Air Power. Available at http://tigger.uic.edu/~jensen/military.html #k.

BIBLIOGRAPHY

Berg, A. Scott. *Lindbergh.* New York: G. P. Putnam Sons, 1998.

Burns, James MacGregor. *Roosevelt: The Soldier of Freedom.* San Diego: Harcourt, Brace, Jovanovich, 1970.

Cole, Wayne S. *Charles Lindbergh and the Battle against American Intervention in World War II.* New York: Harcourt, Brace, Jovanovich, 1974.

———. *Roosevelt and the Isolationists, 1932–1945.* Lincoln: University of Nebraska Press, 1983.

Churchill, Winston. *The Grand Alliance.* Boston: Houghton Mifflin, 1950.

Davis, Kenneth S. *FDR: The War President, 1940–1943.* New York: Random House, 2000.

Keegan, John. "How Hitler Could Have Won the War." In *What If? The World's Foremost Military Historians Imagine What Might Have Been,* edited by Robert Cowley. New York: G. P. Putnam's Sons, 1999.

Kennedy, David M. *Freedom from Fear: The American People in Depression and War, 1929–1945.* New York: Oxford University Press, 1999.

Lash, Joseph P. *Roosevelt and Churchill, 1939–1941: The Partnership that Saved the West.* New York: W. W. Norton, 1976.

Russett, Bruce M. *No Clear and Present Danger: A Skeptical View of the United States Entry into World War II.* New York: Harper and Row, 1972.

Solberg, Carl. *Conquest of the Skies: A History of Commercial Aviation in America.* Boston: Little, Brown, 1979.

PRIMARY SOURCES

1. Statement of the Committee to Defend America by Aiding the Allies, November 20, 1940

The Committee to Defend America by Aiding the Allies advocated a policy closely parallel to the position of the Roosevelt administration that aid to Great Britain was critical to the security of the United States. In a statement issued on November 20, 1940, the committee opposed "appeasement" of Hitler's territorial demands and greater power of the president to act in the defense of the country.

Defeat of Britain and her allies would leave the United States alone, confronted with a totalitarian world which not only scorns our freedom and is greedy for our wealth but would not leave us free to maintain our way of life and our institutions. Sooner or later, with Britain defeated, war inevitably would come to this hemisphere.

The war which Britain is now waging looms larger than a national issue for empire advantage; it is a moral issue of world import to civilization itself. The fate of human freedom, freedom of thought, of religion, of individual initiative, is dependent upon victory of Britain and her allies.

Also we say regretfully that no one can guarantee that the United States can avoid active military involvement. But one thing is certain; the only chance of avoiding war is by giving all material assistance to Great Britain and her allies immediately.

In addition to previous suggestions the committee urges the following steps to increase aid to the Allies:

1. Aid to the Allies and American defense, which are parts of the same problem, can only be accomplished by very greatly increased American arms production. The battle for civilization and democracy may be won or lost on the American assembly line.

2. The life line between Great Britain and the United States is the sea route to the Western Hemisphere. Under no circumstances must this line be cut and the United States must be prepared to maintain it. The United States should supply Great Britain with all possible merchant vessels to fly the British flag. The United States should produce boats as rapidly as in the World War days, for lease or rent to the British. . . .

3. The time has come when Congress should assume a larger share of responsibility, with the President, for the policy of aid to the Allies. Consequently, we favor . . . a repeal or modification of restrictive statutes which hamper this nation in its freedom of action when it would cooperate with nations defending themselves from attack by nations at war in violation of treaties of the United States. . . .

Source: Committee to Defend America Papers, Princeton University Library, Princeton, N.J.

2. President Franklin D. Roosevelt, "Arsenal of Democracy" Fireside Chat, December 29, 1940

In one of his most famous "fireside chats" on the radio, President Frank-lin D. Roosevelt outlined to the nation on December 29, 1940, why he thought that Britain's ability to defeat the Nazi threat was fundamental to the defense of the United States. The president said that "we must be the great arsenal of democracy."

My friends:

This is not a fireside chat on war. It is a talk on national security; because the nub of the whole purpose of your President is to keep you now, and your children later, and your grandchildren much later, out of a last-ditch war for the preservation of American independence. . . .

We face this new crisis—this new threat to the security of our nation—with the same courage and realism.

Does anyone seriously believe that we need to fear attack anywhere in the Americas while a free Britain remains our most powerful naval neighbor in the Atlantic? Does anyone seriously believe, on the other hand, that we could rest easy if the Axis powers were our neighbors there?

If Great Britain goes down, the Axis powers will control the conti-nents of Europe, Asia, Africa, Australasia, and the high seas—and they will be in a position to bring enormous military and naval resources against this hemisphere. It is no exaggeration to say that all of us, in all the Americas, would be living at the point of a gun—a gun loaded with explosive bullets, economic as well as military.

We should enter upon a new and terrible era in which the whole world, our hemisphere included, would be run by threats of brute force. To survive in such a world, we would have to convert ourselves perma-nently into a militaristic power on the basis of war economy.

Some of us like to believe that even if Great Britain falls, we are still safe, because of the broad expanse of the Atlantic and of the Pacific.

But the width of those oceans is not what it was in the days of clipper ships. At one point between Africa and Brazil the distance is less than from Washington to Denver, Colorado-five hours for the latest type of bomber. And at the North end of the Pacific Ocean America and Asia almost touch each other.

Even today we have planes that could fly from the British Isles to New England and back again without refueling. And remember that the range of the modern bomber is ever being increased.

The people of Europe who are defending themselves do not ask us to do their fighting. They ask us for the implements of war, the planes, the tanks, the guns, the freighters which will enable them to fight for their liberty and for our security. Emphatically we must get these weapons to them in sufficient volume and quickly enough, so that we and our children will be saved the agony and suffering of war which others have had to endure.

In a military sense Great Britain and the British Empire are today the spearhead of resistance to world conquest. They are putting up a fight which will live forever in the story of human gallantry.

I want to make it clear that it is the purpose of the nation to build now with all possible speed every machine, every arsenal, every factory that we need to manufacture our defense material.

We must be the great arsenal of democracy.

Source: Samuel I. Rosenman, comp., *The Public Papers and Addresses of Franklin D. Roosevelt.* Vol. 9. New York: Macmillan, 1938–1950, 633–636, 640, 643.

—⁂—

3. President Franklin D. Roosevelt, Proclamation of Unlimited National Emergency, May 27, 1941

In a radio broadcast from the White House on May 27, 1941, President Franklin D. Roosevelt issued one of his most comprehensive statements about the nature of the German threat to the United States. Referring to the geography of the Atlantic community and new technologies, the president warned about the potential of a sudden German surprise attack on the United States.

The Axis Powers can never achieve their objective of world domination unless they first obtain control of the seas. This is their supreme purpose today; and to achieve it, they must capture Great Britain.

They could then have the power to dictate to the Western Hemisphere. No spurious argument, no appeal to sentiment, and no false pledges like those given by Hitler at Munich, can deceive the American people into believing that he and his Axis partners would not, with Britain defeated, close in relentlessly on this hemisphere.

But if the Axis Powers fail to gain control of the seas, they are certainly defeated. Their dreams of world domination will then go by the board; and the criminal leaders who started this war will suffer inevitable disaster.

Both they and their people know this—and they are afraid. That is why they are risking everything they have, conducting desperate attempts to break through to the command of the ocean. Once they are limited to a continuing land war, their cruel forces of occupation will be unable to keep their heel on the necks of the millions of innocent, oppressed peoples on the Continent of Europe; and in the end, their whole structure will break into little pieces. And the wider the Nazi land effort, the greater the danger. . . .

Attacks on shipping off the very shores of land which we are determined to protect, present an actual military danger to the Americas. And that danger has recently been heavily underlined by the presence in Western Hemisphere waters of Nazi battleships of great striking power.

I have said on many occasions that the United States is mustering its men and its resources only for purposes of defense—only to repel attack. I repeat that statement now. But we must be realistic when we use the word "attack"; we have to relate it to the lightning speed of modern warfare.

Some people seem to think that we are not attacked until bombs actually drop on New York or San Francisco or New Orleans or Chicago. But they are simply shutting their eyes to the lesson we must learn from the fate of every nation that the Nazis have conquered. . . .

Nobody can foretell tonight just when the acts of the dictators will ripen into attack on this hemisphere and us. But we know enough by now to realize that it would be suicide to wait until they are in our front yard.

When your enemy comes at you in a tank or a bombing plane, if you hold your fire until you see the whites of his eyes, you will never know what hit you. Our Bunker Hill of tomorrow may be several thousand miles from Boston.

Source: Samuel I. Rosenman, comp., *The Public Papers and Addresses of Franklin D. Roosevelt,* vol. 10. New York: Macmillan, 1938–1950, 185–186, 188–189.

—⁓—

4. Charles Lindbergh, "The Air Defense of America," May 19, 1940

Charles Lindbergh, America's famous airman, rebutted President Roosevelt's argument that the German air force posed a significant threat to the United States. In this radio address from Chicago on May 19, 1940, he argued that it would take "whole armies" to endanger the United States, something that was beyond the capacity of Germany to undertake.

Let us not be confused by this talk of invasion by European Aircraft.

It is true that bombing planes can be built with sufficient range to cross the Atlantic and return. They can be built either in America or Europe. Aeronautical engineers have known this for many years. But the cost is high, the target large, and the military effectiveness small. Such planes do not exist today in any air force. A foreign power could not conquer us by dropping bombs in this country unless the bombing were accompanied by an invading army. And an invading army requires thousands of small bombers and pursuit planes; it would have little use for high trans-Atlantic aircraft.

No, the advantage lies with us, for great armies must still cross oceans by ship. Only relatively small forces can be transported by air today, and over distances of a few hundred miles at most. This has great significance in Europe, but it is not an element that we have to contend with in America. Such a danger can come, in any predictable future, only through division and war among our own peoples. As long as American nations work together [to] maintain reasonable defense forces, there will be no invasion by foreign air-craft. And no foreign navy will dare to approach within bombing range of our coasts.

Let us turn again to America's traditional role—that of building and guarding our own destiny. We need a greater air force, a greater army, and a greater navy; they have been inadequate for many years.

The only reason that we are in danger of becoming involved in this war is because there are powerful elements in America [urging] us to take part. They represent a small minority of the people, but they control much of the machinery of influence and propaganda. They seize every opportunity to push us closer to the edge.

Source: The Charles A. Lindbergh Papers, Yale University.

—⁓—

5. America First Committee, Principles, 1941

The America First Committee was the major organization combating President Roosevelt's policy that brought the United States into a de facto alliance with Great Britain. In 1941, the committee issued a set of principles, the first of which was to avoid "foreign wars."

Our first duty is to keep America out of foreign wars. Our entry would only destroy democracy, not save it. The path to war is a false path to freedom.

Not by acts of war abroad but by preserving and extending democracy at home can we aid democracy and freedom in other lands.

In 1917 we sent our American ships into the war zone and this led us to war. In 1941 we must keep our naval convoys and merchant vessels on this side of the Atlantic.

We must build a defense for our own shores so strong that no foreign power or combination of powers can invade our country by sea, air or land.

Humanitarian aid is the duty of a strong, free country at peace. With proper safeguard for the distribution of supplies we should feed and clothe the needy people of England and other occupied countries and so keep alive their hope for the return of better days.

The America First Committee advocates a National Advisory Referendum on the Question of Peace or War. (We exclude from our rolls Fascists, Nazis, Communists and members of subversive organizations.)

Source: America First Committee Principles, 1941. America First Committee Papers, Hoover Library on War, Revolution, and Peace. Stanford University, Palo Alto, Calif.

—⁓—

6. Robert M. Hutchins, "America and the War," January 23, 1941

On January 23, 1941, Robert Hutchins, the president of the University of Chicago, delivered a radio address on NBC offering a lengthy criticism of President Roosevelt's "aid short-of-war" policy. Hutchins questioned whether the Axis powers contemplated an attack on the Western Hemisphere or could mount one. America's first priority, he declared, should be to promote real democracy at home.

I speak tonight because I believe that the American people are about to commit suicide.

I wish to disassociate myself from all Nazis, Fascists, Communists and appeasers. I regard the doctrine of all totalitarian regimes as wrong in theory, evil in execution. . . .

The lease-lend bill contains provisions that we should regard as acts of war up to last week. The conclusion is inescapable that the President is reconciled to active military intervention. . . .

How can the United States better serve suffering humanity everywhere: by going into this war, or by staying out? I hold that the United States can better serve suffering humanity everywhere by staying out.

We have it on the highest authority that one-third of the nation is ill-fed, ill-clothed, and ill-housed. The latest figures of the National Resources Board show that almost precisely 55 percent of our people are living on family incomes of less than $1,250 a year. This sum, says *Fortune* magazine, will not support a family of four. On this basis more than half our people are living below the minimum level of subsistence. More than half the army which will defend democracy will be drawn from those who have had this experience of the economic benefits of "the American way of life."

We know that we have had till lately 9 million unemployed and that we should have them still if it were not for our military preparations. When our military preparations cease, we shall, for all we know, have 9 million unemployed again.

As for democracy, we know that millions of men and women are disfranchised in this country because of their race, color, or condition of economic servitude.

We have made some notable advances in the long march toward justice, freedom, and democracy.

If we go to war, we cast away our opportunity and cancel our gains.

What, then, should our policy be? . . . we should do everything we can to say at peace.

At the same time we should prepare to defend ourselves against military or political penetration.

Source: Robert Hutchins, "America and the War" radio address on NBC, Jan. 23, 1941. Reprinted by permission of the Special Collections Research Center, University of Chicago Library.

8

THE COLD WAR:
Did Russia Start the Cold War?

—∿—

THE CONTROVERSY

The Issue

Even before the fighting stopped in World War II, tensions between the United States and the Soviet Union (Russia) emerged. These suspicions between the world's two superpowers blossomed in 1946 and 1947 into a diplomatic standoff, which evolved into the cold war. President Harry Truman formally announced this new foreign challenge in a speech to Congress in March 1947. Did Russia start the cold war?

♦ ***Arguments that Russia started the cold war:*** President Truman's March 1947 speech blamed the Russians, without naming them explicitly, for seeking to export communism beyond their own borders. His speech to Congress outlined the Truman Doctrine, which stated that Western nations had a duty to defend their values from the advance of police-state totalitarianism. Truman aides fed the president ominous warnings about Soviet intentions.

♦ ***Arguments that Russia alone did not start the cold war:*** Most Americans were inclined to accept the president's outlook, but a few did not. Some, such as Henry Wallace, Truman's Secretary of Commerce, criticized his administration's hard line toward the Soviets, arguing that Truman's policy worsened relations with the Russians and disposed them to act defensively. Other observers pointed out that supposed Soviet aggressiveness was in reality Russian efforts to ensure their national security, not to export communism throughout the world. This point of view credited the United States with partial responsibility for starting the cold war.

—∿—

INTRODUCTION

On July 15, 1945, President Harry Truman arrived in Potsdam, a suburb of Berlin, Germany, for his first meeting with the leaders of Britain and the Soviet Union. The Allies' fight against Hitler and the Nazis had ended, yet critical issues remained to be resolved, including the future of Germany and Europe and the war against Japan. These were formidable challenges for Truman, who was new to the job as chief executive, which he had held for just three months. Previously a U.S. senator from Missouri, he had served as vice president for only 82 days until Franklin Roosevelt's death on April 12, 1945, elevated him to the presidency.

Now President Truman was about to meet Joseph Stalin, the dictator of Soviet Russia and one of the most powerful men in the world. Truman was nervous as he waited for Stalin, a man with years of practice in world affairs and a reputation for hard-nosed negotiations. Truman had no diplomatic experience. When the Russian leader eventually arrived at the president's suite, Truman was surprised to see that Stalin was only five feet, five inches tall. To his surprise, as well, he thought he could work with the tough-minded Russian ruler, especially after Stalin agreed to join the United States in the war against Japan, Truman's top priority in Potsdam.

While in Potsdam, the president got word that the tests of the first atomic bomb explosion had gone off successfully in New Mexico. Several days later, Truman consulted his advisers who had traveled with him to Germany, including Secretary of State James Byrnes and Army Chief of Staff George Marshall. They all agreed to use the bomb against Japan, and the president took their advice. Truman's reference to America's new superweapon in a conversation with Stalin did not surprise the Russian dictator. He probably knew more about the development of the A-bomb than Truman, who had not learned about the weapon until his 12th day as president.

Truman's hope that he could work amicably with Stalin faded quickly after Potsdam. By 1946, the president's optimistic tone changed to a resolution to "get tough with the Russians." Truman came to the conclusion that "the Russians were planning world conquest." This determination followed the advice of his closest counselors, most of whom he inherited from the Roosevelt administration. They urged steadfast opposition to what they saw as the Soviet Union's intent to spread communist regimes in Europe and elsewhere.

A revolt in Greece gave the president the opportunity to show his resolve. In a speech to Congress on March 12, 1947, the president told Congress of his decision to aid the Greek government, which was battling rebels that included communists. Truman described the conflict in

As much as any person, President Harry S. Truman shaped America's containment policy, aimed at blocking Soviet advances. (© Trinity Mirror/Mirrorpix/Alamy)

Greece in terms of a worldwide struggle that pitted the free world and western values against totalitarian rule and police-state tactics. Military aid to Greece, the president said, was necessary to block the advance of communism. Failure to act would allow communism to triumph in Greece and then spread to neighboring countries. The idea that communism was a contagion that needed to be contained became known as the Truman Doctrine. The president's March 12 speech dates the first major public announcement of the cold war, a diplomatic-political struggle between the Soviet Union and the United States that lasted until the late 1980s. During these years, the United States fought the Korean and Vietnam Wars but never directly engaged Soviets on the battlefield.

Who was responsible for starting this new conflict? Truman and his advisers had no doubt that the aggressive intentions of the Soviet Union caused it. Russia's behavior, especially its continued military occupation of Eastern Europe, its failure to withdraw its forces from Iran, and its pressure on Turkey for concessions, was seen as evidence of the Soviet plan to spread its influence and control. Several American officials helped to shape this viewpoint. George F. Kennan, the U.S. diplomatic attaché in Moscow, wrote an influential memo early in 1946 that warned of the consequences of Russia's "traditional and instinctive" sense of insecurity. The Soviet Union distrusted western regimes and would marshal its vast military power and skill at subversion to retain its world position. Former British prime minister Winston Churchill called on the United States to stop the advance of the communist "Iron Curtain" that had settled across Europe. Under-Secretary of State Dean Acheson argued that communism would spread if the United States did not block "Soviet penetration."

Most Americans accepted these analyses and assumed the worst from totalitarian Russia, whose leaders embraced communist ideology. A few Americans, however, criticized their government's harsh anti-Russian policy. Henry Wallace, U.S. Secretary of Commerce, argued that Soviet actions were rooted in historic fears of invasion and concerns about the country's shattered economy. America's hostility to the Soviets was bound to cause a breach in relations. The respected journalist Walter Lippmann thought that the global inclusiveness of Truman's containment policy was foolhardy and impossible to enforce. And Stalin stressed his concerns to U.S. officials over American efforts to undermine Russia's security, particularly in regard to the rebuilding of Germany, Soviet access to the Mediterranean Sea, and protection of its oil fields. Together, these criticisms put much of the blame on the United States for starting the cold war.

BACKGROUND

American cold war attitudes were rooted in earlier views of Russia and an antiradical tradition. Before 1917, Americans saw Russia as a backward land whose people were subjugated by a landed nobility and undemocratic czars. Elation over the country's democratic revolution in 1917 was quickly dashed by the Communist Revolution (1917–18), which installed the Bolshevik regime. Bolshevik communism was seen as the antithesis of capitalism and democracy, two core American beliefs. Repressive government under the Russian czars was replaced by a communist police state that repressed individualism. Intolerance for individual liberties included discrimination against religion, leading to charges that the Soviets were a threat to Christianity. Britain's Winston Churchill drew on these ideological assumptions in his "Iron Curtain" speech in 1946.

Events during and after World War I fed these older fears of communism. The United States had contributed troops to a British-French expedition in 1917 that aided opponents of the Bolsheviks in Russia. American soldiers remained in Russia until 1919. That was the year a "Red Scare" swept the United States. This political hysteria swirled around allegations that subversives and revolutionaries were loose in the land. A series of bombings, including one that destroyed part of the home of the U.S. attorney general, had triggered the alarm. In response, the Justice Department orchestrated a dragnet that arrested 6,000 suspected political radicals and deported 556 aliens to Russia. The crusade launched the career of J. Edgar Hoover, longtime head of the Federal Bureau of Investigation (FBI) and dedicated anticommunist. Lingering suspicion of the Russian Revolution is evidenced by the failure of the United States to extend diplomatic recognition to the Soviet Union until 1933. While fears of radicalism diminished in the mid-1930s, they revived later in the decade and once again in the late 1940s and 1950s.

During World War II, the United States and Russia had cooperated to defeat Germany and Italy. Relations between the Soviet Union's Stalin and Western leaders (primarily Roosevelt and Churchill), however, were tense and contentious. The key disagreement was the opening of a second military front against Germany. Hitler attacked Russia in June 1941 and by 1942 had taken vast areas of western Russia and killed millions of soldiers and civilians. As Russia struggled desperately to hold off the Nazi juggernaut, Stalin pleaded with British prime minister Winston Churchill and Roosevelt to relieve the pressure on Russia by launching a drive against Germany from the west. Churchill, an avowed anticommunist, was in no rush to help Russia. The Americans agreed to

Churchill's preference for a thrust at Germany from the Mediterranean region and then stalled for time in order to prepare adequately for an epic assault on German defenses, which began on June 6, 1944 (D-day), when the Allies stormed the beaches of northern France. Eventually, American, British, and Canadian forces pushed into Germany from France and the Low Countries. By this time, Stalin's forces had driven the Germans out of Russia and were moving into central Europe. On May 7, 1945, when Hitler's military surrendered, both Soviet and western Allied forces occupied Germany. Soviet troops remained in eastern European countries, including Poland.

During the war, Roosevelt had worked effectively with Stalin, who could be difficult because of his suspicions of western leaders. The president's skill at handling difficult personalities enabled him to function as a buffer between the obstreperous Churchill and the distrustful Stalin. The question before the press and citizens in the United States in April 1945, when Roosevelt died, was whether Truman could handle the job as president, especially relations with the Russians. Roosevelt had kept his vice president in the dark about wartime diplomacy, including the development of the atomic bomb. Truman had limited experienced as an executive or with foreign policy. He had never participated directly in diplomatic discussions. His experience as an executive consisted primarily of his service as an administrative "judge" for Jackson County, Missouri, and his short tenure as vice president. Although a vociferous reader, Truman's formal education ended with a high school diploma, earned in Independence, Missouri, and two years of law school. His first year in office presented him with one crisis after another, as inflation, strikes in major industries (such as coal and autos), charges of disloyalty in the federal government, constant partisan sniping, and, until August 1945, the possibility of a bloody invasion of Japan confronted the president. Truman also had to deal with the presence of Soviet troops in Germany and eastern Europe and a revolution in China that threatened to install another communist regime. Occasionally, the president stumbled during this time of trouble, leading the wife of Senator Robert A. Taft, an influential Republican leader, to quip, "To err is Truman."

The Potsdam Conference resolved few of the disagreements between Russia and United States, whose mutual suspicion and antagonism deepened in late 1945 and 1946. Like much of central Europe,

After consolidating power in the late 1920s, Joseph Stalin ruled the Soviet Union until his death in 1953. (Keystone-France/Gamma-Keystone via Getty Images)

Russia had been ravaged by the war. Economic reconstruction was a top priority to Stalin, but the rebuilding of destroyed factories and public facilities required capital. The United States extended loans to England and France for postwar reconstruction projects but denied a request from the Soviet Union for financial assistance, because the Russians would not agree to American conditions, such as guaranteeing free elections and free trade in Eastern Europe. The decision of U.S. military commanders in Germany to halt reparations destined for Russia from the American-occupied zone further irritated the Soviets. Soon thereafter, the Americans began a program of amnesty for ex-Nazis in Germany. At the end of 1945, the British and the Americans merged their zones of occupation in Germany and invited France to join the unified region. The ever-suspicious Soviet leaders saw these actions as signs of a concerted western resistance to Russian interests.

The future of Germany, Poland, and Iran were major sources of disagreement between the superpowers. Despite a vague promise given at the Yalta Conference to President Roosevelt in early 1945, Stalin did not allow free elections in Poland, which he viewed as a military gateway to Russia from the west. Germany had launched attacks on the Soviet Union from Poland in World Wars I and II. During the latter conflict, between 15 and 17 million Russians, half of them civilians, had perished, largely at the hands of German invaders. Stalin opposed any plan that would produce a resurgent Germany or a Poland allied to the west. The presence of the Soviet army in the German occupation zone, which Stalin refused to combine with the Allied sectors, apparently reflected similar Soviet apprehensions about possible western actions. The Soviets also left troops in other European countries where their forces had routed the Germans. During the war, the Allies and Russians had jointly occupied Iran, but the Soviets reneged on a deal to withdraw their forces when hostilities ended. Officials in the Truman administration presumed that the Soviets wanted to obtain control of an oil-rich province in the country.

To Truman and his close circle of advisers, Stalin's actions in 1945 and early 1946 were taken as signs of purposeful Soviet aggression. Stalin's pressure on Turkey to obtain a Soviet naval base along the passageway from the Black Sea to the Mediterranean Sea via the Straits of Bosporus and the narrower water passageway known as the Dardanelles constituted additional proof of this thesis to Truman officials. (See the sidebar "Russia and the Sea" on page 244.) Greece and locations in the Middle East had historically been sites of British influence or control. The Truman administration had no intention of allowing the Russians to replace the British as the dominant power in this petroleum-laden region. Truman ordered a U.S. battleship to the coast of Turkey to underscore the point. The Americans had already decided not to share atomic energy technology (including A-bomb details) with the Soviet

Union. Stalin contributed to American apprehensions by stating publicly in early 1946 that communism and capitalism were incompatible. The Russian leader said that the Soviet Union must rearm for a confrontation with the west, which he predicted would occur in the 1950s.

The optimism that Truman had envisioned about amicable Russian-American relations following the Potsdam meeting dissolved into the president's conviction over the next year that the Soviets sought to dominate Europe and the Middle East. Some of the rancor between the two superpowers seems partially the result of the personalities of their leaders. Observers acknowledged, many remorsefully but others with admiration, that Harry Truman was no FDR. Franklin Roosevelt, the Harvard-educated scion of an established northeastern family, was urbane, tactful, and usually inscrutable. By contrast, the man from Missouri was a blunt and folksy product of the Midwest, with limited formal education and humble parental origins. FDR's diplomatic style featured patience, compromise, and, when needed, evasiveness. Truman's approach was direct, sometimes "brash," and focused on achieving decisive action. At Potsdam, Truman wanted results, not talk. Roosevelt had kept his ideological feelings about the Russians to himself. Truman was more open about how he saw the Soviet Union. He told his daughter that Russia was a police state, no different from the way the Nazis had governed. Irked by what he interpreted as Stalin's refusal to accept American offers of cooperation and compromise, Truman apparently had made up his mind by early 1946 that the Soviets would seek to expand their power and influence by political intrigue if not by force. He told his Secretary of State, James Byrnes, at the time that "I'm tired of babying the Soviets."

By 1946, Truman had come to think the worst of the Russians. His advisers played an influential role in shaping the president's outlook toward the Soviets. His inner circle of advisers included Byrnes; Averell Harriman; Army Chief of Staff George Marshall; Admiral William Leahy, who headed the Navy; Assistant Secretary of State Dean Acheson; George Kennan (the Soviet expert in the U.S. embassy in Moscow and later a key policy planner in the State Department); and Clark Clifford, a young attorney whom Truman appointed as his special assistant. They believed that Russia was bent on geographic expansion, either by force or subversion, and saw the Soviet leadership as a Red version of the Nazis. This outlook was encapsulated in a report prepared under

RUSSIA AND THE SEA

The United States is blessed with numerous ocean ports on two oceans. The East Coast has a dozen deep-harbor ports and many other minor ones that face the Atlantic Ocean, ranging from Portland, Maine, in the north to Houston, Texas, in the Gulf of Mexico. There are six major Pacific ports, from Anchorage, Alaska, to San Diego, California. San Francisco has one the world's finest harbors. With the exception of Anchorage, all American harbors are located in the temperate zone and seldom, if ever, experience closures due to ice. Russia, by contrast is port poor. Before its dissolution in the early 1990s, the Soviet Union contained a landmass two and a half times larger than the area of the United States, but most of its area lay in higher latitudes than the United States, and some portions much higher. Moscow, Russia's largest city, sits closer to the North Pole than any of Canada's major cities.

A glance at a map shows that the Soviet Union had no European port that rivaled any of America's Atlantic harbors. Russia's port at Murmansk is located above the Arctic Circle and experiences icing an average of 50 days a year. St. Petersburg, known as Leningrad during the Soviet era, provides access to the North Sea via the Baltic Sea, but it is too shallow for large naval vessels, which must pass through narrow passages that separate Denmark and Sweden. Still, the Soviet Union regarded control of the Baltic republics (Estonia, Latvia, and Lithuania) as well as Poland as critical to its access to the open ocean.

Farther south, the Soviet Union kept much of its navy at Sevastopol on the Black Sea. Access to the Atlantic Ocean from this location came by

Clifford's direction but with input from Acheson and Kennan. Reaching Truman in September 1946, the document expressed alarm about Soviet conduct in Europe and Asia since the end of the war. The Clifford Report charged that Russia wanted to make Turkey a puppet state, which would give it a launching pad for controlling the Middle East. The report fit comfortably with Truman's decision to "get tough" with the Russians.

Truman's increasing hard line toward the Soviet Union probably reflected pressures from politics at home, where the president faced a way of the Mediterranean, which requires a voyage through the Straits of Bosporus (where Istanbul is situated) and the Dardanelles, both long, narrow strips of water more like rivers than inlets. These water passages were controlled for centuries by the Ottoman Empire and later Turkey and were easily defended. Russia's unsuccessful war against the Turks in the Crimean War (1853–56) was partially motivated by a desire to establish a naval base on the Dardanelles.

Russia's Pacific ports lay in Asia, many time zones distant from Moscow, the capital. At the end of the 19th century, Russia gained access to Port Arthur, located at the head of the Yellow Sea, until the Russo-Japanese War in 1905. It took seven months for the Russian Atlantic fleet to steam from its base in the Baltic to challenge the Japanese navy, which defeated the Soviet armada in the Battle of Tsushima. The remnants of the Russian navy limped to Vladivostok, the one remaining Russian port on the Pacific. But Vladivostok was located 5,600 miles from Moscow, which lay on the western side of the vast Siberian wilderness. Vladivostok served more as a satellite naval station than as a major port city.

Russia's distinct geography has influenced its national history. The country's rulers, from Peter the Great (1682–1725) through Joseph Stalin in the 20th century, have seen expansion partly in terms of securing reliable access to the sea. Moreover, the huge Russian landmass and its few outlets to the sea probably helped to create an insular sense in relation to the outside world. The expansion of the United States, by contrast, gave it unrivaled access to the oceans, while its leaders denied that Americans possessed aspirations for empire. Despite its tradition of diplomatic "isolation" from European affairs, America was a nation of oceanic travelers.

series of problems. Prices skyrocketed in 1946 as American consumers demanded goods they had been forced to forgo during the war; political pressures forced an abrupt end to government price controls. The unsettled economy provoked numerous strikes, with major work stoppages occurring among coal miners, autoworkers, steelworkers, electricians, dockworkers on the West coast, and railroad workers. Truman threatened to draft the trainmen if they did not reach an agreement with management.

These economic woes worked to the advantage of the Republican Party, which unleashed a steady stream of criticism of the president. Members of the opposition party charged that Truman was soft on the Soviet Union and harbored "fellow-travelers" (people sympathetic to communism) on the federal payroll. Richard Nixon, a candidate for Congress in 1946 and later president of the United States, claimed that the Truman administration was "un-American." The difficulties at home and on the diplomatic front showed up in Truman's popularity rating, which slipped from 80 percent in late 1945 to 32 percent in October 1946. A few weeks after this poll was taken, the Republicans won control of both the House and the Senate in the 1946 elections. It was the first time they had enjoyed undisputed control of Congress since 1928. When the new Congress opened in 1947, the GOP mounted a campaign to cut taxes.

This political attack framed the backdrop for one of the most critical decisions of the Truman presidency. Britain informed the State Department that it could no longer support the Greek government. By agreement with the Soviets, British forces remained in Greece at the end of the war after driving out the Germans. During its occupation, Great Britain assisted the right-wing monarchy, which fought a civil war against guerrillas that included communists. Josip Broz, Marshal Tito, the communist head of neighboring Yugoslavia, provided aid and refuge to the rebels. By early 1947, British leaders announced that financial difficulties forced them to abandon Britain's military presence in Greece. Anticipating this development and assuming that Stalin was involved in the Greek revolt, at least in sympathy if not actual aid, Truman and his advisers decided to act.

Their plan was to support the Greek monarchy by providing military aid and military advisers. The political problem with the proposal was that implementation required congressional approval of funding. Republicans were skeptical of both committing the United States to a new venture in southern Europe and appropriating additional monies. The Truman team, including Dean Acheson, met with congressional leaders in the White House to plead their case. Acheson claimed that Russia had launched a campaign of expansion that threatened the West, aggression that needed to be blocked. Republican leaders reputedly were "stunned" at Acheson's contention. Persuaded of the dangers that the Greek crisis presented, Arthur Vandenberg, chairman of the Senate

Foreign Relations Committee and a Republican, said he would support the president if he warned Congress about the situation with language that echoed Acheson's analysis of Russian adventurism. Vandenberg and Truman both realized that in early 1947 Americans were focused on disbanding the army and getting back to civilian life, not on a new foreign conflict.

Truman was up to the task of breaking through this complacency. Addressing a joint session of Congress on March 12, 1947, in a speech broadcast on radio, the president warned of a looming crisis in Greece and of the failure to stand up to the advances of the communists. He requested an appropriation of $400 million in military aid, which would include the assignment of American military advisers to the Greek government. The president justified these steps by arguing that the failure to stand firm against communism in Greece would allow this malignancy to advance to neighboring countries. The idea that communism was a contagion that would spread if not confronted wherever it appeared became known as the Truman Doctrine. American commitments to block this "disease" were subsequently called the containment policy. Newspaper editorials were widely favorable to the speech, providing support that helped move Truman's financial request through Congress by comfortable margins. Truman's March 12 speech represented the official public announcement that the United States was embroiled in a new foreign conflict, known now as the cold war.

THE DEBATE

The Argument that Russia Started the Cold War

President Truman did not specifically name the Soviet Union in his speech to Congress on March 12, 1947, but the implication was clear. The source of the danger to global stability was Joseph Stalin and the Russian leadership, who had set their sights on exporting communism around the world. While Stalin did not publicly announce this objective, he had stated that communism was incompatible with capitalism. Distinctions between Stalin's motivations, the national interests of the Soviet Union, and the influence of communist ideology on Soviet leaders were difficult to discern. How much Truman separated these elements is unclear. He may never have even thought any difference between them existed. In his view, Russia was a police-state run by a dictator who wanted to expand communist influence and ideology. The situation, he believed, threatened the security of the United States and the West and had to be blocked. The vast majority of Americans apparently came to the same conclusion, many influenced, no doubt, by the president's analysis of the new danger in the world.

Truman had plenty of advice about how to size up the Russian threat. Most of his close advisers worried about Soviet intentions in 1944 and 1945. George F. Kennan put forward an influential assessment of Soviet behavior in February 1946. A specialist in Russian affairs and deputy head of the American embassy in Moscow in 1946, Kennan sent a "long telegram" to the State Department outlining his analysis of Soviet politics and diplomacy. (See "George F. Kennan's 'Long Telegram' from Moscow, February 22, 1946," on page 260 in the Primary Sources section.). Kennan's premise was that "At bottom of [the] Kremlin's neurotic view of world affairs is [a] traditional and instinctive Russian sense of insecurity." Stretching back to the era of the czars, Russian insecurity derived from its authoritarian rule, which lacked popular support, and feelings of inadequacy compared with Western regimes. This sense of inferiority toward the West, as well as apprehension of foreign military invasion, put Russian rulers in a constant state of alertness and suspicion.

Kennan held that Marxism-Leninism (the ideological inspiration of Russian communism) "became a perfect vehicle for this sense of insecurity," offering a "justification for their instinctive fear of the outside world." In later writings, Kennan indicated that communism as an ideology did not drive Soviet expansionism. Soviet leaders used communism as a justification for their actions, but their drive for control was really Russian nationalism in a new guise. However, the Soviet worldview was dangerous because it held that there could be no accord with the West. Kennan thought that Russia was not inherently expansionistic, yet its "neurotic" worldview propelled it to control its rivals. In acting on this instinct, the Soviet Union would avoid taking military risks, preferring to rely on its "elaborate and far flung apparatus" of underground subversion. Kennan's analysis predicted Soviet intrigue in the politics of neighboring lands, especially eastern and southern Europe.

Kennan turned his "long telegram" and subsequent communiqués from Moscow into an article in *Foreign Affairs* (July 1947). Signed "Mr. X," he called for a policy that contained Soviet expansion. Kennan's

George F. Kennan in 1947, the year the "Mr. X" article was published (Library of Congress)

posts from Moscow had so impressed officials in the Truman administration that he was transferred to Washington in 1947 to lecture at the newly created National War College. The next year, he became director of policy planning in the State Department. By then, he was considered a father of the "containment" policy, which lasted in various forms until the end of the cold war in 1989.

A month after Kennan sent his "long telegram," Winston Churchill delivered a talk at Westminster College, a small institution in Fulton, Missouri. Truman had invited the former British prime minister to give an address, and he was on hand to introduce him, calling Churchill one of the outstanding men of the age. Churchill observed that the United States currently stood "at the pinnacle of world power," a status that incurred duties and opportunities. (See "Winston Churchill's 'Iron Curtain' Speech, March 5, 1946," on page 262 in the Primary Sources section.) America's chief responsibility was confronting Russian adventurism. "From Stettin in the Baltic to Trieste in the Atlantic," he declared, "an iron curtain has descended across the continent." Churchill was referring to the presence of Soviet troops that had remained in Eastern Europe, where "Police governments are prevailing in nearly every case." Furthermore, Churchill warned that Russia intended to spread communism elsewhere, which presented "a growing challenge and peril to Christian civilization." The western democracies must stand together, within the framework of the United Nations, to block the spread of these malignant tendencies.

Most of Truman's close foreign affairs advisers accepted Churchill's premises. Many in Congress, on the other hand, were skeptical that Russia constituted a threat of sufficient magnitude to justify a renewed military buildup, especially if it meant spending money. The Republican majority in Congress made tax cuts and expenditure reduction a centerpiece of their legislative agenda in 1947. As the crisis over Greece reached a climax, Truman invited congressional leaders, including Senator Arthur Vandenberg, to meet with him at the White House in late February 1947. Under-Secretary of State Dean Acheson, who was present at the meeting, offered a succinct summary of the crisis as he saw it, reviewing the instances of Soviet pressure and "penetration." (See "Dean Acheson Argues for Containment in Greece, February 27, 1947," on page 263 in the Primary Sources section.) The challenge in Greece, he warned, threatened to spread the communist "infection" to Africa and Asia Minor and then to Europe. "The Soviet Union," he charged, "was playing one of the greatest gambles in history at minimal cost." Only the United States could block the aggression. Acheson's analysis impressed Vandenberg, who urged Truman to repeat these ideas in his speech to Congress. Truman took the advice. According to Vandenberg, Truman's apocalyptic description of the crisis over Greece "scared hell" out of the American people.

President Truman addressed a joint meeting of Congress on March 12, 1947. Truman told lawmakers that the government of Greece had asked for American assistance in its battle against "terrorist activities . . . led by Communists." (See "President Harry S. Truman, Speech to Congress, March 12, 1947," on page 264 in the Primary Sources section.) It was critical for the United States to intervene, the president explained, because "At the present moment in world history nearly every nation must choose between alternative ways of life." One way was based on democratic values; the other "relies upon terror and oppression, a controlled press and fixed elections, and the suppression of personal freedoms." The president did not specifically cite Russia as exemplary of the second way of life, but his listeners knew who he meant. The failure of the United States to help suppress the rebellion in Greece could lead to instability in Turkey, which could spread to the Middle East and then infect Europe and the rest of the world. The president called for a $400 million appropriation to assist the Greek and Turkish governments. "The free peoples of the world look to us for support in maintaining their freedom." Truman made it plain that communists had started the cold war.

Historians now consider Truman's address the official announcement in the United States that a cold war had begun. The speech had been drafted in the State Department, revised by Dean Acheson, and polished by Clark Clifford and his assistant, George Elsey, in accordance with Truman's tastes. The idea that communism would spread like malignant cancer, infecting one country after another unless contained, became known as the Domino Theory, a term used by President Dwight Eisenhower in 1954. Truman's decision to use American money and military might to fight the disease became central components of the containment policy, which aimed to block the advance of Soviet-induced communism.

The Argument that Russia Alone Did Not Start the Cold War

Given the hallowed place of democracy and individualism in American culture, most residents of the United States had little difficulty understanding the gravity of the president's warning, but the president's role as the nation's leader in foreign policy helps explain the public acceptance, too. Few citizens followed international relations closely. They depended on their elected leaders to identify friends and foes in the world at large. As the cold war dragged on decade after decade, especially during the Vietnam War (1963–73), doubts about the credibility of American leaders collided with this conventional acquiescence to presidential leadership. During the opening rounds of the cold war, however, most thought Truman had sized up the world scene pretty well.

Some observers, however, did find fault with American foreign policy during the late 1940s. Few of these critics claimed the United States alone had started the cold war, but they argued that American behavior contributed to the conflict. The most prominent of these opponents was Henry A. Wallace, Truman's secretary of commerce and his predecessor as vice president of the United States (1941–45). Wallace faulted American policy makers for failing to understand the motives behind Soviet actions in Europe. (See "Secretary of Commerce Henry Wallace Criticizes Truman's 'Get Tough' Policy, 1946," on page 265 in the Primary Sources section.) "The Russians," he wrote in 1946, "see themselves fighting for their own existence in a hostile world." The Soviets distrusted the United States and the western nations for historical reasons. Numerous foreign invasions of Russia dating back centuries to the Mongols and the Turks and more recently to the Germans twice in the 20th century had occurred. American actions that blocked Russian efforts to enhance their security, as in the case of securing access to the Mediterranean, was interpreted in Moscow as part of the United States' effort to encircle Russia with unfriendly regimes. Rather than provoke the Russians, Wallace urged Americans to accept the Soviet sphere of influence in eastern Europe. He recommended the opening of trade relations with the Soviets and extending postwar redevelopment loans to them.

After Wallace aired his criticisms publicly in a speech at Madison Square Garden in New York in September 1946, Truman fired him. Writing in his memoirs after retiring from the presidency, Truman called Wallace a "pacifist 100 per cent" who wanted to "disband our armed forces, give Russia our atomic secrets and trust a bunch of adventurers in the Kremlin Politburo." His dismissal afforded Wallace greater opportunity to criticize Truman's approach to the Soviet Union. The Truman Doctrine, he thought, was an excuse for the United States to replace Great Britain as a world policeman. He was critical of relying on military force to ensure stability and called military aid to Greece and Turkey a "reckless adventure." What the world needed was economic development, and here the United States was uniquely situated to provide leadership. Putting bread on the table would win America friends around the world. Wallace repeated these ideas in a campaign for the presidency in 1948 as the nominee of the newly formed Progressive Party. He won barely 2 percent of the popular vote, however, attracting less electoral support than Strom Thurmond, a breakaway Democrat and racial segregationist who challenged the president on a states' rights Democratic Party ("Dixiecrat") ticket. To the surprise of many, Truman won the election in a razor-close race over Republican Thomas Dewey.

Whereas Wallace was vilified for his supposed disloyalty to the president and to the nation, Walter Lippmann's criticism of Truman's foreign policy evoked less hostile responses. An influential author, editor, and social philosopher, Lippmann may have been America's most famous journalist in the 1930s and 1940s. In his position as a columnist on public affairs, he was expected to express his opinions and assess policy decisions. Moreover, his criticism of the Truman hard line against Russia was muted, focused more on tactics than strategic assumptions. Lippmann set his sights on the way Truman and Kennan had framed the containment policy and not on whether the Soviet Union posed a danger to American security. Lippmann faulted containment as too broad and open-ended. (See "Walter Lippmann Assesses American Policy Toward Russia, 1946," on page 267 in the Primary Sources section.) The United States did not have the resources or political resolve to take on Russia or its clients everywhere in the world. Moreover, Lippmann pointed to the Soviet army, a vast force that remained in Poland, east Germany, and other eastern European countries, not communist doctrine, as the primary threat. Americans, he thought, needed to understand Russia's fear of a resurrected Germany and formulate policy that recognized this apprehension. Provoking Russia in its own backyard (eastern Europe) would only deepen and prolong the cold war. Lippmann, in essence, argued that the Truman administration shared responsibility for starting the cold war.

This assessment probably was too ambivalent for Joseph Stalin. When American ambassador Walter Bedell Smith asked the Russian dictator in 1946 who threatened Russia, Stalin answered Winston Churchill. (See "Ambassador Walter Bedell Smith's Conversation with Joseph Stalin, 1946," on page 268 in the Primary Sources section.) The British leader had persuaded the United States to join an armed intervention of Russia in 1919 and "Lately he has been at it again." Stalin said Soviet troops had lingered in Iran largely to protect Russian oil fields in Baku, which were close to the Iranian border and susceptible to sabotage. Russia had no intention of attacking Turkey, either, but Stalin noted that the country was weak, which left the Straits of Bosporus and the Dardanelles vulnerable. On a previous occasion Stalin had noted that German warships had used this critical waterway to attack Russia during World War II. Placing a Soviet base on the Dardanelles was, the Russian leader argued, "a matter of our security." Stalin saw American action to block the Russian effort to gain a warmwater port, either in Turkey or Iran, as an act of aggression.

OUTCOME AND IMPACT

The Truman administration adamantly opposed allowing Russia to establish a foothold in Turkey. Officials feared if Russia gained control of Turkey, the Soviets would be in a position to extend their influence throughout the Middle East. Although Truman did not refer to oil in the region in his March 12 speech nor name Russia as the primary aggressor, he had both ideas in mind. Oil as a factor in defense strategy figured prominently among American military leaders, who had learned from World War II that modern wars run on gasoline. Some analysts had predicted a diminishing supply of domestically produced gasoline in the United States, although the possibility of American dependence on foreign oil was not the primary concern of American military planners. They were interested in denying Russia access to oil. The crisis over Greece was largely seen as a way for the United States to establish influence in Turkey, which American strategists saw as a gateway to the Middle East. Moreover, military leaders saw Turkey as strategically vital because it could serve as a base from which American bombers could reach Moscow.

Control of petroleum was a key objective in the world outlook of strategists in the Truman administration. In a larger sense, American access to resources was a driving concern, because some officials feared a resumption of the Great Depression once World War II ended. Truman officials thought that American influence in the postwar economy and the revival of Europe could help prevent a renewed business slump. This thinking helped to frame George Marshall's plan to provide reconstruction aid to Europe, a measure that Congress approved in 1948. An economically healthy Europe was seen as essential for warding off indigenous communist and leftist political parties. Nurturing Germany back to economic health was a key part of this plan, one that conflicted with Soviet intentions of preventing the rebirth of a strong Germany. In 1949, the American, British, and French zones of occupation were merged into the new state of West Germany.

A second assumption of the American cold warriors was that an international communist movement existed and that it was directed by Soviet officials in Moscow. Potential advances of communism, whether by subversion or other means, constituted a threat to American security that had to be opposed by political, economic, and military means. Through 1949, American policy makers thought that their monopoly of nuclear weapons gave them an advantage in confronting the Russians. Some historians speculate that this factor contributed to the decision to "get tough" with the Russians in 1946. The establishment of the Department of Defense and the National Security Council in 1947 reflected the commitment to enhance American military capability. The 1947 National Security Act created a unified Joint Chiefs of Staff to coordinate the units of the military. The law also created the Central Intelligence Agency, which would keep tabs on the Russians, especially their subversive activities. (See the sidebar "CIA" on page 256.)

The formation of the North Atlantic Treaty Alliance (NATO) in 1949, a military pact among western European nations, the United States, and Canada, represented a key step in building a military barrier to contain the Soviet Union. In 1951, Greece and Turkey joined the 12 original NATO members. West Germany was admitted to the alliance in 1955. Stalin expressed concerns about a revived Germany even before Hitler was defeated. Alarmed by western plans to unify their zones in Germany, Stalin blocked land access to Berlin, which lay in Russia's zone of occupation but which the allies jointly occupied. In June 1948, Truman authorized an airlift that supplied the city until Stalin lifted the blockade in May 1949.

In 1949, Russia exploded an atomic bomb, ending the American monopoly on nuclear weapons. This ominous development prompted the National Security Council to issue its famed NSC-68 report (April 1950), which called for the development of a hydrogen bomb and substantial increases in American military capability. The report was instrumental in ratcheting up an arms race between the United States and the Soviet Union during the cold war. The outbreak of the Korean War in June 1950 had a decisive influence on producing the massive increases in the American defense budget over the decade and later. The arms race proved to be a costly aspect of the cold war.

A third and pivotal assumption of American cold warriors was the superiority of western democracy over Soviet totalitarianism. Truman dramatized this ideological gulf in his March 12 speech. In part, the cold war was a battle between belief systems fanned by sentiments of nationalism and patriotism. Convinced of the virtue of their values,

CIA

Before the cold war, the United States did not have a permanent spy agency. For generations, Americans had embraced the idea that their nation should refrain from involvement in foreign intrigues. The term *isolation* sums up the feeling. Americans should not snoop on other governments and should avoid involvement in international politics whenever possible. The Senate's rejection of President Woodrow Wilson's plan for a League of Nations in 1919 following World War I symbolizes this insular outlook. World War II changed American ideas about intelligence gathering, and the cold war radically changed the way Americans thought about their role in the world. The creation of the Central Intelligence Agency (CIA) in 1947 emerged out of this transformation.

The CIA traces its lineage to World War II. Prior to the Japanese attack on the United States at Pearl Harbor in 1941, the nation lacked a central clearing house of information concerning foreign powers. At the time, President Franklin Roosevelt received intelligence reports from 10 different agencies, which sometimes contradicted one another. Entrance into the war prodded Roosevelt to create the Office of Strategic Services (OSS), which collected information about foreign governments and military operations and engaged in covert (undercover) operations, such as supporting guerilla movements, sabotage, and espionage. It even had plans to kidnap Adolf Hitler. Despite the plea of OSS director William Donovan to extend the life of the office beyond the war, President Harry Truman disbanded the OSS in September 1945.

By 1946, however, Truman's hope to work amicably with the Russians changed to a conviction that they threatened the United States. In this new, more dangerous international environment, a professional and centralized intelligence gathering agency made sense to the president and his staff. Truman later wrote in his memoirs that "the war taught us this lesson—that we had to collect intelligence." The statutory authority for an intelligence agency (the Central Intelligence Agency) was part of the National Security the Truman team believed that the Russians ran an atheistic police state that would eventually rot from within and collapse. Until that happened, Americans had to be vigilant against communist subversion

Act of 1947. The director of the CIA reported directly to the president via the National Security Council, an advisory group chaired by the president.

Initially, the CIA was to collect and analyze information, not engage in spy operations. The job description soon changed, and the agency dove into undercover operations outside the United States. Spying on the Soviets and their spies throughout Europe was a big part of its mission, but the agency aimed for grander achievements. Its operatives played major, even critical, roles in many notable events of the cold war. In 1953, the CIA, working through Kermit Roosevelt, the grandson of President Theodore Roosevelt, orchestrated a coup in Iran that overthrew a nationalist, anti-American government and installed the shah (Muhammad Reza Pahlavi), who ruled until the Islamic Revolution of 1979. The CIA fomented the coup in Guatemala in 1954 that overthrew the leftist president Jacob Arbenz. In 1956, "the Agency," as many called it, began flying spy planes over Russia. These U-2 aircraft flew at 70,000 feet and took pictures of areas as wide as 125 miles at very high resolution. The Soviet Union shot down a U-2 in 1960, to the embarrassment of the CIA and President Dwight Eisenhower, who had denied the secret missions.

The CIA's biggest blunder in the early years of the cold war was the failed invasion of Cuba. In 1959, Fidel Castro overthrew the conservative regime in Cuba and embraced a form of nationalist communism that was vigorously anti-American. The CIA immediately began planning attempts to assassinate Castro. None of these efforts worked, but the agency had a bigger plan: recruiting, training, and supporting "La Brigada," a brigade of anti-Castro Cuban exiles, who stormed Cuba at a location called the Bay of Pigs in April 1961. The mission was a disaster. Momentarily stalled by this fiasco, the agency quickly recovered, returning to the business of fomenting coups and undercover operations during the 1960s and 1970s. In 1980, the agency had a staff of 16,500 and purportedly a budget of three-quarters of a billion dollars, although its finances were secret. The end of the cold war in 1989 did not mean the demise of the agency, which played an active role in the Iraq and Afghan wars.

and fellow-traveler sympathizers. As the conflict with Russia evolved in the 1940s and 1950s, charges of disloyalty were raised repeatedly, especially by Republicans. Regardless of which side bears the most blame for starting the cold war, the conflict imposed numerous costs. One price was a narrowing of permissible criticism of American foreign policy.

WHAT IF

What if President Roosevelt had lived to finish his fourth term?

Franklin Roosevelt died on April 12, 1945. Harry Truman, vice president for less than three months, took over the responsibility for American foreign policy. By most modern historical assessments, Truman's hard line against the Soviets contributed to the outbreak of the cold war. Would the foreign policy history of the United States have been different if FDR had lived?

Probably yes. Roosevelt and Truman were very different in background, temperament, and political experience. FDR was cautious, was disposed toward compromise, and could be evasive. He seldom revealed his intentions. Certainly, he had kept Truman in the dark about his postwar plans. Truman, on the other hand, tended to see matters in black and white. He was impatient and at times acted impulsively. He prided himself in being decisive. Truman possessed little of the experience that FDR had acquired in dealing with world leaders. Roosevelt had developed a working relationship with Joseph Stalin, meeting a second time with the Soviet leader at Yalta in February 1945. One of Roosevelt's achievements during the war was acting as a mediator between Stalin and Churchill, neither of whom trusted the other. Roosevelt also was adroit in managing his advisers. There is a good probability that he would have been more able to modulate the hard-line anti-Soviet advice that some of these aides gave. Further, Roosevelt's political skills may have enabled him to resist the blandishments of Republican criticism more than Truman appeared to do. The stark ideological dichotomy that Truman painted in his March 1947 speech, designed in part to rouse Republican support, cast cold war politics into an either-or scenario, a life-or-death struggle. Perhaps Roosevelt would have framed policy toward Russia less as a worldwide crusade and more in terms of immediate, concrete, and very specific diplomatic disagreements.

If FDR had lived a year longer, through 1946, the cold war might have unfolded differently. Still, the chances are that a cold war of some form would have emerged. Stalin was a ruthless dictator, suspicious of the West and apprehensive of Russian security. His armies lingered in Eastern Europe and East Germany long after World War II ended. Stalin thought it perfectly normal for the Soviets to exercise hegemonic control over their own sphere of influence, an idea American strategists opposed. For their part, Americans had thought poorly of czarist Russia and found its current communist regime even less appealing. American opinion of its role in the world no doubt was influenced by recent history. The United States had scored victories in two military theaters during World War II, acquired the atomic bomb in 1945, and emerged from the war with a robust economy. The notion that political and moral values in the United States were universal and unique reaches deep into the nation's history. For American leaders to have refrained from exercising their new power in the postwar world is an optimistic expectation.

DISCUSSION QUESTIONS

1. How influential was Harry Truman to the start or the cold war?
2. Evaluate the role of technology and partisan politics in the origins of the cold war.
3. Is the term *war* appropriate for naming the confrontation between the Soviet Union and the United States between 1945 and 1950? If not, what terms work better?
4. How realistic is it to argue that a cold war between the Soviet Union and the United States was avoidable?

WEB SITES

Cold War. Timelines, documents, multimedia, biographies. Available at http://www.wilsoncenter.org/coldwarfiles/index.cfm?thisunit=0&fuseaction=events.list.

George C. Marshall Foundation. Historical resources concerning a key figure in World War II and the early cold war. Available at http://www.marshallfoundation.org/.

Joseph Stalin biographical chronicle (in English and Russian). Available at http://www.stel.ru/stalin/.

Harry S. Truman Library and Museum. Features photos, cartoons, documents, history, and timelines. Available at http://www.trumanlibrary.org/photos/av-photo.htm.

BIBLIOGRAPHY

Gaddis, John Lewis. *George F. Kennan: An American Life*. New York: Penguin, 2011.

——. *Strategies of Containment*. New York: Oxford University Press, 2005.

——. *The United States and the Origins of the Cold War*. New York: Columbia University Press, 1972.

McCullough, David. *Truman*. New York: Simon and Schuster, 1992.

Paterson, Thomas G. *Cold War Critics: Alternatives to American Foreign Policy in the Truman Years*. Chicago: Quadrangle Books, 1971.

——. *On Every Front: The Making and Unmaking of the Cold War*. New York: W. W. Norton, 1993.

Patterson, James T. *Grand Expectations: The United States, 1945–1971*. New York: Oxford University Press, 1996.

Ranelagh, John. *The Agency: The Rise and Decline of the CIA*. New York: Simon and Schuster, 1986.

Truman, Harry S. *Memoirs*. 2 vols. New York: New American Library, 1955–1956.

Yergin, Daniel. *Shattered Peace: The Origins of the Cold War and the National Security State*. London: Andre Deutsch, 1978.

PRIMARY SOURCES

1. George F. Kennan's "Long Telegram" from Moscow, February 22, 1946

In what became known as the "long telegram," George F. Kennan, the U.S. diplomatic attaché in Moscow, assessed the historical and political factors that drove Soviet foreign policy in a communication dated February 22, 1946. The statement was widely read among officials in the U.S. government.

At bottom of Kremlin's neurotic view of world affairs is traditional and instinctive Russian sense of insecurity. Originally, this was insecurity of a peaceful agricultural people trying to live on vast exposed plain in neighborhood of fierce nomadic peoples. To this was added, as Russia came into contact with economically advanced West, fear of more competent, more powerful, more highly organized societies in that area. But this latter type of insecurity was one which afflicted rather Russian rulers than Russian people; for Russian rulers have invariably sensed that their rule was relatively archaic in form, fragile and artificial in its psychological foundation, unable to stand comparison or contact with political systems of Western countries. For this reason they' have always feared foreign penetration, feared direct contact between Western world and their own, feared what would happen if Russians learned truth about world without or if foreigners learned truth about world within. And they have learned to seek security only in patient but deadly struggle for total destruction of rival power, never in compacts and compromises with it.

It was no coincidence that Marxism, which had smouldered ineffectively for half a century in Western Europe, caught hold and blazed for first time in Russia. Only in this land which had never known a friendly neighbor or indeed any tolerant equilibrium of separate powers, either internal or international, could a doctrine thrive which viewed economic conflicts of society as insoluble by peaceful means. After establishment of Bolshevist regime, Marxist dogma, rendered even more truculent and intolerant by Lenin's interpretation, became a perfect vehicle for sense of insecurity with which Bolsheviks, even-more than previous Russian rulers, were afflicted. In this dogma, with its basic altruism of purpose, they found justification for their instinctive fear of outside world.

Thus Soviet leaders are driven [by] necessities of their own past and present position to put forward a dogma which [apparent omission] outside world as evil, hostile and menacing, but as bearing within itself germs of creeping disease and destined to be wracked with growing internal convulsions until it is given final coup de grace by rising power of socialism and yields to new and better world. This thesis provides justification for that increase of military and police power of Russian state, for that isolation of Russian population from outside world, and for that fluid and constant pressure to extend limits of Russian police power which are together the natural and instinctive urges of Russian rulers. Basically this is only the steady advance of uneasy Russian nationalism, a centuries old movement in which conceptions of offense and defense are inextricably confused. But in new guise of international Marxism, with its honeyed promises to a desperate and war torn outside world, it is more dangerous and insidious than ever before.

It should not be thought from above that Soviet party line is necessarily disingenuous and insincere on part of all those who put it forward.

Many of them are too ignorant of outside world and mentally too dependent to question [apparent omission] self-hypnotism, and who have no
difficulty making themselves believe what they find it comforting and
convenient to believe.

There is good reason to suspect that this Government is actually a
conspiracy within a conspiracy; and I for one am reluctant to believe
that Stalin himself receives anything like an objective picture of outside
world. Here there is ample scope for the type of subtle intrigue at which
Russians are past masters.

Source: George F. Kennan to James F. Byrnes, February 22, 1946, U.S. Department of State, *Foreign Relations of the United States, 1946, Eastern Europe: The
Soviet Union,* vol. 6. Washington, D.C., 1969, 697–709.

—⁂—

2. Winston Churchill's "Iron Curtain" Speech, March 5, 1946

*In a speech in Fulton, Missouri, on March 5, 1946, Winston Churchill,
the former prime minister of Great Britain, issued a warning to Americans about Soviet aggression and called for Western democracies to
oppose it. His phrase "iron curtain" became a popular way of referring to
Soviet control of Eastern Europe.*

The United States stands at this time at the pinnacle of world power. It
is a solemn moment for the American Democracy. For with primacy in
power is also joined an awe inspiring accountability to the future. If you
look around you, you must feel not only the sense of duty done but also
you must feel anxiety lest you fall below the level of achievement. . . . It is
necessary that constancy of mind, persistency of purpose, and the grand
simplicity of decision shall guide and rule the conduct of the English-
speaking peoples in peace as they did in war.

A shadow has fallen upon the scenes so lately lighted by the Allied
victory. Nobody knows what Soviet Russia and its Communist international organisation intends to do in the immediate future, or what are
the limits, if any, to their expansive and proselytising tendencies.

From Stettin in the Baltic to Trieste in the Adriatic, an iron curtain
has descended across the Continent. Behind that line lie all the capitals of the ancient states of Central and Eastern Europe. Warsaw, Berlin, Prague, Vienna, Budapest, Belgrade, Bucharest and Sofia, all these
famous cities and the populations around them lie in what I must call

the Soviet sphere, and all are subject in one form or another, not only to Soviet influence but to a very high and, in many cases, increasing measure of control from Moscow.

However, in a great number of countries, far from the Russian frontiers and throughout the world, Communist fifth columns are established and work in complete unity and absolute obedience to the directions they receive from the Communist centre. Except in the British Commonwealth and in the United States where Communism is in its infancy, the Communist parties or fifth columns constitute a growing challenge and peril to Christian civilisation.

Source: Churchill Centre and Museum, London. Available at http://www.winstonchurchill.org/.

—⬯—

3. Dean Acheson Argues for Containment in Greece, February 27, 1947

President Truman called congressional leaders to the White House for a meeting on February 27, 1947, to discuss the "crisis" in Greece. Dean Acheson, the deputy secretary of state, informed the lawmakers that the Soviets were behind the revolt in Greece and that unless the United States intervened, the danger of communism spreading from country to country loomed. Acheson recounted his remarks in his memoirs of 1969.

When we convened . . . in the White House to open the subject with our congressional masters, I knew we were met at Armageddon. We faced the "leaders of Congress"—all the majority and minority potentates except Senator Taft, an accidental omission to which Senator Vandenberg swiftly drew the President's attention.

My distinguished chief, most unusually and unhappily, flubbed his opening statement. In desperation I whispered to him a request to speak. This was my crisis. For a week I had nurtured it. These congressmen had no conception of what challenged them; it was my task to bring it home. Both my superiors, equally perturbed, gave me the floor. Never have I spoken under such a pressing sense that the issue was up to me alone. No time was left for measured appraisal. In the past eighteen months, I said, Soviet pressure on the Straits, on Iran, and on northern Greece had brought the Balkans to the point where a highly possible Soviet breakthrough might open three continents to Soviet penetration. Like apples in a barrel infected by one rotten one, the corruption of Greece would infect Iran and all to the east. It would also carry infection to Africa through Asia Minor and Egypt, and to Europe through Italy and France, already threatened by the strongest domestic Communist parties in Western Europe. The Soviet Union was playing one of the greatest gambles in history at minimal cost. It did not need to win all the possibilities. Even one or two offered immense gains. We and we alone were in a position to break up the play. These were the stakes that British withdrawal from the eastern Mediterranean offered to an eager and ruthless opponent.

A long silence followed. Then Arthur Vandenberg said solemnly, "Mr. President, if you will say that to the Congress and the country, I will support you and I believe that most of its members will do the same." Without much further talk the meeting broke up to convene again, enlarged, in a week to consider a more detailed program of action.

Source: Dean Acheson. *Present at the Creation.* New York: W.W. Norton, 1969, 219.

—⁓—

4. President Harry S. Truman, Speech to Congress, March 12, 1947

In a major speech on March 12, 1947, President Truman told Congress that the United States faced a new foreign policy danger from totalitarian powers, implying but not explicitly naming the Soviet Union. Outlining a policy that became known as the Truman Doctrine, the president requested American aid to keep communism from advancing in Greece and Turkey.

The gravity of the situation which confronts the world today necessitates my appearance before a joint session of the Congress.

The United States has received from the Greek Government an urgent appeal for financial and economic assistance. Preliminary reports from the American Economic Mission now in Greece and reports from the American Ambassador in Greece corroborate the statement of the Greek Government that assistance is imperative if Greece is to survive as a free nation.

The very existence of the Greek state is today threatened by the terrorist activities of several thousand armed men, led by Communists, who defy the government's authority at a number of points, particularly along the northern boundaries.

Greece must have assistance if it is to become a self-supporting and self-respecting democracy.

The future of Turkey as an independent and economically sound state is clearly no less important to the freedom-loving peoples of the world than the future of Greece. . . . Turkey now needs our support.

At the present moment in world history nearly every nation must choose between alternative ways of life. The choice is too often not a free one. One way of life is based upon the will of the majority, and is distinguished by free institutions, representative government, free elections, guarantees of individual liberty, freedom of speech and religion, and freedom from political oppression.

The second way of life is based upon the will of a minority forcibly imposed upon the majority. It relies upon terror and oppression, a controlled press and radio, fixed elections, and the suppression of personal freedoms.

It is necessary only to glance at a map to realize that the survival and integrity of the Greek nation are of grave importance in a much wider situation. If Greece should fall under the control of an armed minority, the effect upon its neighbor, Turkey, would be immediate and serious. Confusion and disorder might well spread throughout the entire Middle East.

Moreover, the disappearance of Greece as an independent state would have a profound effect upon those countries in Europe whose peoples are struggling against great difficulties to maintain their freedoms and their independence while they repair the damages of war.

The free peoples of the world look to us for support in maintaining their freedoms.

If we falter in our leadership, we may endanger the peace of the world—and we shall surely endanger the welfare of this Nation.

Source: Truman papers. Harry S. Truman Library and Museum. Available at http://www.trumanlibrary.org/publicpapers/index.

—⁓—

5. Secretary of Commerce Henry Wallace Criticizes Truman's "Get Tough" Policy, 1946

Henry Wallace, the secretary of commerce and former vice president, wrote an article in The New Republic *in 1946 that criticized President Truman's policy toward the Soviet Union. Wallace faulted the Truman administration for not understanding Russia's long-standing concerns over its national security and the new realities of a world with atomic weapons.*

How do American actions since V-J Day appear to other nations? I mean by actions the concrete things like $13 billion for the War and Navy Departments, the Bikini tests of the atomic bomb and continued production of bombs, the plan to arm Latin America with our weapons, production of B-29s and planned production of B-36s, and the effort to secure air bases spread over half the globe from which the other half of the globe can be bombed. I cannot but feel that these actions must make it look to the rest of the world as if we were only paying lip service to peace at the conference table. These facts rather make it appear either (1) that we are preparing ourselves to win the war which we regard as inevitable or (2) that we are trying to build up a predominance of force to intimidate the rest of mankind. How would it look to us if Russia had the atomic bomb and we did not, if Russia had ten thousand-mile bombers and air bases within a thousand miles of our coast lines and we did not?

The flaw in this policy is simply that it will not work. In a world of atomic bombs and other revolutionary new weapons, such as radioactive poison gases and biological warfare, a peace maintained by a predominance of force is no longer possible.

Why is this so?

First. Atomic warfare is cheap and easy compared with old-fashioned war. Within a very few years several countries can have atomic bombs and other atomic weapons. Compared with the cost of large armies and the manufacture of old-fashioned weapons, atomic bombs cost very little and require only a relatively small part of a nation's production plant and labor force.

Second. So far as winning a war is concerned, having more bombs—even many more bombs—than the other fellow is no longer a decisive advantage. If another nation had enough bombs to eliminate all of our principal cities and our heavy industry, it wouldn't help us very much if we had ten times as many bombs as we needed to do the same to them.

Third. The most important, the very fact that several nations have atomic bombs will inevitably result in a neurotic, fear-ridden, itching-trigger psychology in all the peoples of the world, and because of our wealth and vulnerability we would be among the most seriously affected. . . . In a world armed with atomic weapons, some incident will lead to the use of those weapons.

Our basic distrust of the Russians, which has been greatly intensified in recent months by the playing up of conflict in the press, stems from differences in political and economic organizations. For the first time in our history defeatists among us have raised the fear of another system as a successful rival to democracy and free enterprise in other countries and perhaps even our own.

We must recognize that the world has changed and that today there can be no "one world" unless the United States and Russia can find some way of living together.

Source: The New Republic 115 (1946), 401–406.

—⁓—

6. Walter Lippmann Assesses American Policy Toward Russia, 1946

Walter Lippmann, one of America's most respected journalists, faulted the Truman administration for confusing ideological differences between democracy and communism with the actual threat of the Soviet army, which remained in Eastern Europe after World War II. In the excerpts below from several of his newspaper columns in 1946, which were later collected into a book, Lippmann argued that Truman's containment policy was too broad and hence impractical as a guide for American foreign relations. Lippmann's reference to "Mr. X" was George F. Kennan.

I agree entirely with Mr. X that the Soviet pressure cannot "be charmed or talked out of existence:" I agree entirely that the Soviet power will expand unless it is prevented from expanding because it is confronted with power, primarily American power, that it must respect. But I believe: and shall argue, that the strategical conception and plan which Mr. X recommends is fundamentally unsound and that it cannot be made to work, and that the attempt to make it work will cause us to squander our substance and our prestige.

Now the strength of the western world is great, and we may assume that its resourcefulness is considerable. Nevertheless, there are weighty reasons for thinking that the kind of strength we have and the kind of resourcefulness we are capable of showing are peculiarly unsuited to operating a policy of containment.

How, for example, under the Constitution of the United States is Mr. X going to work out an arrangement by which the Department of State has the money and the military power always available in sufficient amounts to apply "counterforce" at constantly shifting points all over the world? Is he going to ask Congress for a blank check on the Treasury and for a blank authorization to use the armed forces? Not if the American constitutional system is to be maintained.

The westward expansion of the Russian frontier and of the Russian sphere of influence, though always a Russian aim, was accomplished when, as, and because the Red Army defeated the German army and advanced to the center of Europe. It was the mighty power of the Red Army, not the ideology of Karl Marx, which enabled the Russian government to expand its frontiers.

Mr. X has reached the conclusion that all we can do is to "contain" Russia until Russia changes, ceases to be our rival, and becomes our partner.

The conclusion is, it seems to me, quite unwarranted. The history of diplomacy is the history of relations among rival powers, which did not enjoy political intimacy and, did not respond to appeals to common purposes. Nevertheless, there have been settlements. . . . For a diplomat to think that rival and unfriendly powers cannot be brought to a settlement is to forget what diplomacy is about.

Source: Walter Lippmann. *The Cold War: A Study in U.S. Foreign Policy.* New York: Harper and Brothers, 1948, 10, 15, 33, 60. Copyright 1947 by Walter Lippmann. Copyright renewed ©1975 by Walter Lippmann. Reprinted by permission from HarperCollins Publishers.

—∞—

7. Ambassador Walter Bedell Smith's Conversation with Joseph Stalin, 1946

In U.S. ambassador Walter Bedell Smith's conversation with the leader of the Soviet Union, Joseph Stalin explains his country's interest in the oil fields around Baku in Russia and Iran. Stalin also emphasized that Turkey could block Russia's access to the Mediterranean Sea.

He discussed in detail the Iranian oil question, including a history of Soviet-Iranian relations from the time of the Treaty of Versailles. He commented rather bitterly on the fact that the United States had pressed for debate on Iran's complaint before the United Nations, and had opposed Gromyko's request for postponement. He stressed the need of the Soviet Union for a great share in the exploitation of the world's oil resources, and said that Great Britain and later the United States had placed obstacles in the way of Russia when she sought oil concessions.

"You don't understand our situation as regards oil and Iran," he said. "The Baku oil fields are our major source of supply. They are close to the Iranian border and they are very vulnerable. Beria [the head of the MVD] and others tell me that saboteurs—even a man with a box of matches—might cause us serious damage. We are not going to risk our oil supply."

Later in the conversation I asked Stalin why he thought that any power or group of powers seemed a threat to the U.S.S.R.

"Churchill," Stalin replied. "He tried to instigate war against Russia, and persuaded the United States to join him in an armed occupation against part of our territory in 1919. Lately he has been at it again."

I asked . . . "How far is Russia going to go?"

Looking directly at me, Stalin replied, "We're not going much further."

You say "not much further," I observed, but does that "much" have any reference to Turkey?

"I have assured President Truman and have stated publicly that the Soviet Union has no intention of attacking Turkey, nor does this intention exist," Stalin said. "But Turkey is weak, and the Soviet Union is very conscious of the danger of foreign control of the Straits, which Turkey is not strong enough to protect. The Turkish Government is unfriendly to us. That is why the Soviet Union has demanded a base in the Dardanelles. It is a matter of our own security."

Source: Walter Bedell Smith. *My Three Years in Moscow.* New York: J. B. Lippincott, 1949, 52–53.

9

THE KOREAN WAR:
Should the United States Attack China?

—⚭—

The Issue

Sometimes called the "forgotten war," the conflict in Korea was a key event in the cold war and the containment of communism. President Harry S. Truman did not hesitate to rush American military forces to the defense of the Republic of South Korea when it was attacked by North Korea on June 25, 1950. The intervention of the Chinese communists transformed the clash into a much larger war and threatened to push American forces off the Korean Peninsula. To counter this enemy thrust, should the United States attack China?

♦ **Arguments that the United States should attack China:** General Douglas MacArthur, commander of American and United Nations forces in Korea, urged the Truman administration to bomb China, using atomic weapons if necessary. To fight a limited war against communism, he said, was tantamount to "appeasement." Dwight Eisenhower, Truman's successor as president, intimated that he would consider nuclear weapons if the Chinese did not agree to an armistice.

♦ **Arguments that the United States should not attack China:** President Harry Truman resisted calls to widen the war to China, refusing even to bomb the bridges over the Yalu River on Korea's northern border. Confining the military campaign to a "limited war" would avoid provoking World War III, eliminating a need to consider the use of atomic bombs. The president's top generals supported his decision.

—⚭—

INTRODUCTION

On September 15, 1950, General Douglas MacArthur launched an amphibious attack on the port of Inchon on the east coast of South

Korea, close to its capital of Seoul. It was a daring plan, as the 32-foot tidal swings in Inchon Harbor, its extensive mud flats, and the seawalls at the water's edge, plus an unknown number of North Korean defenders, made the assault extremely risky. That was fine with MacArthur. He reasoned that the very audacity of his attack would surprise the North Koreans. MacArthur had lobbied long and hard with the Joint Chiefs of Staff of the American military for permission to undertake the venture. He overcame their skepticism in part because of his gift of persuasion but also because American and United Nations forces, dug-in around the port of Pusan in South Korea, were in danger of being pushed off the peninsula. America's effort in the Korean War needed a shot in the arm.

Chinese intelligence warned Kim Il Sung, the North Korean leader, that the Americans were planning an amphibious attack somewhere, possibly at Inchon Harbor, which had not been mined. Kim brushed aside the advice, sure that his drive to clear the enemy from Korea was succeeding. His short-sightedness was a lucky break for MacArthur. At dawn, the first of 13,000 marines, supported by 261 ships of the United Nations fleet, stormed the seawalls of Inchon. They took the city with relatively few casualties and pushed on toward Seoul, now held by the North Korean invaders. Seoul was recaptured on September 26. Within 15 days, MacArthur had completely transformed the Korean War from a situation of desperation to one of euphoria. MacArthur's exploits in World War II and his command of the Japanese occupation had already made him an American hero. The Inchon Landing reaffirmed his standing as a military genius. Not only did he reverse the American gloom about the Korea War, he also persuaded President Harry S. Truman to push American forces deep into North Korea, with the objective of disabling Kim's army. Then Chinese soldiers crossed the Yalu River into North Korea and came close to overwhelming United Nations forces. A calamitous retreat from the Yalu raised a new question for Truman and American leaders: Should the United States attack China?

General MacArthur said yes. He urged that the United Nations should blockade the coast of China and bomb its major cities and the bridges over the Yalu River. He favored using divisions from the Nationalist Chinese leader, Chiang Kai-shek, who had fled to the island of Formosa (known today as Taiwan) when Mao Zedong and the communists gained control of the mainland in the Chinese Civil War. In addition, MacArthur recommended the use of atomic weapons. The general's

General Douglas MacArthur, commander of U.S. forces in the Far East, is pictured here with President Harry S. Truman at their meeting on Wake Island, October 15, 1950. (George Skadding/Time & Life Pictures/Getty Images)

proposal had numerous supporters in the United States, mainly in the Republican Party, who concurred with MacArthur that "There is no substitute for victory." To MacArthur, this meant: Win the Korean War and punish the Chinese communists.

President Truman said no. The war should not be escalated into Chinese territory, and it was unthinkable to consider the use of atomic weapons unless the security of the United States was clearly at risk.

Truman and his key advisers, especially Secretary of State Dean Acheson and Secretary of Defense George Marshall, saw the Soviet Union as the prime instigator of the Korean conflict. To take the war to China opened up the prospect of a military confrontation with the Soviets, which threatened to provoke World War III. All key personnel in the Truman administration sought to avoid such a calamity. They were willing to fight a "limited war," designed to maintain South Korean independence and contained to the Korean Peninsula. This restricted objective would be sufficient to deter Soviet adventurism.

BACKGROUND

Korea seems an unlikely spot for an American war. A peninsula jutting southward from China roughly 300 miles into the Sea of Japan, Korea measures about 75 to 100 miles wide. Much of the terrain is mountainous, rugged, and barren. The Yalu River in the north marks the boundary with China. Russia touches a sliver of Korea's far northwestern corner. Japan lies 70 miles to the east, and 5,000 miles of Pacific Ocean separates Korea from the United States. Korea's 20 million inhabitants certainly did not threaten the security of Americans in any direct way in 1950. Nonetheless, the "Hermit Kingdom," as it was once known, became the site for the United States' first significant military engagement of the cold war.

Korea had repeatedly suffered from foreign intrusions. The nation had been a colony of Japan from 1910 until 1945, when the Americans and the Soviets agreed to disarm the Japanese and administer the country. The two superpowers made a hasty decision to divide Korea into two zones of occupation at the 38th parallel. A proposal for a four-power trusteeship led by the United States and the Soviet Union that would oversee eventual reunification of the country never got off the ground. Instead, the Russians installed Kim Il Sung in the northern zone. A guerrilla leader against the Japanese occupation forces in Korea and China, Kim had joined the Chinese Communist Party and became a major in the Soviet army during World War II. He was the ideal candidate to place in charge of Korea, where he could impose a Soviet-style regime, aided and armed by Stalin.

The Americans helped put Syngman Rhee, a conservative, Christian, and Harvard-educated Korean exile living in the United States, in charge of the southern zone. Under United Nations auspices, the southern zone was transformed into the Republic of Korea (ROK) on August 15, 1948, with Rhee as president. In 1948, both the Soviets and the United States withdrew their troops from a divided Korea. Rhee and Kim, both fervent nationalists, longed to reunite their country, by force if necessary. Although the United States helped Rhee create an army, it deliberately underarmed it to prevent Rhee from launching a rash attack on the north. Kim beat his southern rival to the punch. On June 25, 1950, North Korean troops streamed into the southern zone, routing ROK defenders.

Several factors influenced the timing of the invasion. Both Mao Zedong of China and Joseph Stalin of the Soviet Union played instrumental roles in Kim's decision to invade the south. Mao took control of the Chinese government in late 1949, when the communists emerged victorious in the country's long civil war. After vigorous lobbying, Kim secured the approval of both leaders to mount an attack, although neither was enthusiastic about the plan. Not wanting to appear powerless, Mao pledged military intervention if the United States sent forces into North Korea. Stalin acquiesced in Kim's venture, largely to maintain Russia's influence with Asian regimes. Later, he reneged on a promise of air support south of the Yalu River. Stalin was cautious, anxious to avoid a war with the United States. The timing was also affected by news that the United States planned to strengthen Rhee's military.

A remark by Secretary of State Dean Acheson may also have been instrumental in the North Korean attack. Acheson gave a speech in January 1950 in which he implied that Korea lay outside America's defense perimeter in Asia. Republican critics of Truman's foreign policy later charged that Acheson had "given up" Korea and in effect invited the North Korean advance. It is unclear how the Acheson remark affected the strategic calculation of Asian leaders. It does seem clear that Kim dreamed of unifying Korea by force and picked the timing to launch the invasion. The Korean conflict began, in part, as a civil war, but it soon unfolded into the largest global conflict of the cold war to that point.

The rapid disintegration of the ROK forces in face of the North Korean invaders presented President Truman with a crisis that demanded an immediate decision. The president and his close advisers—Acheson, George Marshall, General Omar Bradley (chairman of the Joint Chiefs of Staff), and special assistant Averill Harriman—had no doubt about the cause of the attack in Korea. It was an assault on the free world directed by Stalin and leaders in the Soviet Kremlin. The Korean crisis presented the first real test of the Truman Doctrine—the president's commitment to block the expansion of communism, first announced in March 1947. If the United States did not draw a line in the sand and stand up to the communists, Soviet-style aggression would leap-frog from place to place. Truman and his advisers were unanimous that the containment of communist military aggression included Korea. Truman ordered U.S. air and naval support for ROK troops on June 26. On June 30, as the ROK army fled southward, Truman followed the advice of General Douglas MacArthur, commander of U.S. forces in Asia, to insert American ground troops into the fight.

Dean Acheson presented the Korean crisis to the Security Council of the United Nations (UN), which then endorsed the American decision to resist the North Korean attack. By chance, the Soviet Union—one of five nations on the UN Security Council—was absent from the council due to its boycott of the United Nation's failure to seat Communist China. UN resolutions condemned the attack and endorsed a multination military response, which the United States would lead, under the command of General MacArthur. Eventually, 15 nations joined the ROK and the United States in committing ground troops to the Korean War. Truman did not ask Congress for a resolution of support, nor did he submit a request for a declaration of war. From a constitutional viewpoint, Korea was a presidential war. Few public figures challenged this exercise of presidential authority.

Why did President Truman commit American troops to Korea? Several reasons propelled his decision, but the primary factor was his belief that the United States was locked in a historic conflict with Soviet Russia, whose leaders were presumed to be intent on the expansion of communism throughout the world. Korea was just an outcropping of this plan. Virtually all of Truman's key advisers accepted this explanation as an axiomatic premise. They had witnessed Hitler's aggressive actions in Europe in the 1930s and had participated in World War II. These experiences provided a lesson that an aggressor would continue unless confronted with force. Truman held to this belief throughout his presidency. He later wrote in his memoirs that "If the Communists were permitted to force their way into the Republic of Korea without opposition from the free world, no small nation would have the courage to resist threats and aggression by stronger communist neighbors. If this was allowed to go unchallenged, it would mean a third world war. . . ."

Events in 1949 reinforced this thinking. Truman announced in September that Soviet Russia had exploded a nuclear device in September, joining the United States as a nation in possession of weapons of mass destruction. The communists then won the civil war in China in October. Republican critics blamed the Truman administration and Secretary of State Acheson in particular for "losing China." The Soviets were alarmed by the creation of the NATO alliance between the United States and the Western European democracies and the establishment of the German Republic. Truman's critics warned that there were communists or their agents lurking in the Truman administration. In January 1950, Alger Hiss, a former employee of the State Department, was convicted of spying for the Soviets. That month, Klaus Fuchs was arrested and later convicted for turning atomic bomb secrets over to the Soviets.

In February 1950, Senator Joseph McCarthy (R-WI) inaugurated a stream of charges that communists worked in the federal government. McCarthy's allegations over the next four years that communists (sometimes referred to as "fellow-travelers") had infiltrated the national government—charges that some Republicans echoed—became known as "McCarthyism." Like most Americans, Truman instinctively saw Soviet communism as an alien force and a threat to American institutions. Still, charges about disloyalty in his administration appeared to have spurred the president to accentuate his hard-line position on Russia and to stand firm on his containment policy.

The introduction of American troops gradually slowed the southward advance of the North Korean army, which had driven UN forces into an enclave around the port city of Pusan by late summer 1950. Then MacArthur sprung his September surprise by executing an amphibious assault on the port city of Inchon. Bewildered and fearful of entrapment, the North Koreans fled northward, with UN troops in pursuit. When ROK units crossed the 38th parallel into North Korea, Truman gave approval for MacArthur to send Americans in pursuit, an order that the UN later ratified (October 7, 1950). This decision fundamentally changed the goal of the war, which originally had been to preserve the Republic of Korea. Now the objective became the destruction of North Korea's army and perhaps the reunification of Korea under UN supervision.

A truck loaded with soldiers from the U.S. 1st Calvary Division is greeted by Koreans north of Seoul on the way to the 38th parallel. A South Korean flag flies in the foreground. (Library of Congress)

Zhou Enlai, Mao's foreign minister, had warned on several occasions that China would intervene militarily if the United States pushed across the 38th parallel into North Korean territory. Truman considered the threat a bluff. MacArthur had personally told the president at their one and only meeting, held on Wake Island on October 15, that the Chinese would not enter the fighting and that the war would be over by Thanksgiving. MacArthur's intelligence was faulty. Truman was too enamored with the success of the Inchon Landing to pay close attention to signs that the Chinese warning was serious. Moreover, conservatives in the United States continued to pound the administration for being "soft" on communism. Opinion polls showed that 64 percent of Americans supported the pursuit of the enemy into North Korea. MacArthur and UN forces, steadily growing in strength and audacity, needed no prompting as they dashed north. By early November, they had pushed the North Koreans into the mountains within sight of the Yalu River.

As his advance units reached the Yalu, MacArthur was confident that he had won the war. Then, the third act of the drama unfolded. Perhaps as many as 300,000 Chinese soldiers descended on UN units, which were dispersed across the wide expanse of northern Korea. In an amazing infantry maneuver, the Chinese had crossed the Yalu undetected, traveling at night. MacArthur had personally flown in a reconnaissance aircraft along the length of the Yalu River in late November 1950 without seeing a single Chinese solider. But they were in Korea, hidden from view, sometimes in caves. Plus, they were masters of surprise, which compensated to some extent for their lack of mechanization and firepower. Attacking at night, the Chinese sent UN forces reeling southward, recrossing the 38th parallel. Seoul fell to the North Koreans for a second time in January

---

RETREAT FROM THE YALU

As units of the U.S. and South Korean armies raced toward the Yalu River in autumn 1950, General Douglas MacArthur thought his prize was in his grasp. His goal was to destroy the forces of the North Koreans and capture all of Korea. Since launching the daring but successful Inchon Landing in September, MacArthur had pushed his troops relentlessly. American boys would be done fighting by Thanksgiving and home by Christmas, he said. When an American battalion had been overrun by Chinese troops at Unsun in early November, MacArthur dismissed the surprise attack as incidental. It was just a small group of isolated Chinese volunteers, he said; the Chinese would not dare strike in force at the United States. In fact, he maintained through late November that there were no Chinese regulars in Korea. Because North Korean troops were melting away, the general felt confident that he could disperse his troops into small groups as the UN forces headed toward the Yalu. This decision and the intelligence on which it was based constitute one of the great blunders in American military history.

On November 26, 1950, the Chinese struck in force. They had crossed the Yalu River undetected, traveling along mountain trails at night and hiding in caves and villages during the day. Their plan was to lure the Americans far into Korea's fan shaped northern region. Some American field officers thought MacArthur's strategy, which denied the existence of a Chinese army in Korea and which dispersed his forces into smaller, largely isolated units in

1951. (See the sidebar "Retreat from the Yalu" below.) When he learned of the Chinese entrance into Korea in December, Truman recorded in his diary that "it looks like World War III is here."

Why had China joined the conflict? The reversal of fortunes in the war was an immediate factor. In broad political terms, Mao wanted to demonstrate the power of the new Chinese Republic. Moreover, Mao had good reason to be suspicious of American objectives. The United States had supported the noncommunist Nationalist Chinese right up to the communist victory in October 1949. Republicans heaped abuse on the Truman administration for its failure to prevent this communist advance. When the Korean War erupted, Truman had ordered the U.S. Seventh Fleet to Taiwan, ostensibly to prevent Chiang Kai-shek

the dead of a subfreezing winter, carried enormous risks. These battle-tested officers proved to be right. The Chinese did strike. They attacked at night, signaling their men to advance by blowing bugles and horns. They came by the thousands, both in frontal assaults at American positions but also along the flanks and deep behind American lines. The Americans traveled narrow Korean roads in vehicles. The Chinese moved on foot and set ambush after ambush from the hills overlooking escape routes. One of the worse of these nightmarish withdrawals occurred at the "Gauntlet" on the road from Kunuri, where thousands of Americans perished and thousands more were captured. The Chinese were good at stopping the lead vehicle in a convoy, which left the vehicles and men in the rear sitting ducks.

The only real bright spot in the surprise Chinese offensive was the First Marines' breakout at Chosin Reservoir, where they had been surrounded. Regular army units did not fare as well. Communications dissolved; units became leaderless; battalions lost fighting effectiveness. UN forces retreated 120 miles in 10 days, falling back below Seoul, the South Korean capital, by late December. It was the worst military defeat for the United States since the First Battle of Bull Run in the Civil War. Junior officers in the field cursed MacArthur's stupidity and arrogance, equating his leadership with Colonel George Custer's fiasco at the Battle of Little Bighorn. Claiming that he faced "an entirely new war," MacArthur predicted that the United Nations would have to evacuate the Korean Peninsula. He was wrong again. His days as supreme commander in Korea were numbered.

from invading China, the general's long-term objective. Mao saw this naval redeployment as American aggression. (See "The Chinese Foreign Ministry Explains China's Entry into the Korean War, November 1950," on page 293 in the Primary Sources section.) The Chinese accused the United States of violating Chinese airspace and killing Chinese civilians, charging that the "bloodthirsty United States aggressors" were threatening their national security.

THE DEBATE

China's entry into the Korean War presented the president with a critical decision. General Douglas MacArthur, Truman's Far Eastern commander, advised taking the war to the mainland of China, principally by bombing its major cities, attacking air bases in Manchuria (the Chinese province that bordered Korea), blockading the coast, and, if necessary, using atomic bombs. Truman overruled his field commander and refused permission to widen the war. Military activities would be confined to the Korean Peninsula. The president was willing to fight a "limited war" for very specific objectives. MacArthur was not.

The debate raged from December 1950 to April 11, 1951, when Truman fired MacArthur. The debate over strategy became entangled in a clash between two tough-minded leaders whose personalities differed like night and day. (See the sidebar "President Truman Fires General MacArthur" on page 282.) When Truman rejected the general's advice about how to conduct the war, MacArthur countermanded Truman's cease-fire proposal with his own ultimatum to China. Then the general went public with criticism of Truman's policy of "limited war." MacArthur wrote a letter to Representative Joseph Martin (R-MA), leader of the Republican opposition in the House of Representatives, that he suspected would be released to the press. The Truman policy was wrong, MacArthur wrote, because "There is no substitute for victory." The president was livid, telling Senator Harley Kilgore (D-WV), "I'll show that son-of-a-bitch who's boss, who does he think he is—God?" Both Truman and the Joint Chiefs of Staff agreed that the general was insubordinate and thus a liability. The MacArthur-Truman controversy raised a fundamental constitutional issue: Who would make American foreign policy, the general or the president? In relieving MacArthur of his Korean command, Truman upheld the tradition of civil control of the military.

The Argument that the United States Should Attack China

The entrance of 300,000 Chinese into the Korean War caught MacArthur by surprise. In his hot pursuit of the North Koreans toward the Yalu River, he had dangerously dispersed his forces. When it became clear that Chinese troops had slipped into Korea, the general sought permission to bomb the bridges over the Yalu. The Joint Chiefs denied the request. MacArthur responded immediately over the telecom (telephone-typewriter communication device) that the refusal to take the war into China "will be paid for dearly in American and other United Nations blood. . . . I believe your instructions may well result in a calamity of major proportion. . . ." Then Truman approved some bombing, but only the Korean side of the bridges. That was technically impossible, MacArthur replied, adding that handcuffing him on bombing the Yalu bridges was "the most indefensible and ill-conceived decision ever forced on a field commander in our nation's history." MacArthur was not one to mince words.

MacArthur requested authority to engage in "hot pursuit" of enemy aircraft (some piloted by Russians) that flew missions over North Korea from bases in Manchuria. Permission was denied because the allies objected. The appointment of Matthew B. Ridgway as commander of the Eighth Army at the end of 1950 was a blow to MacArthur's inflated ego and sense of omnipotence. Ridgway's reports from the field contradicted MacArthur's alarmist predictions that the Chinese would force the Americans to evacuate Korea. The Americans could hold South Korea, he reported, and under his leadership, they did. By 1951, the war settled into a prolonged stalemate around the 38th parallel. The impasse did not sit well with MacArthur; he sought victory, which at a minimum meant military control of all of Korea. He proposed use of Chinese Nationalist troops (who had taken refuge on Formosa) in Korea, a naval blockade of China, and tactical bombing along the Yalu River and in Manchuria. If these steps failed, MacArthur recommended the use of atomic bombs.

MacArthur did not worry about widening the Korean War. He probably welcomed it. In his view, Truman's concept of "limited war" was "appeasement," a term that had gained currency during the late 1930s when England and France acquiesced in Hitler's expansionism into

(continues on page 284)

PRESIDENT TRUMAN FIRES GENERAL MacARTHUR

On April 11, 1951, President Harry S. Truman relieved General Douglas MacArthur of command of United Nations troops in Korea. Truman accused the general of insubordination, because the general had publicly contradicted the president's foreign policy. The immediate issue in the controversy was how to conduct military operations in Korea after Communist China intervened in the war. Truman wanted to fight a "limited war" that sought to preserve the South Korean government and confine combat exclusively to the Korean Peninsula. MacArthur urged total victory over his communist adversaries, which he said required taking the war to the Chinese mainland. He intimated that he considered the use of atomic bombs on Chinese cities. MacArthur went public with his criticism of the administration's truncated objectives. Truman refused to tolerate this breech of presidential authority. A reporter asked the president if it took courage to sack America's most beloved general. Truman replied that courage had nothing to do it: "He was insubordinate, and I fired him."

Behind the conflict over strategy and political protocol lay a clash between two tough-minded personalities who had very different styles. Vain and egotistical, MacArthur exuded confidence in the extreme, expressing no reservation about his ability to drive the Chinese from Korea and "win" the war. There was "no substitute for victory," he said. The folksy, down-to-earth Truman was equally adamant about the nature of his authority as president. The job, as he saw it, required making difficult decisions, and once rendered, he stuck to them; nor was he willing to have the general upstage him. He had long thought MacArthur was a "Prima Donna" who had become too big for his britches.

Truman also remained firmly committed to the historical American tradition that civil authority should control the military. He was willing to act on this principle even if the decision was politically damaging. In the instance of General MacArthur, Truman took on America's most famous general, who enjoyed broad support from the nation's conservatives. Truman anticipated that he would trigger a whirlwind of criticism for sacking the general, which is probably a major reason why he waited so long for a showdown.

MacArthur returned to a hero's welcome in the United States. The same day he set foot in California, he traveled to Washington, D.C., to address Congress. Some lawmakers wept publicly during his 35-minute speech. So did, no doubt, many everyday Americans who saw the general on television (the largest TV audience up to that time) or listened to him on the radio. Then the general traveled to New York City for a mammoth ticker tape parade in his honor. The turnout was estimated as larger than the crowd that had cheered for Charles Lindbergh in 1927. Letters to the White House on the MacArthur decision ran 20 to one against the president, whose popularity slipped to 26 percent in a Gallup Poll. Many Republicans thought they had found the ideal presidential nominee.

The relationship between a president and top military officials demands a delicate balance. Generals must be afforded a degree of autonomy in the field, where military judgment is required. Yet presidents have final responsibility for conducting diplomacy and setting foreign policy goals. Sometimes these competing demands are buffeted by political factors, as was the case with Republican criticism of Truman's handling of the Korean War. Moreover, some of the nation's most popular generals have run successfully for the presidency.

It is rare for a president to fire a top general, but it is not unprecedented. One of the most famous firings was President Abraham Lincoln's removal of General George B. McClellan from command of the Army of the North during the Civil War. McClellan enjoyed wide popularity and became the Democrats' candidate for president in 1864. President James Madison relieved a number of generals from command during the War of 1812. President James Polk, a Democrat, ordered a court-martial trial for General Winfield Scott, hero of the U.S. victory over Mexico in 1848. Scott ran as the Whig candidate for president in 1852. The officers in charge of American forces in Hawaii were sacked after Japan's attack on Pearl Harbor in 1941. The tradition of civilian control of the military continued into the 21st century, when President Barack Obama relieved General Stanley McChrystal of command of American forces in Afghanistan in June 2010 because of remarks made to the press.

MacArthur concluded his address to Congress on April 19, 1951, with a line from an old Army ballad: "Old soldiers never die; they just fade away." He correctly predicted his own future. Truman's military advisers rebutted MacArthur's China strategy in hearings before Congress, upholding the president's position. MacArthur did not come close to winning the Republican nomination for president in 1952. He soon faded away from public view and died in 1964.

(continued from page 281)
neighboring countries. Appeasement to MacArthur was tantamount to surrender and a sign of weakness. As he explained to Congress in May 1951 in hearings over his firing, the Korean struggle was a global struggle against communism. (See "General Douglas MacArthur, Testifying to the U.S. Senate, May 1951," on page 293 in the Primary Sources section.) The threat to America was worldwide communist efforts "to enslave the individual to the concept of the state." When Senator J. William Fulbright (D-AR) remarked, "I thought the enemy was Russia," MacArthur disagreed. It was global communism, which the United States should resist everywhere in the world.

MacArthur's recommendation to use nuclear weapons had military support. Truman and the Joint Chiefs had considered the possibility, but objections from the British, a major U.S. ally in Europe and a member of NATO, the defensive alliance designed to block Russian advances, was the major obstacle to approval of the proposal. General Ridgway intimated that the United States may have to resort to atomic weapons if the stalemate continued in Korea. General Dwight D. Eisenhower, who became president in January 1953, agreed. Eisenhower wrote in his memoirs that atomic weapons were vital to American military commitments. The president let it be known in 1953 that if the stalled peace talks did not make progress, he would consider a "more aggressive military campaign." (See "Former President Dwight D. Eisenhower Recollects His Position on Peace Talks and the Korean War, 1963," on page 295 in the Primary Sources section.) Ike was as popular a military hero as MacArthur, and he won the presidency as a Republican.

The Argument that the United States Should Not Attack China

President Truman justified his decision to commit American military forces to Korea in June 1950 and on numerous subsequent occasions as a response to communist aggression. Joseph Stalin and the Soviet leaders in Russia, he said in his nationally televised speech on April 11, 1951, "are engaged in a monstrous conspiracy to stamp out freedom all over the world. . . ." (See "President Harry S. Truman Explains the American Role in Korea, April 1951," on page 296 in the Primary Sources section.) Free nations must "check the aggressive designs of the Soviet Union before they result in a third world war." In fall 1952, Truman said that "We are fighting in Korea so we won't have to fight in Wichita, or in Chicago, or in New Orleans, or in San Francisco Bay."

In the broader context of the cold war, the president explained that America's stand in Korea was implementation of the goals of the Truman Doctrine, which was the containment of communist expansion into "free" countries. Initially, the administration (and UN) entered the Korean War to drive the North Koreans out of the south in order to preserve the Republic of Korea. The momentum of MacArthur's success at Inchon and his race north of the 38th parallel, however, enticed the administration to endorse a new objective: Destroy the North Korean army and allow the UN to oversee unification of the country. But the optimism of October 1950 turned into the disaster of November, when the Chinese army forced the UN retreat from the Yalu. MacArthur urged an attack on China itself. Truman rejected the idea and stood by his position that the United States was engaged in a "limited war." To follow MacArthur's advice would threaten to ensnare the United Nations "in a vast conflict on the continent of Asia," which was fraught with military hazards and compromised American cold war strategy.

Truman maintained several assumptions during the two and a half years that he oversaw the American commitment in Korea. First, enforce the Truman Doctrine by opposing Soviet aggression as he saw it unfold around the world. Second, avoid a third world war, which the president dreaded. Third, avoid the use of atomic weapons, which Truman regarded as an absolute last resort to protect the security of the United States. And fourth, put Europe before Asia in terms of implementing a global strategy of containment. To conduct an unlimited military operation in Asia by attacking China would weaken the American presence in Europe and thus work to the advantage of the Soviets. Moreover, a full-scale American thrust at China, perhaps using nuclear weapons, might prompt Stalin to join the war. Under this scenario, the United States would become mired in a costly and perhaps unwinnable land war in Asia. Unlike MacArthur, most American military leaders shuddered at such a prospect.

Defense secretary George Marshall reiterated the outline of this argument at the congressional hearings over the firing of General MacArthur in May and June 1951. Marshall was one of the triumvirate of top American military heroes of World War II, along with Eisenhower and MacArthur. Marshall had served as President Franklin Roosevelt's army chief (1939–45) and was a key architect of the U.S. victory in Europe. He served as Secretary of State from 1947 to 1949 and helped shape the Truman Doctrine. Among many in Congress and millions of citizens, Marshall commanded enormous respect and credibility.

The secretary told a Senate panel in 1951 that MacArthur's proposal to take the war to China would increase the possibility of a Soviet attack in Western Europe, which he said could occur "at any moment." (See "Secretary of Defense George C. Marshall, Testifying to the U.S. Senate, May 1951," on page 298 in the Primary Sources section.) It was the Soviet army, not communism per se, that threatened American interests. Do not declare war on China, Marshall counseled, it is a Soviet trap. Moreover, an adventure in China would alienate America's allies, which were vital to the maintenance of containment. Maintaining good relations with the British was pivotal in this regard, because an American nuclear attack on Russia would be launched largely from the United Kingdom. Furthermore, the British opposed the use of atomic bombs in the Asian conflict. Marshall also reported to Congress that he had advised the president to fire MacArthur for attempting to reformulate American foreign policy publicly. As early as January 1951, the allies had sought to negotiate a cease-fire in Korea through the United Nations. Truman drew up a similar proposal in March, a step that apparently provoked MacArthur to go public with criticism of the administration's policy toward Korea.

General Omar N. Bradley, the chairman of the Joint Chiefs of Staff, seconded Marshall's argument. Like Marshall, he saw Russia as the culprit behind the Korean conflict, which he characterized as "Kremlin-inspired imperialism" implemented via "guerrilla diplomacy." (See "General Omar Bradley, Testifying to the U.S. Senate, May 1951," on page 299 in the Primary Sources section.) Bradley saw the world divided into two power centers—the United States and the Soviet Union—and viewed their confrontation in global terms. Expanding the Korean War into a wider Asian campaign, he told Congress in May 1951, would "probably delight" the Soviets. Such an adventure would certainly cost much more than the current limited war. Bradley and other Truman officials were highly sensitive to the politics of the defense budget, which had ballooned with expenditures for the Korean War and a military buildup in Europe in conjunction with the NATO alliance. Attacking China, Bradley advised, was "the wrong war, at the wrong place, at the wrong time, and with the wrong enemy." This was the most quoted phrase of the administration's presentation to Congress on the MacArthur firing.

OUTCOME AND IMPACT

By late January 1951, the Chinese and North Koreans had pushed UN forces 50 miles south of the 38th parallel. The anticommunist coalition then held its ground and drove the enemy back to the 38th parallel by the spring. The Chinese offensive had run out of steam, in good part because its supply line was stretched too thin. The Chinese had relatively few vehicles, and those they had were vulnerable to American air attacks. The use of human and animal porters to carry food and ammunition could not sustain an army of 300,000 far down the Korean Peninsula. Moreover, the Chinese now faced a revitalized U.S. Army, commanded by General Matthew Ridgway, a tough, smart, and determined soldier who replaced MacArthur. Ridgway revised tactics against the Chinese. No longer would the Americans push isolated units along mountainous roads, where they would be vulnerable to ambushes. The Americans dug in and waited for the enemy to come, using "lure and destroy" tactics and relying on superior firepower and radio communications. The Americans had another advantage: airpower, which grew in strength as the conflict lengthened. The Korean weather more than enemy fire set limits on the effectiveness of the air force.

With the war settled into a stalemate around the 38th parallel in spring 1951, both sides signaled a willingness to discuss a cease-fire. Talks began in July 1951 and dragged on for two years. An armistice was finally signed on July 27, 1953. Fighting continued during this interlude, with each side launching probes and minor offenses. By early 1953, China had moved 1.35 million troops into Korea. Negotiations were bitter and acrimonious as two very different cultures clashed over military etiquette and political fundamentals. Mao and Kim saw cease-fire negotiations as an opportunity to expose the aggression of the imperialist Western nations. American negotiators suspected their communist adversaries of calculated treachery, looking to milk every opportunity to score propaganda points. A major sticking point in the negotiations was the exchange of prisoners. UN forces held 10 times more prisoners than the communists, who wanted the return of all detained soldiers. President Truman refused to hand over individuals who wished not to be repatriated, claiming that it violated the American principle of freedom of choice. Some UN prisoners were Nationalist Chinese who had been forcibly inducted into the Chinese army; others were South Koreans who had been forced into the North Korean army.

Korean civilians pass a tank at Haengju, Korea. (Major R. V. Spencer/U.S. Army National Archives)

Several developments broke the impasse. On March 5, 1953, Joseph Stalin died. Mao thus lost his chief supporter, as a power vacuum developed while three Russians vied for control of the Kremlin. Six weeks earlier, General Dwight D. Eisenhower had been inaugurated president of the United States. Eisenhower, known as "Ike," had pledged during the campaign to "go to Korea" and to end the war with "deeds" not "words." In office, he hinted that he would approve an escalated military campaign against China and implied that the Soviet Union might also be vulnerable. To put a point on this new attitude, Ike had held a well-publicized meeting with General MacArthur. He also withdrew the American Seventh Fleet from the Taiwan Straits, which removed the constraint on potential Nationalist raids on the Chinese mainland. And, American bombers ranged widely over Korea, hitting irrigation facilities and military storage dumps. Under attack and with an economy overtaxed by war, Mao agreed to a deal. The shooting stopped. The armed forces of both adversaries, however, stayed put along the cease-fire line and remained there through 2012—including American troops—more than 60 years later.

The Korean War was a deadly affair. Approximately 10 percent of the Korean population (including civilians) was killed or wounded. China reported 148,000 combat deaths, in all likelihood an undercount. The American military suffered more than 54,000 deaths and 105,000 nonfatal casualties, many to frostbite. American fatalities were the cost of President Truman's decision to implement the containment policy in Korea with military force.

The strategic value of Korea to American security was debatable, but its location was secondary to the very act of a military attack on South Korea. Almost instinctively, the Truman administration saw the North Korean act as a test of the will of the West to contain communist expansion. Truman's version of containment relied mainly on military force; the president and his advisers used the Korean War to leverage a major expansion of American defense capability, a policy recommended by the National Security Council in 1950. Defense appropriations quadrupled during the Korean War and remained high afterward. New taxes were levied to pay for the increased military spending. This enhanced defense capacity may have deterred Soviet adventurism elsewhere in the world, but it also accelerated an arms race, including improved delivery systems for nuclear weapons.

Truman did refuse to use atomic bombs in Korea. He opted for "limited war," restricting the fighting to only the Korean Peninsula. The president achieved his goal of stopping communist aggression in Korea while avoiding a third world war, but he paid a heavy price for his middle way between an all-out attack on China and disengagement from Korean politics. Few Americans wanted another global war, but many were uneasy with a military campaign that imposed restrictions on how generals could fight it. Shortly after Truman fired MacArthur, the president's approval rating dropped to 26 percent, one of the lowest readings ever. Republican conservatives pounded the administration for "softness" on world communism and supposedly harboring "red" sympathizers in the State Department. Public dissatisfaction with the conduct of the Korean War helps to explain the victory of Eisenhower and the Republican Party in the 1952 elections.

While Truman's Korean policy hurt the Democratic Party, the president did leave another lasting legacy. The president did not seek a declaration of war from Congress; he relied on his interpretation of presidential authority to conduct American military operations in a foreign country. The Korean War marks the moment when a declaration of war under the provisions of the Constitution was discarded and the inauguration of virtually unrestricted presidential power to deploy American troops in a major military engagement anywhere in the world. This legacy continued into the 21st century.

WHAT IF?

What if the United States had attacked China?

Speculation about an attack on China depends in part on whether actions would have been tactical as opposed to strategic. Some of General MacArthur's recommendations were tactical in nature: Blockade the Chinese coast, bomb the bridges over the Yalu River, and undertake hot pursuits of enemy aircraft into airspace over Manchuria. These strikes probably would have slowed the Chinese offensive, especially if the bridges over the Yalu had been destroyed before the Chinese army entered Korea. Whatever the impact of these steps, the Joint Chiefs of Staff doubted that MacArthur's plan would have changed much of the outcome in Korea.

Escalating a war on China by bombing its major cities, sending American combat troops into Chinese territory, and using atomic bombs offers a more ambiguous scenario. China is a huge country, containing as much territory as the United States. China's coastline stretches some 2,000 miles from Manchuria to Vietnam. Its population in 1950 was roughly four times that of the United States, giving China a massive pool of manpower. America's economy was far more developed than the preindustrial conditions of China. American spending on defense in 1952 was 15 times higher than that of China. Nevertheless, China's military campaign in Korea demonstrated that a "peasant" army that lacked mechanization, naval support, and modern communications could be a formidable opponent, even outside its own territory. Transporting American infantry over the Pacific to fight in China would have been a recipe for disaster.

Bombing Chinese cities would have hindered Mao's fighting capacity but also risked the active intervention of the Soviet Union in the process. This step would have taken the United States toward the "world war three" scenario that Truman feared. But even if the Soviets had continued to sit on the sidelines, bombing alone is unlikely to have caused Mao to cave in to the "imperialists." Air raids on German cities during World War II did not force Hitler to surrender. Until atomic bombs were dropped on Hiroshima and Nagasaki, conventional bombing of Japanese cities did not cause the capitulation of the island nation, despite devastation of its urban environment. U.S. Air Force chief Hoyt Vandenberg told Congress during the MacArthur hearings that American air strikes against China would undermine the ability of the United States to attack the Soviets. The Soviets were always America's prime adversary during the cold war. Most American military leaders recognized that an attack on China was a recipe for disaster.

CHRONOLOGY

1945 *August 15:* With Japan's surrender ending World War II, Korea is divided into two zones at the 38th parallel.

1949 *April 4:* North Atlantic Treaty Organization (NATO) is formed.

May 12: German Republic is established.

June: Alger Hiss perjury trial begins.

September 23: President Truman announces Soviets' explosion of an atomic bomb in August.

October 1: Mao Zedong and communists seize power in China.

1950 *January 21:* Alger Hiss is convicted of perjury related to spying.

February 9: Senator Joseph McCarthy charges that communists are employed by the U.S. State Department.

April 14: National Security Council Report (NSC-68) advises military buildup.

June 25: North Korea invades South Korea.

June 26: President Truman orders U.S. military opposition to the North Korean invasion.

June 27: United Nations authorizes resistance to North Korean invasion.

June 30: Truman agrees to use U.S. ground combat troops in Korea.

September 15: General MacArthur launches Inchon Landing.

September 23: Congress passes the Internal Security Act over the veto of President Truman.

October 25: South Korean troops clash with Chinese soldiers.

November–December: U.S. retreats from the Yalu River.

1951 *April 11:* Truman relieves MacArthur of Korean command.

July 10: Negotiations for an armistice begin.

1952 *November 4:* Dwight D. Eisenhower is elected president.

1953 *March 5:* Soviet leader Joseph Stalin dies.

July 27: Korean War armistice agreement is signed.

DISCUSSION QUESTIONS

1. How is Korean history before 1950 relevant to the Korean War?
2. How should one assess General Douglas MacArthur: a brilliant strategist or an uncontrolled egoist?
3. Explain how the Korean War fit into the containment policy of the United States.
4. Why is the Korean conflict called the "Forgotten War?"

WEB SITES

Harry S. Truman Library and Museum. Available at http://www.truman library.org/whistlestop/study_collections/koreanwar/index.php.

Harry S. Truman public papers. Available at http://www.trumanlibrary. org/publicpapers/index.php.

Korean War Project. Available at http://www.koreanwar.org/.

BIBLIOGRAPHY

Cumings, Bruce. *The Korean War: A History.* New York: Modern Library, 2010.

Eisenhower, Dwight D. *Mandate for Change, 1953–1956.* Garden City, N.Y.: Doubleday, 1963.

Goncharov, Sergei, John W. Lewis, and Xue Litai. *Uncertain Partners: Stalin, Mao, and the Korean War.* Palo Alto, Calif.: Stanford University Press, 1993.

Halberstam, David. *The Coldest Winter: America and the Cold War.* New York: Hyperion, 2007.

Manchester, William. *American Caesar: Douglas MacArthur, 1880–1964.* Boston: Little, Brown, 1978.

McCullough, David. *Truman.* New York: Simon and Schuster, 1992.

Stueck, William W. *Rethinking the Korean War: A New Diplomatic and Strategic History.* Princeton, N.J.: Princeton University Press, 2002.

Truman, Harry S. *Memoirs.* 2 vols. New York: New American Library, 1955–1956.

PRIMARY SOURCES

1. The Chinese Foreign Ministry Explains China's Entry into the Korean War, November 1950

In a document printed by the United Nations and dated November 11, 1950, the Chinese Foreign Ministry provided its official explanation for entering the Korean War. The Chinese accused the United States of violating Chinese airspace and killing Chinese civilians and charged that "bloodthirsty United States aggressors" were threatening their national security.

Immediately after the beginning of its aggressive war in Korea, the United states sent its fleet into the waters of Taiwan, which belongs to China. It then sent its air forces to invade the air space of north-east China and carried out bombings. . . . In the last three months numerous cases have been noted of United States aircraft violating the air borders of China, bombing Chinese territory, killing Chinese civilians and destroying Chinese property.

The spontaneous assistance of the Chinese people in Korea and their resistance to United States aggression has a firm moral foundation. The Chinese people will never forget how the Korean people magnanimously gave the Chinese people voluntary assistance in its revolutionary struggle. The Korean people took part not only in the Chinese war of national liberation, but also in the northern march of the Chinese people in 1925 to 1927, in the war against Japan from 1937 to 1945. Through the four stages of the Chinese people's revolution the Korean people always fought shoulder to shoulder with the Chinese people to overthrow imperialism and feudalism.

The American aggressors have gone too far. After making a five-thousand mile journey across the Pacific, they invaded the territories of China and Korea. . . . The United States Government itself provoked civil war in Korea. . . .

Source: United Nations Document S902, November 15, 1950, 2–4.

—ᴍ—

2. General Douglas MacArthur, Testifying to the U.S. Senate, May 1951

Testifying before the U.S. Senate Committee on Armed Services and Committee on Foreign Relations in May 1951, General Douglas MacArthur defended his recommendation to take the war into China. He charged that Truman's policy of limited war constituted "appeasement" of the expansion of global communism.

The Chairman [Richard Russell, Democrat of George]: General, did your intelligence have any previous knowledge of the fact that the Chinese were crossing the boundaries in any considerable force, prior to the attack . . . last December?

General MacArthur: We had knowledge that the Chinese Communists had collected large forces along the Yalu River.

The Red Chinese, at that time, were putting out, almost daily, statements that they were not intervening. . . .

In November, our Central Intelligence Agency, here, had said that they felt there was little chance of any major intervention on the part of the Chinese forces. . . .

Senator Saltonstall [Leverett Saltonstall, Republican of Massachusetts]: Now, on April 15, the Assistant Secretary of State, Dean Rusk, in a television address and press broadcast, stated, in part—and this is the pertinent part of his speech, as I read it:

"What we are trying to do is to maintain peace and security without a general war. We are saying to the aggressors, 'You will not be allowed to get away with your crime. You must stop it.' At the same time, we are trying to prevent a general conflagration. . . ."

General MacArthur: That policy . . . seems to me to introduce a new concept into military operations—the concept of appeasement, the concept that when you use force, you can limit that force.

The concept that I have is that when you go into war, you have exhausted all other potentialities of bringing the disagreement to an end.

Senator Fulbright [J. William Fulbright, Democrat of Arkansas]: What is your concept of communism? I mean is this the communism of Marx and Engels, or is it the communism practiced by the Kremlin. . . ?

General MacArthur: Communism has many various factors. The great threat in what is called present communism is the imperialistic tendency or the lust of power beyond their own geographical confines. It is their effort to enslave the individual to the concepts of the state. It is the establishment of autocracy that squeezes out every one of the freedoms which we value so greatly. . . .

I believe the problem is a global one. I believe we should defend every place from communism. I believe we can.

Source: U.S. Senate, Committee on Armed Services and Committee on Foreign Relations, Military Situation in the Far East. Washington, D.C.: Government Printing Office, 1951, 18, 39, 142, 120.

—⚹—

3. Former President Dwight D. Eisenhower Recollects His Position on Peace Talks and the Korean War, 1963

Former president Dwight D. Eisenhower wrote in his memoirs, published in 1963, that he would have considered the use of atomic weapons during the Korean War if the Chinese did not move forward with peace talks. Eisenhower assumes that Russia would have entered the war if the United States had used nuclear weapons against China.

An attack launched merely to move the line of contact to the narrow waist of the peninsula between Sinanju and Hungnam would not in itself prove decisive and would never merit the cost in lives. Clearly, then, a course of action other than a conventional ground attack in Korea was necessary.

In the light of my unwillingness to accept the status quo, several other moves were considered in the event that the Chinese Communists refused to accede to an armistice in a reasonable time. These possibilities differed in detail, but in order to back up any of them, we had to face several facts.

First, it was obvious that if we were to go over to a major offensive, the war would have to be expanded outside of Korea—with strikes against the supporting Chinese airfields in Manchuria, a blockade of the Chinese coast, and similar measures. Second, a build-up of both United States and ROK forces would be necessary. I had already authorized the raising of military aid to the ROK Army to permit an increase from 460,000 to 525,000 troops and the organization of two new divisions. This would bring the ROK Army up to fourteen divisions, as a step toward a total of twenty. In addition, there were more United States units available. In Japan, for example, the 24th Infantry Division and the 1st Cavalry Divisions were made up largely of personnel experienced in Korean fighting. A second Marine division was available from the United States. Build-up of Korean ammunition stocks would also be required, which would cut, undesirably but not fatally, into ammunition already committed to NATO.

Finally, to keep the attack from becoming overly costly, it was clear that we would have to use atomic weapons.

This necessity was suggested to me by General MacArthur while I, as President-elect, was still living in New York. The Joint Chiefs of Staff were pessimistic about the feasibility of using tactical atomic weapons on front-line positions, in view of the extensive underground fortifications which the Chinese Communists had been able to construct; but such weapons would obviously be effective for strategic targets in North Korea, Manchuria, and on the Chinese coast.

If we decided upon a major, new type of offensive, the present policies would have to be changed and the new ones agreed to by our allies. Foremost would be the proposed use of atomic weapons. In this respect American views have always differed somewhat from those of some of our allies. For the British, for example, the use of atomic weapons in war at that time would have been a decision of the gravest kind. My feeling was then, and still remains, that it would be impossible for the United States to maintain the military commitments which it now sustains around the world (without turning into a garrison state) did we not possess atomic weapons and the will to use them when necessary. But an American decision to use them at that time would have created strong disrupting feelings between ourselves and our allies. However, if an all-out offensive should be highly successful, I felt that the rifts so caused could, in time, be repaired.

Of course, there were other problems, not the least of which would be the possibility of the Soviet Union entering the war. In nuclear warfare the Chinese Communists would have been able to do little. But we knew that the Soviets had atomic weapons in quantity and estimated that they would soon explode a hydrogen device. Of all the Asian targets which might be subjected to Soviet bombing, I was most concerned about the unprotected cities of Japan.

Source: Dwight D. Eisenhower. *Dwight D. Mandate for Change, 1953–1956.* Garden City, N.Y.: Doubleday, 1963, 179–180.

—⚭—

4. President Harry S. Truman Explains the American Role in Korea, April 1951

In a broadcast from the White House at 10:30 P.M. on April 11, 1951, President Harry S. Truman used the firing of General Douglas

MacArthur as Far Eastern Commander as an occasion to explain his policy toward Korea. Truman charged the communists with aggression in Asia but argued that the limited American response to Korea would prevent a third world war.

My fellow Americans:

I want to talk to you plainly tonight about what we are doing in Korea and about our policy in the Far East.

In the simplest terms, what we are doing in Korea is this: We are trying to prevent a third world war.

I think most people in this country recognized that fact last June. And they warmly supported the decision of the Government to help the Republic of Korea against the Communist aggressors. It is right for us to be in Korea now. It was right last June. It is right today.

I want to remind you why this is true.

The Communists in the Kremlin are engaged in a monstrous conspiracy to stamp out freedom all over the world. If they were to succeed, the United States would be numbered among their principal victims. It must be clear to everyone that the United States cannot—and will not—sit idly by and await foreign conquest.

And the best way to meet the threat of aggression is for the peace-loving nations to act together. If they don't act together, they are likely to be picked off, one by one.

This is the basic reason why we joined in creating the United Nations. And, since the end of World War II, we have been putting that lesson into practice—we have been working with other free nations to check the aggressive designs of the Soviet Union before they can result in a third world war.

The aggression against Korea is the boldest and most dangerous move the Communists have yet made.

The attack on Korea was part of a greater plan for conquering all of Asia.

The whole Communist imperialism is back of the attack on peace in the Far East. It was the Soviet Union that trained and equipped the North Koreans for aggression.

The question we have had to face is whether the Communist plan of conquest can be stopped without a general war.

So far, we have prevented world war III.

So far, by fighting a limited war in Korea, we have prevented aggression from succeeding, and bringing on a general war.

But you may ask why can't we take other steps to punish the aggressor. Why don't we bomb Manchuria and China itself? Why don't we assist the Chinese Nationalist troops to land on the mainland of China?

If we were to do these things, we would become entangled in a vast conflict on the continent of Asia. . . .

Behind the North Koreans and Chinese Communists in the front lines stand additional millions of Chinese soldiers. And behind the Chinese stand the tanks, the planes, the submarines, the soldiers, and the scheming rulers of the Soviet Union.

I believe that we must try to limit the war to Korea for these vital reasons: to make sure that the precious lives of our fighting men are not wasted; to see that the security of our country and the free world is not needlessly jeopardized; and to prevent a third world war.

A number of events have made it evident that General MacArthur did not agree with that policy. I have therefore considered it essential to relieve General MacArthur so that there would be no doubt or confusion as to the real purpose and aim of our policy.

Source: Truman Library, Independence Mo., Public Papers of President Harry S. Truman, address April 11, 1951. http://www.trumanlibrary.org/index.php.

—∞—

5. Secretary of Defense George C. Marshall, Testifying to the U.S. Senate, May 1951

Secretary of Defense George Marshall testified to the Senate committees investigating U.S. policy in Asia in May 1951 that General Douglas MacArthur's plans for taking the Korean War to China ran the risk of widening the conflict and leaving Europe vulnerable to Soviet attack. He supported President Truman's firing of MacArthur.

Secretary Marshall: Our objective in Korea continues to be the defeat of the aggression and the restoration of peace. We have persistently sought to confine the conflict to Korea and to prevent its spreading into a third world war. In this effort, we stand allied with the great majority of our fellow-members of the United Nations.

General MacArthur, on the other hand, would have us, on our own initiative, carry the conflict beyond Korea against the mainland of

Communist China, both from the sea and from the air. He would have us accept the risk of involvement not only in an extension of the war with Red China, but in an all-out war with the Soviet Union. . . . He would have us do this even though the effect of such action might expose Western Europe to attack by the millions of Soviet troops poised in Middle and Eastern Europe.

Source: U.S. Senate, Committee on Armed Services and Committee on Foreign Relations, Military Situation in the Far East. Washington, D.C.: Government Printing Office, 1951, 324–25.

—⁓—

6. General Omar Bradley, Testifying to the U.S. Senate, May 1951

General Omar Bradley, chair of the Joint Chiefs of Staff, defended President Truman's limited war policy in Korea at the U.S. Senate hearings on Korea on May 15, 1951. The general argued that it was necessary to block "Kremlin-inspired . . . guerrilla diplomacy." But taking the action to China was "the wrong war, at the wrong place, at the wrong time, and with the wrong enemy."

General MacArthur has stated that there are certain additional measures which can and should be taken, and that by so doing no unacceptable increased risk of global war will result.

The Joint Chiefs of Staff believe that these same measures do increase the risk of global war. . . .

From a global viewpoint . . our military mission is to support a policy of preventing communism from gaining the manpower, the resources, the raw materials, and the industrial capacity essential to world domination. If Soviet Russia ever controls the entire Eurasian land mass, then the Soviet-satellite imperialism may have the broad base upon which to build the military power to rule the world.

Korea, in spite of the importance of the engagement, must be looked upon with proper perspective. It is just one engagement, just one phase of this battle that we are having with the other power center in the world which opposed us and all we stand for. For five years this 'guerrilla diplomacy' has been going on. In each of the actions in which we have participated to oppose gangster conduct, we have risked World War III. But each time we have used methods short of total war. As costly as Berlin and Greece and Korea may be, they are less expensive than the vast destruction which would be inflicted upon all sides if a total war were to be precipitated.

The course of action often described as a "limited war" with Red China would increase the risk we are taking by engaging too much of our power in an area that is not the critical strategic prize

Red China is not the powerful nation seeking to dominate the world. Frankly, in the opinion of the Joint Chiefs of Staff, this strategy would involve us in the wrong war, at the wrong place, at the wrong time, and with the wrong enemy. . . .

Source: U.S. Senate, Committee on Armed Services and Committee on Foreign Relations, Military Situation in the Far East. Washington, D.C.: Government Printing Office, 1951, 730–732.

10

THE VIETNAM WAR:
Should the United States Use Combat Troops in Vietnam?

—ᴧ—

The Issue

The Vietnam War arose out of the U.S. effort to "contain" the spread of communism in Asia. Following France's failure to defeat anticolonial insurgents, Vietnam was divided into two zones in 1954, with a procommunist regime in the north and an anticommunist regime in the south, supported by the United States. When a guerrilla insurgency threatened to topple the Republic of South Vietnam, President Lyndon Johnson in 1965 sent American combat troops to bolster the regime. The United States battled South Vietnamese insurgents and troops from North Vietnam until a cease-fire agreement was reached in 1973. A debate raged in the United States over whether American combat soldiers should be used in Vietnam.

♦ *Arguments that the United States should use combat troops in Vietnam:* Presidents from Harry Truman through Richard Nixon accepted as an article of faith that communist powers sought to expand their ideology and control around the world and should be blocked. President Johnson acted on this premise in 1965 by sending combat troops to Vietnam, explaining that the country of South Vietnam had been attacked by North Vietnam. He claimed that the United States had made irrevocable commitments to South Vietnam to defend its "freedom."

♦ *Arguments that the United States should not use combat troops in Vietnam:* A variety of critics faulted the Johnson administration for intervening in what many saw as a civil war among the Vietnamese. From this perspective, South Vietnamese guerrillas and the army of North Vietnam switched their anticolonial resistance from the French, who previously had controlled Indochina, to the Americans. Senator William Fulbright (D-AR) argued that Americans exhibited an "arrogance of power" by attempting to thwart a "war of liberation." Other critics, such as George Kennan, questioned the relevance of Vietnam to the basic cold war objectives of containing communism.

—ᴍ—

INTRODUCTION

On May 3, 1971, the so-called May Day Tribe, a collection of young antiwar demonstrators, blocked traffic and public buildings in Washington, D.C. At the request of President Richard Nixon's White House staff, the city's chief of police ordered mass detentions, arresting 7,000 protesters by day's end. Since the Washington police lacked facilities to house so many arrestees, many were bused to the Washington Coliseum. The May Day Tribe's protests in the nation's capital were the culmination of more than a week of antiwar activity, which had been kicked off by the arrival in Washington of thousands of Vietnam War veterans. Frustrated at Congress's disinterest in their complaints about the war, many veterans threw their war medals over a fence erected around the national Capitol.

President Nixon urged his staff not to hassle the Vietnam vets, fearing a public backlash, but the administration was less restrained regarding what it called the "crazies" and "hippies" that descended on Washington for a mass demonstration scheduled for April 24. Perhaps half a million people attended the rally, while another 200,000 had gathered in San Francisco to protest the war. Although Nixon had pledged to bring the troops home from Vietnam, he fumed that citizen groups challenged his authority to manage American policy. He held round-the-clock conferences with White House aides discussing how to discredit the protesters, including John Kerry, a leader of the Vietnam Veterans Against the War. White House chief of staff H. R. Haldeman told Nixon that managing the media would be helped by the fact that the demonstrators were "bad-looking people." The Nixon aides, many sporting crew-cuts and usually wearing neckties, saw long hair and jeans as the uniform of the enemy.

The May Day demonstrations were a caricature of public protests of the Vietnam War. From a policy standpoint, dissenters objected to a national policy that nurtured and supported the Republic of South Vietnam. At the time, the antiwar movement was complex, pulling in various groups and airing numerous complaints about the conditions of American life. In many respects, the protest against the Vietnam War became a cultural battle at home between younger and older Americans. Many parents recoiled at the vehement denunciations of American policy that their children exhibited, creating what some called a "generation gap." Some critics of the war broadened their indictment of policy toward Vietnam to include racism and sexism at home as well as institutions, such as multinational corporations, that supposedly sustained these tendencies. This criticism of the "establishment" and its alleged misdeeds at times spilled out onto the streets, where some protesters vandalized the surroundings. These acts of civil disobedience often obscured the fundamental questions about America's military involvement in Vietnam. Was it appropriate for the United States to use American combat troops to save the government of South Vietnam? Was communist aggression the real reason for American involvement in Vietnam?

Presidents Harry S. Truman, Dwight D. Eisenhower, John F. Kennedy, and Lyndon B. Johnson all were in fundamental agreement on the answers to these questions. Since World War II, communists in Asia had sought to extend their system by force into surrounding territories. President Truman authorized aid to the French in 1950 to counter the advance of communism in Indochina (which included Vietnam). President Eisenhower pledged support to the new regime of South Vietnam, created in 1954, pointing to the threat of communist subversion that could topple one free regime after another. President Johnson put the case simply and directly. He said that South Vietnam, an independent nation, was under attack from North Vietnam, which was urged on by the Chinese. He reiterated the "domino" theory that presumed that when one nation succumbed to "communism," others were likely to follow. Johnson claimed the United States had "a promise to keep" in supporting freedom in South Vietnam.

President Johnson's decision to bolster the regime in South Vietnam with American combat troops began in earnest in 1965. As the troop level rose, so did the doubters and critics of his policy. Some questioned whether events in Vietnam actually arose from a master plan of international communists. These critics emphasized the long Vietnamese effort to oust French colonialism in Indochina. They acknowledged that Ho Chi Minh, the leader of North Vietnam, was a communist but

Ho Chi Minh led the struggle to expel France from Vietnam and opposed U.S. support of the Diem regime in South Vietnam. (Associated Press)

emphasized that he was equally as fervent a nationalist working for independence. This line of thinking saw the government of South Vietnam as an American client, a regime created by the United States to facilitate its containment policy.

Some opponents of America's Vietnam policy thought that the truth in this debate was immaterial. Their criticism of U.S. policy contended that Vietnam had little strategic value to broader diplomatic objectives of the United States. A related concern challenged the assumption that the United States possessed the capacity and moral authority to remake a small nation into a Western-style democracy. And some war protesters demanded a halt to a military campaign that killed civilians in a poor nation on the other side of the globe. From 1964 to the early 1970s, debate raged in the United States over whether the United States should use American troops to stop communist aggression in Vietnam.

BACKGROUND

The roots of the Vietnam War lie in the European colonization of Southeast Asia. In the mid-19th century, the French had established a foothold on the Indochinese peninsula and built colonies in regions formerly known as Annam, Tonkin, and Cochin (now Vietnam) as well as in Cambodia and Laos. Japan occupied Indochina in World War II but delegated administration of the region to the Vichy French government that cooperated with their German invaders in Europe. Japan's defeat in World War II led to its exodus from the colony in late 1945, which provided a political opportunity for Ho Chi Minh. A Vietnamese nationalist and also a communist, Ho became the nemesis of the United States from the late 1940s until his death in 1969. (See the sidebar "Ho Chi Minh" on page 306.) Aided by his talented general Vo Nguyen Giap, Ho organized the Vietminh, an organization dedicated to winning independence for the Vietnamese. In September 1945, Ho proclaimed the independence of Vietnam, a step that had received tacit approval from President Franklin Roosevelt.

French leaders, however, sought to reassert control of their colonies in southeastern Asia. In 1946, fighting erupted between the French army and the Vietminh. Ho's campaign to oust the French reached a crescendo in 1954 at the Battle of Dien Bien Phu, a town in Vietnam's northwestern highlands. A Vietminh victory forced the French to retreat to southern Vietnam. At a conference at Geneva, Switzerland, the same year, negotiators adopted an agreement, the Geneva Accords, that partitioned the country into two temporary zones, assigning Ho's Vietminh control of the northern zone, with its capital at Hanoi, and the French supervision of the southern zone, with Saigon as its capital. The Geneva Accords scheduled elections in 1956 to determine the unification of the country. France decided to exit Vietnam entirely and placed its zone in the hands of a former Vietnamese emperor, Bao Dai, who appointed Ngo Dinh Diem as premier. Most observers conceded that Ho Chi Minh's side would win the unification elections, with the likely result that a communist regime would be established in the country.

The elections were never held. Beginning with President Truman in 1950, the United States began to provide aid to France's military effort against the Vietminh. By 1954, the United States was paying 80 percent of the cost of France's resistance against the anticolonial insurgency. Both Truman and his successor, President Dwight D. Eisenhower, saw Ho Chi Minh as part of the communist conspiracy that sought to expand its control in Asia. The victory of Mao Zedong and the communists in China in 1949 was still fresh in their minds. Concern about the advance of communism in Asia was reinforced by the outbreak of the Korean War in 1950. The French claimed they were fighting communism in Vietnam. They were also displaying reluctance to join NATO, the military alliance that the United States and other Western

HO CHI MINH

Ho Chi Minh, the president of the Democratic Republic of Vietnam from 1945 until his death in 1969, is hailed in his country as the leading nationalist and hero of the victory over French colonialism. To most Americans during the cold war, he was the head of an insurgency that sought to turn Vietnam into a communist dictatorship.

Ho was born Nguyen Sihn Cung in a rural province of central Vietnam around 1890. After a limited education, he taught school and then signed on as a mess boy on a French ocean liner, which took him to ports throughout Africa and the Mediterranean. He worked for a time in Boston, New York, and London before locating to Paris in 1917. A committed anticolonialist and a socialist, Ho joined a small group of Vietnamese who petitioned President Woodrow Wilson during the World War I peace conference at Versailles, France, to end French rule in Indochina. The request seemed in accordance with Wilson's support of self-determination for nationalist groups, but the Vietnamese delegation was denied an audience with conference leaders. While in Paris, Ho became a founding member of the French Communist Party in 1920. An admirer of Vladimir Lenin, the revolutionary leader of Russia, Ho journeyed to Moscow in 1923, where he studied and wrote.

In 1924, Ho left Russia for China, where he spent most of the next 20 years, working both for Vietnamese independence and the Communist Party. In 1930, he organized the Vietnamese Communist Party in Hong Kong, where he had fled from areas controlled by the Chiang Kai-shek Nationalists, who were battling the Chinese communists. World War II gave Ho an opportunity to win national unification for Vietnam. As part of their thrust into China and southeastern Asia, the Japanese occupied Indochina,

democracies had formed to block a Russian advance in Europe. The Americans thought that aiding France in Vietnam might entice their European ally to change its mind about joining NATO.

The Eisenhower administration considered the Geneva Accords a "disaster," because it opened up the likelihood of communist control over all of Vietnam and perhaps other places in Indochina. Eisenhower and his Secretary of State, John Foster Dulles, took steps to prevent this development. First, the administration authorized the Central but they allowed the Vichy French (collaborators with the German occupation of France) to continue everyday administration. In 1941, Ho formed the Vietminh, a political organization to resist French and Japanese occupation of Indochina. When Japan was defeated in 1945, the Vietminh declared the independent Republic of Vietnam, with Ho as president. The Vietnamese declaration of independence drew on the American Declaration of Independence and the French Declaration of the Rights of Man and the Citizen.

Aspirations for a free Vietnam met bitter disappointment in 1946, when France reasserted its control over its former colony. Eight years of war between the French and the Vietminh followed, until Ho's brilliant general Vo Nguyen Giap defeated the French at the battle of Dien Bien Phu. At the armistice arrangement embodied in the Geneva Accords of 1954, the French assumed temporary control over South Vietnam until elections could be held to unify the country. Few observers doubted that Ho would win and become leader of a unified Vietnam.

But American cold war politics blocked the agreement. Ignoring the 1954 accords, the United States pushed to established a Republic of South Vietnam under the leadership of Ngo Dinh Diem. Authoritarian in style, Diem became increasingly oppressive, which steeled Ho's determination to oust a leader whose power rested on American support. The elections to unify Vietnam were never held. Ho aided the Vietcong guerrilla resistance to Diem in 1959 and later sent divisions of North Vietnamese regulars into the south. By the early 1960s, a war commenced that lasted more than a decade. Ho did not live to see its end. He died in 1969 at approximately the age of 79, but he probably foresaw the outcome. Patience and persistence were his two chief attributes.

Intelligence Agency (CIA) to launch secret operations against North Vietnam, designed to impede Ho's regime from consolidating its hold on the region. Second, the Eisenhower administration engineered the appointment of Ngo Dinh Diem, a staunch anticommunist and Catholic and a former French collaborator who had been living in exile in the United States, as Bao Dai's premier in the government in the southern zone of Vietnam. Diem won a rigged election in 1955 that gave him control of the government in the southern zone and, with American encouragement, declared the Republic of Vietnam. The United States recognized the new country three days later. The Eisenhower administration lavished financial aid on the Diem regime and sent advisers to build an army.

Diem proved to be a poor bet for the United States. He was an authoritarian leader who could not tolerate dissent and who played favorites in a government that some observers likened to a medieval court. The regime was corrupt, nonrepresentative, and opposed to reforms that could help the rural peasants. He suppressed Buddhist monks—in a country 80 percent Buddhist—and others who dared to complain about his policies. Diem also targeted the Vietminh, who launched a guerrilla insurgency against his regime in 1957. The following year, North Vietnam began giving aid to the Vietminh. Encouraged by Ho in North Vietnam, the southern Vietminh formed the National Liberation Front (NLF) in 1960 as a political organization to oppose Diem. Americans dubbed the indigenous guerrillas in South Vietnam the Vietcong.

By the time John Kennedy became president in January 1961, the Diem regime was wavering under protests and insurgency. Like Truman and Eisenhower before him, Kennedy was committed to the containment policy and was determined not to "lose" more territory to the communists. As a United States senator, Kennedy (D-MA) had said that "Vietnam represents the cornerstone of the Free World in Southeast Asia." Publicly, at least, he held to this position as president. His goal was to maintain a noncommunist buffer state, even if it meant supporting an undemocratic leader. Kennedy authorized an increase of American military advisers to help stabilize South Vietnam and hold Diem in power. By November 1963, 17,000 U.S. military personnel were in Vietnam aiding in counterinsurgency activities. Diem's inability to mollify his critics in South Vietnam or contain the Vietminh insurgency convinced the Americans that his effectiveness was over. The Kennedy administration gave tacit consent to conspirators to overthrow Diem in a military coup, which occurred on November 1, 1963. Diem was found in the trunk of a car, murdered. Three weeks later, on November 22, 1963, Kennedy was assassinated. The Vietnam baton now passed to Lyndon Johnson.

Lyndon B. Johnson (LBJ) did not want to be a war president. His dream was to build a "Great Society" at home through legislation that tackled domestic problems such as health care for the elderly, voting rights for African Americans, better public schools, preserving the wilderness, elimination of poverty, and protections for consumers. Early in his presidency, it looked as if LBJ might realize his hope to achieve political fame on a par with his idol, Franklin D. Roosevelt. Then Vietnam encroached on his presidency.

Johnson viewed Vietnam through the same lens that had guided presidents Truman, Eisenhower, and Kennedy. He saw communism as a malignant force that undermined freedom in emerging countries around the world. If he did not completely accept the "domino theory" that communism would spread from one

President Lyndon B. Johnson mired the United States in a war in Vietnam that he did not want and was unable to win. (Library of Congress)

location to another, he did not disavow the idea. LBJ supported the containment policy as a necessary step to thwart communist aggression in Vietnam, which he contended was instigated by rulers in Beijing and Moscow. Politically, the memory of charges that Truman had "lost" China to the Communists bolstered his determination not to fall victim to the same charge in Vietnam.

As a consummate deal maker who got things done in the United States, Johnson thought that he could fix the Vietnam problem, largely by convincing Ho Chi Minh of the reasonableness of negotiating with the Americans. Johnson never understood Ho's commitment to win independence for Vietnam on his own terms, nor did he realize the difficulty of turning a former colonial regime in Asia into a stable democratic state. South Vietnam underwent a sequence of governmental coups after Diem's murder, as one general after another seized power. In February 1965, Air Marshal Nguyen Cao Ky became prime minister, and Nguyen Van Thieu assumed control of the South Vietnamese army.

The duo were not successful in stemming the widening control of the Vietcong over the villages in the countryside.

In August 1964, a fateful turn in the Vietnam War occurred. Armed vessels of North Vietnam, President Johnson informed Congress, had attacked two American destroyers in the Gulf of Tonkin off the coast of North Vietnam. The president asked for congressional authority to respond to the attacks as part of the nation's policy of "assisting the free nations of the area to defend their freedom." Without hearings on the request, following Johnson's wishes, Congress passed the Gulf of Tonkin Resolution on August 7, with only two senators in dissent, and no opposition in the House. The Johnson administration later claimed that the resolution provided ample authority for the president to commit offensive military forces to Vietnam. Neither Johnson nor prior presidents involved in the conflict submitted a declaration of war to Congress concerning the use of troops in Vietnam. The circumstances surrounding the Gulf of Tonkin Resolution remain controversial, in part because of doubt that North Vietnam had actually fired on the American ships. Johnson did not tell most members of Congress at the time that the American destroyers were part of a larger campaign that sought to destabilize the North Vietnamese regime.

The Gulf of Tonkin Resolution provided Johnson with authority to order reprisals on North Vietnam, including, presumably, a bombing campaign. The president hung back from launching air attacks, however, probably for political reasons, since 1964 was an election year, and Johnson wanted to win the White House on his own. His opponent was Arizona senator Barry Goldwater, a dedicated cold warrior and vocal opponent of communism. Referring to the Soviet Union, he wrote in his political manifesto, *Conscience of a Conservative* (1960): "We are confronted by a revolutionary world movement that possesses . . . the will to dominate absolutely every square mile of the globe." During the presidential campaign, the Arizona senator repeatedly charged that Johnson was failing to meet the communist challenge. Goldwater proposed greater military pressure against North Vietnam, including the use of nuclear weapons. The Democrats painted Goldwater as trigger happy and reckless. Johnson wanted to show that he was the moderate in comparison to Goldwater's "hawkish" bellicosity.

Johnson used the Gulf of Tonkin Resolution to show that he could be tough on the communists, too, while his restraint in ordering air attacks on North Vietnam offered support to the claim that he was the peace candidate in 1964. Johnson's victory and the polls suggest that the public sided with the "doves" (people who support military restraint) over the "hawks" regarding approaches to Vietnam. But secretly, the Johnson administration had planned a bombing campaign before the November election. "Rolling Thunder," as the air operation was code-named, was launched from aircraft carriers in the South China Sea in March 1965.

The president hoped that pressure from an air campaign would drive Ho Chi Minh to the bargaining table—on American terms. Attempting to apply just the right amount of pressure, Johnson restricted the scope of the bombing campaign, personally approving targets. But he had few illusions that bombing alone could win the war. The "jungle war" in Southeast Asia was largely a guerrilla campaign. The Vietcong and the regular army of North Vietnam seldom appeared in large formations willing to engage in set-piece battles such as occurred in Europe and Russia during World War II. The Vietnamese style was to hit and hide. Supplies were carted from North Vietnam into the South via a trail that snaked into Laos and Cambodia, under a jungle canopy, usually at night, sometimes by truck, and sometimes by human porters. Underground tunnels were used for storage dumps. Later in the war, the U.S. Air Force used napalm and other chemical products to defoliate what became known as the "Ho Chi Minh Trail."

As 1965 unfolded, it became clear that neither American bombing nor the government of South Vietnam was gaining over the Vietcong and North Vietnam. Faced with this situation, Johnson authorized the deployment of combat troops to Vietnam. At first, their mission was only defense of American air bases in South Vietnam. This restriction was soon lifted. The final phase of the "Americanization" of the war in Vietnam had commenced. By the end of 1965, 184,000 American troops were serving in Vietnam. In 1966, the number rose to 385,000, and by 1967 it had grown to 485,000. At the peak of the American troop commitment in 1968, 535,000 military personnel served in Vietnam. This gradual enlargement of American combat troops over a four-year period was called "escalation." This incremental increase in force, tempered by restrictions on their actions, became a highly controversial aspect of the war.

Why did Johnson escalate? There are several reasons, although historians have not completely unraveled the psychology behind the

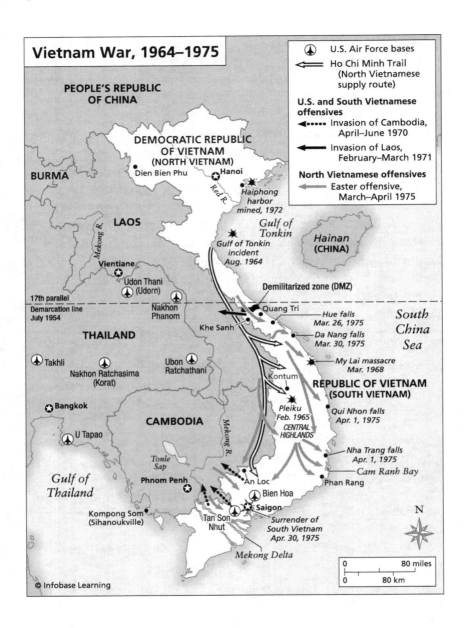

Vietnam War, 1964–1975

U.S. Air Force bases

⬅ Ho Chi Minh Trail
(North Vietnamese
supply route)

**U.S. and South Vietnamese
offensives**

◄••••• Invasion of Cambodia,
April–June 1970

◄— Invasion of Laos,
February–March 1971

North Vietnamese offensives

— Easter offensive,
March–April 1975

PEOPLE'S REPUBLIC
OF CHINA

DEMOCRATIC REPUBLIC
OF VIETNAM
(NORTH VIETNAM)

BURMA

Dien Bien Phu • ❀Hanoi

Red R.

Haiphong
harbor
mined, 1972

LAOS

Mekong R.

*Gulf of
Tonkin*

Gulf of Tonkin
incident
Aug. 1964

Hainan
(CHINA)

Vientiane

Udon Thani
(Udorn)

17th parallel

Demarcation line
July 1954

Nakhon
Phanom

Khe Sanh

Quang Tri

Demilitarized zone (DMZ)

Hue falls
Mar. 26, 1975

Da Nang falls
Mar. 30, 1975

*South
China
Sea*

THAILAND

Takhli

Nakhon Ratchasima
(Korat)

Ubon
Ratchathani

Kontum

My Lai massacre
Mar. 1968

**REPUBLIC OF VIETNAM
(SOUTH VIETNAM)**

Bangkok

CAMBODIA

Mekong R.

Pleiku
Feb. 1965

*CENTRAL
HIGHLANDS*

Qui Nhon falls
Apr. 1, 1975

U Tapao

*Tonle
Sap*

Phnom Penh

An Loc

Nha Trang falls
Apr. 1, 1975

Cam Ranh Bay

Phan Rang

*Gulf of
Thailand*

Phan Hoa

Kompong Som
(Sihanoukville)

Tan Son
Nhut

Saigon

Surrender of
South Vietnam
Apr. 30, 1975

N

Mekong Delta

0   80 miles

0   80 km

© Infobase Learning

president's decision. First and most apparent to American policy makers, the government of South Vietnam was losing the war to the communists. A crisis loomed, and a decision was required, fast. Second, Johnson and his small circle of advisers, especially Secretary of Defense Robert McNamara, special assistant McGeorge Bundy, Secretary of State Dean Rusk, and General William Westmoreland, argued that the Vietnam problem could be solved by military force. "Peace-feelers" to North Vietnam had failed, largely because the United States refused to allow the Vietcong a role in negotiations. Once Johnson and his small team of inside players committed to a military solution, however, it became increasingly difficult to cut loose from it. Adopting a new approach meant admitting that their original plan was a mistake. In effect, the group became a prisoner of their own decision making. As events proved, the generals had overestimated their capacity to win a guerrilla war.

Moreover, Johnson tried to fine-tune his Asia policy to minimize political damage at home. Ever mindful of the criticism that President Truman received when the communists won in China, Johnson believed that the "loss" of Vietnam to communist control would have devastating political consequences. Doing nothing would allow the communists to win on the battlefield. Negotiations harbored the possibility of bargaining from weakness. On the other hand, the president continually minimized the level of military commitment needed to succeed in Vietnam. He concluded that a middle path—neither too little force nor too much—was the optimum course for defusing political criticism at home.

Finally, Johnson did not want to lure China or Russia into the war. If the warnings of the communist superpowers were to be believed, an American invasion of North Vietnam would have triggered their intervention and expanded the war. A bombing campaign without targeting restrictions may have had the same result. Therefore, Johnson played it cautiously, limiting bombing targets and applying measured levels of troop increases, but never as many soldiers as his generals requested. This middle path, the president hoped, would eventually exhaust North Vietnam, which would then be willing to negotiate. Escalation did not force Ho Chi Minh to the bargaining table; it did impale Johnson on a policy dilemma of his own making.

THE DEBATE

The debate over Vietnam was not just about tactics, it was also about fundamental questions of American policy toward Southeast Asia and "wars of liberation" in the postcolonial era. The central issue at stake was: Did the communist insurgency in Vietnam pose a threat to American security and national interest? Were the freedoms cherished in the

Western democracies dependent on affairs in Vietnam? This debate went beyond an intellectual discussion about the best policy solutions. The Vietnam issue often degenerated during the mid-1960s into an emotional yelling match in which many families were split between parents on the one side and their children, some of whom were liable to the military draft, on the other. When words were insufficient, some dissenters took to the streets to protest. Violence sometimes erupted when young antiwar demonstrators were confronted by prowar opponents and the police. "Debate" is a polite way of referring to the political cleavage in America over Vietnam.

The Argument that the United States Should Use Combat Troops in Vietnam

The Johnson administration saw the war as communist aggression in which North Vietnam sought to conquer the independent nation of South Vietnam. It thought that Russia and China were the kingpins behind this adventure, with Ho their tool to spread communism in Asia. The administration considered the "domino theory" as established truth, not a conjecture. Since President Truman's influential speech in 1947 that warned of communist threats to the West, Washington diplomats had stood by the "containment" of communist powers. Most administration officials believed the only logic that the Russians understood was military force.

President Dwight Eisenhower had subscribed to this thinking. In April 1954, as he pondered the wisdom of helping the French avoid defeat at Dien Bien Phu, he was asked to comment on the strategic importance of Indochina "to the free world." The president drew a vivid picture of "the 'falling domino' principle." (See "President Dwight D. Eisenhower, Comments on Indochina, 1954," on page 327 in the Primary Sources section.) The loss of Indochina, he said, would trigger the loss of Burma (now Myanmar), then Thailand, and perhaps Indonesia. Not only would the "free world" become smaller, but a sweep of "communist dictatorship" through Asia would threaten Western access to strategic natural resources.

The Eisenhower view of tittering dominos was conventional wisdom to President Johnson and his advisers in 1965. They saw communist aggression in Vietnam and believed that had it had to stopped. Johnson summed up the case for military intervention in Vietnam at a speech in Baltimore on April 7, 1965. (See "President Lyndon B. Johnson, 'Peace

Without Conquest' Speech on Vietnam, 1965," on page 328 in the Primary Sources section.) The president charged that China had egged on North Vietnam to attack "the independent nation of South Vietnam." Johnson gave three reasons the United States had to resist this aggression. First, he claimed that the United States had a "promise" to keep, namely, of supporting the South Vietnamese resistance to communism. Not to do so would undermine the world's confidence in America's "word." Second, the domino theory was at stake. Insuring the "independence" of Vietnam would deter China and defend freedom in the world. Third, the president said "our own security is at stake" when one nation attempts to conquer another. Johnson did not elaborate on this idea, but he did offer to fund a massive redevelopment program in Vietnam if Hanoi accepted a bid to come to the bargaining table.

Johnson offered a condensed version of a view that the U.S. State Department had developed over the years. William P. Bundy, assistant secretary of state for Far Eastern affairs (and brother of McGeorge Bundy), offered a more detailed review of this history. (See "William P. Bundy, Address on 'Myth and Reality Concerning South Vietnam,' 1965," on page 329 in the Primary Sources section.) After the Geneva Accords in 1954, Ngo Dinh Diem had drawn on his anticommunist fervor to battle for a stable, free Vietnam. Refugees that streamed from North to South were testimony that "the great mass of the people of South Vietnam do not wish to be ruled by communism or from Hanoi." However, the Diem regime stumbled and mistakenly turned away from reform, creating dissent in the country; at the same time, Hanoi sent its divisions south. William Bundy explicitly rejected the suggestion that the fighting in South Vietnam was a "civil war." North Vietnam, aided and encouraged by the leadership in "Peiping" (Beijing), he argued, directed the fight in the South. Because infiltration from Hanoi increased in early 1965, President Johnson, acting on the "request from the South Vietnamese Government," ordered carefully targeted air attacks on North Vietnam. American policy had not changed in 1965, Bundy concluded, only the level of its execution.

The Argument that the United States Should Not Use Combat Troops in Vietnam

Bundy's version of the facts failed to convince skeptics. Some observers scoffed at the contention that the Republic of South Vietnam was an "independent" nation. Critics argued that the regime was largely a creation of the United States as a makeshift bulwark against communist control, a development that violated the terms of the Geneva Accords. This criticism maintained that the struggle in Vietnam was essentially an anticolonial movement that happened to be associated with communists.

Senator J. William Fulbright (D-AR), chairman of the Senate Foreign Relations Committee, came around to this view by 1966. Fulbright had sponsored President Johnson's Gulf of Tonkin Resolution in 1964, to the senator's later regret. Johnson never forgave the senator's criticism of his Vietnam policy. By 1966, Fulbright called American intervention in Vietnam an exercise in "the arrogance of power." (See "J. William Fulbright, On the "Arrogance of Power," 1966," on page 330 in the Primary Sources section.) American leaders had lost their sensibility about the realities of world developments. They had, Fulbright charged, equated use of the nation's unprecedented power with virtue, whereby military intervention in other lands was deemed fitting and appropriate. Fulbright argued that the administration had chosen to disregard the nationalistic fervor in Vietnam's struggle against French colonialism and then against the Americans. Instead, the administration saw only communism. The effort to refashion Vietnam into a democracy overlooked historic realities in Southeast Asia. Not only was the effort likely to fail, but also the way the administration pursued this objective alienated America's allies and many of its own citizens at home. The solution was to admit the limitations of nation-building by military force and bring all parties, including Ho Chi Minh and the National Liberation Front, to the bargaining table to work out the future of their own country. Unlike LBJ, Fulbright rejected the use of military power to force the enemy to negotiate.

The alienation at home was manifest on the nation's college campuses, at first among small groups of radicals, such as the Students for a Democratic Society (SDS), and later by major segments of the college-aged population. Some of this concern was influenced by the likelihood that the draft would put some young males in a war whose purposes they questioned. Paul Potter, president of SDS, raised these issues at an antiwar rally in 1965. (See "Paul Potter, 'Incredible War' Speech, 1965," on page 331 in the Primary Sources section.) Potter scoffed at the notion that the United States was defending freedom in South Vietnam, given that Diem had "systematically" suppressed political opposition. One of the assignments for American soldiers, he charged, was to control indigenous opponents to the dictatorship that ran South Vietnam. Beyond this misuse of military power, Potter denounced the destruction of "the very fabric of the country." The institutional structure of the United States allowed American leaders to conduct war without considering the human consequences of their actions. Changing the policy, Potter argued, required changing the political system at home. These were radical ideas for most Americans. The majority of the public supported President Johnson's military escalation in Vietnam into 1967. Still, dissent grew year by year.

Some criticism of Johnson's approach came from individuals who were not radicals by any stretch of the imagination. George F. Kennan, one of the founding fathers of containment policy and a specialist in international relations, clearly fit this description. Kennan accepted the legitimacy of the government of South Vietnam and agreed that the war was caused by the invasion from North Vietnam. What he questioned was the relevance of Vietnam to America's strategic interests. (See "George F. Kennan, Statement on Vietnam, 1966," on page 333 in the Primary Sources section.) Testifying at a Senate hearing in 1966, Kennan stated flatly that "Vietnam is not a region of major military and industrial importance" to the United States. Contrary to assertions from the Johnson administration, Kennan thought it likely that South Vietnam would follow an independent course rather than kowtow to Russia or China. Kennan wondered how others around the world reacted to the efforts of the United States to reshape the politics of another country, especially when the press distributed photographs of Americans "inflicting grievous injury on the lives of a poor and helpless people." Moreover, Kennan doubted that the United States could win a military victory in Vietnam. In 1967 and 1968, this belief gained increasing acceptance.

OUTCOME AND IMPACT

Some of Johnson's former colleagues in the Senate expressed reservations about the "Americanization" of the war as the escalation commenced. Senators Richard Russell (D-GA), John Sparkman (D-AL), and Mike Mansfield (D-MT), the majority leader, warned the president that he was headed down the wrong road. Johnson brushed aside their misgivings and listened to his close circle of advisers, which initially included Secretary of Defense Robert McNamara. By late 1966, however, McNamara revealed a change of heart. In a document dated October 14, 1966, and printed in the Pentagon Papers, the secret government history of the Vietnam War published in 1970, McNamara reported to

THE PENTAGON PAPERS

On Sunday, June 13, 1971, the *New York Times* began publication of secret government documents concerning the war in Vietnam. Produced at the urging of Robert McNamara, the secretary of defense, the collection became known as the Pentagon Papers. Disillusioned with the pace of the Vietnam War, McNamara ordered officials in the Pentagon (the headquarters of the U.S. military) in June 1967 to compile a history of U.S. policy toward Vietnam. Some 30 governmental officials worked a year and a half compiling 47 volumes of narrative history and supporting government documents. Spanning a period between 1950 and early 1968, the compilation totaled 7,000 pages.

The Pentagon Papers was a secret project, not intended for public consumption. Originally, only 15 copies of the report were produced. A distraught Pentagon researcher, Daniel Ellsberg, gave copies to the *New York Times* and other newspapers. The *Times* published excerpts for several days, until a suit in district federal court brought by the Nixon administration produced a judicial order to suspend publication. The *Times* appealed to the Supreme Court, which reversed the stay of publication. The Nixon Justice Department had argued that public distribution of the documents would cause "irreparable" injury to the United States. The Supreme Court disagreed, noting that never had prior restraint on speech been permissible in the United States (*New York Times Co. v. United States,* 1971). The remedy, if any was warranted, should be taken after publication.

The Pentagon Papers had an electrifying effect on the debate over the Vietnam War. The *Times* rushed out a 677-page paperback book condensation in July 1971. The papers documented a broad gap between what the administration said was happening and what governmental officials actually knew about the war. The confidence that the Johnson White House emanated stood in sharp contrast to doubts of officials behind the scenes, groping for a workable policy. Moreover, the papers revealed that the United the president that "I see no reasonable way to bring the war to an end soon." (See the sidebar "The Pentagon Papers" below.) Even though the enemy was suffering huge casualties, he wrote, "there is no sign of an impending break in enemy morale . . . they can replace their losses."

States had a history of undertaking dirty tricks in Vietnam. The ink was barely dry on the Geneva Accords when President Dwight D. Eisenhower approved clandestine CIA missions into North Vietnam. These actions, under the supervision of Colonel Edward Lansdale, included paramilitary activities, sabotage, and psychological warfare (they called it "psywar") in an effort to disrupt and discredit the communist government in the North. Moreover, intelligence officials had written memos expressing the view that the war began largely as a rebellion in South Vietnam against the oppressive Diem regime.

Revealing as they were, the Pentagon Papers did not constitute a full history of the war. The researchers did not have access to White House archives, nor did they interview individuals, including current and former government officials. The project was secret, done from within the Pentagon bureaucracy. Nonetheless, the papers confirmed the allegations of many critics that much of what several presidential administrations had said about the war was a public relations campaign, with little regard for the truth. The Pentagon Papers contributed to the "credibility" gap, wherein the public distrusted what its leaders said.

However, the story does not end here. President Nixon was incensed that the Pentagon Papers had been made public. He wanted to plug leaks of confidential information. The president authorized the formation of the "Plumbers" group in the White House, with instructions to find and stop unauthorized leaks. The Plumbers burglarized the office of Ellsberg's psychiatrist in an effort to find information to discredit the research. The Plumbers were disbanded soon afterward, with some of its personnel assigned to the Committee to Re-elect the President. These insiders ordered the break-in into Democratic Party headquarters in the Watergate Hotel in Washington in 1972. When the burglars were apprehended and their trial revealed connections to the Nixon White House, the president approved a cover-up so as not to reveal his involvement in the Ellsberg episode. The Watergate scandal ultimately led to Nixon's resignation in 1974.

The war must be won by the Vietnamese, yet "we have not found the formula" for "inspiring them into action." Johnson eased McNamara out of his job in February 1968. In reflecting later on his initial support of the president, McNamara said: "None of our allies supported us. . . . If we can't persuade nations with comparable values of the merit of our cause, we'd better reexamine our reasoning."

The Joint Chiefs of Staff submitted a dissenting memo to McNamara's report, rejecting his analysis and calling for increased military pressure. Many military leaders complained to Johnson that restrictions on their scope of action, especially on bombing, threatened to undermine their mission in Vietnam. Nonetheless, through 1967, generals such as William Westmoreland saw "light at the end of the tunnel," a phrased uttered frequently to underscore the statement that the tide was turning in America's favor.

The Tet Offensive lifted the veil of this forced optimism. On January 30, 1968, the Vietnamese New Year Holiday known as Tet, Vietcong guerrillas struck at targets in more than 100 cities and 36 of 44 provincial capitals in South Vietnam. A band of insurgents even breached the walls of the American embassy in Saigon, where they conducted a gun battle with military police. American and South Vietnamese soldiers regained the upper hand in most locales within days, inflicting heavy casualties on the Vietcong and North Vietnamese regulars. Tet was a tactical defeat for the communists, but it was a strategic defeat for the United States. The communist offensive had demonstrated that Johnson's escalation had not subdued the insurgency and that the Americans were not on the verge of victory. The situation on the ground in South Vietnam remained as tenuous as in prior years, indicating that the war remained an unresolved stalemate.

Tet had a dramatic effect on public attitudes toward the war. Polls registered plummeting confidence in the administration's optimistic predictions. In March 1968, a Gallup Poll found that half of respondents believed it wrong to have become involved in Vietnam. On March 12, Senator Eugene McCarthy (D-MN), an outspoken critic of escalation, nearly beat Johnson in the New Hampshire presidential primary, the first in the nation's nominating canvases. Johnson's group of "Wise Men," retired governmental officials who met periodically to advise him, now concluded that the war could not be won. At the end of the month, Johnson announced on national TV that he would not run for reelection.

Vietnam was not the only factor that soured Johnson on running again. Great Society programs, especially civil rights legislation, and deadly, destructive riots in dozens of American cities had alienated southern and white working-class Democrats. Still, the divisive Vietnam War was key to the fracturing of the Democratic Party; its liberal wing increasingly criticized the president's Asian policy.

Senator Robert Kennedy (D-NY), the slain president's brother, led the challenges to the administration's Vietnam policy until he was assassinated in Los Angeles on June 5, 1968. The antiwar faction never found a viable replacement for Kennedy—McCarthy amassed only a limited following—but protest against the war turned the 1968 Democratic National Convention in Chicago into a battleground. Thousands of young protesters who had journeyed to the city to demonstrate against the war were assaulted by police over several days of rioting. The clash spilled over to the convention floor, where pro-Johnson supporters and antiwar Democrats engaged in a screaming match, captured on TV.

Activism against the Vietnam War reached a fever pitch at the Democratic National Convention in August 1968, when thousands of young activists gathered in Chicago and clashed with a hostile police force. (CBS Photo Archive/Getty Images)

Outside the convention hall, police smashed protesters with batons in the streets of Chicago. In the end, the Democrats nominated Vice President Hubert Humphrey, who lost the election to Richard Nixon, the former vice president in the Eisenhower administration. During the campaign, Nixon claimed that he had a secret plan to end the war in Vietnam. Johnson's withdrawal and Nixon's victory in 1968 framed an extraordinary year in America's political history.

President Nixon's outlook on the cold war differed little from his successors' in the White House. He had entered national politics in 1946 charging that his Democratic opponent for Congress was soft on communism. Like Johnson, he feared the "loss" of Vietnam on his watch, but he was astute enough to realize that the public had wearied of American combat. Nixon's solution was "vietnamization," which meant turning the fighting over to the army of South Vietnam. Beginning in June 1969, Nixon began the withdrawal of American ground forces from Vietnam. By mid-1972, when the next presidential campaign season was in full swing, less than 50,000 American combat troops remained in the country; by August, the last contingent departed. To compensate for the reduction in ground forces, Nixon escalated the bombing of North Vietnam, mined and blockaded Haiphong Harbor in North Vietnam, and invaded Cambodia to destroy enemy sanctuaries. The Cambodian invasion in late April 1970 ignited antiwar demonstrations on college campuses; the next month in Kent, Ohio, National Guardsmen killed four students at Kent State University. Nixon's widening of the war raised the level of anger over Vietnam, evidenced in the May Day protests in Washington, D.C., in 1971. The president denounced the radicalism of young protesters, but he also sensed the political fallout from failure to extricate the nation from Vietnam.

In 1969, Henry Kissinger, the president's National Security Advisor, began secret talks with representatives of North Vietnam. Progress was stalled until 1972, an election year in the United States; facing a reelection campaign, Nixon had to account for his earlier pledge to end the war. The president's interest in concluding the conflict and increased bombing of North Vietnam helped move the peace talks to a conclusion. North Vietnamese leaders saw Nixon's reelection as likely to bring more destruction to their country. An Agreement on Ending the War was announced on January 24, 1973, to go into effect on January 27. Adding to pressures to reach an agreement, Nixon had held summit meetings with both the Russians and the Chinese in 1972, which reduced tensions with the United States and secured pledges of decreased aid to North Vietnam. Nixon's historic visit to the People's Republic of China in February 1972 had reopened official contact between the United States and China, ending several decades of American nonrecognition. All of these developments disposed North Vietnam to approach negotiations more seriously. Likewise, the Nixon administration faced pressure from Congress, which repealed the Gulf of Tonkin Resolution in 1971 and voted reduced funding for the war.

The cease-fire agreement left political arrangements for Vietnam vague. Two years later, North Vietnamese tanks rolled into Saigon virtually unopposed. The last TV images of the war showed desperate Vietnamese trying to squeeze into overloaded U.S. helicopters as they lifted off from the American embassy in Saigon, just ahead of communist troops entering the city.

WHAT IF?

What if the United States had not sent ground troops to Vietnam?

President Johnson's Vietnam legacy rests on his deployment of American combat troops to the country. While he inherited a U.S. commitment to support the Republic of South Vietnam, he also made a deliberate decision to initiate American offensive actions to bolster the shaky regime. He could have chosen an alternative path. Many eminent observers, some hardened cold warriors, urged Johnson to avoid a land war in Asia. Johnson and his close-knit team of advisers, none of whom were experts on Asian culture, turned aside such counsel. They could have followed George Kennan's advice and scratched Vietnam off the list of places critical to the containment of communism. Or, they could have anticipated Richard Nixon's vietnamization policy and ramped up training and armament of the army of South Vietnam. Johnson rejected these alternatives.

Had Kennedy lived, might he have avoided the Vietnam quagmire? Historians have wrestled with this question ever since his assassination, with no consensus. Still, the transition of power from Kennedy to Johnson suggests that the particular person holding the presidency was a critical determinant of military escalation. Vietnam was essentially Lyndon Johnson's war.

Vietnam had enormous consequences for American society. The war brought down two presidents, first Johnson and then Richard Nixon, who resigned because of the Watergate Scandal, which evolved from issues embedded in the intervention in Vietnam. The misinformation about the situation in Vietnam disseminated by the Johnson and Nixon administrations exacerbated the "credibility gap," whereby public trust in government plummeted during the 1970s. That decade witnessed extraordinarily high rates of inflation, which hampered the economy. Some economists blame Johnson's attempt to fight the Vietnam War without raising taxes as the trigger that ignited the 1970s price increases. Congressional investigating committees unearthed numerous instances in which the U.S. government violated civil liberties by spying on Americans in order to monitor antiwar protesters.

The Vietnam War claimed 47,000 Americans lives in combat and cost $141 billion (more than $675 billion in 2011 dollars). The stress of fighting a guerrilla war in the jungles and rice paddies of Vietnam turned many American soldiers on to narcotic drugs or sent them home with disabling psychoses, making readjustment to civilian life difficult, if not impossible. Perhaps a million Vietnamese were killed; much of the country's economy was devastated by war. The backlash against the use of combat troops in Vietnam resulted in reduced congressional support for the American military for the remainder of the 1970s. While the final assessment of the Vietnam War continues to be debated, few would deny that the conflict significantly affected American history.

CHRONOLOGY

1945 Republic of Vietnam is proclaimed.

1950 Korean War begins.

1954 *April 27:* Geneva Accords are signed.

1955 *October 26:* Ngo Dinh Diem proclaims the Republic of South Vietnam.

1960 National Liberation Front is formed in South Vietnam.

1963 *November 1:* Ngo Dinh Diem is murdered in a coup.
November 22: President Kennedy is assassinated in Dallas; Lyndon Johnson becomes president.

1964 *August 7:* Gulf of Tonkin Resolution passes Congress.
November 3: Johnson is elected president.

1965 *March 8:* Two Marine combat battalions arrive in Vietnam.
Summer: Johnson approves sending 100,000 more troops to Vietnam.

1968 *January 31:* Tet offensive

March 12: Eugene McCarthy nearly beats Johnson in the New Hampshire primary.

March 16: My Lai Massacre

March 31: President Johnson announces he will not seek reelection. Paris Peace Talks begin.

August 28: Protest in Chicago during the Democratic National Convention

November 5: Richard Nixon defeats Hubert Humphrey for the presidency.

1970   *April 30:* Nixon announces the invasion of Cambodia.

May 4: National Guardsmen kill four students at Kent State University.

1971   *February 8:* South Vietnam army invades Laos.

April–May: March on Washington antiwar protest, with mass arrests

June 13: New York Times publishes parts of the Pentagon Papers.

1972   *June 17:* Break-in at Democratic Party headquarters at the Watergate Hotel in Washington, D.C.

November 7: Richard Nixon is elected president.

1973   *January 24:* Paris Peace Agreement for a cease-fire in Vietnam is announced.

1974   *August 8:* President Nixon announces his resignation, effective the following day.

1975   *April 30:* North Vietnamese and National Liberation Front troops enter Saigon.

DISCUSSION QUESTIONS

1. How did the Vietnam War differ from the Korean War?
2. Explain how the Vietnam War related to the cold war policy of the United States.
3. Discuss the role of domestic politics in the United States in influencing the decisions concerning Vietnam.
4. How much responsibility should Lyndon Johnson bear for the Vietnam War? Consider the role played by his advisers, other presidents, political opponents, and the public.

WEB SITES

Annotated links to other Vietnam sites. Available at www.sparatcus. schoolnet.co.uk.vietnam.htm.

Lyndon Baines Johnson Presidential Library. Available at http://www. lbjlibrary.org/.

President Lyndon B. Johnson. Available at http://www.ipl.org/div/potus/ lbjohnson.html.

Vietnam timelines, documents, multimedia, biographies. Available at http://www.pbs.org/wgbh/pages/amex/vietnam/index.html.

The Wilson Center, "The Cold War Files." Available at http://www.wilson center.org/coldwarfiles/.

BIBLIOGRAPHY

Fulbright, J. William. *The Arrogance of Power.* New York: Random House, 1966.

Gardner, Lloyd C. *Pay Any Price and the Wars for Vietnam.* Chicago: Ivan Dee, 1995.

Halberstam, David. *The Best and the Brightest.* New York: Ballantine Books, 1992.

Herring, George. *America's Longest War.* 4th ed. New York: John Wiley and Sons, 2002.

Hess, Gary. *Presidential Decisions for War: Korea, Vietnam, the Persian Gulf and Iraq,* 2d ed. Baltimore: Johns Hopkins University Press, 2009.

Kaiser, David E. *American Tragedy: Kennedy, Johnson and the Origins of the Vietnam War.* Cambridge, Mass.: Harvard University Press, 2000.

Lacouture, Jean. *Ho Chi Minh: A Political Biography.* New York: Vintage Books, 1968.

Morris, Errol. *The Fog of War: Eleven Lessons from the Life of Robert S. McNamara.* Documentary. Sony Film Classics, 2003.

Small, Melvin. *Johnson, Nixon, and the Doves.* New Brunswick, N.J.: Rutgers University Press, 1988.

New York Times. *The Pentagon Papers.* New York: Bantam Books, 1971.

Wells, Tom. *The War Within: America's Battle over Vietnam.* Berkeley: University of California Press, 1994.

PRIMARY SOURCES

1. President Dwight D. Eisenhower, Comments on Indochina, 1954

At a news conference on April 7, 1954, President Dwight D. Eisenhower offered a folksy description of the "domino theory" to explain why Vietnam was important to American interests. In this paraphrase of remarks made at the news conference, the president also cited the importance of strategic resources in the region.

Question. Mr. President, would you mind commenting on the strategic importance of Indo-China to the free world? I think there has been across the country some lack of understanding on just what it means to us.

President Eisenhower. Mr. Eisenhower said that the question could be approached both specifically and generally. First of all, he said, there is the specific value of a locality in its production of materials that the world needs.

Then, he continued, there is the possibility that many human beings could pass under a dictatorship that is inimical to the free world; and, finally, there are broader considerations that might follow the "falling domino" principle.

If someone sets up a row of dominoes, and knocks over the first one, the President said, it is certain that the last one will go over very quickly. It would be the beginning of a disintegration that would have the most profound influences.

With respect to Indo-China's specific value, Mr. Eisenhower explained, this area produces two items that the world uses, tin and tungsten. They are very important, he said, and Indo-China also produces other materials, including rubber.

With respect to the possibility that more people might pass under a dictatorship, Mr. Eisenhower pointed out that Asia has already lost some 450 million of its peoples to the Communist dictatorship. He asserted that the U.S. simply can't afford greater losses.

The third possibility, said the President, is that the loss of Indo-China would set off the loss of Burma, of Thailand, of the Malay Peninsula and Indonesia. This would not only multiply the disadvantages the U.S. would suffer through loss of materials, or sources of materials, but it would involve millions and millions and millions of people, and would create a new geographical position, he said.

Source: *Public Papers of the Presidents of the United States: Dwight D. Eisenhower. 1954.* Washington, D.C.: Government Printing Office, 1958–61, 382–383.

—⁓—

2. President Lyndon Johnson, "Peace Without Conquest" Speech on Vietnam, 1965

Speaking at Johns Hopkins University on April 7, 1965, President Lyndon Johnson outlined his reasons for U.S. military intervention in Vietnam. The president said that the "independent nation" of South Vietnam was attacked by North Vietnam and that the security of the United States and the world hinged on repulsing the invasion.

We fight because we must fight if we are to live in a world where every country can shape its own destiny. And only in such a world will our own freedom be finally secure. The first reality is that North Viet-Nam has attacked the independent nation of South Viet-Nam. Its object is total conquest.

Of course, some of the people of South Viet-Nam are participating in attack on their own government. But trained men and supplies, orders and arms, flow in a constant stream from north to south.

Over this war—and all Asia—is another reality: the deepening shadow of Communist China. The rulers in Hanoi are urged on by Peking. This is a regime which has destroyed freedom in Tibet, which has attacked India, and has been condemned by the United Nations for aggression in Korea. It is a nation which is helping the forces of violence in almost every continent. The contest in Viet-Nam is part of a wider pattern of aggressive purposes.

Why are we in South Viet-Nam?

We are there because we have a promise to keep. Since 1954 every American President has offered support to the people of South Viet-Nam. We have helped to build, and we have helped to defend. Thus, over many years, we have made a national pledge to help South Viet-Nam defend its independence.

We are also there to strengthen world order. Around the globe, from Berlin to Thailand, are people whose well-being rests, in part, on the belief that they can count on us if they are attacked. To leave Viet-Nam to its fate would shake the confidence of all these people in the value of an American commitment and in the value of America's word. The result would be increased unrest and instability, and even wider war.

The central lesson of our time is that the appetite of aggression is never satisfied. To withdraw from one battlefield means only to prepare for the next. We must say in southeast Asia—as we did in Europe—in the words of the Bible: "Hitherto shalt thou come, but no further."

Source: Lyndon Baines Johnson Library. http://www.lbjlib.utexas.edu/.

—⚏—

3. William P. Bundy, Address on "Myth and Reality Concerning South Vietnam," 1965

In an address to the Dallas Council on World Affairs on May 13, 1965, Assistant Secretary of State for Far Eastern Affairs William Bundy claimed that the Vietnam War was not a civil war but a result of North Vietnam's invasion of South Vietnam. Bundy acknowledged the failures of South Vietnamese premier Ngo Dinh Diem.

When the Republic of Viet-Nam was formed in 1955 . . . [t]he Government and people of South Viet-Nam had all the aspirations and hopes of any lesser developed country.

So, from 1954 to 1959 great progress was made. In Ngo Dinh Diem a staunchly nationalist and anti-Communists leader was found. Against all odds, including the opposition in 1954–55 of old-line military leaders and religious groups, he took hold. Under his rule the nationalist feeling of the newly formed country . . . was aroused, and it soon became and has remained clear in their own country that the great mass of the people of South Viet-Nam do not wish to be ruled by communism or from Hanoi.

Then, beginning roughly in 1959, two trends got underway that are still today at the heart of the problem.

First, the Diem government, instead of steadily broadening its base and training key groups for responsibility, began to narrow it. More and more the regime became personal in character. Opposition parties, which had previously been active in relatively free elections, were driven underground, and there began a process of repression which, while never drastic by the standards we should apply to governments in new nations—much less by those of Communist countries—nevertheless alienated increasing numbers of the all-too-small pool of trained men capable of helping to govern effectively.

Second, Hanoi went on the march. Seeing itself thwarted in both South Viet-Nam and Laos, Hanoi began to send trained guerrillas into the South and increasing cadres to assist the Communist Pathet Lao forces in Laos. In South Viet-Nam there had been from the start thousands of agents and many pockets of Communist influence left behind in the division of Viet-Nam, and as early as 1957 a campaign of assassination of local officials had begun that tallies on the map almost exactly with the areas under strongest Communist control today. In 1959 such activity was stepped up, guerrilla units formed, and the real campaign got underway.

That campaign is sometimes referred to as a civil war. But let us not delude ourselves. Discontent there may have been, and local recruiting by the Viet Cong, largely through intimidation. But the whole campaign would never have been possible without the direction, personnel, key material, and total support coming from Hanoi, and without, too, the strong moral support, and key material when needed, provided by Peiping and, up to 1962 at least, by the Soviet Union. Thousands of highly trained men coming from the North, along with the crucial items of equipment and munitions—these have been from the start the mainspring of the Viet Cong insurgency. This has been all along a Communist subversive aggression, in total violation of the Geneva accords as well as general principles of international behavior.

Source: Department of State, Bulletin, LII (June 7, 1965), 890–893.

—⁓—

4. Senator J. William Fulbright, On the "Arrogance of Power," 1966

Senator J. William Fulbright (D-AR), chair of the Senate Foreign Relations Committee at the time of the Gulf of Tonkin Resolution (1964), became a staunch critic of escalation in Vietnam. Fulbright faulted the Johnson administration for misunderstanding the power of nationalism in Vietnam.

The attitude above all others which I feel sure is no longer valid is the arrogance of power, the tendency of great nations to equate power with virtue and major responsibilities with a universal mission. The dilemmas involved are preeminently American dilemmas, not because America has weaknesses that others do not have but because America is powerful as no nation has ever been before and the discrepancy between its power and the power of others appears to be increasing. . . .

I do not question the power of our weapons and the efficiency of our logistics; . . . What I do question is the ability of the United States, or France or any other Western nation, to go into a small, alien, undeveloped Asian nation and create stability where there is chaos, the will to fight where there is defeatism, democracy where there is no tradition of it and honest government where corruption is almost a way of life.

The cause of our difficulties in southeast Asia is not a deficiency of power but an excess of the wrong kind of power which results in a feeling of impotence when it fails to achieve its desired ends. We are still acting like boy scouts dragging reluctant old ladies across the streets they do not want to cross. We are trying to remake Vietnamese society, a task which certainly cannot be accomplished by force and which probably cannot be accomplished by any means available to outsiders. The objective may be desirable, but it is not feasible. . . .

If America has a service to perform in the world and I believe it has, it is in large part the service of its own example. In our excessive involvement in the affairs of other countries, we are not only living off our assets and denying our own people the proper enjoyment of their resources; we are also denying the world the example of a free society enjoying its freedom to the fullest. This is regrettable indeed for a nation that aspires to teach democracy to other nations, because, as Burke said! "Example is the school of mankind, and they will learn at no other."

Source: J. William Fulbright. *The Arrogance of Power.* New York: Random House, 1966, 9, 15–21. Copyright ©1966 by J. William Fulbright. Used by permission of Random House, Inc.

—⁓—

5. Paul Potter, "Incredible War" Speech, 1965

In a speech at the Washington Antiwar March on April 17, 1965, Paul Potter, president of the Students for a Democratic Society, scoffed at the claim that the United States was protecting "freedom" in Vietnam. He charged that the United States was raining down destruction on women and children, dehumanizing Americans in the process.

MOST OF US grew up thinking that the United States was a strong but humble nation, that involved itself in world affairs only reluctantly, that respected the integrity of other nations and other systems, and that engaged in wars only as a last resort. This was a nation with no large standing army, with no design for external conquest, that sought primarily the opportunity to develop its own resources and its own mode of living. If at some point we began to hear vague and disturbing things about what this country had done in Latin America, China, Spain and other places, we somehow remained confident about the basic integrity of this nation's foreign policy. The Cold War with all of its neat categories and black and white descriptions did much to assure us that what we had been taught to believe was true.

But in recent years, the withdrawal from the hysteria of the Cold War era and the development of a more aggressive, activist foreign policy have done much to force many of us to rethink attitudes that were deep and basic sentiments about our country. The incredible war in Vietnam has provided the razor, the terrifying sharp cutting edge that has finally severed the last vestige of illusion that morality and democracy are the guiding principles of American foreign policy. The saccharine self-righteous moralism that promises the Vietnamese a billion dollars of economic aid at the very moment we are delivering billions for economic and social destruction and political repression is rapidly losing what power it might ever have had to reassure us about the decency of our foreign policy. The further we explore the reality of what this country is doing and planning in Vietnam the more we are driven toward the conclusion of Senator Morse that the United States may well be the greatest threat to peace in the world today.

The President says that we are defending freedom in Vietnam. Whose freedom? Not the freedom of the Vietnamese. The first act of the first dictator, Diem, the United States installed in Vietnam, was to systematically begin the persecution of all political opposition, non-Communist as well as Communist. The first American military supplies were not used to fight Communist insurgents; they were used to control, imprison or kill any who sought something better for Vietnam than the personal aggrandizement, political corruption and the profiteering of the Diem regime. The elite of the forces that we have trained and equipped are still used to control political unrest in Saigon and defend the latest dictator from the people.

The pattern of repression and destruction that we have developed and justified in the war is so thorough that it can only be called cultural genocide. I am not simply talking about napalm or gas or crop destruction or torture, hurled indiscriminately on women and children, insurgent and neutral, upon the first suspicion of rebel activity. That in itself is horrendous and incredible beyond belief. But it is only part of a larger pattern of destruction to the very fabric of the country. We have uprooted the people from the land and imprisoned them in concentration camps called "sunrise villages." Through conscription and direct political intervention and control, we have destroyed local customs and traditions, trampled upon those things of value which give dignity and purpose to life.

If the people of this country are to end the war in Vietnam, and to change the institutions which create it, then the people of this country must create a massive social movement—and if that can be built around the issue of Vietnam then that is what we must do.

Source: http://voicesofdemocracy.umd.edu/potter_the_incredible_war_speech _text/.

—⁜—

6. George F. Kennan, Statement on Vietnam, 1966

At hearings before the Senate Committee on Foreign Relations on February 10, 1966, the longtime diplomat and scholar George F. Kennan doubted that Vietnam was a region of strategic importance to the United States. The so-called father of the containment policy also thought that "victory" over the Vietcong and the army of North Vietnam was unlikely.

Vietnam is not a region of major military and industrial importance. It is difficult to believe that any decisive developments of the world situation would be determined in normal circumstances by what happens on that territory.

Given the situation that exists today in the relations among the leading Communist powers, and by that I have, of course, in mind primarily the Soviet-Chinese conflict, there is every likelihood that a Communist regime in South Vietnam would follow a fairly independent course.

I think it should be our Government's aim to liquidate this involvement as soon as this can be done without inordinate damage to our own prestige or to the stability of conditions in that area. . . .

I have great misgivings about any deliberate expansion of hostilities on our part directed to the achievement of something called victory. . . . The North Vietnamese and the Vietcong have between them a great deal of space and manpower to give up if they have to, and the Chinese can give them more if they need it.

But our country should not be asked and should not ask of itself, to shoulder the main burden of determining the political realities in any other country. . . .

Our motives are widely misinterpreted, and the spectacle emphasized and reproduced in thousands of press photographs and stories that appear in the press of the world, the spectacle of America inflicting grievous injury on the lives of a poor and helpless people, a people of different race and color. . . .

But our country should not be asked . . . to shoulder the main burden of determining the political realities in any other country, and particularly not in one remote from our shores, from our culture, and from the experience of our people.

Source: United States Senate Hearings, 89th Cong, 2d sess. Washington, D.C.: U.S. Government Printing Office, 331–336.

THE PERSIAN GULF WAR:
Should the United States Use
Military Force to Liberate Kuwait?

—ɯ—

THE CONTROVERSY

The Issue

On August 2, 1990, Saddam Hussein, the dictator of Iraq, invaded the neigh-boring country of Kuwait. President George H. W. Bush denounced the attack as aggression that had to be reversed. Working with the United Nations, the United States joined a trade embargo against Iraq, hoping that sanctions would force the Iraqi strongman to negotiate a withdrawal. Impatient with sanctions, Bush received congressional authorization to use military force to "liberate" Kuwait. Was the use of military force the appropriate way of resolving the Per-sian Gulf crisis?

♦ **Arguments that military force is necessary to liberate Kuwait:** Bush and his supporters doubted that trade sanctions would persuade Sad-dam Hussein to withdraw from Kuwait. As the international community waited for results, Hussein would strengthen his military position, thus complicating the task of forcing his withdrawal. Advocates of using force observed that the coalition of nations that Bush had organized to confront Iraq would fracture as time passed. Some who favored military action emphasized Hussein's abuse of human rights; he was, they said, a ruthless dictator who possessed chemical and wanted nuclear weapons, which were justification to remove him from power. Moreover, Saddam might invade Saudi Arabia and gain a stranglehold on the world's oil reserves.

♦ **Arguments that military power is not necessary to liberate Kuwait:** Opponents of using force against Iraq did not approve of its invasion of Kuwait or of Hussein's dictatorship. Rather, they questioned the timing of Bush's decision for war. The "doves" called for time to allow sanctions to work. Some antiwar lawmakers wondered why American soldiers would do the bulk of the fighting, given that Arab nations had much to lose from Iraq's aggression. Some in the opposition thought that a formal declaration of war was required for the use of the U.S. military in a foreign country.

—⚏—

INTRODUCTION

On the evening of January 16, 1991, Americans witnessed an incredible sight on CNN news. Bombs from American and coalition aircraft were falling on downtown Baghdad. The destruction aimed at the Iraqi capital was not totally unanticipated. Signs were in the wind that a hammer would fall. President George Herbert Walker Bush had told Iraq's leader, Saddam Hussein, on numerous occasions that his invasion of the tiny Persian Gulf nation of Kuwait "would not stand." Since late August 1990, American and coalition partners had built up "Desert Shield," a huge military force in Saudi Arabia. UN Resolution 678 had given Hussein until January 15 to pull his military out of Kuwait or face the consequences. Hussein refused to budge.

Despite these warnings, it is unlikely that many Americans expected to see a war unfolding right before their eyes. CNN's cameras, placed on the roof of the Rasheed Hotel and elsewhere around Baghdad, recorded explosion after explosion, each sending plumes of light across the night sky. Cruise missiles were launched from B-52 bombers that flew from bases in Louisiana to Iraq and back home nonstop. F-117 stealth fighters from airfields in Saudi Arabia and Navy A-6s from aircraft carriers in the Persian Gulf flew hundreds of sorties over Baghdad. Coalition warships in the Persian Gulf and Red Sea fired Tomahawk missiles. Trails of light streaking across the TV screen and the crackling sound of gunfire hinted that Iraqi air defenses were mounting a frantic response. These bizarre images framed the beginning of what Saddam Hussein called "the mother of all battles." And this was but night one of an aerial barrage that went on for five weeks.

The aerial attack on Baghdad represented the opening scene of the final act in a complex play that began on August 2, when Saddam Hussein, the Iraqi dictator, invaded neighboring Kuwait. (See the sidebar "Saddam Hussein and Iraq" on page 338.) President Bush saw the attack as illegal aggression that had to be condemned and reversed. The United Nations agreed with Bush's stand and adopted a resolution that imposed a trade embargo, or "sanctions," on Iraq. But this step did not go far enough to suit the president, who gravitated toward the use of the military to force Hussein out of Kuwait. Bush stood resolute in the face of numerous efforts to broker a negotiated settlement with Hussein, who demanded that his Kuwait venture be linked to discussions about the Israeli-Palestinian dispute. The United States persuaded the UN Security Council to adopt a resolution in December that gave Saddam until January 15, 1991, to vacate Kuwait or face possible military action. On January 12, the president sent a resolution to Congress seeking authority to use military force, if necessary, to resolve the Persian Gulf crisis. Was the use of American force the appropriate remedy for the Kuwait invasion?

Bush and his supporters in Congress, strongest among Republicans, said yes, that the president needed the authority to wage war to compel Hussein to take the demands of the international community seriously. Otherwise, the Iraqi dictator would wait for the UN coalition to fragment, while strengthening his defenses in Kuwait. Only if the president was armed with this authority would the United States and the United Nations have the means to restore stability in what Bush called the "new world order," referring to the post–cold war era. Some supporters of the president argued that Hussein's brutality toward opponents demanded his removal from power. Knowledge that Hussein possessed chemical weapons and was developing nuclear weapons persuaded some in Congress to grant the president the power he sought to counter these threats. Oil also played a role in this debate. Proponents of the Bush resolution on military force argued that Hussein's invasion gave him control of a quarter of the world's known petroleum supply, posing an unacceptable threat to the world economy

Not so fast, responded the opponents to the Bush resolution on Kuwait. Virtually all participants in the debate on the Gulf crisis agreed that Hussein was an unsavory dictator and that his invasion of Kuwait should "not stand." Nonetheless, some argued that economic sanctions should be given time to work. Members of Congress noted that sanctions had been in place only five months; it might require a year for them to pressure Hussein to withdraw. Some congressional opponents of American military intervention wondered why Arabs were not taking a more proactive role in the crisis, which occurred in their own region. Some in the opposition also resisted handing President Bush a blank check to wage war. The Constitution, they argued, clearly lodged

SADDAM HUSSEIN AND IRAQ

Saddam Hussein was born in the Tikrit region of Iraq north of Baghdad on April 28, 1937, to Sunni Muslim parents of humble means. His country had been carved out of the remnants of the Ottoman Empire, which disintegrated as a result of World War I. In 1920, the League of Nations assigned oversight of the region, once called Mesopotamia, as a "mandate" territory to Great Britain. Winston Churchill, head of Britain's Colonial Office and later prime minister, and T. E. Lawrence (the famed Lawrence of Arabia), were instrumental in designing the new state. In 1921, the British installed a tribal leader as king over an area that incorporated three former Ottoman provinces, centered on the cities of Mosul, Baghdad, and Basra.

Continuing Ottoman practice, the new government and its army were dominated by Sunni Muslim Arabs, while the more numerous Shiite Muslims, who looked to the Ottoman's rival of Persia (now Iran) for religious leadership, were shunned. Iraq gained full independence in 1932. Four years later, a military coup overthrew the king. Within a year, the new military leader was assassinated, and the monarchy was reinstated. In 1958, another military coup overthrew the monarchy and established a republic.

Saddam Hussein matured in a land where coups and assassinations were frequent and the ties of family, tribal identities, and Muslim sectarian loyalties guided political leaders. He drew on these traditions in his rise to power. In 1957, Hussein joined the Baath Party, an organization based more on personal loyalty and self-interest than ideology, to climb to dominance in Iraq. A coup in 1968 put Baathists in power, with Hussein second

the power to declare war with Congress. Despite this constitutional argument, Congress voted to give Bush a free hand in confronting Hussein, but the resolution barely passed the Senate.

BACKGROUND

From its beginning, the historian William Spencer has written, Iraq was an "artificial nation-state patched together by outsiders." This patching was an artifact of World War I, when Allied forces defeated Germany in command. In charge of security and the military, Hussein played his hand ruthlessly, organizing networks of loyalists and clients and purging opponents and dissidents, often by assassination or execution. In the late 1970s, he doubled the size of the army and in 1972 personally took control of the state-run oil company, which replaced a private consortium. In 1979, Hussein obtained the presidency and immediately launched a purge of individuals he regarded as disloyal, executing perhaps 500 Baath Party members. Once in power, his brutality had few limits. He arrested and executed leading Muslim Shiites. In northern Iraq, his military used poison gas against Kurds, a minority fighting for an autonomous region in northwestern Iraq. He enriched himself, his family, and his hangers-on with oil revenue, building lavish palaces.

In a land with little tradition of democracy or civil liberties, Hussein fashioned a police state that created a huge bureaucracy, a network of informants, and a climate of fear. British prime minister Tony Blair described him as "profoundly wicked" and a "very bad bastard." Several members of Congress compared him to Adolf Hitler when they debated whether to use American soldiers to liberate Kuwait in 1991. Hussein survived his army's forcible expulsion from Kuwait, only to experience a more complete defeat in 2003 in the Iraq War. U.S. troops captured him, and the provisional Iraqi government sentenced him to death. He was hanged on December 30, 2006. Some in the Arab Middle East admired his defiance of Western imperialism. The *Manchester Guardian* newspaper, on the other hand, saw him as a "thug." As a dictator of modern-day Mesopotamia, his epitaph might read: "Live by the sword, die by the sword."

and dismembered the Ottoman Empire, which had controlled the Arabian peninsula for centuries. Great Britain was assigned control of three former Ottoman provinces—Basra, Baghdad, and Mosul—which the League of Nations joined together under a "mandate" territory it named Iraq. In 1921, the British established a constitutional monarchy for Iraq, appointed a king, and helped to create a functioning government. The new nation gained its sovereignty in 1932.

But Iraq was a nation more in name than in political cohesiveness. Its history from the 1920s revolved around coups, assassinations, tribal

Saddam Hussein's 1990 invasion of Kuwait triggered the Persian Gulf War. (© Peter Jordan/Alamy)

feuds, ethnic conflict, and religious hatreds. Saddam Hussein was born into this chaotic society in 1937. He rose to power in a tangle of Iraqi politics that revolved around family, regional, tribal, and religious connections, interlaced with personal loyalties wherever they could be found. Force, organization, and personal magnetism more than ideology forged his path to power. Saddam played this game in earnest, executing his opponents when convenient. He was ruthless toward his ethnic rivals. A Sunni Muslim, Hussein continued the Ottoman tradition of snubbing the Shiite Muslim majority, whose concentration lay in southern Iraq, and suppressing the Kurds, who sought an autonomous state in northern Iraq. Consolidating his authority by gaining the loyalty of the military, forming networks of informants, and controlling the state-owned oil company, which fed his treasury, Hussein sat atop a police state by 1979. The next year, he attacked neighboring Iran, in part because he saw it as a rival to his aspiration to lead the Arab world. The Iraq-Iran War lasted eight years and exhausted Saddam's financial resources.

That year, 1979, was also the year of the Iranian Revolution, in which a religiously based Shiite regime replaced the Shah (Muhammad Reza Pahlavi), a military strongman whom the United States had helped place in power in 1953 and who had cooperated with the United States during the cold war years. This fundamentalist Islamic revolution produced the background for the Iran Hostage Crisis, in which young Iranian radicals stormed the U.S. embassy in Tehran, Iran's capital city, in late 1979 and held more than 50 Americans captive for more than a year. The frustration and embarrassment that resulted from this crisis partially explains American support for Hussein during the Iraq-Iran War. Moreover, Hussein was seen as a moderate within the Arab Middle East, despite his reputation as the "Butcher of Baghdad." Hussein's favor with American leaders dissolved when he invaded Kuwait on August 2, 1990. About the size of New Jersey, Kuwait had been a British protectorate until the small sheikhdom gained its independence in 1961. The country's petroleum resources made its royal family very rich, a fact important to Hussein. He had borrowed heavily from Kuwait to finance his war against Iran. With his treasury broke, Hussein demanded that Kuwait suspend its loan. He also accused the sheikhdom of overproducing oil, which flooded the market, lowering its price and reducing Iraqi petroleum revenues. Besides this charge of "stolen oil," Saddam claimed that Kuwait had been historically part of Basra Province. Hussein's occupation of Kuwait gave Iraq control of an estimated one-quarter of the world's known petroleum reserves. If Saddam overran Saudi Arabia, he would control 45 percent of the world's oil.

Iraq's invasion caught the Bush administration, including the Central Intelligence Agency, by surprise. Nonetheless, the president reacted swiftly, immediately urging the United Nations to renounce Hussein's action. UN Resolution 660, adopted on August 2, condemned the invasion. Then Bush met with his National Security Council, which concluded that the United States needed to prevent Iraq from attacking Saudi Arabia. On August 5, Bush condemned Iraq's "brutal, naked aggression," indicating that he was building an international coalition to "reverse this awful aggression." The president vowed that Saddam Hussein's brazen step "will not stand, this aggression against Kuwait." Aided by Secretary of State James Baker, Bush assembled a broad international coalition in support of a trade embargo of Iraq. The United Nations ratified the adoption of the "sanctions" in Resolution 661 on August 6.

Worried that Hussein's army might move south, Bush devised a plan to send 250,000 American troops to Saudi Arabia as a "defensive" measure. This deployment, labeled "Desert Shield," would put American and other foreign soldiers on Muslim territory, a touchy subject with most Arabs. The step required careful diplomatic handling. Bush dispatched Secretary of Defense Dick Cheney and General Colin Powell, chairman of the Joint Chiefs of Staff, to convince the Saudi royal family that Desert Shield was in their interest. (See the sidebar "General Colin Powell" on page 344.) Aiding this effort was agreement among the majority of Arab nations that Hussein's annexation of Kuwait was illegal and that they would contribute troops to a military force in the Gulf region. As the deployment of troops to the Middle East progressed, the president worried that his international coalition would split before sanctions had sufficient time to work. That apprehension was partially buffered by Hussein's belligerent rejection of offers to negotiate and his rants against the United States. Saddam Hussein let it be known that he was not easily intimidated.

As the size of the American force in Saudi Arabia grew, Bush's strategy changed. Initially the president sought UN condemnation of Iraq's invasion and a trade embargo against the invader. He got both. He also received support of an international coalition for Desert Shield, which he characterized as a defensive measure to protect Saudi Arabia. Then the president assumed a more belligerent posture. In early October, Bush asked Colin Powell and General H. Norman Schwarzkopf,

Jr., commander of American forces in the Middle East, to formulate an offensive plan, one capable of driving Hussein out of Kuwait. Bush, Cheney, and Brent Scowcroft, the president's national security adviser, all rejected the generals' proposal as inadequate. Powell and Schwarzkopf explained that the plan's weakness derived largely from an insufficient force level. When Powell presented the president with a revised, beefed-up offensive plan, with double the force size on October 30, the general later recalled that "this is what he wanted to hear." Could bombing alone drive Hussein from Kuwait, Bushed asked? No, Powell replied: History had shown that air power alone never won a war. Then Powell coached Schwarzkopf on how to prepare for an offensive operation. Drawing on lessons learned in Vietnam, Powell advised, "Go in big, and end it quickly."

A flurry of initiatives swirled in diplomatic channels between the United States and Iraq, trying to find a peaceful solution to the crisis. Hussein complicated these overtures by demanding that the Israeli-Palestinian conflict be included in a diplomatic settlement. Bush rejected any solution that included "linkage" to issues beyond the liberation of Kuwait. After the midterm elections in early November, the president announced that he had ordered the deployment of another 200,000 American soldiers to Desert Shield in Saudi Arabia. He also sought UN approval to use coalition forces if Hussein did not withdraw from Kuwait. Secretary of State Baker guided the proposition through the United Nations on November 29. UN Resolution 678 stated that if Hussein did not withdraw from Kuwait by January 15, 1991, UN members were authorized "to use all necessary means" to restore the status quo.

The president's embrace of a military solution for the Kuwait crisis disturbed many in Congress. Some Democrats had drafted an "expression of concern," forwarded to the president, that outlined their opposition to offensive military action before sanctions were given time to work. Democrats also filed a suit in federal court seeking an injunction that would prohibit the president from using force without congressional authorization. The court rejected this move. In late November, the House and Senate Armed Services Committees held hearings that solicited opinions on the Gulf crisis from current and former government officials. Several influential figures from earlier administrations testified that rushing American soldiers into combat was wrong and that sanctions should be given time to work.

GENERAL COLIN POWELL

It is fashionable in some quarters to see the U.S. Army as a conservative bureaucracy stifled by traditionalism and elitism. Colin Powell saw the army as an equal opportunity employer. He not only took advantage of its merit-oriented philosophy but thrived in the military environment. He became the youngest officer to be named chairman of the Joint Chiefs of Staff, the nation's highest military position. He also was the first African American to hold the post.

Powell was born in New York City in 1937 to parents who both had emigrated from Jamaica, a former British colony. He grew up in an integrated neighborhood of the Bronx, where racial prejudice was not pronounced. A so-so student from a family of very modest means, he was admitted to the City College of New York and joined its Reserve Officers Training Corp (ROTC) program. The ROTC's military style suited Powell's desire for structure and purpose, providing an environment in which his determination to achieve paid dividends. He rose to top leadership posts by the time he graduated in 1958. Shortly afterward, he was commissioned a second lieutenant in the U.S. Army, the service in which he decided to launch his career.

Powell honed his leadership skills during two tours of duty in Vietnam, where he experienced the dangers and frustrations of jungle warfare. Looking back at his career in his autobiography, *My American Journey*, Powell was sharply critical of American misadventures in Southeast Asia, writing, "We had lost touch with reality." He took away valuable lessons from the Vietnam War, including the requirement that leaders have a clear objective in mind before entering a war and that they then provide the military with all the means necessary to achieve it.

Bright, energetic, diplomatic, and ambitious, Powell advanced rapidly up the ranks, winning his first general's star in 1979 at age 42. His ability to

The president claimed that he possessed the legal authority to take military action on his own initiative, regardless of what Congress said about the crisis. Nonetheless, Bush thought it politically prudent to gain congressional support for a military solution. On January 8, 1991, he submitted a joint resolution to Congress that requested authority for the president to use American military force, if necessary, to resolve the articulate military options in clear English made him attractive to civilian leaders. After serving as the senior military adviser to the secretary of defense in the early 1980s, he became President Ronald Reagan's National Security Advisor in 1987. Two years later, he was a four-star general and became President George H. W. Bush's chairman of the Joint Chiefs of Staff. The crowning moment in this assignment was his supervision of the American victory in the Persian Gulf War. Remembering the agony and restraints of war in Vietnam, Powell's strategy for driving Saddam Hussein out of Kuwait was "Go in big, and end it quickly." He did.

Powell stepped down from the chairmanship after two terms of service and retired from the army in 1993. As both a military hero and admired statesman, Powell was urged to run for president in 1996 but declined. He returned to government as Secretary of State under President George W. Bush in 2001, taking part in the second thrust at Hussein's military machine during the Iraq War.

Colin Powell will be best remembered for two extraordinary achievements. First will be his victory over Saddam Hussein's war machine in 1991, with minimal casualties. The lightning fast strike returned a sense of pride among the U.S. military, erasing some of the disappointments that lingered from the Vietnam War. Second, Powell overcame racial prejudice by his ability to focus on his primary objective, which was to do his job well. The army offered an organization in which he could apply this philosophy. On numerous occasions, he observed that the army "had given African-Americans more equal opportunity than any other institution in American society." Powell urged young blacks not to get caught up in racial resentment but to find places that allowed an individual to thrive by merit. Colin Powell epitomizes how this model could work in late 20th-century America.

Kuwaiti dispute. Congress considered the request on January 10 and 11 in a historic debate that was televised and given detailed newspaper coverage. The debate in the Senate, which has greater authority over diplomatic affairs than the House and no time restrictions on senators' speeches, offered a detailed and comprehensive examination of the relevant issues.

President George H. W. Bush, pictured here in the White House Oval Office, led the international coalition that ousted Saddam Hussein's army from Kuwait. (David Valdez/White House/Time & Life Pictures/Getty Images)

Few members of Congress doubted that Saddam Hussein was despicable and should withdraw from Kuwait. Two questions dominated discussions in the House and Senate. First, was a declaration of war by Congress necessary prior to the military deployment of U.S. troops in the Middle East? And second, should sanctions be given sufficient time to work?

THE DEBATE

The Argument that the United States Should Use Military Force to Liberate Kuwait

Both President Bush and congressional proponents of the Bush resolution raised numerous points in support of a military solution to the Gulf crisis. The debate in the Senate touched on all these considerations. Not every senator mentioned oil in these discussion, but the subject was never far from the surface. All lawmakers understood that petroleum was integral to American life. Americans may not have loved their cars, but most were forced to rely on them and did so increasingly as the 20th century unfolded. Consumers bought more and more vehicles in the latter half of the century, and they drove them farther and faster, on average, each year. Suburban sprawl spread as automobility accelerated. By 1990, many driveways contained an SUV, which essentially was a large sedan body placed on a truck frame. Light trucks were exempt from auto fuel standards. Critics called these beefed-up cars "gas-guzzlers." American consumption of oil on a per capita basis rose steadily during the course of the 20th century. The price of gasoline per gallon at the pump had fallen during the 1980s, but an increasing proportion of petroleum was imported. In 1973, when Middle Eastern nations embargoed oil to the United States, imports made up 36 percent of American petroleum usage; by 1990, this figure had risen to 44 percent. An Iraqi invasion of Saudi Arabia would have allowed Saddam Hussein to control 45 percent of the world's known oil reserves. Many senators said that they were unwilling to hold the American economy hostage to an unpredictable "petro-dictator."

Senator John Danforth (R-MO) put the connection of oil to America very directly: "Like it or not, our country . . . is utterly dependent on oil. Our economy, our jobs, our ability to defend ourselves are dependent on our access to oil." (See "Senator John Danforth, Speech in the U.S. Senate, January 10, 1991," on page 358 in the Primary Sources section.) "To control the world's supply of oil is in a real sense to control the world." Danforth argued that the Gulf crisis was, in part, about the economic security of the United States. Senator William Roth (R-DE) seconded this analysis, claiming that petroleum "is as basic to the economy as water is to life." (See "Senator William Roth, Speech in the U.S. Senate, January 10, 1991," on page 358 in the Primary Sources section.) Oil not only was "critical for the industrial democracies" but also for the "fragile Third World nations." He warned that "any attempt to disrupt those supplies will send a devastating quake through these economies." Roth urged Congress to support the president's determination to prevent these dreadful possibilities from occurring.

Pro-Bush senators saw more immediate reasons for the president to have the authority to confront Hussein with military force. Senator Orrin Hatch (R-UT) outlined four reasons for supporting the war resolution. (See "Senator Orrin Hatch, Speech in the U.S. Senate, January 10, 1991," on page 359 in the Primary Sources section.) First, if not "decisively reversed," Iraq's aggression against Kuwait would establish a dangerous precedent of one country invading another. In essence, Hatch reiterated Bush's emphasis on ensuring stability in the post–cold war world. Several senators observed that this was the first serious challenge to international stability since the fall of communism began in 1989. Second, the United States had a moral interest in liberating Kuwait. Hatch referred to the "baby-killing" story that charged Iraqis with stealing incubators, leaving infants to die. The story was false, although President Bush repeated it. Still, Saddam Hussein would take no prizes as a champion of human rights. Senator Roth agreed that Hussein "offends our sense of morality." He called him a "despotic madman" who used chemical weapons "on his own people." The charge was true; Saddam had used poison gas on Kurds in northern Iraq.

Third, Hatch said that the United States had a security interest in thwarting Hussein's terrorist network. He claimed that the Iraqi leader was the mastermind of several terrorist plots, including the bombing of Pan Am flight 103 in 1988 (although an international court found no such links). Fourth, Hatch contended that "we have the vital security interests in stopping Hussein's development of weapons of mass destruction." This madman, Hatch warned, could soon be heavily armed and even more dangerous.

Why not give sanctions more time to work, Hatch asked. The longer we wait, he answered, the more time Iraq had to fortify its position in Kuwait. "If Congress stalls," the senator continued, "we will be responsible for the loss of thousands of lives." Senator John Warner (R-VA) voiced further skepticism about the effectiveness of sanctions. He cited the testimony of Central Intelligence Agency director William Webster to the House Armed Services Committee on December 4, which predicted that sanctions would not seriously degrade the capacity of Iraqi ground forces for six to 12 months. Warner added that "This is especially true if Iraq does not believe a coalition attack is likely during this period." Few Republicans saw much to be gained by waiting indefinitely for sanctions to force Hussein to withdraw.

The proresolution position carried the day. The president lost little time in using his congressional authority. Within 24 hours of the expiration of the UN ultimatum to Hussein, Bush ordered an air attack on Iraq. Two hours later, he explained to the public why he had acted. (See "President George H. W. Bush, 'The Liberation of Kuwait Has Begun,' January 16, 1991," on page 360 in the Primary Sources section.) "This conflict started August 2nd when the dictator of Iraq invaded a small and helpless neighbor. Kuwait—a member of the Arab League and a member of the United Nations—was crushed; its people, brutalized."

Coalition strikes, the president explained, included the targeting of Hussein's nuclear weapons and chemical weapons facilities. He said that sanctions were not working. Instead, "while the world waited, Saddam Hussein systematically raped, pillaged, and plundered a tiny nation," committing "unspeakable atrocities" that included the murder of innocent children. Concluding, Bush predicted that "When we are successful . . . we have a real chance at this new world order, an order in which a credible United Nations can use its peacekeeping role to fulfill the promise and vision of the U.N.'s founders."

The Argument that the United States Should Not Use Military Force to Liberate Kuwait

Democrats in the House and Senate agreed with much of the argument presented by their Republican colleagues. Senator George Mitchell (D-ME), the majority leader, summed up this feeling: "Most Americans and most Members of Congress, myself included, supported the President's initial decision to deploy American forces to Saudi Arabia to deter further Iraqi aggression. We supported the President's effort in marshaling international diplomatic pressure and the most comprehensive economic embargo in history against Iraq." (See "Senator George Mitchell, Speech in the U.S. Senate, January 10, 1991," on page 362 in the Primary Sources section.) But then the president changed course, Mitchell argued, and took a more warlike path. The Bush resolution was open-ended, which let the president himself decide on war and thus abandon the international effort to rebuke Iraq. By giving up on sanctions, Bush placed the country "on a course toward war." Mitchell urged that sanctions be given time to work.

The majority leader allowed other senators to address the second grievance that Democrats had with Bush's approach to Kuwait. These opponents charged that the president was attempting to usurp the constitutional authority of Congress to declare war. Senator (and future vice president) Joe Biden (D-DE) reviewed the argument in this complaint. (See "Senator Joe Biden, Speech in the U.S. Senate, January 10, 1991," on page 363 in the Primary Sources section.) Although Bush, Secretary of Defense Cheney, and Secretary of State Baker claimed that the president had sufficient authority to take military action in Kuwait, Biden countered that Article I of the Constitution clearly and explicitly gave Congress—"and Congress alone"—the power to declare war. The senator referred to numerous constitutional scholars who supported this interpretation. The leaders of other countries might have the power to act alone, but the authority to wage war unilaterally was not given to the president of the United States. Biden conceded that this constitutional provision would be satisfied if Congress gave "a clear, unambiguous authorization," evidently meaning a vote that might fall short of an actual declaration of war. Congressional adoption of the Bush resolution presumably passed this lesser constitutional test.

Even if Congress could not prevent the president from initiating war, the question remained whether it was an appropriate action to take in January 1991. Senator John D. Exon (D-NE) said no. Combat should be considered as the last resort, not the first. (See "Senator John D. Exon, Speech in the U.S. Senate, January 10, 1991," on page 364 in the Primary Sources section.) Exon wondered why the president was rushing to war without giving sanctions "a chance to work." He also questioned the propriety of going beyond the objectives established by the United Nations to attack Iraq's "potential nuclear capability." Plus, while the Arab nations had urged an Arab solution to the crisis, he charged that their military commitment to the crisis was inadequate; 75 percent of the ground forces facing Iraqi tanks in Saudi Arabia were Americans.

The historian Arthur Schlesinger, Jr., had answered Exon's question about the whereabouts of Arab troops several days earlier in the *Wall Street Journal*. (See "Arthur Schlesinger, Jr., 'White Slaves in the Persian Gulf,' January 7, 1991," on page 365 in the Primary Sources section.) Schlesinger pointed to a recent interview with an official from the Gulf region, who remarked: "You think I want to send my teen-aged son to die for Kuwait? . . . We have our white slaves from America to do that." Schlesinger was unimpressed by the long list of "peripheral justifications" to use American soldiers in Kuwait. He argued that the plan for the United States to establish stability in Iraq ignored history. It was "a region characterized from time immemorial by artificial frontiers, tribal antagonism, religious fanaticisms, and desperate inequalities. I doubt that the U.S. has the capacity or the desire to replace the Ottoman Empire. . . ." Intervening before sanctions were given a chance was likely to reap contempt, not respect, from Arab rulers. Schlesinger thought that "War against Iraq will be the most unnecessary war in American history."

Senator Daniel Patrick Moynihan (D-NY), displaying his well-known sarcasm and wit, wondered why George Bush had turned the crisis in Iraq into a personal conflict "with this particular thug in Baghdad—the recent thug in Baghdad, not the last by any means. . . ." He scoffed at the idea that the United States was in an international crisis. To Moynihan, the Iraqi occupation of Kuwait represented "A nasty little country invaded a littler, but just as nasty country." Moynihan thought that Bush's vision of upholding a world order was overblown puffery.

OUTCOME AND IMPACT

Bush got his congressional authorization on January 12, 1991. The House of Representatives approved the proposal 251-182; the Senate narrowly passed the resolution, dividing 52-47. The Senate vote broke sharply along party lines, with Republicans supporting their president (42-2), while most Democrats (10-45) opposed giving the president unilateral authority to commit Americans troops to war. The defection of 10 Democrats gave the president his victory in the Senate. The vote was closest on the authorization of war in the history of the U.S. Senate.

Four days after Congress approved the resolution authorizing the use of military force, American aircraft struck Baghdad and other targets in Iraq. Saddam Hussein had not blinked. His troops remained ensconced in Kuwait. Perhaps he thought that Bush's saber rattling was a bluff. The president's commitment to war, in public at least, occurred abruptly, in early November. Why did the president choose force over sanctions? Attempting to read George Bush's mind became a popular indoor sport in 1991, yet no one completely uncovered the president's motivation for abandoning sanctions in favor of military intervention. A variety of factors probably impelled his decision. The first stems from Bush's memories of World War II. He had lived during the years of German and Japanese aggressiveness in the 1930s, and he served as a navy combat pilot in the Pacific during the war. When the president said he would not let aggression stand, no doubt he meant it. Bush was also worried about unity among the international coalition, especially if Hussein attacked Israel. An Israeli military response was sure to drive Arab nations out of the UN coalition. The more time that passed, the more Hussein had the opportunity to extricate himself from Kuwait, perhaps by some half-way measure. Such an eventuality would have made a military strike problematic and thus left Hussein unpunished for his invasion of Kuwait. Furthermore, Scowcroft and Cheney, who were nearly as hawkish as the president, believed that Hussein's development of chemical and nuclear weapons posed a growing threat to peace in the Middle East.

An additional consideration derives from Bush's position as president. He commanded the military, which had built a formidable presence in the Gulf region. Congress had given him authority to use this force, and it was a tempting tool. The use of the American military to force Iraq out of Kuwait had a high likelihood of success. As the president, Bush could exercise this option when he chose to do so, and he was also the military's commander in chief. Waiting for sanctions to force a negotiated settlement that won the approval of the UN coalition faced numerous uncertainties, including the possibility that they would not work. Instead, Bush reached for his most accessible tool for resolving the Gulf conflict.

Bush was determined to push Hussein out of Kuwait. Despite threats and appeals for negotiations (on Bush's terms), the dictator had not flinched. Some had suggested that a sense of Arab machismo may have compelled him to stand firm in the face of the approaching storm. It was not long in coming. Some 17 hours after the expiration of the UN deadline for Saddam Hussein to withdraw from Kuwait, the coalition unleashed an aerial barrage on Baghdad and other locations in Iraq. The Americans used 700 aircraft on the first night; only one was lost (cause unknown). Some of the ordnance dropped were "smart bombs," which were guided to their targets by computers and lasers. At news conferences reviewing the aerial onslaught, General Schwarzkopf showed videos that supposedly proved the on-target precision of these high-tech weapons.

Postwar assessments questioned the touted accuracy of the smart bombs. Still, there is no question that allied air power eliminated the Iraqi air force as a military factor. Hussein ordered some of his surviving airplanes flown to Iran for safekeeping and parked others in secure bunkers. Five weeks of bombing demoralized Hussein's forces that were dug in around Kuwait. When coalition ground forces struck, they had the advantage of air cover, including Apache Attack helicopters with tank-killing missiles. Ranged in Saudi Arabia near the border of Kuwait were 430,000 American troops with 2,000 tanks and 1,800 combat aircraft. Another 130,000 troops from other nations, mainly Saudi Arabia, Great Britain, and Egypt, joined the force. The ground attack began on February 23, 1991. The plan had three components. The first was to strike directly at Kuwait, headed in the direction of Kuwait City. The second

U.S. Air Force aircraft fly over burning Kuwaiti oil wells, set by the retreating Iraqi army, 1991. (U.S. Air Force)

element of the plan launched several diversionary strikes, mainly on the coast of Kuwait. Third, the bulk of American forces moved secretly to locations in western Saudi Arabia, which were lightly defended. These units, supported by the British and French, would attack from the west, and thrust eastward, attempting to envelop and cut off Iraq military units that escaped from Kuwait.

The concept was sound, but the timing of the flanking maneuver was off. U.S. Marines, supported by forces from some Arab nations, were given the job of attacking Iraqi forces in southern Kuwait. The going was tough, due not only to Iraqi resistance and mines seeded along invasion routes, but also because the enemy ignited oil wells, which produced a blinding smoke. Even with night-vision goggles, Marines could not see their hands in front of them at times. The Iraqis put up a token defense and retreated, many fleeing in civilian vehicles stolen from Kuwaitis. This stream of traffic out of Kuwait City became sitting ducks for U.S. Air Force planes; 1,400 vehicles were destroyed on what became nicknamed "the highway of death." Contrary to some expectations, the Iraqi defenders were no match for coalition forces. Demoralization, partly from incessant bombing, had sucked the will to fight from many defenders. Their rapid retreat from Kuwait put pressure on the American units in western Iraq to race across the desert (the Iraqis were astonished that U.S. forces could travel over terrain that lacked roads) to close the trap door in the flanking operation. They never did.

U.S. and British units engaged Iraqi troops in a massive tank battle during the final hours of fighting before President Bush ordered a cease-fire on February 27, 100 hours after the coalition had launched its attack. Iraq had been driven out of Kuwait, the primary coalition objective. Neither the United Nations nor President Bush had made removal of Saddam Hussein from power a goal of the war. Moreover, the Bush administration did not want to give the impression that they were slaughtering helpless Iraqi soldiers as they fled.

On the surface, the Gulf War was an impressive American victory. Generals Colin Powell and Norman Schwarzkopf were honored in a ticker tape parade in New York City. By showing that the military could do the job assigned to it if given adequate support, they had thrown the Vietnam "monkey" off the back of the American armed forces. The coalition had destroyed 75 percent of all Iraqi tanks in southern Iraq. Had the war continued, many more Iraqi armored vehicles would have been lost. The Iraqis were no match for American firepower. American M1 Abrams tanks were far superior to the older model Russian T-72s that Iraq used. The M1s had a longer firing range, much better fire guidance systems, and stronger armor, which could survive direct frontal hits from the T-72s.

Beneath the surface, however, cracks appeared in the military's victory cup. Faulty intelligence had given the impression that most of Hussein's army in the south had been destroyed. Hussein's elite Republican Guards, however, escaped with half of their force intact, including half of their armored vehicles. American command and control coordination had broken down at points during war. The army used 40-year-old radios to communicate in the field. Poor communications between air and army services occurred. Some of the army's maps were outdated. Fratricide—killing members of your own side (mainly accidently in the Gulf conflict)—was a problem, especially during night fighting. Dust storms and oil smoke both gave a new twist to the old saying about the "fog of war."

President Bush glowed from his victory in the Persian Gulf. Immediately after the cease-fire, he received an 89 percent approval rating in the polls, an extraordinarily high reading. The public opinion survey no doubt reflected Americans' relief that only 148 Americans were killed in the war, in comparison to an estimated 10,000 Iraqi soldiers and 2,000 civilians, but the bloom on America's Persian Gulf War victory wilted quickly. Saddam Hussein remained in power, and much of his army survived, which he later used to suppress rebellious Shiites in southern Iraq and Kurds in the north. Because Bush had stuck by his prewar objective of liberating Kuwait, he had denied the time his generals needed to annihilate Saddam's army. The decision was politically costly. At the onset of the war, 82 percent of Americans saw the overthrow of Hussein as one of the goals of the war. By April 1991, 55 percent said that allowing Hussein to remain in power meant the war was not a victory. By summer, the feeling that Hussein should have been driven from power had grown. This negative opinion, plus the weakening of the economy, are primary reasons that Bush lost his bid for reelection and Bill Clinton won the presidency in 1992.

One lesson of the Persian Gulf War is that a victory does not ensure electoral success. Another is that presidents can go to war essentially on their own initiative; formal congressional declarations of war appear to have become passé. The last declaration of war was voted in 1941. Third, the American military had embraced the world of high tech, as illustrated by the use of smart bombs and computer-guided missiles. "For most citizens," wrote the author David Halberstam, "the Gulf War was like watching a movie." Perhaps more appropriately from today's perspective, the Gulf War was like a video game. Increasingly tight controls on media coverage of battlefield actions helped to sanitize the horrors of war. These factors may have misled Americans when the next crisis in the Middle East arose.

WHAT IF?

What if the United States military had conquered Baghdad and forced Hussein from power?

If history can serve as a guide, this speculation is easy to answer. One need only look at the Iraq War (2003–10) under President George W. Bush, George Bush's son. Ruthless as he was, Hussein held together an artificial state. His removal from power probably would have allowed Iraq to sink into a guerrilla insurgency and ethnic violence, as occurred between 2004 and 2010. Possibly, a full-scale civil war would have ensued. Moreover, an American occupation of Iraq may have hastened a 9/11-type attack on the United States, which took place 10 years after the Gulf

War. Osama bin Laden, the al-Qaeda leader and mastermind of 9/11, was incensed at the deployment of American soldiers in Saudi Arabia during the Gulf Crisis and afterward.

A second scenario warrants consideration. What if the United States had not launched a military campaign and given sanctions more time to work? This course had no certain outcome. Quite possibly, sanctions would not have forced Hussein to withdraw from Kuwait. It is also unlikely that Arab nations would have mounted their own expedition to "liberate" Kuwait. If Iraqi history offers any guidance, a coup or assassination would have offered the best chance to topple Hussein. In the meantime, the global demand for petroleum suggests that the world community would soon have been back buying Iraqi oil.

CHRONOLOGY

1979   Saddam Hussein assumes power in Iraq.

1980–88   Iraq-Iran War

1988   George H. W. Bush elected president.

1990   *August 2:* Iraq invades Kuwait.

August 6: UN Resolution 661 approves economic sanctions against Iraq.

November 29: UN Resolution 678 authorizes use of force after January 15, 1991, to compel Iraq to withdraw from Kuwait.

1991   *January 8:* President Bush requests Congress to approve a resolution authorizing the use of force against Iraq.

January 12: Congress approves presidential use of force.

January 16: U.S. bombs Iraq, including Baghdad.

February 23–27: UN ground forces drive Iraq army from Kuwait.

February 27: Cease-fire in the Gulf War

1993   United States launches missile attack on Iraq.

DISCUSSION QUESTIONS

1. What is the United States' interest in the Middle East?
2. Did Saddam Hussein's disregard for human rights qualify as a reason for the United States to intervene militarily in his country?

3. Is continued access to oil at a reasonable price a legitimate reason for the United States to use military force in its foreign policy activities?
4. Should Congress have insisted on adopting a formal declaration of war prior to American military intervention in the Gulf crisis?

WEB SITES

The Air and Missile Attack on Baghdad, as recorded by CNN. Available at http://www.youtube.com/watch?v=3xhDkzH9z80&feature=related.

The Gulf War. Available at http://www.pbs.org/wgbh/pages/frontline/gulf/.

Photos of Gulf War. Available at http://www.history.army.mil/photos/gulf_war/INDEX.HTM

BIBLIOGRAPHY

Congressional Quarterly. "Special Report: Persian Gulf War." In *Congress and the Nation, 1989–1993*. Washington, D.C.: CQ Press, 1993, 300–319.

Gordon, Michael, and Bernard Trainor. *The General's War*. Boston: Little, Brown, 1995.

Hess, Gary. *Presidential Decisions for War: Korea, Vietnam, the Persian Gulf and Iraq*, 2d ed. Baltimore: Johns Hopkins University Press, 2009.

Miller, Judith, and Laurie Mylroie. *Saddam Hussein and the Crisis in the Gulf*. New York: Times Books, 1990.

Parmet, Herbert. *George Bush: The Life of the Lone Star Yankee*. New York: Scribner, 1997.

Powell, Colin L. *My American Journey*. New York: Random House, 1995.

Sifry, Micah L., and Christopher Cerf, eds. *The Gulf War Reader: History, Documents, Opinions*. New York: Times Books, 1991.

Spencer, William. *The Middle East*, 12th ed. Boston: McGraw Hill, 2009.

Tripp, Charles. *A History of Iraq*, 3rd ed. New York: Cambridge University Press, 2007.

Woodward, Bob. *The Commanders: The Pentagon and the First Gulf War, 1989–1991*. New York: Simon and Schuster, 1991.

PRIMARY SOURCES

1. Senator John Danforth, Speech in the U.S. Senate, January 10, 1991

In the Senate debate over the Bush resolution authorizing the president's use of military force to liberate Kuwait, Senator John Danforth (R-MO) raised several points in support. In his speech in the Senate on January 10, 1991, he included a concise statement about the importance of oil in American society.

This is the first major test of the post–cold-war world order. With the recent collapse of the Soviet Empire, the great threat we have feared since 1945 is no longer real. The likelihood is zero that the Soviet Union will precipitate war by invading Western Europe. But the events of August 2 have demonstrated to all that to be rid of one threat does not make the world safe. A growing list of countries now possess or soon will possess the instruments of mass destruction. One of those countries is Iraq. It is simply not sufficient to check the possibility of terrifying aggression at one of its sources. We must be prepared to check terrifying aggression at all of its sources.

Some people have asked whether this conflict is not "just about" oil. To me, that is like asking whether it is not just about oxygen. Like it or not, our country, together with the rest of the world, is utterly dependent on oil. Our economy, our jobs, our ability to defend ourselves are dependent on our access to oil. To control the world's supply of oil is in a real sense to control the world. So what is involved in the Persian Gulf today is not only the preservation of the world order and the prevention of brutal aggression; it is the vital economic and security interests of the United States and the rest of the world as well.

Source: Congressional Record, January 10, 1991, S122–123.

—⚏—

2. Senator William Roth, Speech in the U.S. Senate, January 10, 1991

In his defense of the Bush resolution to authorize military force against Iraq on January 10, 1991, Senator William Roth (R-DE) called Saddam Hussein a "despotic madman." Roth also discussed the importance of Middle Eastern oil to the world economy.

What Hussein has done not only offends our sense of morality, but threatens our sense of security. It is not enough that he violently and illegally annexed Kuwait, that he held innocent men, women, and children hostage, and that he has denied his own citizens basic rights and needs to build the third largest war machine in the world. It is not enough that this dictator is little more than a despotic madman who has demonstrated his ruthless behavior by using chemical weapons on his own people and killing members of his own family.

One can only imagine what devastating consequence would follow should his dominance be allowed in the oil-rich Middle East—and this is the second reason he must be stopped.

Oil runs the economies of the world. It fuels our factories, heats our homes, carries our products from manufacturer to market. It is as basic to the economy as water is to life, and the free trade in international energy supplies is critical for not only the Industrial democracies but the fragile Third World nations that depend on this precious resource even more than we do. Any attempt to disrupt those supplies will send a devastating quake through these economies—lengthening unemployment lines and boosting inflation in the industrial democracies and crushing the economies of developing countries where day-to-day existence depends on imported energy sources.

Source: Congressional Record, January 10, 1991, S137–138.

—〰—

3. Senator Orrin Hatch, Speech in the U.S. Senate, January 10, 1991

In a speech delivered on January 10, 1991, Senator Orrin Hatch (R-UT) offered a convenient summary of the four major arguments articulated on behalf of the president's authority to use military force in Iraq. His use of the term "weapons of mass destruction" would later surface in charges against Saddam Hussein in the Iraq War.

The only way to avoid war, in my opinion, in this particular situation, is to be prepared to go to war and to show our resolve is for real.

If we back the President overwhelmingly, we will maximize the pressure on Iraq. We will enhance the chances that we can avoid war.

What are our U.S. interests over there?

No. 1, we have a vital interest in stopping and reversing Iraqi aggression. Saddam Hussein is a man who has invaded two of his neighbors, and he will strike again unless his invasion of Kuwait is decisively reversed. If we fail to do so, then we will set the precedent that aggression can succeed, that aggression can pay, that aggressors need not fear even when the United States votes to take positive action against them.

No. 2, we have a moral interest in liberating the Kuwaiti nation and stopping the brutal violations of human rights committed by Iraq's occupying forces. Even ailing infants have been left to die as their incubators were carted away by Saddam Hussein and his people.

No. 3, we have a security interest in thwarting Hussein's threat to launch a major international terror campaign. He has assembled the world's most vicious terrorists, including those behind the Pan Am 103 bombing, the Rome airport massacre, the *Achille Lauro* hijacking.

No. 4, we have the vital security interest in stopping Hussein's development of weapons of mass destruction. His chemical, biological, and nuclear programs have been well documented in the press. He has already used chemical weapons. He almost certainly has the means to deliver biological weapons. He could develop a crude nuclear device within a year.

Why not wait for the sanctions to work? Even if we wait a few more months, the cost in terms of U.S. lives will escalate dramatically. That will give Iraq's forces more time to build up the greatest fortified work since the Maginot Line. He has already put in place vast mine fields, fire ditches, dug in armor, infantry positions with overlapping fields of fire, all designed to channel attacking forces into preplanned killing zones.

If Congress stalls, we will be responsible for the loss of thousands of lives, not only American casualties, but the others as well.

Source: Congressional Record, January 10, 1991, S141, 143.

—ᴍ—

4. President George H. W. Bush, "The Liberation of Kuwait Has Begun," January 16, 1991

On January 16, 1991, President George H. W. Bush addressed the nation from the White House several hours after the bombing campaign against Iraq had begun. He condemned Iraq's invasion of Kuwait and human rights atrocities against its own people. The president also promised to eliminate Iraq's potential for producing nuclear weapons.

Just 2 hours ago, allied air forces began an attack on military targets in Iraq and Kuwait. These attacks continue as I speak. Ground forces are not engaged.

This conflict started August 2nd when the dictator of Iraq invaded a small and helpless neighbor. Kuwait—a member of the Arab League and a member of the United Nations—was crushed; its people, brutalized. Five months ago, Saddam Hussein started this cruel war against Kuwait. Tonight, the battle has been joined.

This military action, taken in accord with United Nations resolutions and with the consent of the United States Congress, follows months of constant and virtually endless diplomatic activity on the part of the United Nations, the United States, and many, many other countries. Arab leaders sought what became known as an Arab solution, only to conclude that Saddam Hussein was unwilling to leave Kuwait.

Now the 28 countries with forces in the Gulf area have exhausted all reasonable efforts to reach a peaceful resolution—we have no choice but to drive Saddam from Kuwait by force. We will not fail.

As I report to you, air attacks are underway against military targets in Iraq. We are determined to knock out Saddam Hussein's nuclear bomb potential. We will also destroy his chemical weapons facilities.

Our objectives are clear: Saddam Hussein's forces will leave Kuwait. The legitimate government of Kuwait will be restored to its rightful place, and Kuwait will once again be free.

Some may ask: Why act now? Why not wait? The answer is clear: The world could wait no longer. Sanctions, though having some effect, showed no signs of accomplishing their objective. Sanctions were tried for well over 5 months, and we and our allies concluded that sanctions alone would not force Saddam from Kuwait.

While the world waited, Saddam Hussein systematically raped, pillaged, and plundered a tiny nation, no threat to his own. He subjected the people of Kuwait to unspeakable atrocities—and among those maimed and murdered, innocent children.

While the world waited, Saddam sought to add to the chemical weapons arsenal he now possesses, an infinitely more dangerous weapon of mass destruction—a nuclear weapon. And while the world waited, while the world talked peace and withdrawal, Saddam Hussein dug in and moved massive forces into Kuwait.

When we are successful—and we will be—we have a real chance at this new world order, an order in which a credible United Nations can use its peacekeeping role to fulfill the promise and vision of the U.N.'s founders.

Source: Public Papers of the Presidents of the United States: George H. W. Bush, 1991, Book I (US Government Printing Office, Washington, D.C.: 1992), 42–44 http://www.gpoaccess.gov/pubpapers/ghwbush.html.

—⁓—

5. Senator George Mitchell, Speech in the U.S. Senate, January 10, 1991

Senator George Mitchell (D-ME), the majority leader of the Senate, led the Democratic opposition to President George H. W. Bush's request for authority to use force to remove Iraq from Kuwait. In a speech in the Senate on January 10, 1991, Mitchell charged that the president had made an abrupt about-face change in policy without consulting Congress and now wanted open-ended authority to wage war unilaterally.

Most Americans and most Members of Congress, myself included, supported the President's initial decision to deploy American forces to Saudi Arabia to deter further Iraqi aggression. We supported the President's effort in marshaling international diplomatic pressure and the most comprehensive economic embargo in history against Iraq.

I support that policy. I believe it remains the correct policy, even though the President abandoned his own policy before it had time to work. The change began on November 8, when President Bush announced that he was doubling the number of American troops in the Persian Gulf to 430,000 in order to attain a "credible offensive option." The President did not consult with Congress about that decision. He did not try to build support for it among the American people. He just did it.

In so doing, President Bush transformed the U.S. role and its risk in the Persian Gulf crisis. In effect, the President—overnight, with no consultation and no public debate—changed American policy from being part of a collective effort to enforce economic and diplomatic sanctions into a predominantly American effort relying upon the use of American military force. By definition, sanctions require many nations to participate and share the burden. War does not. Despite the fact that his own policy of international economic sanctions was having a significant effect upon the Iraqi economy, the President, without explanation, abandoned that approach and instead adopted a policy based first and foremost upon the use of American military force.

As a result, this country has been placed on a course toward war.

Source: Congressional Record, January 10, 1991, S101.

—⚏—

6. Senator Joe Biden, Speech in the U.S. Senate, January 10, 1991

On January 10, 1991, Senator Joe Biden (D-DE) argued during the Senate debate over the Gulf crisis that the president should not be handed authority to use military force on his own discretion. Citing numerous legal scholars to support this argument, Biden said that only Congress possessed the power to declare war.

On this point the Constitution is as clear as it is plain. While article II of the Constitution gives the President the power to command our troops, article I of the Constitution commits to Congress—and Congress alone—the power to decide if this Nation will go to war. The Framers of our Constitution took great pains to ensure that the Government they established for us would differ from the rule of the British monarchs. They knew firsthand of the consequences of leaving the choice between war and peace to one man.

The Constitution's language says that the war power rests with the Congress, and from James Madison to John Marshall, the Constitution's fathers all understood this to be a key principle of the Republic.

Lest anyone in this body or anyone listening wonder why I am raising this question—since we will soon vote on a resolution authorizing the use of force—I am raising it because the President continues to insist he does not need the will of the people, spoken through the Congress as envisioned by the Constitution, to decide whether or not to go to war. I assume that means he would believe he had the constitutional authority even if we vote down a resolution authorizing him to use force. Whether he would politically do that or not is another question. But at least it should be somewhere on the record that there is ample evidence, constitutional scholarship to suggest that he has no such authority. On Tuesday, President Bush asked this Congress to debate and decide whether to take the Nation to war. Unfortunately, the President stopped short of abandoning his previous claim that he has the power, acting alone, to start a war. His Secretary of Defense has said, "We do not believe that the President requires any additional authorization from the Congress before committing U.S. forces to achieve our objectives in the gulf." And his Secretary of State has said, "The President has the right as a matter of practice and principle to initiate military action."

Just yesterday, as I mentioned earlier, the President himself said that he alone has the constitutional authority to initiate war.

To put it simply, these views are at odds with the Constitution. They may accurately describe the power of leaders of other countries, but they do not describe the power of the President of the United States.

Source: Congressional Record, January 10, 1991, S120, 122.

—∽—

7. Senator John D. Exon, Speech in the U.S. Senate, January 10, 1991

In a speech on January 10, 1991, Senator John D. Exon (D-NE) charged that President George H. W. Bush was rushing to war in the Persian Gulf before economic sanctions against Iraq were given a chance to work. He also was critical of the Americanization of the conflict with Iraq, wondering why the Arabs "are nowhere to be found."

[T]he rush to combat now, early in 1991, before the embargo and sanctions have been afforded a chance to work, is in my view tragically shortsighted. There never has been an explanation as to why the administration abruptly changed course on November 8, 1990; abandoning its defense strategy for an offensive one which 60 days later has us all but launching all-out combat.

Also, I am concerned by the recent Americanization of the conflict and the perception that war is no longer the last resort in removing Hussein's army from Kuwait. More specifically, I am concerned with the shift in administration rhetoric and policy to use offensive force for reasons, such as Iraq's potential nuclear capability or its large conventional military strength, which are beyond those listed in U.N. Resolution 660 or any other measure approved by the international community. I am disappointed that the military force in Saudi Arabia is predominantly American, with American troops representing approximately 75 percent of the ground forces facing Iraqi tanks. While many Arab States express a desire for an Arab solution and have a combined military power superior to Iraq, their military commitment in this crisis is inadequate. Other nations which heavily depend on Iraqi and Kuwaiti oil are nowhere to be found when it comes to defending their interests. Fairness has given way to expediency.

Experienced and proven experts in military and international channels, including the immediate past two Chairmen of the Joint Chiefs of Staff and a former Secretary of the Navy under the Reagan administration, cautioned strongly against the immediate combat option as opposed to some deal by means of the sanctions and embargo.

My question is: Are wise heads prevailing in our rush to early battle?

Source: Congressional Record, January 10, 1991, S146.

—◊◊◊—

8. Arthur Schlesinger, Jr., "White Slaves in the Persian Gulf," January 7, 1991

An eminent historian and scholar of the American presidency, Arthur Schlesinger, Jr., wrote a critique of President Bush's policy on Kuwait for the Wall Street Journal, *one of the nation's most conservative newspapers, on January 7, 1991. Noting that the Americans were preparing to do a job that the Arabs themselves should do, he wondered whether the United States was replacing the old Ottoman Empire as the overlord of the Middle East.*

In this newspaper a few days ago Geraldine Brooks and Tony Horwitz described the reluctance of the Arabs to fight in their own defense. The Gulf states have a population almost as large as Iraq's but no serious armies and limited inclination to raise them. Why should they? The *Journal* quotes a senior Gulf official: "You think I want to send my teenaged son to die for Kuwait?" He chuckles and adds. "We have our white slaves from America to do that."

In defining our vital interests in the Gulf, the administration's trumpet gives an awfully uncertain sound. It has offered a rolling series of peripheral justifications—oil, jobs, regional stability, the menace of a nuclear Iraq, the creation of a new world order. These pretexts for war grow increasingly thin.

As for the stabilization of the Middle East, this is a goal that has never been attained for long in history. Stability is not a likely prospect for a region characterized from time immemorial by artificial frontiers, tribal antagonism, religious fanaticisms and desperate inequalities. I doubt that the U.S. has the capacity or the desire to replace the Ottoman Empire, and our efforts thus far have won us not the respect of the Arab rulers but their contempt.

As for the new world order, the United Nations will be far stronger if it succeeds through resolute application of economic sanctions than if it only provides a multilateral facade for a unilateral U.S. war. Nor would we strengthen the U.N. by wreaking mass destruction that will appall the world and discredit collective security for years to come.

War against Iraq will be the most unnecessary war in American history, and it well may cause the gravest damage to the vital interests of the republic.

Source: Arthur Schlesinger, Jr. "White Slaves in the Persian Gulf." *Wall Street Journal,* January 7, 1991. Reprinted by permission of *The Wall Street Journal,* Copyright © 1991 Dow Jones & Company, Inc. All Rights Reserved Worldwide. License number 2697150253501.

THE IRAQ WAR:
Will the American Invasion of Iraq Reduce Terrorism?

—ᴍ—

THE CONTROVERSY

The Issue

On March 19, 2003, the United States invaded Iraq, overwhelming its army and sending dictator Saddam Hussein into hiding. President George W. Bush said that the military strike on Iraq was linked to the terrorist attacks of September 11, 2001, on the United States, because Saddam Hussein had aided al-Qaeda and would provide them with nuclear weapons. Defeating Saddam Hussein, Bush argued, would aid the fight against terrorism. After the invasion, the Iraq War settled into a guerrilla insurgency and sectarian violence that had killed more than 4,000 American soldiers through 2010. Did the American invasion of Iraq reduce terrorism?

♦ *Arguments that the invasion of Iraq will reduce terrorism:* President George W. Bush and his advisers claimed that Saddam Hussein possessed weapons of mass destruction, including a program to build nuclear bombs. His regime, they charged, aided and abetted terrorist groups such as Osama bin Laden's al-Qaeda and would give them nuclear weapons. In light of this threat, a preemptive strike was justified.

♦ *Arguments that the invasion of Iraq will not reduce terrorism:* Opponents of the Iraq War responded that the American invasion increased the likelihood of terrorism, not diminished it. They argued that the American invasion increased Arab anti-American hostility. Critics observed that no evidence of a nuclear program in Iraq was ever found or that the Saddam Hussein regime had provided assistance to al-Qaeda.

—ᴍ—

INTRODUCTION

On September 11, 2001, two airliners loaded with passengers slammed into the twin towers of the World Trade Center in New York City.

The first aircraft struck the North Tower between the 93rd and 99th floors of the 110-story building at 8:46 A.M., trapping the occupants on the floors above. The second plane hit the South Tower between the 78th and 85th floors at 9:03 A.M. Both aircraft had been hijacked in the United States and deliberately flown into the World Trade Center. By late morning, both towers collapsed, killing nearly 3,000 employees, visitors, and rescue workers. Even before the buildings came crashing down, another hijacked commercial airliner plowed into the Pentagon building in Arlington, Virginia, leaving 189 people dead. Minutes later a fourth plane, presumably headed for Washington, D.C., crashed into a field in Pennsylvania, east of Pittsburgh, following a struggle between passengers and hijackers. All 44 onboard the aircraft died. The toll in human life from the four crashes eventually climbed to 2,973, making the 9/11 attack the most deadly on American soil in the history of the United States.

All 19 hijackers involved in the 9/11 attack were of Middle Eastern descent; 15 had links to Saudi Arabia. Subsequent investigation revealed that the hijackers were members of al-Qaeda, a radical Islamic organization headed by Osama bin Laden. In October, bin Laden justified the

A New York City firefighter calls for 10 more rescue workers to make their way into the rubble of the World Trade Center. (1st Class Preston Keres/U.S. Navy)

attacks as retribution for what "Our Islamic nation has been tasting . . . for more than 80 years, of humiliation and disgrace, its sons killed and their blood spilled. . . . God has blessed a group of vanguard Muslims, the forefront of Islam, to destroy America." The following month, bin Laden claimed that "America and its allies" were "massacring us in Palestine, Chechnya, Kashmir, and Iraq." In retaliation, he said, Muslims battle "America's icons of military and economic power," but he also blamed all Americans for its "anti-Muslim policies."

Most Americans had probably never heard of Osama bin Laden before 9/11. By the next day, he was enemy number one in the United States. The attack that he masterminded had a transformative effect on U.S. foreign policy. With the cold war over, Russia no longer loomed as a major threat to American security. In its place, a new danger developed, centered around radical Muslims from the Arab-speaking world. Unlike the cold war, when the United States faced the power of nations and their military establishments, the new enemy operated as individuals and small groups in clandestine cells of civilian terrorists. Bin Laden's headquarters was located in Afghanistan, whose Taliban regime, a radicalized organization of Afghan Muslims, gave al-Qaeda a safe haven. President George W. Bush demanded that the Taliban leaders turn bin Laden over to the United States. When they refused, Bush ordered the bombing of al-Qaeda facilities in Afghanistan on October 7, 2001. Subsequently, ground troops of the United States invaded and in partnership with Afghan allies overthrew Taliban rule. Bin Laden, however, eluded capture and went into hiding. But another despised figure, Saddam Hussein, remained very visible and in power in Iraq. On March 19, 2003, the United States invaded Iraq with the intent of toppling Saddam's regime, which President Bush claimed supported Islamic terrorists. Would the Iraq invasion reduce the threat of terrorism to Americans?

President Bush contended that Saddam Hussein threatened world stability and the security of the United States. He accused Iraq of developing weapons of mass destruction (WMD) and claimed that Saddam was certain to use them against the United States and its allies Furthermore, Iraq hosted terrorist organizations such as al-Qaeda, which hoped to acquire nuclear weapons. The president asserted that Iraq's nuclear program, along with Saddam Hussein's cooperation with al-Qaeda, was grounds for taking "preemptive" action against the dictator's regime.

Once Saddam was toppled, the United States would hand power over to law-abiding Iraqis, who could build a stable democracy in their new nation. U.S. military intervention in Iraq would protect Americans, spread democracy, and build a more stable Middle East.

Initially, most Americans supported the president's plan, although a few dissenters questioned the connection between Saddam and al-Qaeda. Others thought that the United Nations, which had mandated that Iraq cease the development of WMD, should be allowed to verify that Saddam was abiding by UN resolutions. After American forces overpowered the Saddam Hussein regime, inspection of his occupied country failed to find facilities for producing nuclear weapons. What Americans did encounter was stiff resistance from guerrilla insurgents. The Bush administration claimed that the insurgency embodied terrorist activity. Critics responded that the American invasion had triggered a civil war among Iraq's religious-ethnic groups. Instead of installing a stable democracy, they argued, the occupation of Iraq created a breeding ground for Islamic terrorism and new hostility toward the United States.

BACKGROUND

During the Persian Gulf War in February 1991, U.S. and coalition partners had driven Saddam Hussein's army out of Kuwait, which it had invaded in 1990. Encouraged by the rout of Iraqi forces, Kurds in northern Iraq and Shiite Muslims in the south staged rebellions in quest of greater political autonomy, but Saddam's army remained sufficiently intact to crush these regional uprisings. Responding to Saddam Hussein's brutalities, the United States, Britain, and France, claiming authority under United Nations resolutions, imposed "no-fly" zones north of the 36th parallel in 1991 and south of the 33rd parallel in 1992 that were designed to deter further Iraqi reprisals against the restive groups. The United Nations also adopted a resolution that directed Iraq to dismantle its long-range ballistic missiles and dismantle its facilities for manufacturing nuclear weapons. Its embargo on the sale of Iraqi oil established in the wake of its invasion of Kuwait in 1990 remained in place, contingent on Saddam Hussein's compliance with all UN mandates. Saddam was ordered to open his country to UN inspectors, who

Osama bin Laden, leader of al-Qaeda, plotted the 9/11 attacks on the United States. (AFP/Getty Images)

would verify his compliance with the destruction of WMD. His refusal to allow inspections and violations of the no-fly zone prompted the United States to bomb Iraqi military installations several times during the administration of President Bill Clinton (1993–2001). Nonetheless, 10 years after the Persian Gulf War, Saddam Hussein still thumbed his nose at his adversaries.

The 9/11 attacks changed this inconclusive policy toward Iraq. President George W. Bush had been in office less than nine months when the hijackers struck. The events of 9/11 revitalized his administration, providing Bush an opportunity to rally a nation shocked by a terrorist attack of unimaginable proportion. Bush pledged to hunt down the al-Qaeda perpetrators and bring them to justice. First on this list was Osama bin Laden.

American intelligence personnel were aware of al-Qaeda terrorists and of threats that bin Laden had issued before 9/11. Nevertheless, neither the Clinton nor Bush administrations had taken decisive action, either by mounting a concerted antiterrorist campaign abroad, particularly in Afghanistan, where al-Qaeda had set up training camps, or by instituting adequate security precautions in the United States. There were numerous suggestions that al-Qaeda was planning an attack on American soil, although the nature, place, and time was unknown. Perhaps clearer intelligence and greater diligence in analyzing it could have prevented a 9/11-type attack.

Osama bin Laden's virulent hostility toward the United States was a matter of public record. Committed to a radical version of Islam that harbored little tolerance of alternative faiths, bin Laden saw Americans as the new crusaders in Arab lands. He had issued several jihads, declaration of holy war, since 1996, denouncing the United States for military intrusion on the Arabian Peninsula, which he regarded as sacred Islamic soil. "[F]or over seven years," his 1998 declaration stated, "the United States has been occupying the lands of Islam in the holiest of places, the Arabian Peninsula, plundering its riches, dictating to its rulers, humiliating its people, terrorizing its neighbors, and turning its bases in the Peninsula into a spearhead through which to fight the neighboring Muslim peoples." (See "Osama bin Laden, 'Jihad Against Jews and Crusaders,' February 23, 1998," on page 393 in the Primary Sources section.) Bin Laden, in short, had declared a holy war against foreign invaders.

George Bush's response to 9/11 centered on the capture of bin Laden and the destruction of his training camps in Afghanistan, which were controlled by the Taliban, a radical Islamic group. Bombing of al-Qaeda facilities began on October 7, 2001. The American ground invasion that followed quickly dispersed the Taliban but failed to get bin Laden, who allegedly hid in the Tora Bora mountains bordering Pakistan and then in Pakistan itself. With bin Laden on the loose, the United States turned its efforts to building a secular regime in Afghanistan that would cooperate in preventing a return of al-Qaeda. In time, however, Taliban fighters drifted back into Afghanistan, where they battled American soldiers for more than 10 years. Like the British and Russians before them, Americans found Afghan guerrilla fighters tough to subdue.

The American incursion into Afghanistan killed or captured various al-Qaeda figures, but bin Laden remained a fugitive. Failing to deliver on his promise to bring the mastermind of 9/11 to justice, President Bush turned to a more accessible villain: Saddam Hussein. Early in 2002, Bush began to focus publicly on Saddam Hussein, who remained defiant of the United Nations and the United States. In his January 2002 State of the Union message, Bush sounded an alert about regimes that were developing nuclear weapons, specifically pointing to North Korea, Iran, and Iraq, which he called "an axis of evil." These rogue nations were not only developing WMD, but "they could provide these arms to terrorists." Bush singled out Iraq for continuing "to support terror" In a speech at West Point five months later, the president repeated his January implication that the United States might not wait for these regimes to become hostile but might take "preemptive action" to eliminate the threat of WMD.

By the summer of 2002, Bush had fixed his sights on Iraq for "preemptive action." The shift from concern about al-Qaeda in Afghanistan to Saddam Hussein in Iraq derived from several factors. First, Bush entered the presidency with virtually no experience in foreign affairs. Unlike his father, George H. W. Bush, the younger Bush had not served overseas, either in the military or as a governmental official. His only public office prior to the presidency was as governor of Texas, a job that required little attention to foreign policy matters. This inexperience left the president especially dependent on his advisers, something the president had admitted during the 2000 presidential campaign. Second, many Americans, conservatives in particular, were angry that the first president Bush had not removed Saddam Hussein from power during the Persian Gulf War. Saddam's survival had taken the bloom off the coalition victory over the Iraqi army.

Finally, third, George W. Bush picked a team of foreign policy advisers who brought a distinct vision about foreign policy to the White House. Nicknaming themselves the Vulcans, after the Greek god of fire and metal, Bush's choices for his inner circle of advisers possessed decades of experience in the federal government and in matters of defense policy. Three individuals formed a hawkish wing of the Vulcans: Vice President Dick Cheney, Secretary of Defense Donald Rumsfeld, and Deputy Secretary of Defense Paul D. Wolfowitz. This trio had worked together during several earlier Republican administrations (Richard Nixon, Gerald Ford, Ronald Reagan, and George H. W. Bush). Vice President Cheney had been secretary of defense during the Persian Gulf War and had served under Donald Rumsfeld, who was President Gerald Ford's chief of staff in the 1970s until he was appointed secretary of defense. Wolfowitz had a long career in Pentagon and State Department policy positions and served as under secretary of defense during Cheney's tenure as secretary of defense. The trio had similar outlooks about how to shape foreign policy; they agreed that the United States should assert its objectives as a superpower in the post–cold war world.

Two other individuals, also with experience in Republican administrations, rounded out Bush's inner circle. Condoleezza Rice served as George W. Bush's national security adviser. An academic with expertise in the Soviet Union, she had assisted Brent Scowcroft, who had been George H. W. Bush's national security adviser. General (retired) Colin Powell was secretary of state. Powell had served as a military adviser in the Nixon and Reagan administrations and had been military chief of staff during the Gulf War under President George H. W. Bush. Powell was the least hawkish of the Vulcans. Rice (who replaced Powell as secretary of state in 2005) took a quiet, consensus-building role within the inner circle.

Expressing views called "neoconservative," the Vulcans believed that the old cold war doctrine of containment, whereby the United States blocked adversaries from spreading their influence, had become outmoded. Former president Harry Truman and former British prime minister Winston Churchill were seen as models because of their fierce defense of "freedom" during World War II and the cold war. They advocated the rebuilding of the nation's military power with the objective of becoming the unchallengeable superpower in the wake of the collapse of the Soviet Union in the early 1990s. America should not shrink from using this power to advance its objectives, they charged, even if allies, such as western European nations, objected. Military power, not diplomacy, they believed, was the most potent tool in world affairs. The Vulcans were prepared to take preemptive military action (strike before being attacked) if necessary, including for the purpose of regime change—overthrowing unfriendly governments—if it advanced democracy, which they regarded as a universal moral value. Wolfowitz in particular had urged regime change in Iraq before 2001. George W. Bush's elevation to the presidency along with 9/11 gave the Vulcans a platform on which to put their ideas into practice.

Because of his personal outlook or because of his dependency on experienced foreign policy hands, or both, George Bush followed the Vulcans' recommendations. The evidence suggests that Bush contemplated a preemptive strike against Iraq late in 2001 and decided on war no later than July 2002. Various tasks remained to be completed, however, before the United States undertook the invasion. First, Congress had to be brought on board. Second, the United Nations would be asked to approve military action against Iraq. Third, Bush would try to assemble a coalition of nations to join a preemptive strike at Iraq. Fourth, an adequate military force had to be assembled in the Middle East.

Getting Congress on board was the easiest of these objectives. The president claimed that he did not need congressional approval to take military action against Iraq, yet he realized that its support was politically sensible. With the memories of 9/11 still in the air and bin Laden still on the loose, Congress was in no mood to deny the president authority to proceed against Iraq if Saddam Hussein continued to drag his feet over WMD. The House of Representatives approved a resolution giving the president authority to use military force against Iraq by a vote of 296-133 on October 10, 2002. The following day, the Senate passed the measure 77-23. Partisan conflict in Congress was muted, in part because many leading Democrats, some of whom were considering a run for the presidency in 2004, sided with the president and because the president indicated his willingness to seek approval from the United Nations. Moreover, public opinion polls showed the majority of Americans believed that Saddam Hussein was involved in 9/11. A very large majority indicated that Iraq's alleged possession of WMD justified war.

The United Nations and potential coalition partners proved less cooperative. In November 2002, Secretary of State Colin Powell shepherded Resolution 1441 through the United Nations, which mandated stricter standards of inspection concerning WMD in Iraq. However, despite his claim that Saddam Hussein possessed chemical and biologic weapons and was developing facilities for manufacturing nuclear weapons, Powell was unable to persuade the UN Security Council to authorize military action. Only Great Britain was willing to commit a sizeable number of troops to an offensive operation against Iraq. Tony Blair, Britain's prime minister, was a Vulcan in all but name. Calling Saddam Hussein "a profoundly wicked . . . almost psychopathic man," Blair believed that removing the dictator was the morally correct path to take. Bush took whatever help he could get, calling his small contingent of supporters "the coalition of the willing." By March 2003, the United States had assembled a force of more than 150,000 in Kuwait, at sea, and in several air bases in the region. On March 19, the coalition struck, commencing "Operation Iraqi Freedom."

THE DEBATE

The debate over the U.S. invasion of Iraq and its link to terrorism took a twisting path. The shock of 9/11 disposed the American public and most political leaders to support the president's effort to bring the terrorists to justice. In the immediacy of the attack on the World Trade Center and the Pentagon, Americans displayed patriotism and rallied behind their nation and its leader much as they had done following the Japanese attack on Pearl Harbor on December 7, 1941. The debate over an invasion of Iraq initially concerned techniques, especially regarding the president's right to order a preemptive strike at his discretion without congressional approval. After the invasion turned into a military occupation, criticism of the Iraq War grew. Dissent was fanned by revelations in 2004 and subsequent years that contradicted administration assertions that Saddam Hussein had aided al-Qaeda.

The Argument that the Invasion of Iraq Will Reduce Terrorism

In many ways, the Iraq War was Vice President Dick Cheney's war. He became committed to a preemptive strike after 9/11, if not before. Usually operating behind the scenes, Cheney apparently felt passionate enough about confronting Saddam to go public, accepting a speaking engagement at the national convention of the Veterans of Foreign Wars in Nashville, Tennessee, on August 26, 2002. Cheney offered a rationale

Vice President Dick Cheney (The White House)

for invading Iraq that lay at the center of the administration's argument for a military confrontation with Saddam Hussein. (See "Vice President Dick Cheney, Speech, August 26, 2002," on page 394 in the Primary Sources section.) The vice president asserted that al-Qaeda sought to acquire nuclear weapons and that Saddam Hussein had resumed efforts to acquire them. It was known that Iraq possessed chemical weapons. Cheney believed Saddam Hussein would be successful in getting nuclear weapons, too, and then would share these weapons with "terrorists."

Instead of waiting for this danger to materialize, Cheney advocated "regime change" in Iraq, which he believed would lessen terrorism. Without directly tying al-Qaeda to Saddam Hussein, the vice president implied that these two malignant elements were collaborators.

President Bush seconded Cheney's contention about Saddam Hussein's quest for nuclear weapons on numerous occasions, including in his State of the Union addresses in 2002 and 2003. At a news conference on March 6, 2003, Bush went beyond his earlier allegations. He stated that not only did Saddam Hussein possess WMD but that he also funded, trained, and provided "safe havens" to terrorists. (See "President George W. Bush, News Conference, March 6, 2003," on page 395 in the Primary Sources section.) Iraq, he said, "is part of the war on terror. Iraq is a country that has got terrorist ties. . . . It's a country that trains terrorists." He continued that "we not only must chase down al-Qaeda terrorists, we must deal with weapons of mass destruction as well." The president did not explicitly say that Saddam had helped al-Qaeda with the 9/11 attack on the United States, but he left the impression that this was the case. Bush implied that he would take preemptive action rather than "wait to see what terrorists or terrorist states could do with weapons of mass destruction."

Later in the month, on March 17, 2003, the president indicated that his patience was exhausted. He repeated his conviction that Saddam was developing nuclear weapons and "aided, trained, and harbored terrorists." Saddam also continued to defy UN mandates concerning WMD. Bush announced that he would order an invasion of Iraq unless "Saddam Hussein and his sons . . . leave Iraq within 48 hours." (See "President George W. Bush, Ultimatum to Iraq, March 17, 2003," on page 397 in the Primary Sources section.) Saddam stayed put, and the U.S.-British coalition, which also included soldiers from a few other countries, invaded on March 19, quickly overpowering Iraqi resistance. Less than three weeks later, on April 8, Bush announced the end of Saddam's rule over Iraq. With the invasion over, and as the occupation of Iraq unfolded, doubts about administration claims concerning Saddam's regime grew. The president, however, clung tenaciously to his original position. On the TV news show *Meet the Press* in February 2004, Bush reiterated his belief that U.S. intelligence had left no doubt that Saddam possessed WMD and that he funded terrorists.

Nonetheless, Bush did add another reason for invading Iraq as the occupation proceeded. In his State of the Union address on January 20,

2004, the president defended the goal of regime change in Iraq. (See "President George W. Bush, State of the Union Speech, January 20, 2004," on page 398 in the Primary Sources section.) "The work of building a new Iraq is hard, and it is right." The aspiration to transform Iraq into a democracy, the president said, embodied a key "mission" of America, emanating from "our basic beliefs." Not only did the hope for democracy stem from American traditions, it also was divinely endowed: "I believe that God has planted in every heart the desire to live in freedom." Democracy, Bush pledged, would replace the brutal dictator's "torture chambers" and "killing-fields." The president had embraced the Vulcans' objective of spreading democratic institutions around the world.

Preventing Saddam Hussein from developing nuclear weapons, preventing him from harboring terrorists, and replacing Iraq's police state with a democracy were the three chief justifications that the administration gave for the Iraq War. One heard little about oil in the buildup to the invasion and virtually nothing about oil during the immediate aftermath of the attack. This omission was clearly a political calculation, despite the disavowal of Secretary of Defense Donald Rumsfeld in late 2002 that "regime change" in Iraq "has nothing to do with oil." Perhaps access to oil was not the immediate objective in toppling Saddam, yet all American politicians—indeed, virtually every world leader—understood the critical importance of oil to modern economies. Even average Americans knew that Iraq contained immense petroleum wealth buried in its sands. (See the sidebar "Oil and the Middle East" on page 380.) Iraq held 11 percent of the world's known petroleum resources, not far behind the deposits in Saudi Arabia. Further exploration could possibly put Iraq in first place. Petroleum exports from the Middle East were predicted to grow in significance, not decline, in the years ahead. Given that Bush, Cheney, and Rice all had business connections with the oil industry before taking office in 2001, the suggestion that oil played no part in their formulation of policy toward Iraq stretches credulity.

The Argument that the Invasion of Iraq Will Not Reduce Terrorism

Misgivings about the Bush buildup for war in 2002 were heard among a few members of Congress, journalists, and others, yet most politicians and the majority of the public, according to polls, gave the president the benefit of the doubt concerning his decision to invade Iraq. The

OIL AND THE MIDDLE EAST

Four axioms of oil have had immense influence on American foreign policy in the late 20th and early 21st centuries. First, petroleum is crucial to industrial societies, particularly the United States. As a key source of power to run machines and generate electricity and as a resource base for products such as plastics, oil is an indispensable commodity. If its availability declines or its price becomes unaffordable, economies will falter and may collapse. Second, the United States is heavily dependent on imported petroleum. In 2001, more than half of the oil consumed in the United States was purchased from foreign sources. This figure had risen from virtually zero in the early 1950s. Third, the Middle East has the largest known petroleum reserves in the world. In 2000, Saudi Arabia, Kuwait, and Iraq held roughly 45 percent of the world's known oil deposits. Iran and the small oil-rich sheikhdoms in the Persian Gulf also possess sizeable petroleum deposits. Fourth, world demand for petroleum keeps rising. Economic development in China, India, Brazil, and other emerging countries has spurred increased consumption of oil products. Unless alternative sources of energy are developed, which is highly unlikely in the near future, further economic growth in these countries is bound to push the price of oil higher.

These four axioms set the stage for discussion of American policy toward the Middle East. Oil in the Persian Gulf region assumed major importance following discoveries in Iraq in 1927 and in Saudi Arab, Kuwait, and the United Arab Emirates in 1938. World War II demonstrated the dependence of modern armed forces on petroleum, particularly for aviation, motor vehicles, and ships. The first major diplomatic crisis of the postwar era for the United States centered on Greece and Turkey, which some scholars conclude had as much to do with protecting access to oil and denying it to enemies as any other factor. The oil embargo of 1973, orchestrated by

emotional shock of the terrorist attack in September 2001 led to a resurgence of patriotism in the United States through March 2003. After the U.S. invasion and the fall of the Saddam Hussein regime, however, the difficulties of the occupation became front-page news. From this point on, the Bush administration's justifications for the intervention in Iraq came under closer scrutiny. The argument that regime change in Iraq the Organization of Petroleum Exporting Countries (OPEC), in which Saudi Arabia is the dominant member, created an energy crisis in the United States and demonstrated the dependence of the American economy on petroleum exports from the Gulf region. Despite talk of conservation and developing alternative sources of energy in the wake of the 1973 oil crisis, the U.S. reliance on petroleum exports from the Persian Gulf increased during the remainder of the 20th century. Energy planners predicted an even greater reliance in future years. The National Energy Policy Development Group, a body assembled by Vice President Dick Cheney, reported in 2001 that "Middle East oil producers will remain central to world oil security." Possessing around 11 percent of known petroleum reserves, Iraq held second place behind Saudi Arabia.

The Iraq War was the second conflict in which the U.S. military fought in the Persian Gulf since 1991. A Bush was president during each war. President George W. Bush had worked in the oil industry before turning to politics, as had his father, President George H. W. Bush, who maintained commercial ties to the Saudi royal family after his presidency. George W. Bush's vice president, Dick Cheney, had worked for Halliburton, a firm engaged in oil extraction. Bush's secretary of the army and secretary of commerce also had backgrounds in the oil business. Condoleezza Rice sat on the board of directors of Chevron, an oil company, prior to becoming Bush's national security adviser. Secretary of Defense Donald Rumsfeld stated in late 2002 that the Bush administration's interest in "regime change" in Iraq "has nothing to do with oil." Maybe so, at least in the very short run, but oil certainly counts from the standpoint of political economy. When Saddam Hussein ruled Iraq, he barred American and British oil companies from gaining access to his country's oil but entertained deals with Russia, China, and France. With Saddam out of the way, the opportunity opened for American firms to tap one of the world's richest oil pools.

would lessen terrorism was increasingly challenged. The 2006 midterm elections, which put Democrats in control of both houses of Congress, contributed to this escalation of second-guessing about the purposes of the Iraq War.

The 9/11 Commission provided an occasion for examining links between al-Qaeda and Iraq. Created in November 2002, the commission held hearings in early 2004 and issued its major report in July 2004. The commission was primarily interested in the intelligence failures in anticipating an attack on the United States before 9/11, yet its report did not confirm cooperation between Iraqis and al-Qaeda prior to 9/11. The testimony of Richard A. Clarke, who chaired the National Security Council's Counter-Terrorism Security Group from 1998 to 2003, was a highlight of the public hearings in March 2004. Clarke's job had been to advise the president (first Clinton, then Bush) on terrorist threats to the United States. Bush, Clarke charged, had largely ignored his advice in 2001 to take aggressive actions against al-Qaeda despite mounting evidence of plans to attack Americans. Equally explosive was Clarke's charge at the hearing that "by invading Iraq, the President of the United States has greatly undermined the war on terrorism."

Clarke expanded on this these points in his 2004 book, *Against All Enemies*. (See "Richard A. Clarke, *Against All Enemies*, 2004," on page 398 in the Primary Sources section.) The former chief of American anti-terrorism intelligence wrote that there had not been any Iraq-sponsored foreign terrorism. Bush and his advisers had primarily stitched together conflicting bits of information into a rationale to invade Iraq. The president wanted, Clarke surmised, to "do something big" to compensate for the 9/11 attack. The invasion of Iraq, however, increased the likelihood of terrorism, not diminished it. Contrary to the predictions of the Vulcans, Americans were not seen as liberators in Iraq but as modern crusaders, bullying their way around Iraq and Arab nations. Iraq posed no "imminent threat" to the United States, he claimed, but the invasion may have increased the possibility of a radical Islamic revolution in Saudi Arabia, similar to what had happened in Iran in 1979. Osama bin Laden represented a strand of Islam that had become disaffected with the Saudi rulers. Clarke believed that the United States should be working to encourage ideological counterweights to radical Islam.

Bush supporters denounced Clarke's claims as blatant antiadministration partisanship. Despite increased guerrilla opposition to the American occupation—and increasing casualties—many Republicans fiercely defended the president's actions in the Middle East, but some Republicans had misgivings. In 2005, Pat Buchanan, a national columnist, former Reagan aide, and former contender for the Republican presidential nomination, agreed with Clarke that attacking Iraq "is not a cure for terrorism, it is the cause." (See "Pat Buchanan on Inaugurating

Endless War," January 26, 2005," on page 399 in the Primary Sources section.) The president failed to understand that bin Laden was not angry at Americans because of their reverence for constitutional rights but because they stationed soldiers in the Middle East. As a result of Bush's misguided policy, he charged, America had suffered 10,000 dead and wounded, spent $200 billion (through 2004), and created a "new training ground and haven for terrorists" in Iraq. Buchanan also sharply criticized Bush's quest for regime change as nothing but "a formula for endless collisions between this nation and every autocratic regime on earth."

The Bush administration alleged that Saddam Hussein was developing nuclear weapons and assisting al-Qaeda. Bush and his Vulcan advisers claimed that these assertions rested on information provided by the United States intelligence community. Both contentions were put forward as justifications for a preemptive strike on Iraq, which would remove Saddam and allow a democracy to replace his police state. In 2004, the Senate Committee on Intelligence appointed a select committee to investigate the accuracy of these allegations.

The committee issued its report in June 2008. While containing few surprises for critics of the Bush administration, the report was a bombshell nonetheless, as it directly contradicted every major contention the Bush administration had used in support of its Iraq invasion. The majority of Republicans on the select committee rebutted the conclusion of the report and issued their own minority statement. By 2008, with a presidential election looming, the Iraq War had become highly politicized and partisan.

The select committee found that the intelligence community had been divided about the credibility of the evidence concerning a nuclear weapons program in Iraq *prior to* the invasion. (See "Senate Select Intelligence Committee Report, June 5, 2008," on page 400 in the Primary Sources section.) After the invasion of March 2003, when a thorough reconnaissance inside Iraq was undertaken, inspection teams found that Saddam had ended his nuclear program in 1991. The Vulcans had argued, both indirectly and sometimes directly, that Saddam harbored al-Qaeda terrorists. Before March 2003, the intelligence community had believed that Saddam "was unwilling to conduct terrorist attacks [on] the US." After March 2003, the intelligence assessment found that Saddam had "refused all requests from al-Qaida to provide material or operational support." The select committee also threw cold water on the Vulcans' contention that Iraqis would welcome the Americans as liberators and look forward to establishing a democratic regime. The committee cited a 2002 CIA finding "that Iraqi political culture has been inhospitable to democracy," in part because its society lacked the "economic and politico-cultural prerequisites that political scientists generally regard as necessary to nurture democracy." In his concluding remarks to the report, Committee Chairman John D. Rockefeller IV (D-WV) charged that the president had "led the Nation to war on false premises." The Republican minority on the committee denounced the report as part of a "partisan agenda," claiming that the Democratic majority had cherry-picked statements from the evidence to discredit the president.

OUTCOME AND IMPACT

On March 19, 2003, approximately 150,000 American and British troops, supported by small contingents from several other countries, invaded Iraq. General Tommy Franks, a veteran of the Persian Gulf War, commanded the assault, called Operation Iraqi Freedom. Franks and his staff spent months planning the attack, including a covert campaign to persuade Iraqi commanders along the Kuwait border of the futility of resisting the coalition. This effort was surprisingly successful, as numerous Iraqi divisions became ineffective when their troops "melted away" rather than confront coalition soldiers.

Iraq's regular army had already shrunk considerably since the first Gulf War. Losses in that conflict, subsequent desertions, and poor administration had reduced its strength to 17 divisions, or about 150,000 to 200,000 men. The army had less than half its tank total of 1991, and those in service were 50 old models, the Russian T-72. Saddam's air force was virtually nonexistent; his radar defense system had been knocked out by American and British pilots who had enforced the "no-fly" zones over Iraq. Saddam still had his Republican Guard, units composed largely of Sunnis and designed principally as a security force to keep the dictator in power. Saddam also had the *fedayeen* (martyrs), guerrilla fighters from paramilitary political organizations that his regime had created. American commanders had underestimated the resistance that they would pose.

A second challenge to the coalition campaign was where to launch the assault. Coalition plans to use Turkey as a site to strike at Iraq from the north had to be scrapped when Turkish leaders, under increased pressure from Muslim factions, refused permission for American and British troops to stage operations from their territory. Fears of arousing Arab resentment eliminated Syria, Jordan, and Saudi Arabia from consideration as launching points. Iran, on Iraq's eastern border, was controlled by radical Islamists and was a sworn foe of the Americans. This left Kuwait as the staging area for Operation Iraqi Freedom.

The Iraqis mounted an ineffective resistance as U.S. Marine and Army units drove toward Baghdad and British forces surrounded Basra, Iraq's second largest city, located near the Persian Gulf. Iraqi tanks were no match for the range and accuracy of the 155-millimeter canon on American M1 Abrams tanks. Iraqi armor that escaped destruction by U.S. tanks and Bradley fighting vehicles were picked off by attack aircraft, including Apache helicopters equipped with Hellfire missiles. *Fedayeen* jihadists, armed with rifles and rocket-propelled grenades, attacked advancing American units in towns surrounding Baghdad and inside the city. While dangerous, the *fedayeen* were hardly a match when they faced American armored units, whose firepower overwhelmed these lightly armed irregulars. The United States closed

Apache Longbow helicopters can be equipped with an arsenal of weapons capable of destroying tanks and armored vehicles. (Stephen Morton/Getty Images)

President George W. Bush declares the end of major combat in Iraq, as he speaks aboard the aircraft carrier USS *Abraham Lincoln*, May 1, 2003. (J. Scott Applewhite/ Associated Press)

off escape routes from Baghdad, yet Saddam Hussein managed to elude the Americans for nine months. By April 8, Baghdad was in American hands. On May 1, 2003, President Bush announced from the deck of the aircraft carrier USS *Abraham Lincoln,* cruising off the California coast, that "the battle of Iraq is one victory in a war on terrorism that began on September 11, 2001." With a banner proclaiming "Mission Accomplished" waving behind him, he implied that the war was over.

Overturning the Saddam regime during Operation Iraqi Freedom cost the Americans 139 dead and 542 wounded, matched against uncounted thousands of Iraqi casualties. Saddam was captured on December 13, 2003, and executed three years later by the Iraqi provisional government. While the battle between large-scale units had ended quickly, guerrilla insurgents fought American soldiers in occupied Iraq for years. The insurgency surprised the Bush administration, whose subsequent actions probably made the situation worse. Bush supported the 2003 decision of Paul Bremer III, appointed ambassador to head the occupation, to remove members of the Baath Party, Saddam's political organization, from government positions in Iraq, which the United States replaced with a provisional regime. The "de-Baathification" program not only weakened the national police and civil service, but also led to the disbanding of the Iraqi army. This latter action stripped 200,000 young men of a job, sending them into the ranks of the unemployed with a new grievance against the United States. By restricting the size of the American occupation force, Secretary of Defense Rumsfeld bore some responsibility for this development. Rumsfeld had publicly overruled his army chief of staff, who recommended a force at least twice as large. The use of "private security" personnel partially compensated for the deficiency of American soldiers in postwar Iraq. (See the sidebar "Blackwater" on page 388.)

The lack of sufficient American coalition and Iraqi military personnel was a major reason that Iraq descended into a bloody insurgency. Disaffected Sunni and foreign fighters, some from Syria, mounted hit-and-run guerrilla attacks on Americans and their Iraqi collaborators. The use of roadside bombs (improvised explosive devises, or IEDs) was particularly hazardous. Instability in Iraq was compounded by sectarian violence between Shiites and Sunnis and hostility between Arabs and Kurds, conflicts that were embedded deep in Iraqi history and culture. Deposed Sunnis were especially resentful of American favoritism toward Shiites and Kurds in the provisional government.

As Iraq spiraled into hit-and-run attacks, suicide bombings, and roadside explosions, American casualties mounted. Criticism of the Bush administration for failing to plan properly for the occupation increased. Public opinion polls registered this dissatisfaction. In November 2006, 64 percent of Americans surveyed said the war was not going well, and 51 percent said the war had been the wrong decision. These sentiments influenced the 2006 congressional elections, which returned Democrats to the majority in the House and Senate. Days later, Rumsfeld stepped down as secretary of defense. The Bush administration, however, persevered and sent a "surge" of American troops to Iraq in 2007, a step that was partially successful in reducing violence. Still, Iraq remained a problem to the majority of the American electorate, a sentiment that contributed to Democrat Barack Obama's victory in the 2008 presidential election. During the campaign, Obama pledged to remove American combat troops from Iraq, a promise he honored in office. On August 31, 2010, President Obama announced in a televised speech from the White House that the United States had ended its combat mission in Iraq.

The Iraq War was a costly campaign in terms of personnel and money. American military fatalities exceeded 4,400 through 2010. The cost of the war totaled three-quarters of a billion dollars, 15 times

BLACKWATER

On September 16, 2007, private security guards killed 17 Iraqi civilians at an intersection in Baghdad. The shooters were employees of Blackwater USA, an American firm under contract with the U.S. government to provide protection for personnel of the State Department. Blackwater claimed that a convoy carrying civilian officials had been attacked during the September incident, with Blackwater agents returning fire. Iraqi witnesses disputed the allegation. The facts regarding the incident and its resolution remained in dispute for years. But the shooting did have one immediate impact: Many Americans were shocked to learn that some of the fighting in Iraq was being done by paid civilians.

Founded in 1998 by Erik Prince, a former Navy Seal, Blackwater trained law enforcement and military personnel. Its headquarters was initially located in Moyock, North Carolina, on a 7,000-acre property in the Great Dismal Swamp. Prince had great ambitions for Blackwater, maintaining a vision "to do for the national security apparatus what FedEx did to the postal service." The invasion of Iraq in 2003 transformed the company from a small training firm into a global security operation that employed thousands of individuals and operated in numerous countries. Prince won a contract to provide security to Paul Bremer, the man in charge of the American occupation of Iraq. This was a formidable task in 2003 and 2004, when Americans became targets of insurgents in the guerrilla war raging in Iraq. Blackwater kept Bremer alive and went on to win other contracts from the State Department to provide security. By 2007, Blackwater had obtained $1 billion worth of U.S. government contracts, mainly for duties in Iraq.

Most Blackwater security guards were former military and law enforcement agents. Sporting crew cuts and wrap-around sunglasses and highly paid, Blackwater protectors were armed, drove armored SUVs, and flew company-owned helicopters that provided sniper coverage for vehicle convoys. Security work in Iraq was dangerous and unpredictable. Blackwater employees were involved in 195 shooting incidents between 2005

the initial Bush estimate. Outlays for prime contracts, which included private contractors operating in Iraq, more than doubled between 2000 and 2006 (to $257 billion). Much of this money was borrowed, and 2007, according to hearings before the House Committee on Oversight and Governmental Reform in October 2007. Blackwater was the star of this investigation, but it was only one of many private companies operating in Iraq. According to Prince, 170 other firms were engaged in security activities in Iraq. Private contractors employed up to 100,000 individuals, rivaling the size of the U.S. military occupation. While theoretically assigned defensive tasks, some firms, Blackwater included, participated in clandestine CIA operations, including alleged assassinations of al-Qaeda leaders and the capture of Iraqi insurgents. Granted immunity from prosecution by the Iraqi government and minimally supervised by the U.S. government, private security contractors operated in a legal grey zone. In some aspects, the war in Iraq had been privatized, using mercenaries to do the business of the U.S. military.

Three factors help to explain Blackwater's involvement in the Middle East. First, Republicans in the two Bush administrations pushed "privatization," which contracted various public functions to private businesses. Dick Cheney had been instrumental in developing plans to use private contracts for the Department of Defense when he served as defense secretary under George H. W. Bush in 1989–93. Cheney revived this objective when he became vice president under George W. Bush in 2001. Second, Donald Rumsfeld, secretary of defense under George W. Bush, had initially restricted the number of American military personnel in Iraq to 135,000. This number was two or three times less than military experts thought were needed for the occupation of Iraq. Hence, the United States faced a manpower deficiency in Iraq. Third, Bremer had disbanded the Iraqi army and purged the Iraqi civil service of former Baathist Party members (Saddam Hussein's political organization), which undermined Iraqi security. Bremer also granted legal immunity to private contractors operating in Iraq. The door had been opened for private firms to contract with agencies in Washington for assignments in Iraq. The biggest winner in these sweepstakes was Halliburton, the company that Richard Cheney headed until he became vice president.

because President Bush made tax cuts, not tax increases, a centerpiece of his domestic agenda. Instead of a short and inexpensive war in which Americans were welcomed as liberators, the United States had wandered into a hornet's nest of Arab resentment and insurgency that lasted for more than seven years. Critics of the war argued that the Iraq invasion had increased the level of Arab hostility to the United States and incited more anti-American terrorism. They pointed out that most of America's allies opposed the invasion of Iraq and became alienated from the United States because of Bush's unilateral foreign policy. Public opinion polls of world opinion recorded that favorable attitudes toward the United States plummeted, especially in Europe. On the other hand, Bush supporters could claim that no major terrorist attack on the United States had succeeded since 9/11, that Iraq had been cleansed of WMD, and that Iraq was taking tentative steps toward a representative form of government. The debate over the invasion of Iraq and its consequence will continue for years.

WHAT IF?

What if Osama bin Laden had been captured before the invasion of Iraq?
Bin Laden avoided apprehension when American troops swept into Afghanistan and apparently took refuge in the mountainous "tribal area" of western Pakistan before relocating in Abbottabad, Pakistan. Bin Laden had not been captured during the 16 months between the time that U.S. soldiers entered Afghanistan in November 2001 and the American invasion of Iraq in March 2003. Perhaps if the United States had demanded greater cooperation from Pakistan, whose intelligence service had aided the Taliban, bin Laden might have been caught. In all likelihood, his capture would have reduced political pressure on President Bush to do "something big" in the wake of 9/11. Bringing bin Laden to trial for murder (perhaps as a war criminal) would have provided the nation some measure of justice for the al-Qaeda massacres and probably would have reduced support for driving Saddam Hussein from power in Iraq.

The fact that George W. Bush was president during 9/11 was instrumental in creating the impression that al-Qaeda was linked to Saddam Hussein. What if Al Gore had won the election in 2000 instead? Gore had won more popular votes than Bush but lost the election because the Supreme Court, on a vote of five to four, blocked a recount of votes from Florida. The decision resulted in Bush winning the state's electoral votes and with them the presidential election. Would a Gore presidency have led to an invasion of Iraq? Probably not. Although the Clinton-Gore administration intervened militarily in the Yugoslavian civil war, attacked Iraq's air defense system, and launched missile strikes at al-Qaeda in Afghanistan,

Gore and his supporters were far less hawkish than Bush's. The Vulcans were largely Republicans, while Democrats took a more dovish approach to foreign relations. Given this comparison, it is unlikely that Gore would have abandoned diplomacy to invade Iraq.

CHRONOLOGY

2001 *January 20:* George W. Bush becomes president of the United States.

September 11: Al-Qaeda terrorists attack the World Trade Center twin towers and the Pentagon.

October 7: President Bush orders bombing of Afghanistan.

October 26: Congress passes the USA Patriot Act.

December 7: Taliban is driven from power in Afghanistan.

2002 *January 29:* President George W. Bush identifies Iraq as part of an "axis of evil."

October 10: House passes resolution authorizing the use of force against Iraq.

October 11: Senate passes resolution authorizing the use of force against Iraq.

November 25: Department of Homeland Security is created.

2003 *March 19:* Invasion of Iraq (known as Operation Iraqi Freedom) begins.

May 1: President Bush declares victory in Operation Iraqi Freedom.

May 11: Bush appoints Paul Bremer head of the Coalition Provincial Authority in Iraq.

December 13: Saddam Hussein is captured.

2004 *November 2:* Bush is reelected president.

2006 *December 30:* Saddam Hussein is executed.

2007 *February:* U.S. military "surge" of troops in Iraq

September 16: Blackwater employees shoot and kill 17 Iraqi civilians in Baghdad.

2009 President Barack Obama begins drawdown of U.S. troops in Iraq.

2010 Stalemate over formation of a government in Iraq

August 31: United States President Obama declares an end to the U.S. "combat mission" in Iraq.

December 21: Iraqi parliament forms a government, nine months after national elections.

2011   *May 2:* U.S. forces kill Osama bin Laden in Pakistan.

DISCUSSION QUESTIONS

1. What alternatives to the Iraq invasion existed for fighting terrorism?
2. How important is access to oil in the policy of the United States toward the Middle East?
3. Would the invasion of Iraq have taken place if the 9/11 attack had not occurred?
4. How relevant was the oil factor in the Iraq invasion?

WEB SITES

Links to Web Sites on Iraq and the Iraq War. Available at http://www.mtholyoke.edu/~gktemple/iraq/resources.htm.

Oil in Iraq, U.S. Energy Information Administration (September 2010). Available at http://www.eia.doe.gov/emeu/cabs/Iraq/Background.html.

PBS, *Frontline*, "The Long Road to War." Available at http://www.pbs.org/wgbh/pages/frontline/shows/longroad/.

BIBLIOGRAPHY

Clarke, Richard A. *Against All Enemies: Inside America's War on Terror.* New York: Free Press, 2004.

Gordon, Michael R., and Bernard E. Trainor. *Cobra II: The Inside Story of the Invasion and Occupation of Iraq.* New York: Random House, 2006.

Hess, Gary. *Presidential Decisions for War: Korea, Vietnam, the Persian Gulf and Iraq.* 2d ed. Baltimore: Johns Hopkins University Press, 2009.

Keegan, John. *The Iraq War.* New York: Knopf, 2004.

Mann, James. *Rise of the Vulcans: The History of Bush's War Cabinet.* New York: Penguin, 2004.

Phillips, Kevin. *American Dynasty: Aristocracy, Fortunes, and the Politics of Deceit in the House of Bush.* New York: Viking, 2004.

Scahill, Jeremy. *Blackwater: The Rise of the World's Most Powerful Mercenary Army.* New York: Nation Books, 2007.

Sifry, Micah L., and Christopher Cerf, eds. *The Iraq War Reader: History, Documents, Opinions.* New York: Times Books, 2003.

Spencer, William. *The Middle East.* 12th ed. Boston: McGraw Hill, 2009.

Tripp, Charles. *A History of Iraq.* 3rd ed. New York: Cambridge University Press, 2007.

Woodward, Bob. *Plan of Attack.* New York: Simon and Schuster, 2004.

———. *The War Within: A Secret White House History, 2006–2008.* New York: Simon and Schuster, 2008.

PRIMARY SOURCES

1. Osama bin Laden, "Jihad Against Jews and Crusaders," February 23, 1998

Osama bin Laden, the Saudi Arabian–born leader of al-Qaeda, issued this "jihad" on February 23, 1998. Bin Laden justified his call "to kill Americans" with charges that he repeated on numerous occasions.

No one argues today about three facts that are known to everyone; we will list them, in order to remind everyone.

First, for over seven years the United States has been occupying the lands of Islam in the holiest of places, the Arabian Peninsula, plundering its riches, dictating to its rulers, humiliating its people, terrorizing its neighbors, and turning its bases in the Peninsula into a spearhead through which to fight the neighboring Muslim peoples.

The best proof of this is the Americans' continuing aggression against the Iraqi people using the Peninsula as a staging post, even though all its rulers are against their territories being used to that end, but they are helpless.

Second, despite the great devastation inflicted on the Iraqi people by the crusader-Zionist alliance, and despite the huge number of those killed, which has exceeded 1 million . . . despite all this, the Americans are once again trying to repeat the horrific massacres, as though they are not content with the protracted blockade imposed after the ferocious war or the fragmentation and devastation.

So here they come to annihilate what is left of this people and to humiliate their Muslim neighbors.

Third, if the Americans' aims behind these wars are religious and economic, the aim is also to serve the Jews' petty state and divert attention from its occupation of Jerusalem and murder of Muslims there.

The best proof of this is their eagerness to destroy Iraq, the strongest neighboring Arab state, and their endeavor to fragment all the states of the region such as Iraq, Saudi Arabia, Egypt, and Sudan into paper statelets and through their disunion and weakness to guarantee Israel's survival and the continuation of the brutal crusade occupation of the Peninsula.

All these crimes and sins committed by the Americans are a clear declaration of war on God, his messenger, and Muslims. And *ulema* [Muslim religious leaders] have throughout Islamic history unanimously agreed that the *jihad* is an individual duty if the enemy destroys the Muslim countries.

On that basis, and in compliance with God's order, we issue the following *fatwa* to all Muslims. The ruling to kill the Americans and their allies—civilians and military—is an individual duty for every Muslim who can do it in any country in which it is possible to do it, in order to liberate the al-Aqsa Mosque and the holy mosque [Mecca] from their grip, and in order for their armies to move out of all the lands of Islam, defeated and unable to threaten any Muslim. This is in accordance with the words of Almighty God, "and fight the pagans all together as they fight you all together," and "fight them until there is no more tumult or oppression, and there prevail justice and faith in God."

Source: http://www.mideastweb.org/osamabinladen2.htm.

—ɯ—

2. Vice President Dick Cheney, Speech, August 26, 2002

Vice President Dick Cheney spoke to the Veterans of Foreign Wars national convention in Nashville, Tennessee, on August 26, 2002. He intimated that Saddam Hussein might provide nuclear weapons to al-Qaeda, which was sufficient reason to launch a preemptive attack on Iraq and remove the dictator.

Nine-eleven and its aftermath awakened this nation to danger, to the true ambitions of the global terror network, and to the reality that weapons of mass destruction are being sought by determined enemies who would not hesitate to use them against us.

It is a certainty that the al-Qaeda network is pursuing such weapons, and has succeeded in acquiring at least a crude capability to use them.

And containment is not possible when dictators obtain weapons of mass destruction, and are prepared to share them with terrorists who intend to inflict catastrophic casualties on the United States.

But we now know that Saddam has resumed his efforts to acquire nuclear weapons. Among other sources, we've gotten this from the first-hand testimony of defectors—including Saddam's own son-in-law, who was subsequently murdered at Saddam's direction. Many of us are convinced that Saddam will acquire nuclear weapons fairly soon.

A person would be right to question any suggestion that we should just get inspectors back into Iraq, and then our worries will be over. Saddam has perfected the game of cheat and retreat, and is very skilled in the art of denial and deception. A return of inspectors would provide no assurance whatsoever of his compliance with UN resolutions. Simply stated, there is no doubt that Saddam Hussein now has weapons of mass destruction. There is no doubt he is amassing them to use against our friends, against our allies, and against us.

If the United States could have preempted 9/11, we would have, no question. Should we be able to prevent another, much more devastating attack, we will, no question. This nation will not live at the mercy of terrorists or terror regimes.

Another argument holds that opposing Saddam Hussein would cause even greater troubles in that part of the world, and interfere with the larger war against terror. I believe the opposite is true. Regime change in Iraq would bring about a number of benefits to the region. When the gravest of threats are eliminated, the freedom-loving peoples of the region will have a chance to promote the values that can bring lasting peace. The Middle East expert Professor Fouad Ajami predicts that after liberation, the streets in Basra and Baghdad are "sure to erupt in joy in the same way the throngs in Kabul greeted the Americans."

Source: http://www.newamericancentury.org/iraq-082602.htm.

—⁓—

3. President George W. Bush, News Conference, March 6, 2003

In his news conference of March 6, 2003, President George W. Bush recited key justifications for an invasion of Iraq, unless Saddam Hussein

allowed comprehensive inspections to ensure that he was not manufac-
turing weapons of mass destruction. The president further charged that
the Iraqi leader aided "terrorists."

Saddam Hussein has a long history of reckless aggression and terrible crimes. He possesses weapons of terror. He provides funding and
training and safe haven to terrorists—terrorists who would willingly
use weapons of mass destruction against America and other peace-
loving countries. Saddam Hussein and his weapons are a direct threat
to this country, to our people, and to all free people. If the world fails
to confront the threat posed by the Iraqi regime, refusing to use force
even as a last resort, free nations would assume immense and unacceptable risks. The attacks of September the 11th, 2001, showed what
the enemies of America did with four airplanes. We will not wait to
see what terrorists or terrorist states could do with weapons of mass
destruction. We are determined to confront threats wherever they
arise. I will not leave the American people at the mercy of the Iraqi
dictator and his weapons.

Q. And what harm would it do to give Saddam a final ultimatum, a 2- or
3-day deadline to disarm or face force?

The President. Saddam Hussein hasn't disarmed.

Fourteen forty-one, the Security Council resolution passed unanimously last fall, said clearly that Saddam Hussein has one last chance to
disarm. He hasn't disarmed. . . . Iraq is a part of the war on terror. Iraq
is a country that has got terrorist ties. It's a country with wealth. It's a
country that trains terrorists, a country that could arm terrorists. And
our fellow Americans must understand, in this new war against terror,
that we not only must chase down Al Qaida terrorists, we must deal with
weapons of mass destruction as well.

Saddam Hussein is a threat to our Nation. September the 11th
changed the strategic thinking, at least as far as I was concerned, for
how to protect our country. My job is to protect the American people.
It used to be that we could think that you could contain a person like
Saddam Hussein, that oceans would protect us from his type of terror.
September the 11th should say to the American people that we're now a
battlefield, that weapons of mass destruction in the hands of a terrorist
organization could be deployed here at home.

Q. Mr. President. If you order war, can any military operation be considered a success if the United States does not capture Saddam Hussein, as you once said, dead or alive?

The President. Well, I hope we don't have to go to war, but if we go to war, we will disarm Iraq. And if we go to war, there will be a regime change. And replacing this cancer inside of Iraq will be a Government that represents the rights of all the people, a Government which represents the voices of the Shi'a and Sunni and the Kurds.

Q. Mr. President, are you worried that the United States might be viewed as defiant of the United Nations if you went ahead with military action without specific and explicit authorization from the U.N.?

The President. No, I'm not worried about that.

I'm confident the American people understand that when it comes to our security, if we need to act, we will act, and we really don't need United Nations approval to do so.

Source: http://www.gpoaccess.gov/pubpapers/gwbush.html [March 6, 2003].

—⁂—

4. President George W. Bush, Ultimatum to Iraq, March 17, 2003

On March 17, 2003, President George W. Bush issued an ultimatum to Saddam Hussein to leave Iraq or face invasion. The president repeated his belief that a preemptive strike was justified because the Iraqi leader was developing weapons of mass destruction that could fall into the hands of terrorists.

Intelligence gathered by this and other governments leaves no doubt that the Iraq regime continues to possess and conceal some of the most lethal weapons ever devised. This regime has already used weapons of mass destruction against Iraq's neighbors and against Iraq's people.

The regime has a history of reckless aggression in the Middle East. It has a deep hatred of America and our friends. And it has aided, trained, and harbored terrorists, including operatives of Al Qaida.

The danger is clear: Using chemical, biological or, one day, nuclear weapons obtained with the help of Iraq, the terrorists could fulfill their stated ambitions and kill thousands or hundreds of thousands of innocent people in our country or any other.

The United States and other nations did nothing to deserve or invite this threat. But we will do everything to defeat it. Instead of drifting along toward tragedy, we will set a course toward safety. Before the day of horror can come, before it is too late to act, this danger will be removed.

All the decades of deceit and cruelty have now reached an end. Saddam Hussein and his sons must leave Iraq within 48 hours.

Source: http://www.gpoaccess.gov/pubpapers/gwbush.html.

—⁂—

5. President George W. Bush, State of the Union Speech, January 20, 2004

Nine months after driving Saddam Hussein from office, President Bush used his State of the Union address on January 20, 2004, to argue that the American occupation of Iraq would establish the basis for a democratic regime for the country.

The work of building a new Iraq is hard, and it is right. And America has always been willing to do what it takes for what is right. Last January, Iraq's only law was the whim of one brutal man. Today our coalition is working with the Iraqi Governing Council to draft a basic law, with a bill of rights. We are working with Iraqis and the United Nations to prepare for a transition to full Iraqi sovereignty by the end of June. As democracy takes hold in Iraq, the enemies of freedom will do all in their power to spread violence and fear. They are trying to shake the will of our country and our friends— but the United States of America will never be intimidated by thugs and assassins. The killers will fail, and the Iraqi people will live in freedom.

We also hear doubts that democracy is a realistic goal for the greater Middle East, where freedom is rare. Yet it is mistaken, and condescending, to assume that whole cultures and great religions are incompatible with liberty and self-government. I believe that God has planted in every heart the desire to live in freedom. And even when that desire is crushed by tyranny for decades, it will rise again.

Source: http://www.gpoaccess.gov/pubpapers/gwbush.html.

—⁂—

6. Richard A. Clarke, *Against All Enemies*, 2004

Richard A. Clarke, the counterterrorism chief of the National Security Council in the Clinton and Bush administrations, criticized the invasion of Iraq in a book written after he left government. Clarke argued that the Iraq invasion increased the likelihood of terrorism rather than diminished it and bred new levels of Arab hostility toward the United States.

The second agenda item post-September 11 should have been the creation of a counterweight ideology to the al Qaeda, fundamentalist, radical version of Islam because much of the threat we face is ideological, a perversion of a religion. Bombs and bullets, handcuffs and jail bars will not address the source of that ideological challenge.

When colleagues in the White House asked me what to read to understand the problem after September 11, I urged them instead to get an old black and white French film, *The Battle of Algiers.* In it, French counterterrorism authorities round up all the "known terrorists managers" and leaders but lose the war with the terrorists because they did not address the ideological underpinnings. After the known terrorist leaders were arrested, time passed, and new, unknown terrorists emerged. We are likely face the same situation with al Qaeda. The only way to stop it is to work with leaders of Islamic nations to insure that tolerance of other religions is taught again. . . ."

The invasion . . . lost us many friends. . . . In Muslim countries, the U.S. invasion of Iraq increased support for al Qaeda and radical anti-Americanism. Elsewhere, we are now seen as a super-bully more than a superpower, not just for what we did but for the way we did it, disdaining international mechanisms that we would later need.

Source: Richard A. Clarke. *Against All Enemies: Inside America's War on Terror.* New York: Free Press, 2004, 262–263, 273.

—⁂—

7. Pat Buchanan on Inaugurating Endless War, January 26, 2005

A syndicated columnist, Pat Buchanan sought the Republican presidential nomination in 1992 and 1996 and ran as a Reform Party candidate for president in 2000. He offered a biting indictment of the invasion of Iraq in his newspaper column of January 26, 2005.

President Bush is championing a policy of interventionism in the internal affairs of every nation on earth. But did we not learn from 9/11 that intervention is not a cure for terrorism, it is the cause of terrorism?

Clearly, the president does understand this, or believe it. For in his inaugural, he describes 9/11 as the day "when freedom came under attack." But Osama bin Laden did not dispatch his fanatics to ram planes into the World Trade Center because he hated our Bill of Rights. He did it because he hated our presence and our policies in the Middle East.

The invasion of Iraq has reaped a harvest of hatred in the Arab world, cost us 10,000 dead and wounded and $200 billion, and created a new training ground and haven for terrorists to replace the one we cleaned out in Afghanistan.

Source: Buchanan's column of January 26, 2005, for the Creators Syndicate.

—⚬—

8. Senate Select Intelligence Committee Report, June 5, 2008

In its report issued on June 5, 2008, the Senate Select Intelligence Committee compared Bush administration claims about Saddam Hussein and terrorism as justifications for the invasion of Iraq with known intelligence information before and after the U.S. invasion of Iraq. The committee's report reflected a sharp division of opinion between Democrats and Republicans about the war.

Conclusion 1: Statements by the President, Vice President, Secretary of State and the National Security Advisor regarding a possible Iraqi nuclear weapons program were generally unsubstantiated by intelligence community estimates, but did not convey the substantial disagreements that existed in the intelligence community.

Prior to the October 2002 National Intelligence Estimate, some intelligence agencies assessed that the Iraqi government was reconstituting a nuclear weapons program, while others disagreed or expressed doubts about the evidence. The Estimate itself expressed the majority view that the program was being reconstituted, but included clear dissenting views from the State Department's Bureau of Intelligence and Research, which argued that reconstitution was not underway, and the Department of Energy, which argued that aluminum tubes sought by Iraq were probably not intended for a nuclear program.

POSTWAR FINDINGS

Postwar findings revealed that Iraq ended its nuclear weapons program in 1991, and that Iraq's ability to reconstitute a nuclear weapons program progressively declined after that date. The Iraq Survey Group (ISG) found no evidence that Saddam Hussein ever attempted to restart a nuclear weapons program, although the Group did find that he took steps to retain the intellectual capital generated during the program. That intellectual capital decayed between 1991 and 2003, however, the ISG found no evidence that the relevant scientists were involved in renewed weapons work.

VII LINKS TO TERRORISM

"Indeed, the more time passes the more time Saddam Hussein has to develop his deadly weapons and to acquire more. The more time he has to plant sleeper agents in the United States and other friendly countries or to supply deadly weapons to terrorists he can then disown, the greater the danger."—*Deputy Secretary of Defense Paul Wolfowitz, Remarks at Fletcher Conference, October 16, 2002.*

"After September the 11th, we've entered into a new era and a new war. This is a man that we know had had connections with al Qa'ida. This is a man who, in my judgment, would like to use al Qa'ida as a forward army."—*President George W. Bush, Remarks in Dearborn, Michigan, October 14, 2002.*

"His regime has high-level contacts with al Qa'ida going back a decade and has provided training to al Qa'ida terrorists. And as the President has said, 'Iraq could decide on any given day to provide biological or chemical weapons to a terrorist group or to individual terrorists'— which is why the war on terror will not be won till Iraq is completely and verifiably deprived of weapons of mass destruction."—*Vice President Dick Cheney, Remarks at the Air National Guard Conference, December 2, 2002.*

Conclusion 15: Statements by the President and Vice President indicating that Saddam Hussein was prepared to give weapons of mass destruction to terrorist groups for attacks against the United States were contradicted by available intelligence information.

The October 2000 National Intelligence Estimate assessed that Saddam Hussein did not have nuclear weapons, and was unwilling to conduct terrorist attacks on the US using conventional, chemical or biological weapons at that time, in part because he feared that by doing so would give the US a stronger case for war with Iraq. This judgment was echoed by both earlier and later intelligence community assessments.

All of these assessments note that gauging Saddam's intention was quite difficult, and most suggested that he would be likely to initiate hostilities if he felt that a US invasion was imminent.

POSTWAR FINDINGS

Postwar findings indicate that Saddam Hussein was distrustful of al-Qaida and viewed Islamic extremists as a threat to his regime, and refused all requests from al-Qaida to provide material or operational support. No postwar information indicates that Saddam ever considered using any terrorist group to attack the United States.

REGIME CHANGE IN POST-WAR IRAQ

In August 2002, the CIA produced a report, *Can Iraq Ever Become a Democracy?*, at the request of the National Security Council. In the report's scope note, the CIA stated that:

"This assessment fully accepts that traditional Iraqi political culture has been inhospitable to democracy."

The report stated that, "On the surface, Iraq currently appears to lack both the socio-economic and politico-cultural prerequisites that political scientists generally regard as necessary to nurture democracy. Nevertheless, we believe that Iraq has several advantages that, if buttressed by the West, could foster democracy in post-Saddam Iraq." The advantages cited by the report included the return of exiled elites, a weak tradition of political Islam, near-universal revulsion against Saddam's dictatorship, and economic resources. The report emphasized that "None of these factors should be seen as minimizing the obstacles to democratization in Iraq after Saddam.

Source: U.S. Senate, Select Intelligence Committee, Report on WHETHER PUBLIC STATEMENTS REGARDING IRAQ BY U.S. GOVERNMENT OFFICIALS WERE SUBSTANTIATED BY INTELLIGENCE INFORMATION (June 5, 2008). http://intelligence.senate.gov/080605/phase2a.pdf.

INDEX